THE
WRITING PROCESS

THE WRITING PROCESS

A CONCISE RHETORIC

FIFTH EDITION

JOHN M. LANNON
University of Massachusetts—Dartmouth

HarperCollins*Publishers*

Senior Acquisitions Editor: Jane Kinney
Developmental Editor: Leslie Taggart
Cover Design and Illustration: Louis Fuiano
Electronic Production Manager: Angel Gonzalez Jr.
Manufacturing Manager: Angel Gonzalez Jr.
Publishing Services: Ruttle, Shaw & Wetherill, Inc.
Electronic Page Makeup: Ruttle, Shaw & Wetherill, Inc.
Printer and Binder: RR Donnelley & Sons
Cover Printer: The Lehigh Press, Inc.

The Writing Process: A Concise Rhetoric, Fifth Edition

Library of Congress Cataloging-in-Publication Data

Lannon, John M.
    The writing process : a concise rhetoric / John M. Lannon.—5th
  ed.
      p. cm.
   Includes index.
   ISBN 0-673-52492-2(SE).—ISBN 0-673-52400-0 (IE)
     1. English language—Rhetoric.   I. Title.
  PE1408.L3188 1994
  808′.042—dc20   94-18589
                                    CIP

95 96 97 98 9 8 7 6 5 4 3 2

Brief Contents

Detailed
Contents

SECTION THREE
ESSAYS FOR VARIOUS GOALS 211

SECTION FOUR
RESEARCH AND CORRESPONDENCE 415

APPENDIX C
GUIDELINES FOR WRITING
WITH A COMPUTER   589

APPENDIX D
FORMAT GUIDELINES FOR SUBMITTING
YOUR MANUSCRIPT   593

Preface

This text promotes rhetorical awareness by treating the writing process as a set of deliberate and recursive decisions. It promotes rhetorical effectiveness by helping develop the problem-solving skills essential to reader-centered discourse.

Organization

Section One, THE PROCESS, covers planning, drafting and revising. Students learn to invent, select, organize, and express their material recursively. They see how decisions about purpose and audience influence decisions about what will be said and how it will be said. They see that reading and writing are linked, and that writing is essentially a "thinking" process.

Section Two, THE PRODUCT, expands on composing and evaluation skills by focusing on content, organization, and style. Students learn to support their assertions; to organize for the reader; and to achieve prose maturity, precise diction, and appropriate tone.

Section Three, ESSAYS FOR VARIOUS GOALS, shows how the *strategies* (or modes) of discourse serve the particular *goals* of a discourse; that is, how description, narration, exposition, and argument are variously employed for expressive, referential, or persuasive ends. Offering variations on the standard "formula-essay," a balance of student and professional selections touches on current and lasting issues. Beyond studying these samples as models, students are asked to respond to the issues presented, that is, to write in response to a specific rhetorical situation.

Section Four, RESEARCH AND CORRESPONDENCE, expands rhetorical awareness beyond the traditional composition classroom. The two chapters on library research cover the process, the resources, and the product (a fully annotated research report). A chapter on business letters and memoranda focuses on the audiences, the informational and persuasive considerations, and the composing decisions in writing in the workplace.

Finally, for easy reference, Appendix A is a concise handbook, with exercises for the student. Additional, brief appendices offer advice on collaboration, word processing, and manuscript format.

The Foundations of *The Writing Process*

- Writers with no rhetorical awareness overlook the decisions that are crucial for effective writing. Only by defining their rhetorical problem and asking the important questions can writers formulate an appropriate solution.

- Although it follows no single, predictable sequence, the writing process is not a collection of random activities; rather it is a set of decisions in problem solving. Beyond emulating this or that model essay, students need to understand that effective writing requires critical thinking.

- Students initially are more comfortable with writer-centered discourse (description, narration) than with reader-centered discourse (exposition, argument) because they rarely write for any apparent audience other than teachers or for any apparent purpose other than to complete an assignment. To the extent that they view writing as an exercise in which writer and reader have no higher stake or interest, students cannot possibly understand that each writing situation poses its own rhetorical constraints. Outside the classroom, we write to create specific connections with specific audiences.

- Students at any level of ability can learn to incorporate within their writing the essential rhetorical features: worthwhile content, sensible organization, and readable style.

- As an alternative to reiterating the textbook material, classroom workshops apply textbook principles by focusing on the students' writing. Workshops, then, call for a readable, accessible, and engaging book to serve as a comprehensive resource. (Suggestions for workshop design are in the Instructor's Manual.)

- Finally, most writing classes contain students with all types of strengths and weaknesses. Because books are ordered far in advance, instructors can only hope that their choices will match the general caliber of the particular class. A textbook then should offer explanations that are thorough, examples and models that are broadly intelligible, and goals that are rigorous yet realistic. And the book should be flexible enough to allow for individualized assignments.

This book proceeds from writer-centered to reader-centered discourse. Beginning with personal topics and a basic essay structure, the focus shifts to increasingly complex rhetorical tasks, culminating in argument. Within this cumulative structure, however, each chapter is self-contained for flexible course planning. Exercises (or Applications) in each chapter offer various levels of challenge. All material has been class-tested.

New to This Edition

- Many more sample essays that, in addition to being multicultural in authorship, have meaning for the lives of students today. Following each essay are questions that promote critical analysis of the readings along with suggestions for discussion and written response. (See "Introduction" and Chapters 1, 5, 10, 11, 12, 14, 15, 16, 17, and 18.)

- Explanation of distinctions between conversational tone and usage that is substandard or colloquial. (See Chapter 2, page 49.)

- More applications suitable for collaborative work. (See Applications 1–2, 1–3, 2–10, 2–11, 4–2, 6–5, 6–8, and other easily adaptable applications, such as those in Chapters 8 and 9.)

- Greater emphasis on critical thinking in argument and persuasion. New or expanded topics: measurements of certainty and truth; the influence of personal bias; reasoning versus rationalizing; statistical fallacies; uses and limitations of emotional appeals; satire, irony, and sarcasm as persuasive strategies; audience and ethics guidelines. (See Chapter 18.)

- Two fully revised chapters (20 and 21) on research methods for the information age. New or expanded topics: automated resources (card catalogs and OCLC databases, compact disks, database searches); bias in printed and electronic sources; paraphrase and integration of quoted material; detailed MLA documentation guidelines; introduction to APA documentation; a checklist for assessing one's methods, interpretations, and reasoning in the research process.

- Guidelines for collaboration, word processing, and manuscript format. (See Appendices B, C, and D.)

- A broad range of challenging, class-tested ideas for essay topics.

- All chapters revised for greater clarity, conciseness, and emphasis.

Much of the improvement in this edition was inspired by helpful reviews from Arnold J. Bradford, Northern Virginia Community College; Wayne P. Hubert, Chaffey College; and Craig R. Auge, Kent State University. My thanks to you all.

For examples, advice, and support, I thank colleagues and friends at the University of Massachusetts—Dartmouth, especially Tish Dace, Barbara Jacobskind, Margaret Panos, Louise Habicht, and Richard Larschan. As always, Raymond Dumont helped in countless ways.

A special thanks to my students who allowed me to reproduce versions of their work: Wendy Gianacoples for "Confessions of a Food Addict," Chris Adey for selections on privacy in America, Mike Creeden for a paragraph on physical fitness, Kim Fonteneau for "Suffering Through Gym Class," Suzanne Gilbertson for selections on New Guinea, Shirley Haley for "Sailboats" and other excellent work, Jeff Leonard for "Walk but Don't Run," and the many other writers whose selections appear throughout.

At HarperCollins, my editor Jane Kinney graciously and expertly guided this revision; Marisa L'Heureux and Alison Brill provided assistance of all kinds; Janet Nuciforo did an outstanding job of coordinating production.

For Chega, Daniel, Sarah, and Patrick—without whom not.

JOHN M. LANNON

THE
WRITING PROCESS

SECTION ONE

THE PROCESS— PLANNING, DRAFTING, REVISING

Introduction

Success comes from good decision making. People who succeed usually are those who make the right decisions—about a career, an investment, a relationship, or anything else. Instead of letting things happen, these decision makers take control of their situation—and they stay in control. In one respect, writing is no different from life in general: effective writers stay in control by making the right decisions.

How Writing Occurs

Like any decision making, good writing is hard work. If we had one recipe for all writing, one surefire way of doing it, our labors would be small. We could learn the recipe ("Do this; then do that"), and then apply it to every writing task—from love letters to lab reports. (With a cookbook approach of that kind, I might have spent only an hour or two writing this introduction, instead of nearly a week!) But no two writing tasks are identical; we write about various subjects for various audiences for various purposes—at home, at school, on the job. For every task, writers have to make their own decisions.

Even though we have no one recipe for writing well, most writers in most situations face identical problems: they need to decide who their audience is and how to connect with it; they need to decide what goal they want their writing to achieve and how to make sure the writing achieves that goal; they need to decide what to say and how to say it. Each writer struggles alone, but there *are* decision-making strategies that work for most writing tasks. This book introduces strategies that help writers succeed.

Most writing is a conscious and deliberate process—not the result of divine intervention, magic, miracles, or last-minute inspiration. Nothing ever leaps from the mind to the page in one neat and painless motion—not even for creative geniuses. Instead, worthwhile writing progresses and improves in stages: we plan, draft, and revise—repeating this cycle of decisions until our thinking takes shape, until the writing does precisely what we want it to do. Sometimes we know exactly what we want to do and say as we begin to write, and sometimes we discover our purpose and meaning only as we write. But our finished product takes shape through the decisions we make at different stages in the writing process.

This book provides the ingredients for decision making, but you have to create your own recipes. So that you can make the right decisions, you will be shown how to plan, draft, and revise in a suggested sequence of activities. But just as no two people use an identical sequence of activities to drive, ski, or play tennis, no two people write in the same way. Good writing occurs in many ways, but *each* way requires careful decisions. How you decide to use this book's advice will depend on your writing task and on what works for you.

How Writing Looks

The neat and ordered writing samples throughout this book show the *products* of writing—not the process. Beneath every finished writing product (including this introduction) lie pages and pages of scribbling and things crossed out, lists, arrows, and fragments of ideas. Writing begins in disorder; decision making can be a messy business, as shown in Figure 1, a section from my first draft of this introduction. (Not until I'd written *four* equally messy drafts was it a finished product.) Messiness is a natural and often essential part of writing in its early stages.

Just as the writing process has no one recipe, the finished products have no one shape. In fact, very little writing published in books, magazines, and newspapers looks exactly like the basic college essay discussed in this book's early chapters (an introductory paragraph ending with a thesis statement; three or more support paragraphs, each beginning with a topic sentence; and a concluding paragraph). Published writing may

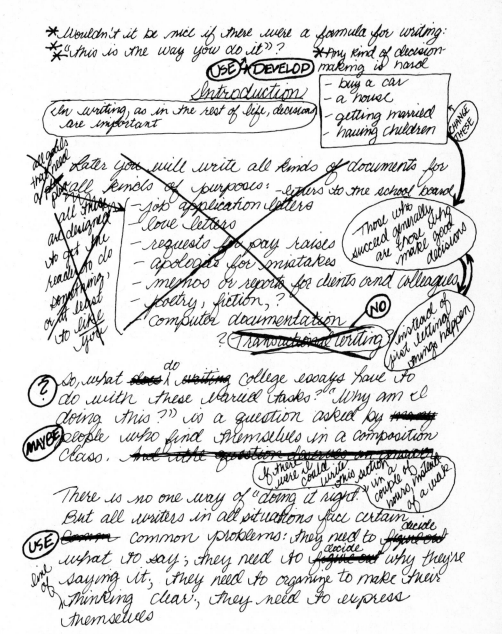

Figure 1 Part of a Typical First Draft

have very short paragraphs, some no longer than one sentence, or even one word.

Despite the countless shapes among the *products* of writing, all effective writers carry out the *process* by using identical skills: they know how to discover something worthwhile to write about, how to organize their material sensibly, and how to express their ideas clearly and gracefully.

College essays offer a good model for developing these skills: first, you begin with personal topics and a basic structure for shaping your thinking; later, as your subjects become more complex, you develop different structures for different goals. Throughout, you learn to make order out of disorder.

College essays also provide you with an immediate, helpful audience—your instructor and classmates. Unlike many audiences who read only your final draft and from whom you could not reasonably expect helpful and sympathetic advice, your teacher and classmates can give you valuable feedback as you continue to shape and rework drafts of your writing. Like any audience, however, your classroom readers will expect you finally to give them something worthwhile—some useful information, a new insight on some topic, an unusual perspective or an entertaining story—in a form that is easy to follow and pleasing to read. Connect with these readers, and you should be able to connect with just about any reader.

In writing college essays, you practice ways of achieving control by attending to all the decisions in the writing process. Here you can learn what a writer needs to know before you set out to face other audiences on your own.

How Writing Makes a Difference

All through school, we write too often for *surface* reasons: to impress teachers, to show we can grind out a few hundred words on some topic, cook up a thesis, and organize paragraphs; to show we can punctuate, spell, and use grammar; to pass the course. Although essential for our survival in school, these surface reasons mask the *deeper* reasons we write: to explore something important to us, to connect with our readers, to be understood, to make a difference—as students, as employees, as citizens, or as friends.

What kind of difference can any writing make? It might move readers to act or reconsider their biases; it might increase their knowledge or win their support; it might broaden their understanding or their insight. Writing might do any of these things or other things. But whether you're giving instructions for running an electric toothbrush or pouring out your feelings to a friend, effective writing almost always brings writer and reader closer together.

Have you read anything lately that has made a difference for you? Can you think of situations in which your own writing could make a difference for others?

As you read the essays in this book, you will see how student and professional writers in all kinds of situations manage to make a difference with their readers. These models, along with the advice and assignments, should help your writing make a difference of its own.

Application

We all hear and read plenty about America's social problems: poverty, inequality, racial strife, violence, and so on. How then could any "ordinary" writer be expected to contribute something new to that conversation? Could only professional writers make a difference?

Read the following essay—by a 19-year-old student—and decide for yourself whether it makes a difference for you. (Use the questions that follow the essay as a guide for your analysis.)

Breaking the Bonds of Hate

Ever since I can remember, I wanted the ideal life: a big house, lots of money, cars. I wanted to find the perfect happiness that so many people have longed for. I wanted more than life in the jungle of Cambodia. America was the place, the land of tall skyscrapers, televisions, cars, and airplanes.

In the jungles of Cambodia I lived in a refugee camp. We didn't have good sanitation or modern conveniences. For example, there were no inside bathrooms—only outside ones made from palm-tree leaves, surrounded by millions of flies. When walking down the street, I could smell the aroma of the outhouse; in the afternoon, the 5- and 6-year-olds played with the dirt in front of it. It was the only thing they had to play with, and the "fragrance" never seemed to bother them. And it never bothered me. Because I smelled it every day, I was used to it.

The only thing that bothered me was the war. I have spent half of my life in war. The killing is still implanted in my mind. I hate Cambodia. When I came to America nine years ago at the age of 10, I thought I was being born into a new life. No more being hungry, no more fighting, no more killing. I thought I had escaped the war.

In America, there are more kinds of material things than Cambodians could ever want. And here we don't have to live in the jungle like monkeys, we don't have to hide from mortar bombing, and we don't have to smell the rotten human carrion. But for the immigrant, America presents a different type of jungle, a different type of war, and a smell as bad as the waste of Cambodia.

Most Americans believe the stereotype that immigrants work hard, get a good education, and have a very good life. Maybe it used to be like that, but not anymore. You have to be deceptive and unscrupulous in order to make it. If you are not, then you will end up like most immigrants I've known. Living in the ghetto in a cockroach-infested house. Working on the assembly line or in the chicken factory to support your family. Getting up at 3 o'clock in the morning to take the bus to work and not getting home until 5 p.m.

If you're a kid my age, you drop out of school to work because your parents don't have enough money to buy you clothes for school. You may end up selling drugs because you want cars, money, and parties, as all teenagers do. You have to depend on your peers for emotional support because your parents are too busy working in the factory trying to make money to pay the bills. You don't get along with your parents because they have a different mentality: you are an American and they are Cambodian. You hate them because they are never there for you, so you join a gang as I did.

You spend your time drinking, doing drugs, and fighting. You beat up people for pleasure. You don't care about anything except your drugs, your beers, and your revenge against adversaries. You shoot at people because they've insulted your pride. You shoot at the police because they are always bothering you. They shoot back and then you're dead like my best friend Sinerth.

Sinerth robbed a gas station. He was shot in the head by the police. I'd known him since the sixth grade from my first school in Minneapolis. I can still remember his voice calling me from California. "Virak, come down here, man," he said. "We need you. There are lots of pretty girls down here." I promised him that I would be there to see him. The following year he was dead. I felt sorry for him. But as I thought it over, maybe it is better for him to be dead than to continue with the cycle of violence, to live with hate. I thought, "It is better to die than live like an angry young fool, thinking that everybody is out to get you."

Mad-dog mind-set: When I was like Sinerth, I didn't care about dying. I thought that I was on top of the world, being immortalized by drugs. I could see that my future would be spent working on the assembly line like most of my friends, spending all my paycheck on the weekend, and being broke again on Monday morning. I hated going to school because I couldn't see a way to get out of the endless cycle. My philosophy was "Live hard and die young."

I hated America because, to me, it was not the place of opportunities or the land of "the melting pot" as I had been told. All I had seen were broken beer bottles on the street and homeless people and drunks using the sky as their roof. I couldn't walk down the street without someone yelling out, "You f—ing gook" from his car. Once again I was caught in the web of hatred. I'd become a mad dog with the mind-set of the past: "When trapped in the corner, just bite." The war mentality of Cambodia came back: get what you can and leave. I thought I came to America to escape war, poverty, fighting, to escape the violence, but I wasn't escaping; I was being introduced to a newer version of war—the war of hatred.

I was lucky. In Minneapolis, I dropped out of school in the ninth grade to join a gang. Then I moved to Louisiana, where I continued my life of "immortality" as a member of another gang. It came to an abrupt halt when I crashed a car. I wasn't badly injured, but I was underage and the fine took all my money. I called a good friend of the Cambodian community in Minneapolis for advice (she'd tried to help me earlier). I didn't know where to go or whom to turn to. I saw friends landing in jail, and I didn't want that. She promised to help me get back in school. And she did.

Since then I've been given a lot of encouragement and caring by American friends and teachers who've helped me turn my life around. They opened my eyes to a kind of education that frees us all from ignorance and slavery. I could have failed so many times except for those people who believed in me and gave me another chance. Individuals who were willing to help me have taught me that I can help myself. I'm now a 12th grader and have been at my school for three years; I plan to attend college in the fall. I am struggling to believe I can reach the other side of the mountain.

—Virak Khiev

QUESTIONS

Identify the Audience

- For whom, exactly, does Virak seem to be writing?

- What assumptions does Virak make about his audience's knowledge and attitudes?

- In your view, are these assumptions accurate? Why or why not?

Identify the Purpose

- What do you suppose Virak wants his audience to be thinking or feeling after reading this piece?

- What point does he want to make, and how does he support it?

- Does the essay achieve its purpose? If so, how?

Explore Your Reactions

- Can you identify any worthwhile information, new insights, unusual perspectives?

- After reading this essay, do you know more than you did? If so, what?

- What are the major issues here? How, exactly, has your thinking about these issues been affected by this essay?

- Do you have a clearer understanding? If so, about what?

Decide on Your Response

- If you had the chance to write your personal response to Virak's essay, what are some things you might want to say?

- What point would you want to make, and how would you support it?

Your instructor may ask you to write out your answers to the above questions, in preparation for class discussion.

1

Decisions
in the
Writing Process

How can writers bring readers closer? By anticipating their needs, by making the message matter, by making the right decisions.

How Writing Is Used

Readers will use your writing to learn something about you, to share your experience and insight, to see things as you do—and maybe even to judge you. Whether your writing succeeds will depend on *what* you decide to say and *how* you decide to say it. A Dear John or Jane letter, a job application, an essay exam, a letter to a newspaper, a note to a sick friend, your written testimony as a witness to a crime—these are just a sampling of the writing situations you might face.

In each of these situations, you write because you feel strongly enough to have a definite viewpoint, to take a definite position, to respond or speak out. Maybe you think X is good (or bad); or maybe you support (or oppose) X; or maybe you see something unique about X; or maybe you think something should be done about X. By asserting your viewpoint, you tell readers where you stand; you announce your position.

11

Here are just a few of the countless possible viewpoints any writer might assert:

> College is not for everyone.
>
> I deserve a raise.
>
> Food can be just as addictive as a drug.
>
> My high school education was a waste of time.
>
> I want my life to be better than that of my parents.

Later you will see how assertions like these serve as thesis statements for essays. But you can see here that the mere expression of a viewpoint is not in itself very useful to readers. To really understand any of these assertions, readers need *explanation*. Whenever you express a viewpoint, you need to explain it. After telling your audience where you stand, show them why.

How Writing Is Shaped

Writers shape their thinking so that readers can follow it. Any useful writing (whether in the form of a book, a chapter, a news article, a memo, a report, or an essay) most often reveals a sensible line of thinking in a shape like this:

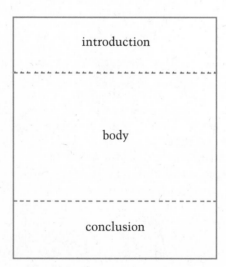

- The *introduction* attracts attention and makes readers take notice, announces the viewpoint, and previews what will follow. Readers like to know what to expect. Some introductions need to be long and involved; others, short and sweet. But all good introductions invite readers in.

- The *body* explains and supports the viewpoint. This section achieves unity by remaining focused on the viewpoint. And it achieves coherence by presenting a line of thinking carried from sentence to sentence in logical order. Body sections come in all different sizes, depending on how much readers need and expect.

- The *conclusion* sums up the meaning of the piece, or it points toward other meanings to be explored. If the issue is straight-forward, the conclusion might be brief and definite. If the issue is complex or controversial, the conclusion might be lengthy and open-ended. But all good conclusions give readers a clear perspective on what they have just read.

Any useful writing usually displays some version of this basic shape, a shape most obvious in the standard college essay—nonfiction writing that supports a viewpoint (expressed as a thesis) in one or more paragraphs.

How an Essay Is Composed

For naming the process that produces a useful essay, *composing* seems more accurate than *writing*. Inscribing words on paper is only one small part of the writing process. Your real challenge lies with the other parts:

1. exploring for things you might want to say (in journals, lists of ideas, and so on) and then deciding what this material means

2. deciding on your audience and how you expect them to use your message

3. deciding on a plan for helping the audience understand your meaning

4. discovering new meanings as you work and deciding on ways of revising your original plan and message to accommodate these new meanings

Writing is a process of transforming the material you discover—by inspiration, research, accident, trial and error, or other means—into a message that makes a difference for readers. In short, *writing is a process of deliberate decisions.*

To appreciate writing as a deliberate process, let's follow one student through two approaches to the same writing situation: first, her quickest effort; then, her best effort. Shirley Haley has been assigned an essay on this topic: How do you want your life to be different from (or similar to) that of your parents? Haley's goal here is twofold: to explore her feelings about this topic and to share that exploration with us. Her first response is a random piece of freewriting that took about 30 minutes:

> When my mother was my age, life was simple. Women really didn't have to study in college. They came primarily to find a husband, and they majored in liberal arts or teaching. They knew they were going to be wives and mothers. My mother says she got an education so she would have "something to fall back on" in case something ever happened to my father—which was a good thing, I suppose. Maybe it was her attitude about "family first, me second" that made our home life so stable.
>
> I appreciate the fact that my parents have given me a stable home life, and I want parts of my life to turn out like theirs. But my parents are slaves to their house; they never go anywhere or do anything with their spare time. They just work on the house and yard. They never seem to do anything they want to do—only what other people expect of them.
>
> I wish my parents would allow themselves to enjoy life, have more adventure. They go to the same place every year for their vacation. They've never even seen a country outside the United States.
>
> I'll have a family some day, and I'll have responsibilities, but I never want to have a boring life. When I'm on my own, I want my life to soar. And even though I want to provide a stable home life for my children and husband some day, I hope I never forget my responsibility to myself as well.

Haley's draft has potential, but she hints at lots of things in general and points at nothing in particular. What exactly does she mean, and what is her purpose? Without a thesis to assert a controlling viewpoint, neither writer nor reader ever finds an orientation. We can't tell what this essay is *about.* We are confused.

At first, the essay seems to be about a change in women's roles, but none of Haley's generalizations (say, "Women . . . came . . . to find a husband") is supported by *evidence.* Then, the end of the first paragraph and the beginning of the second suggest that Haley's topic has shifted to ways in which she wants her life to resemble her parents'. But the second, third, and fourth paragraphs discuss what Haley *dislikes* about her parents' lives. The final sentence adds confusion by looking back to a now-defunct topic in the first paragraph: stable family life. We have no idea where the emphasis belongs.

Not everything that comes to the writer's mind belongs in an essay, but Haley included everything, anyway. Without a definite purpose and thesis, she never could decide which material didn't belong, which was the most important, and which deserved careful development.

Besides its confusing content, the essay has shape and style problems. Without an introduction, we lack a framework for reading, a way of narrowing the possible meanings we might take from the piece. Without a conclusion, we have trouble finding clear perspective on what we have just read.

Also, the paragraphs either are poorly developed or fail to focus on one specific point. And some sentences (such as the last two in paragraph one) seem to have hardly any logical connection. In general, the sentences lack variety and make for dull reading.

Finally, Haley never seems to decide on an appropriate tone. We get almost no sense of a real person speaking to real people, expressing a definite attitude toward her subject. Instead of writing for an audience, Haley has written only for herself—as if writing a journal or diary. Although Haley's quickest effort seems a promising beginning, the piece needs work before it can connect with readers.

A quick effort (as in a journal or diary) can be a good way of getting started, a good source of essay material. But rarely is a quick effort adequate. When writers do nothing more than *draft* whatever comes to mind (as Haley does on page 14), they bypass the essential stages of *planning* and *revising.*

In fact, planning and revising ordinarily take much longer than drafting. Getting some material down on the page is easy. Getting the piece to *work,* to make a difference for readers—this is where tough decisions are made. Indeed, I'm struggling right now to say things that will make a difference for my readers. And if Haley hopes to connect she, too, will have to struggle with decisions such as these:

- *Planning decisions:* about *exactly* what she wants her topic to be and her essay to accomplish; about what her position is and how she will support that viewpoint; about which material, organization, and tone will work best for her specified audience.

- *Drafting decisions:* about how to write an introduction that opens doors to her world, her way of seeing; about how to develop the middle so that it shows a real mind at work and in control; about how to conclude memorably, with emphasis and insight and imagination.

- *Revising decisions:* about whether her material is worth reading; her organization sensible; her style readable; her grammar, spelling, and punctuation correct—rethinking and rewriting until the essay represents her best effort, until it conveys the exact point or feeling she wanted to get across.

Figure 1.1 diagrams the kinds of decisions Haley faces during the writing process. Of course none of these decisions necessarily occurs in the neat sequence shown here. But before turning in a final draft, Haley will need to answer all these questions.

Now let's follow Haley's thinking as she struggles through her planning decisions:

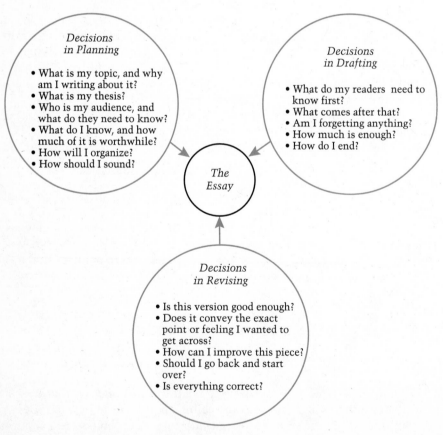

Figure 1.1   Typical Decisions During the Writing Process

What exactly is my topic, and why am I writing about it? My intended topic was "How I Want My Life to Be Different from That of My Parents," but somehow my first draft got off the track. I need to focus on the specific differences!

I'm writing this essay to discover my own feelings and to help readers understand these feelings by showing them specific parts of my parents' life-style that I hope will be different for me.

What is my thesis? After countless tries, I think I've finally settled on my thesis: "As I look at my parents' life, I hope my own will be less ordinary, less duty-bound, and less predictable."

Who is my audience, and what do they need to know? My audience consists of my teacher and classmates (this essay will be discussed in class). Each reader already is familiar with this topic in her or his own way. Everyone, after all, is someone's son or daughter! But I want my audience to understand specifically the differences *I* envision.

What do I know about this topic? A better question might be, "What *don't* I know?" I've spent my life with this topic, and so I certainly don't have to do any research.

Of all the material I've been able to discover on this topic, how much of it is worthwhile (considering my purpose and audience)? Because I could write volumes here, I'll have to resist getting carried away. My readers don't want a life story. They can tolerate only a few paragraphs. I certainly don't want to bury readers in needless detail. I've already decided to focus on the feeling that my parents' lives are too ordinary, duty-bound, and predictable. One paragraph explaining each of these supporting points (and illustrating them with well-chosen examples) should be enough.

How will I organize? I guess I've already made this decision by settling on my thesis: moving from "ordinary" to "duty-bound" to "predictable." Predictability is what bothers me most. It's what I want to emphasize, and so I will save it for last.

How do I want my writing to sound? I'm sharing something intimate with my classmates, and so I want to sound like one of them. My tone should be relaxed and personal, as when people are talking to people they trust.

In completing her essay, Haley went on to make the same kind of deliberate decisions for drafting and revising. And among her many decisions and revisions, Haley discovered in her original draft (page 14) a path worth following. Here is her final draft:

Life in Full Color

I'm probably the only person I know who still has the same two parents she was born with. We have a traditional American family: we go to church and football games; we watch the Olympics on television and argue about politics; and we have Thanksgiving dinner at my grandmother Clancy's and Christmas dinner with my father's sister Jess, who used to let us kids put pitted olives on our fingertips when we were little. Most of my friends are struggling with the problems of broken homes; I'll always be grateful to my parents for giving me a loving and stable background. But sometimes I look at my parents' life and hope my life will be less ordinary, less duty-bound, and less predictable.

I want my life to be imaginative, not ordinary. Instead of honeymooning at Niagara Falls, I want to go to Paris. In my parents' neighborhood, all the houses were built alike about twenty years ago. Different owners have added on or shingled or painted, but the houses basically all look the same. The first thing we did when we moved into our house was plant trees; everyone did. Now the neighborhood is full of family homes on tree-lined streets, which is nice; but I'd prefer a condo in a renovated brick building in Boston. I'd have dozens of plants, and I'd buy great furniture one piece at a time at auctions and dusty shops and not by the roomful from the local furniture store. Instead of spending my time trying to be similar to everyone else, I'd like to explore ways of being different.

My parents have so many obligations, they barely have time for themselves; I don't want to live like that. I'm never quite sure whether they own the house or the house owns them. They worry constantly about taxes, or the old furnace, or the new deck, or mowing the lawn, or weeding the garden. After spending every weekend slaving over their beautiful yard, they have no time left to enjoy it. And when they're not buried in household chores, other people are making endless demands on their time. My mother will stay up past midnight because she promised some telephone voice 3 cakes for the church bazaar, or 5 dozen cookies for the Girl Scout meeting, or 76 little sandwiches for the women's club Christmas party. My father coaches Little League, wears a clown suit for the Lions' flea markets, and both he and my mother are volunteer firefighters. In fact, both my parents get talked into volunteering for everything. I hate to sound selfish, but my first duty is to myself. I'd rather live in a tent than be owned by my house. And I don't want my life to end up being measured out in endless chores.

Although it's nice to be able to take things such as regular meals and paychecks for granted, many other events in my parents' life are too predictable for me. Every Sunday at two o'clock we dine on overdone roast beef, mashed potatoes and gravy, a faded green vegetable, and sometimes that mushy orange squash that comes frozen in bricks. It's not that either of my parents is a bad cook, but Sunday dinner isn't *food* any more; it's a habit. Mom and Dad have become so predictable that they can order each other's food in restaurants. Just once I'd like to see them pack up and go away for a weekend, without telling anybody; they couldn't do it. They can't even go crazy and try a new place for their summer vacation. They've been spending the first two weeks in August on Cape Cod since I was 2 years old. I want variety in my life. I want to travel, see this country and see Europe, do things spontaneously. No one will ever be able to predict *my* order in a restaurant.

Before long, Christmas will be here, and we'll be going to Aunt Jess's. Mom will bake a walnut pie, and Grandpa Frank will say, "Michelle, you sure know how to spoil an old man." It's nice to know that some things never change. In fact, some of the ordinary, obligatory, predictable things in life are the most comfortable. But too much of any routine can make life seem dull and gray. I hope my choices lead to a life in full color.

Haley's deliberate decisions about planning, drafting, and revising have produced a far better essay than her first, random version on page 14. Notice the clear and distinctive shape of this essay:

Introductory paragraph (leads into the thesis)
_____
_____
_____

Thesis statement
_____ But sometimes I look at my parents' life and hope my life will be less ordinary, less duty-bound, and less predictable.

Topic statement and first support paragraph
I want my life to be imaginative, not ordinary. _____
_____
_____
_____

Topic statement and second support paragraph
My parents have so many obligations, they barely have time for themselves; I don't want to live like that. _____
_____
_____

Topic statement and
third support
paragraph

Although it's nice to be able to take things such as regular meals and paychecks for granted, many other things in my parents' life are too predictable for me. _____
_____
_____
_____

Concluding paragraph

_____
_____
_____
_____

Essays can vary from this shape in countless ways, but a good first step for gaining control is to master the standard shape.

Besides seeing how the design of Haley's whole essay has evolved, we recognize other improvements. Above all, we're no longer confused. Somewhere between her first draft and this last one, Haley discovered her exact meaning and found a way of making it clear to us as well. We know *where* she stands because she tells us, with a definite thesis; and we know *why* because she shows us, with plenty of examples. Also, nothing is wasted; everything seems to belong, and everything fits together.

Within the larger design of Haley's whole essay, each paragraph has its own design, a place for things that belong together. The introduction invites us in; each middle paragraph reveals another part of the writer's world; and the conclusion looks back on everything, lets us finish. Each paragraph enriches the whole.

The style, too, is improved. We now see real variety in the ways in which sentences begin and words are put together. We hear a genuine voice. Haley's tone helps create contact.

Because she made careful decisions, Haley produced a final draft that has the qualities of any good writing: *content* that makes it worth reading; *organization* that reveals the line of thinking and emphasizes what is most important; and *style* that is economical and convincingly human.

Every writer struggles with the same decisions about planning, drafting, and revising, but rarely in a predictable sequence. Instead, each writer chooses a sequence that works best for *that* person. And no single stage of decisions is complete until *all three* stages are complete. Figure 1.2 diagrams this looping ("recursive") structure of the writing process.

You might write a draft before or after you have a clear plan, but if the draft has no real potential, you will have to loop back and draft again or even return to your planning stage. Once you do have a usable draft, you revise; but if the revision still fails to convey your exact point or feel-

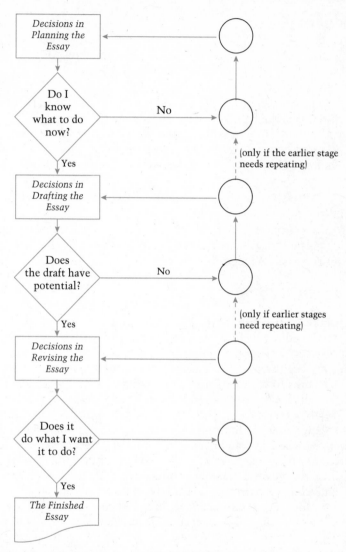

Figure 1.2   The Looping Structure of the Writing Process

ing, you may have to return to the planning or drafting stage. This loop-ing continues until you achieve an essay that does exactly what you want it to do.

Although planning, drafting, and revising are treated separately and sequentially in the next three chapters, during the actual process these decisions often are indistinguishable parts of a writer's thinking.

Application 1–1

The essay that follows (a third draft) was written in response to this assignment:

> Identify a personal trait that is so strong you cannot control it (a quick temper, the need for acceptance, a fear of failure, shyness, a bad habit, a phobia, an obsession, or the like). In a serious or humorous essay, show how this trait affects your behavior. Provide enough details for readers to understand clearly this part of your personality.

Our writer, Wendy Gianacoples, decided to explore a personal obsession: food.

Read the essay once or twice. Then read it again, identifying specific ways the writer connects with her audience. Use the questions that follow the essay as a guide for your analysis.

Confessions of A Food Addict

Like most compulsive eaters, I eat to fill a void—an emptiness within. I feed my feelings. Food can be my best friend, always there when I need it. This friend, however, actually is a tyrant that dominates my life through endless cycles of need, indulgence, and guilt.

Thanks to my food obsession, I seem to have two personalities: the respected, self-controlled Wendy who eats properly all day, and the fat Wendy who emerges after dark to gobble everything in sight. Lying in bed, I wait for the house to be silent. Feeling excited and giddy, I sneak to the kitchen and head straight for the freezer to begin my search. My initial prize is an unopened pint of Ben and Jerry's chocolate chip ice cream. I break the container's seal, dig in with my spoon, and shovel down massive gobs. (I have a love/hate relationship with food: I want all or nothing.) Next thing I know the container is empty.

Stashing the empty container deeply in the trash, I continue my rampage. From the cookie drawer, I snatch a nearly full package of Fig Newtons. As I tiptoe toward the milk, I ask myself what the folks at Weight Watchers would say if they could see me standing half-awake in my ice-cream splattered Lanz nightgown, popping down Fig Newtons and swigging milk from the carton. After pushing the few remaining cookies to the front of the package so it looks fuller, I rummage around for my next "fix."

Beneath a bag of frozen Bird's Eye vegetables, I find a frozen pizza—the ultimate midnight snack. The oven will take too long but the microwave is too noisy—all that beeping could get me busted. Feeling daring, I turn on the kitchen faucet to drown out the beeps, place the pizza in the microwave, set the timer, grab the last handful of Fig Newtons, and wait.

By the time I polish off the pizza, it's 1:00 a.m. and I crave Kraft Macaroni and Cheese. Standing on a chair I reach for a box from the overhead cabinet. Trying to be quiet, I dig out a spaghetti pot from a pile of pots and pans. Grabbing the handle, I hold my breath as I pull the pan from the clutter. While the water boils and the macaroni cooks, I fix a bowl of Rice Krispies. Just as I finish chowing down "Snap, Crackle, and Pop," the macaroni is ready. After eating the whole package, I bury the box in the trash.

After a binge, I panic: "What have I done?" Setting a hand on my bulging stomach, I think of the weight I'll gain this week. Climbing the stairs to my bed, I feel drained, like a person on drugs who is now "coming down." In my bedroom, I study myself in the full-length mirror, looking for visible signs of my sins.

Lying in bed, I feel fat and uncomfortable. Although I usually sleep on my stomach, on "binge" nights, I assume the fetal position, cradling my full belly, feeling ashamed and alone, as if I were the only person who overeats and uses food as a crutch. When the sugar I've consumed keeps me awake, I plead with God to help me overcome this weakness.

The next morning I kick myself and feel guilty. I want to block out last night's memories, but my tight clothes offer a painful reminder. My stomach is sick all day and I have heartburn. During the following week, I'll eat next to nothing and exercise constantly, hoping to break even on the scale at Weight Watchers.

Most people don't consider compulsive eating an addiction. Substance abusers can be easy to spot, but food addicts are less obvious. Unlike drugs, one can't live without food. People would never encourage a drug addict or alcoholic to "have another hit" or "fall off the wagon." However, people constantly push food on over-eaters: "Come on, one brownie won't hurt. I made them especially for you," says a friend. When I decline, she scowls and turns away. Little does she know, while she was in the bathroom, I had four.

—Wendy Gianacoples

QUESTIONS

Does the Content of the Essay Make It Worth Reading?

- Can you find a definite thesis that announces the writer's viewpoint?

- Are you given enough information to understand the viewpoint?

- Do you learn something new and useful?

- Does everything belong, or should any material be cut?

Does the Organization Reveal the Writer's Line of Thinking?

- Is there an introduction that sets the scene, a middle that walks us through, and a conclusion that sums up the meaning?
- Does each support paragraph present a distinct unit of meaning?
- Does each paragraph stick to the point and stick together?

Is the Style Economical and Convincing?

- Can you understand each sentence the first time you read it?
- Should any words be cut?
- Do sentences have variety in the way they're put together?
- Is the writer's meaning always clear?
- Can you hear a real person speaking?
- Do you like the person you hear?

Write out your answers to these questions and be prepared to discuss them in class.

Application 1–2

Collaborative Project: Working in small groups, compare Shirley Haley's first draft (page 14) with her final draft (page 18). Discuss the specific improvements, and give examples. Use the questions from Application 1–1 as a guide for your discussion.

Application 1–3

Collaborative Project: In class, write your "quickest effort" essay about a personal trait, or about this subject: "Important Differences or Similarities Between My Life and That of My Parents." Exchange papers with a classmate, and evaluate your classmate's paper, using the questions from Application 1–1. In one or two paragraphs, give your classmate advice for revising. Don't be afraid to mark up (with your own questions, comments, and suggestions) the paper you're evaluating. Discuss with your classmate your evaluation of his/her paper.

At home, read the evaluation of your paper carefully, and write your "best" version of your original essay. List the improvements you made in moving from your quickest effort to your best effort. Be prepared to discuss your improvements in class.

Also, in two or three paragraphs, trace your own writing process for this essay by describing the decisions you made. Be prepared to discuss your decisions in class.

Note: Don't expect miracles at this stage. You are bound to feel some degree of frustration and confusion. If you find even your best effort disappointing, don't be surprised. Things will improve quickly.

OPTIONS FOR ESSAY WRITING

The following topics offer some ideas for essays that will get you started. People write best about things they know best, and so we begin with personal forms of writing. These topics ask you to explore your feelings, opinions, attitudes, and experience—to discover your insights and viewpoints and to share your thinking with readers. You might want to return to this long list for topic ideas when essays are assigned throughout the early chapters of this book.

Whichever topic(s) you choose, be sure the best version of your essay has a clear thesis supported by a discussion readers will find worthwhile, easy to follow, and understandable. (Save all your writing for revision work in later chapters.)

1. What major effects has television had on your life (your ambitions, hopes, fears, values, consumer habits, awareness of the world, beliefs, outlook, faith in people, and so on)? Overall, has television been a positive or negative influence? Have you learned anything from TV that you couldn't have learned elsewhere? Be sure to support your thesis with specific details.

2. Are today's children growing up too fast by learning so early about sex, violence, drugs, alcohol, money, divorce, suffering, injustice, and death? Or do they need such knowledge in order to cope with an increasingly complex and dangerous world? Discuss this issue in an essay that offers detailed support for your viewpoint. (You might use yourself or a younger sibling as an example here.)

3. How do advertising and commercials shape or mold our values (notions about looking young, being athletic, being thin, smoking, beer drinking, the brands of shoes we wear, and so on)? Does advertising present an unrealistic view of life? In what ways? What kinds of human weaknesses and aspirations do commercials exploit? Support your viewpoint with examples your readers will recognize. (You might focus on how you or someone you know has been victimized by the hype.)

4. How do your notions of "feminine" and "masculine" differ from those of your parents' generation? What do you suppose these changing notions mean for future generations? Support your thesis with specific details.

5. If you had the chance to repeat your high school years, what three or four things would you do differently? Write for a younger brother or sister who is entering high school, and provide enough detail to get your viewpoint across.

6. Has peer pressure had mostly a positive or a negative influence on you? Explain why and how, and give specific examples. Be sure your essay supports a definite viewpoint.

7. Do some music videos communicate distorted and dangerous messages? Discuss specific examples and their effect on viewers. What should be done? Support your viewpoint in a detailed essay.

8. Think about your favorite sport or activity. Identify at least three special features of that activity that contribute to your enjoyment. Describe these features in enough detail to make your classmates share your enjoyment.

9. Americans often are criticized for their emphasis on *competing* and *succeeding* (academically, financially, physically, socially, and so on). Is this criticism valid? Discuss the specific pressures you have experienced. Has emphasis on competition and success been mostly helpful or harmful for you? Why? Support your viewpoint with specific details.

10. Perhaps you belong to a club, sorority, fraternity, environmental or political group, or the like. Encourage your classmates to consider joining the group by writing an essay that describes the organization in terms of its history, goals, philosophy, achievements, activities, or benefits that will have meaning for your readers.

11. Our public schools have been accused of failing to educate America's students. Does your high school typify the so-called failure of American education? Why, or why not? How well did your school prepare you for college—and for life? Give clear and convincing examples to support your thesis.

12. Identify three things that make you angry. Why? Provide enough detail for readers to understand your feelings.

13. Assume that your classmates are about to buy some fairly expensive or specialized item such as ski boots, a stereo, running shoes, a trail bike, roller blades, or the like. Help them make the best choice by giving them clear and useful advice about what qualities and features to look for and what deficiencies to avoid.

14. If a genie could grant you three wishes, what would they be? Describe exactly what you would want, and explain why. Be sure to leave no room for your wishes to be *misinterpreted*.

15. College students commonly are stereotyped as party animals. Explain to a nonstudent audience that college life is harder than people imagine. Make your point without sermonizing, whining, or complaining. Paint a vivid picture for skeptical readers. (For instance, if you attend a public university, you might write for state legislators who want to cut the school budget.)

16. Explain to a skeptical audience the benefits of an alternative lifestyle choice (vegetarianism, co-housing, nontraditional family, male homemaker, or the like). Dispel the negative stereotypes.

2
Planning the Essay

Writing is a battle with impatience, a fight against the natural urge to "be done with it." Effective writers know how to win this battle; they spend plenty of time planning their writing. Of course, "planning" continues throughout the writing process; as your thinking changes, as you explore and discover new meanings and new expressions, your plan might change often. But an initial plan gives you something to aim for, a place to start, and a direction to follow as you work through the process.

Writers plan their essays by deciding on answers to all these questions:

What, exactly, is my topic?

Why do I want to write about it?

What is my viewpoint (expressed as a thesis)?

Who is my audience, and how much information do they need?

What do I know about this topic?

Of all the material I've discovered, how much is worthwhile—considering my purpose and audience?

How will I organize this material?

How do I want my writing to sound?

Although these decisions (about topic, purpose, thesis, audience, material, organization, and tone) are covered here in order, rarely will you follow the same order for your own writing. In Chapter 1, Shirley Haley discovers her thesis *before* brainstorming for material. Other writers begin with an outline. The key is to *make all the decisions*—in whichever order works best for you.

As with any stage in the writing process, you might have to return again and again to your plan while you work toward the finished essay.

Deciding on Your Topic

If the topic is dictated by your situation, you have no problem; this decision is already made in most out-of-school writing ("Why I deserve a promotion"; "Why you should marry me"; "How we repaired your computer"). In school, you might be assigned a topic or asked to choose your own. When the topic decision *is* left to you, remember this one word: *focus*.

Never tackle too broad a topic. Instead of describing your social life last summer or telling how to play tennis, tell us about last night's blind date or how to serve a tennis ball. Begin with a *focused* topic, something you know and really can talk about, something that has real meaning for *you*.

Sometimes we worry about having too little to say, and so we mistakenly choose the broadest possible topic. But a limited topic actually provides *more* to write about by allowing for the nitty-gritty details that help readers see what we mean.

Our world is full of subjects: love, work, sex, drugs, money, lifestyles, or whatever. But none of these huge subjects can be covered in a brief essay. Without a specific focus we end up looking at everything in general and at nothing in particular. For instance, if you wanted to know the "personality" of a particular town, walking around and talking with the people would tell you a lot more than flying over the place at 10,000 feet.

If you try to write about why love is important, we won't get to read about anything we haven't heard or seen or read many times before; if, instead, you share with us your experience in learning to cope with the death of a loved one, we will get to know something about you, about pain, and maybe about courage as well. Reading is hard work; readers expect some reward for their labors. Don't waste their time and yours with a topic you know is too broad.

Within any subject, you need to discover a *topic*, your own angle of vision, a viewpoint. First, make the subject narrow:

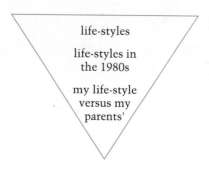

Even the limited subject "my life-style versus my parents'" could be narrowed again—say, to one specific difference (in respective attitudes about money or work or education or the like).

Narrow your subject until you get to where you can take a definite position; then make it a topic by inserting your viewpoint.

Subject   My life-style versus my parents'
                          ↓
Topic   How I want my life to differ from that of my parents

Suppose your instructor asks for an essay about a vivid memory. This time, part of your focusing job is done (memory → a vivid memory). But you need even more focus:

A vivid memory
    ↓
A memory from high school
    ↓
High school gym class
    ↓
Unpleasant memories of my gym class

The last subject seems focused enough for a short essay. But what in this subject do you wish to explore? What do you want readers to know and understand? Make the subject a topic by inserting a viewpoint:

Why I hated high school gym class

Once you have a suitable topic, you're on your way. You might get stuck later and have to discard the whole thing, but for now you have something to work from.

Deciding on Your Purpose

During all stages in the writing process, you will be deciding about priorities: What's most important? What can I leave out? What should I say first? How much is enough? And so on. How you answer those questions will depend on how you answer this one: *Why am I writing this piece?* Once you decide on your exact *purpose,* all other decisions become easier.

Each writing situation has a specific goal. Perhaps you want your audience to see what you saw, to feel what you felt, or to change their thinking. To achieve your goal, you will need a definite plan.

Goal plus plan equals purpose. To define your purpose, then, you need a definite view of your goal and a clear sense of how to reach it. Consider one writer's inadequate answers to the familiar question, "Why am I writing this paper?"

> I'm writing this to pass the course.
>
> My goal is to write an essay about yoga.
>
> My goal is to write an essay to persuade my classmates to try yoga.

The first two responses tell nothing about the specific goal. (We can only reach goals we have *identified.*) The third response does define the goal, but offers no plan. Here, finally, is our writer's purpose statement (goal plus plan):

> My purpose is to write an essay persuading my classmates to try yoga by showing them how it relaxes the body, clears the mind, and stimulates the imagination.*

A well-defined purpose enables you to overcome the problem of trying to make something from nothing—a problem all writers face always. Trying to write anything definite *before* defining your purpose is like trying to cross a wilderness without map and compass. Knowing neither your destination nor your route, you're bound to get lost.

Sometimes you will be unable to define your purpose immediately.

---

* The purpose statement, of course, is not included in the essay; it merely gives the writer a definite orientation.

You might need to jot down as many purposes as possible until one pops up. Or you might need to write a rough draft first or make some type of outline. Assume that you are writing the essay "Why I Hated High School Gym Class." To share with your classmates that painful memory, you will need a plan. Because the essay examines "Why," you organize a rough outline to follow the sequence of causes and effects in your unpleasant experience:

> What the class was like
>
> How I performed
>
> How my peers and teachers reacted to my performance
>
> How I ended up feeling

Now you can compose your statement of purpose:

> My purpose is to explain to my classmates why I have such a painful memory of high school gym class. I'll have to show what the class was like, how I performed, how everyone reacted, and how I ended up feeling.

Besides having a clear direction, you now have a rough map for reaching your goal.

Deciding on Your Thesis

In your purpose statement, you identify exactly what you want to *do*. In your thesis, you announce what you want to *say*. Your thesis statement makes a definite commitment. Think of the thesis as the one sentence you would keep if you could keep only one. A clear thesis is the Great Connector between your exact meaning and the reader's exact understanding; a foggy thesis leaves everyone confused. Tell readers what to expect by making your viewpoint absolutely clear. The viewpoint itself can be expressed in any of several forms:

As an opinion	College is not for everyone.
As an observation	My high school education was a waste of time.
As a suggestion	Computer literacy should be a requirement for all undergraduates.
As an attitude	I want my life to be better than that of my parents.
As a question	What is friendship?

Any of these thesis statements creates clear expectations. Readers don't like to be kept guessing. Make your point, and make it early.

THE THESIS AS FRAMEWORK

Consciously or unconsciously, readers look for a thesis,* and they usually look in the essay's early paragraphs. When they don't know what the essay is about, readers struggle to grasp your meaning. Even a single paragraph is hard to understand if the main point is missing. Read this paragraph *once,* only—and then try answering the questions that follow.

> His [or her] job is not to punish, but to heal. Most students are bad writers, but the more serious the injuries, the more confusing the symptoms, the greater the need for effective diagnostic work. When an accident victim is carried into the hospital emergency ward, the doctor does not start treating the patient at the top and slowly work down without a sense of priority, spending a great deal of time on the black eye before [getting] to the punctured lung. Yet that is exactly what the English teacher too often does. The doctor looks for the most vital problem; he [or she] wants to keep the patient alive, and . . . goes to work on the critical injury.
>
> —Donald Murray

After one reading are you able to identify the paragraph's main idea? Probably not—even after a second reading. Without the orientation provided by a topic sentence, you have no framework for understanding this information in its larger meaning. And you don't know where to place the emphasis: on doctors and hospitals, on students, on English teachers?

Now, insert the following sentence at the beginning and reread the paragraph.

> The writing teacher must be not a judge, but a physician.

With this orientation, the message's exact meaning becomes obvious.

In the *basic* essay framework, each body paragraph supports its own topic statement, which focuses on one aspect of the thesis. In other words, the thesis is the *controlling idea.* And each topic statement treats one part of the controlling idea, as diagrammed here:

---

* Although readers may not *consciously* ask, "Where is the thesis?" they do expect some clear signal to help them approach the whole message and to help them narrow the range of meanings they can create from the essay.

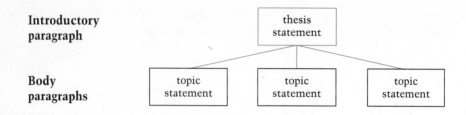

The thesis statement announces the central point—the writer's reason for writing. It is a commitment that everything to follow will support that point.

Some writers include in the thesis a *preview* of supporting points; some don't. An essay titled "Beef Cost and the Cattle Rancher" might have this thesis statement:

> Because of rising costs, unpredictable weather, and long hours, many cattle ranchers have trouble staying in business.

An alternative is to omit such a preview:

> Cattle ranchers' biggest challenge is survival for their business.

Including a preview in their thesis sometimes helps writers stay on track as they develop each support paragraph. Use whichever version works best for you—as long as your thesis announces exactly where you stand. And with or without the preview, be sure that supporting points appear as topic statements in subsequent paragraphs.

FROM PURPOSE STATEMENT TO THESIS

You can make your meaning clear to readers only if you've already made it clear to yourself. Your thesis statement, therefore, often grows out of your purpose statement. Here again is the purpose statement for your gym class essay:

> My purpose is to explain to my classmates why I have such a painful memory of high school gym class. I'll have to show what the class was like, how I performed, how everyone reacted, and how I ended up feeling.

Keep in mind that the purpose statement is part of the discovery process, but the thesis is part of the finished essay. Here is the thesis you've derived from your purpose statement:

Introductory
paragraph
_____
_____
_____

Thesis statement
_____ For three long years, gym
class was my weekly exercise in failure.

Although you decided not to preview the main supporting points, you do
announce each in respective topic statements:

First supporting
paragraph
    Although I respected my gym teacher's focus
on excellence, the standards in this class were
beyond my ability. [*topic statement*] _____
_____
_____

Second supporting
paragraph
    Whatever sport we played, I could count on
being the loser, even when my team won. [*topic
statement*] _____
_____
_____

Third supporting
paragraph
    I was continually reminded of my failures.
[*topic statement*] _____
_____
_____

Concluding paragraph
    The whole experience left me feeling
defeated. [*topic statement*] _____
_____
_____

EVALUATING YOUR THESIS

Always check to see that your thesis has a sharp focus and a definite and
significant viewpoint.

Is the Topic Sharply and Appropriately Focused?   Have you focused on
a topic limited enough to cover in a short essay? Avoid broad topics such
as this one:

Too broad   Some experiences can be unforgettable.

The topic (unforgettable experiences) would require volumes!
    Also, keep your focus appropriate to your purpose. Instead of cata-
loging your disasters in gym class, you might want to focus on the caste

system that grew among the students. You might come up with this thesis:

> Because of the fierce competition in my gym class, each student quickly and indelibly earned the label of "achiever" or of "reject."

Depending on your purpose, you can adjust your thesis to focus on smaller and smaller parts of a topic.

Is a Definite and Informative Viewpoint Expressed?   Let readers know immediately where you stand. Preview your exact meaning. These thesis statements are inadequate, because they offer no such preview:

No clear viewpoint expressed

I will discuss a memory of high school gym class.

In high school, I had a weekly gym class.

High school experiences can be complex.

The first sentence identifies a limited subject but says nothing about the writer's viewpoint. The second is a mere statement of fact. The third signals no exact meaning, thereby arousing no definite expectations in the reader. Always give readers a clear sense of what to expect.

Is the Viewpoint Significant?   Whether your thesis is expressed as an opinion, attitude, observation, suggestion, or question, it should trigger some fresh insight or have some value or importance for readers. A thesis that holds no surprise is worthless:

Insignificant viewpoints

The high school years can be traumatic. [*Everyone would agree, and so why discuss it?*]

Everyone has some vivid memories of high school. [*No big surprise here!*]

Worthless thesis statements usually are a prelude to worthless essays.

To measure the value of your thesis, ask yourself this question: Is my thesis saying something my audience will want to read about?

VARIATIONS IN THE THESIS STATEMENT

The standard thesis statement can have several variations. We have seen, for example, that the main supporting points are not always previewed.

Also, a thesis does not automatically call for only *three* supporting points. Three is a good minimum, but only if the topic actually has only three points for consideration. In later essays, some topics call for more, others for less.

The thesis usually is the final sentence in the introduction. In this position it "bridges" the introduction and the body. But for some purposes it can appear elsewhere in the introduction (as on page 65). Finally, the thesis need not be limited to *one* sentence (as in the abortion paragraph, page 70).

How you phrase your thesis and where you place it depends on your purpose, and audience.

WHEN TO COMPOSE YOUR THESIS

In an ideal world, writers would be able to (1) settle on a topic, (2) compose a purpose statement, and (3) compose a thesis. But these steps rarely occur in such neat order. *If you have trouble coming up with a thesis right away,* go on to some other activity: list some ideas, work on an outline, do some freewriting, or take a walk. Writing, after all, is a way of *discovering* what you want to say—or, writing expert Peter Elbow says, "a way to end up thinking something you couldn't have started out thinking."* As long as you begin with a definite goal, you eventually will discover a purpose and a thesis. Then your later drafts can follow a definite plan. The order of steps is immaterial—as long as you complete them all.

Even if you do begin with a workable thesis, it might not be the one you end up with. As you work and discover new meanings, you might need to revise or even discard your thesis and start again. *Nothing in the writing process is finished until everything is finished.*

Deciding on Your Audience

Except for a diary or a journal, everything you write is for readers who will react to your information. You might write to a prospective employer who wants to know why you quit a recent job; or to a committee who wants to know why you deserve a scholarship; or to a classmate who wants to know you better; or to a professor who wants to know whether you understand the material. For any audience, your task is to deliver a useful message, one that makes a difference with readers, that helps them see things your way.

Out of school you will write for diverse audiences (customers, employers, politicians, and so on). But in school, you can envision a definite audience besides your instructor: your classmates. Like any audience, they expect your writing to be clear, informative, and persuasive. If

---

* *Writing Without Teachers* (New York: Oxford University Press, 1973), p. 15.

you can write for a college audience, you will be prepared to face other audiences later (see Chapter 22).

Whether your audience is the company president or the person next to you in English class, people read your writing because they expect a worthwhile message. They might need it to solve a problem, make a decision, evaluate your performance, or just entertain themselves. Whatever their motives, readers need enough material to understand your position and to react appropriately. Readers *don't* need repetition of material they already know. Instead of telling everything you know about the topic, give readers only what they need.

Based on their specific needs, readers approach any writing with questions:

What is it?

What does it look like?

What are its parts?

What happened?

How does it make you feel?

Who was involved?

When, where, and why did it happen?

How do I do it?

How did you do it?

What are its effects?

Is *X* better than *Y*?

How are they similar or different?

Can you give examples?

What does it mean?

Can you prove it?

Says who?

Why should I?

Who cares?

How am I supposed to react?

To put readers in *your* place, first put yourself in *theirs*. Anticipate their most probable questions.

As author of the gym class essay, for example, you face your own special task: to make an experience that had meaning for you have meaning for your *audience*. At the very least, you need to answer these reader questions:

What was it?

What happened?

When, where, and why did it happen?

How did it make you feel?

Who was involved?

Who cares?

Anticipating your readers' questions gives you a better chance of discovering and selecting material that really makes a difference—that offers readers what they need and expect.

Discovering Useful Material

Discovering useful material is called *invention*. Decisions about purpose, thesis, and audience are all part of invention. These decisions direct your search for content and help you select what to include or exclude. In turn, the material you discover may cause you to revise your original purpose and thesis.

When you begin working with an idea or exploring a topic, you search for useful material, for content: insights, facts, statistics, opinions, examples, images. You search for anything that might help you answer this question: How can I find something worthwhile to say—something that will advance my meaning?

Invention strategies in this section are based on one principle: *No writer can make something from nothing*. Even professional writers have to dredge from memory and imagination things that otherwise would go unrecognized. The goal of invention is to get as much material as possible on paper, through one or more of the following strategies.

KEEPING A JOURNAL

A journal is an excellent way to build a personal inventory of ideas and topics. Here you can write purely *for yourself*.

To start, buy a hardcover notebook with a sewn binding (so that whatever you write becomes a permanent part of your journal). From here on, the journal entries are up to you. Record your reactions to something you've read or seen; ask questions or describe people, places, things, feelings; explore fantasies, daydreams, nightmares, fears, hopes; write conversations or letters that never will be heard or read; examine the things you hate or love. Write several times a day or once a week or whenever you get the urge—or put aside some regular time to write. Every so often, go back and look over your entries—you might be surprised by the things you find.

FREEWRITING

Freewriting is a version of the "quickest-effort" approach discussed in Chapter 1. Shirley Haley's first attempt (page 14) is the product of freewriting. As the term suggests, when freewriting you simply write whatever comes to mind, hoping that the very act of recording your thinking will generate some useful content.

Try freewriting by exploring what makes you angry or happy or frightened or worried. Write about what surprises you or what you think is unfair or what you would like to see happen. Don't stop writing until you've filled a whole page or two, and don't worry about organization or correctness—just get it down. Although your product will be nowhere near a finished essay, freewriting can give you a good start by uncovering all kinds of buried ideas. It can be especially useful if you're suffering from "writer's block."

USING JOURNALISTS' QUESTIONS

To probe the many angles and dimensions of a topic, journalists are taught to ask these questions.

Who was involved?

What happened?

When did it happen?

Where did it happen?

How did it happen?

Why did it happen?

Answering these questions for your gym class essay will enable you to share your experience of the people and events. Unlike freewriting, the journalists' questions offer a built-in organizing strategy—an array of different "perspectives" on your topic.

DISCOVERING USEFUL MATERIAL   41

ASKING YOURSELF QUESTIONS

If you can't seem to settle on a definite viewpoint, try answering any of these questions that apply to your topic.

What is my opinion of X?

Is it good or bad?

Is it beneficial or harmful?

Is it valuable or worthless?

Will it work or fail?

Does it make sense?

What is my attitude toward X?

Am I for it or against it?

Do I like it or dislike it?

Do I accept it or reject it?

Does it make me happy or sad?

Do I approve or disapprove?

What have I observed about X?

What have I seen happen?

What is special or unique about it?

What strikes me about it?

What can I suggest about X?

What would I like to see happen?

What should be done?

What should not be done?

From your answers, you can zero in on the viewpoint that will provide the organizing insight for your essay.

BRAINSTORMING

If you're uncomfortable with freewriting and prefer not to answer a list of questions, try brainstorming—a sure bet for coming up with useful material. Here is how brainstorming works:

1. Find a quiet spot, and bring an alarm clock, a pencil, and plenty of paper.

2. Set the alarm to ring in 30 minutes.

3. Try to protect yourself from interruptions: phones, music, or the like. Sit with eyes closed for two minutes, thinking about *absolutely nothing.*

4. Now, concentrate on your writing situation. If you've already spelled out your purpose and your audience's questions, focus on these. Otherwise, repeat this question: *What can I say about my topic, at all?*

5. As ideas begin to flow, write *every* one down. Don't stop to judge relevance or worth, and don't worry about complete sentences (or even correct spelling). Simply get everything on paper. The more ideas, the better your chance of finding a winner. Trust your imagination. Even the wildest idea might lead to some valuable insight.

6. Keep pushing and sweating until the alarm rings.

7. If the ideas are still flowing, reset the alarm and go on.

8. At the end of this session, you should have a chaotic mixture of junk, irrelevancies, and useful material.

9. Take a break.

10. Now confront your list. Strike out the useless material, and sort what's left into categories. Include any other ideas that crop up. Your finished list should provide plenty of raw material.

For your gym class essay, assume you've developed the brainstorming list that follows.

1. gym teacher expected too much

2. terror every Monday morning

3. like a walk to the guillotine

4. teachers should learn to control their biases

5. they should take courses in dealing with students of all abilities

6. winning was everything

7. drums beating

8. losing teams punished

9. teachers teach *students*, not phys. ed. or other subjects

10. always one of the last players picked

11. always the loser

12. trying hard only made me feel incompetent

13. teacher liked only the athletes

14. fun—instead of victory—should be the goal in athletics

15. teammates groaned at my efforts

16. my gift grade was a C minus

17. I felt blacklisted

18. effort versus performance

19. nicknamed "the athlete"

20. I laughed, but it wasn't funny

21. missed the backboard

22. I had no talent

23. sure to fail

With your raw material collected, you can now move into the selection phase—leaving open the possibility that new material may surface.

Some people use invention as an early writing step, as a way of getting started. Others save the invention stage until they've made other decisions. But regardless of the sequence, all writers use invention throughout the writing process—to ensure they discover *all* the possible material they might want to include in their final draft.

READING AND RESEARCHING

All these earlier invention strategies work well for more personal forms of writing. But some of our best ideas, insights, and questions often come from our reading (as discussed in Chapter 5). Or we might want to consider what others have said or discovered about our topic (as discussed in Chapter 20), before we reach our own conclusions. Reading and research are indispensable tools for any serious writer.

Selecting Your Best Material

From the broad inventory of facts and ideas you've assembled, you will want to select *only* your best material. Invention invariably produces more material than a writer needs. Never expect to use *everything*.

As you review your brainstorming list (page 42) for the gym class essay, let's say you decide to cut items 4, 5, 9, and 14.

- Item 4 sounds too much like a sermon and doesn't relate to the purpose (to describe a memory—not to argue for changes in teaching approaches).

- Item 5, again, is not directly related to experiences in the gym. Also, the notion of such "courses" is too abstract to have real meaning in this context.

- Item 9 is a cliché, which again is too abstract to have real meaning—much less any relevance—to this essay.

- Item 14 is overstated. Athletics could have value other than fun (exercise, relaxation, team spirit, and so on).

If you do find yourself trying to include *all* the material you've discovered, you probably need to refocus on your purpose and audience.*

Organizing for Readers

After selecting worthwhile material, organize it so readers can follow your thinking. With an outline, you move from a random listing of items as they occurred to you to a deliberate map that will guide readers from point to point. Readers more easily understand and remember material organized in a sequence they find logical.

But *how* should you organize to make your writing logical—from your audience's point of view? All readers expect a definite beginning, middle, and ending:

- a beginning (or introduction) that provides orientation by telling readers what they need to know first,

- a middle section (or body) that reveals the writer's exact meaning, with one item logically following another,

- an ending (or conclusion) that emphasizes what is most important and leaves readers reflecting on the material they have just read.

When material is left in its original, unstructured form, readers waste time trying to understand it.

Readers generally expect writing to be organized into orientation,

---

* Chapter 6 offers detailed advice about selecting material that will be fresh and worthwhile for your readers.

discussion, and review sections, such as those just listed. But specific readers want these sections tailored to their expectations. Identify your readers' expectations by (1) anticipating their probable questions about your thesis, and (2) visualizing the sequence in which readers would want these questions answered.

Let's try to anticipate readers' expectations about the gym-class essay. Here again is the thesis: *For three long years, high school gym class was my weekly exercise in failure.* And here are the readers' questions, in the sequence we might anticipate:

Can you set the scene for us, and re-create your feelings or mood?

What were the teacher and the class like?

What did you do that was so bad?

How did everyone react to what you did?

How did you react?

You might think of slightly different questions. But we can assume that most readers would have questions much like these and would want them answered in a similar sequence.

What you have just learned about your readers' expectations gives you a basis for organizing your brainstorming material into definite categories:

I.   How I Dreaded Monday Morning Gym Class

II. How Our Teacher's Standards Were Too High

III. How I Failed to Meet These Standards

IV. How I Was Continually Reminded of My Failures

V.   How the Experience Left Me Feeling Defeated

Within each category, you arrange your brainstorming items, along with any other worthwhile material you have discovered since. Your final outline might resemble this one:

I.   I dreaded Monday morning gym class.
   A.   I knew what was waiting for me.
   B.   I could sense the dampness and the stale smell.
   C.   My hands would tremble, and I would sweat.
   D.   Monday was physical education day.
   E.   I had no athletic talent, and so was terrified.
   F.   It felt like a walk to the guillotine, with drums in the background.

G. *Thesis:* For three long years, my high school gym class was my weekly exercise in failure.

II. Our teacher's standards were too high.
  A. She was not unkind, but not realistic, either.
  B. Athletic prowess was expected of each student.
  C. Only the athletes were liked.
  D. Winning meant everything.
  E. All fun disappeared.

III. I never could measure up to the high standards.
  A. I always lost—even when my team won.
  B. I couldn't hit the backboard.
  C. I tripped over my own feet.
  D. Any sport meant failure.
  E. The more I tried, the more I felt inferior.

IV. I was continually reminded of my failures.
  A. My classmates grew to expect the worst from me.
  B. I was always one of the last picked for teams.
  C. People groaned when I came up to bat.
  D. My friends nicknamed me "the athlete."
  E. I laughed on the outside, but not inside.
  F. My C–"gift grade" killed my otherwise high average.

V. The whole experience left me feeling defeated.
  A. I should have been able to learn something about self-confidence.
  B. But I only felt "blacklisted."
  C. Intimidated, I developed a kind of mental paralysis.
  D. I accepted the certainty of failure.
  E. Never have my personal shortcomings received such public display.

This outline takes the form of short, kernel sentences that include key ideas for later expansion. Some writers might have used a less formal outline—a simple list of phrases without numerals or letters. Use the form that works best for you.

At any stage in the writing process, writers can discover new material. Here are thoughts that might have occurred as you outlined:

My stomach tightened as I walked through the school door. (belongs in IA)

Many classmates seemed to reflect the teacher's attitude. (belongs in IIC)

In baseball, I was the sure strikeout, the right fielder who dropped every fly ball. (belongs in IIIC)

Later, during various drafts, you will discover more material, and probably will delete some original material (as in the final draft, pages 71–72).

Once you have a suitable outline, check it for *unity* and *coherence.* An outline has unity when everything directly supports the thesis. Items 4, 5, 9, and 14 were deleted from the brainstorming list (page 42) because none of that material related directly to the thesis. An outline has coherence when the thesis and all supporting material form one connected line of thought, like links in a chain. Coherence would suffer in the gym class essay if, say, description of the teacher's standards *followed* description of the writer's failures. Readers need to know about the standards to appreciate the writer's sense of failure.

Finally, check for emphasis. An outline has suitable emphasis when the important things stand out. Last things are best remembered; then, first; middles are too easily forgotten. Our gym class outline is organized to emphasize first the writer's fear and last her sense of paralysis. The middle explains the cause of these feelings, but readers will identify most vividly with the feelings themselves.*

Some writers can organize merely by working from a good thesis statement. Others prefer to begin with some sort of outline. And some write a draft and then outline to check the line of thinking. You might outline early or later. But before submitting a final draft, you need to move from a random collection of ideas to an organized list that makes sense to your readers. Organize in the way that will be best for readers to approach your material.

NOTE: A suitable beginning, middle, and ending are essential, but alter your own outline as you see fit. No single form of outline should be followed slavishly by any writer. The organization of any writing ultimately is determined by its audience's needs and expectations.

Deciding on Your Tone

With many planning decisions made, your inventory is nearly complete: you have a topic and a thesis, a clear sense of purpose and audience, a stock of material, and some kind of outline. In fact, if you were writing merely *to get your message across,* you could begin drafting the essay immediately. We write, however, not only to transmit information, but also to connect with readers.

Unlike computers, writers can't be programmed for this profoundly human task. Nor can readers be programmed to react in a particular way. In fact, readers often create their *own* meanings for what they have read!

---

* Because unity, coherence, and emphasis are best illustrated at the paragraph level, they are covered in detail in Chapter 7.

Except for diaries or some technical reports, all writers have to decide how they want their writing to "sound"—what attitude they want to convey about their reader and their topic. The way your writing sounds depends on its *tone,* your personal mark—the voice readers hear between the lines. If readers like the tone, they like the writer; they allow contact. Always labor to get your message across, but never be afraid to express genuine feeling.

Consciously or unconsciously, readers ask three big questions about the writer:

1. *Who is this person* (somebody businesslike, serious, silly, sincere, phony, boring, bored, intense, stuck-up, meek, confident, friendly, hostile, or what)?

2. *How is this person treating me* (as a friend, acquaintance, stranger, enemy, nobody, superior, subordinate, bozo, somebody with a brain and feelings, or what)?

3. *What does this person really think about the topic* (really caring or merely "going through the motions")?

The readers' answers will depend on your tone. Think hard about your words and the meanings they suggest.

Some inexperienced writers mistakenly think that fancy words are better than simple words for sounding more intelligent and important. And sometimes, of course, only the fancy word will convey your exact meaning. Instead of saying "Sexist language *contributes to the ongoing existence of* stereotypes," you could say more accurately and concisely, "Sexist language *perpetuates* stereotypes." (One "fancy" word effectively replaces six "simpler" words.) But when you use fancy words needlessly, and only to impress, your writing sounds stuffy and pretentious.

ACHIEVING A TONE THAT CONNECTS WITH READERS

Readers look for a real person between the lines, just as you do when reading this book or almost anything else. And so when you write, "For three long `years, gym class was my weekly exercise in failure," you invite us in, encourage us to read on; but not when you write, "During the seemingly interminable course of three years, my physical education curriculum served as an effrontery to my self-esteem." This second version probably means pretty much the same as the first, but nothing here is inviting.

Personal essays ordinarily employ a *conversational* tone: you write to your audience as if you were speaking to them. For instance, here again are the opening lines from Shirley Haley's final draft on page 18:

> I'm probably the only person I know who still has the same two parents she was born with. We have a traditional American family: we go to church and football games; we watch the Olympics on television and argue about politics; and we have Thanksgiving dinner at my grandmother Clancy's and Christmas dinner with my father's sister Jess, who used to let us kids put pitted olives on our fingertips when we were little.

Haley's tone is friendly and relaxed—the voice of a writer who seems at home with herself, her subject, and her readers. We are treated to comfortable images of family things. But we sense something else here, too: the long list of "traditional" family activities hints at the writer's restlessness, lets us share her mixed feelings of attraction and repulsion.

Imagine, instead, that Haley had decided to sound "academic" throughout her essay:

> Among my friends and acquaintances, I am apparently the only individual with the good fortune to have parents who remain married. Our family activities are grounded in American tradition: we attend church services and football games; we watch televised sporting events and engage in political debates; at Thanksgiving, we dine at Grandmother's, and at Christmas, with an aunt who has always been quite tolerant of children's behavior.

This second version seems less inviting than the original. To see for yourself, test each version against readers' three big questions on page 48. This second version has words that seem written by no one in particular, about nothing special, for no one who matters—words that deny contact. Let readers hear your voice.*

AVOIDING AN OVERLY INFORMAL TONE

We generally do not write in the same way we would speak to friends at the local burger joint or street corner. Achieving a conversational tone does not mean lapsing into substandard usage, slang, or excessive colloquialisms. *Substandard usage* ("He ain't got none." "I seen it today." "She brang the book.") fails to meet standards of educated expression. *Slang* ("hurling," "belted," "bogus," "bummed") usually has specific meaning only for members of a particular in-group. *Colloquialisms* ("O.K.," "a lot," "snooze," "in the bag,") are understood more widely than slang, but tend to appear more in speaking than in writing.

Slang hardly ever is appropriate in school or workplace writing. The

---

* The more distant and formal tone in the second version might be appropriate in, say, a report for social science class, but not in a personal essay for classmates. For specific ways of adjusting tone, see Chapter 9.

occasional colloquial expression, however, helps soften the tone of any writing—as long as the situation calls for a measure of informality.

A formal or academic tone, in fact, is perfectly appropriate in countless writing situations: a research paper, a job application, a report for the company president, and so on. In a history essay, for example, we would not refer to George Washington and Abraham Lincoln as "those dudes, George and Abe."

Tone is considered offensive when it violates the reader's expectations: when it seems disrespectful or tasteless, or distant and aloof, or too "chummy," casual, or otherwise inappropriate for the topic, the reader, and the situation.

Whenever we begin with freewriting or brainstorming, our tone might be overly informal and is likely to require some adjustment during subsequent drafts.

The Writer's Planning Guide

Decisions and strategies covered in this chapter apply to almost any writing situation. You can make sure your own planning decisions are complete by following the Planning Guide whenever you write. Items in the Planning Guide are reminders of things to be done.

PLANNING GUIDE

Broad subject:

Limited topic:

Purpose statement:

Thesis statement:

Audience:

Probable audience questions:

Brainstorming list (with irrelevant items deleted):

Outline:

Appropriate tone for audience and purpose:

This next Planning Guide has been completed to show a typical set of decisions for the gym class essay.

PLANNING GUIDE

Broad subject: A vivid memory

Limited topic: Why I hated high school gym class

Purpose statement (what you want to do): My purpose is to explain to my classmates why I have such a painful memory of high school gym class. I'll have to show what the class was like, how I performed, how everyone reacted, and how I ended up feeling.

Thesis statement (what you want to say): For three long years, gym class was my weekly exercise in failure.

Audience: Classmates

Probable audience questions:
      Can you set the scene for us, and re-create your feelings
         or mood?
      What were the teacher and the class like?
      What did you do that was so bad?
      How did everyone react to what you did?
      How did you react?
      Who cares?

Brainstorming list:
      1. gym teacher expected too much
      2. terror every Monday morning
      3. like a walk to the guillotine . . . and so on

Outline:
  I. I dreaded Monday morning gym class.
     A.   I knew what was waiting for me.
     B.   I could sense the dampness and the stale smell.
     C.   My hands would tremble, and I would sweat.
     D.   Monday was physical education day . . . and so on.

Appropriate tone for audience and purpose: personal and serious

Remember that your decisions for completing the Planning Guide need not follow the strict order of the items listed—so long as you make all the necessary decisions.

Your instructor might ask you to use the Planning Guide for early assignments and to submit your responses along with your essay.

Application 2–1

Narrow two or three of the subjects in this list to a topic suitable for a short essay. (Review pages 29–30.)

Example

movies
↓
how movies influence viewers
↓
how some movies depict sex
↓
how some movies shown on prime-time television encourage sexual permissiveness

SUBJECTS TO BE NARROWED

television	money	careers	sailing
war	family life	sports	crime
energy	sex	science fiction	automobiles
fashion	forests	animals	music
marriage	jobs	weather	alcohol
camping	studying	junk food	drugs

NOTE: The Options for Essay Writing on pages 25–27 contain certain topics that have been narrowed from some of the subjects listed above (say, "television" or "music"). You might review those topics to get some ideas for this application.

Application 2–2

Compose statements of purpose for essays on three or more of the topics in Application 2–1. (Review pages 31–32.)

Example

Topic   Prime-time television movies that encourage
                      sexual permissiveness

Statement of purpose My purpose is to show a general reading audience
                      how some movies shown on prime-time television
                      encourage sexual permissiveness among immature
                      viewers. I will discuss four misleading ways in
                      which such movies often depict sex: as a ritual of
                      introduction, an educational experience, a device
                      for achieving personal gain, and a form of
                      recreation.

Application 2–3

Convert your statements of purpose from Application 2–2 into thesis
statements. (Review pages 32–35.)

Example

Statement of purpose My purpose is to show a general reading audience
                      how some movies shown on prime-time television
                      encourage sexual permissiveness among immature
                      viewers. I will discuss four misleading ways in
                      which such movies often depict sex: as a ritual of
                      introduction, an educational experience, a device
                      for achieving personal gain, and a form of
                      recreation.

Thesis statement   Too many movies shown on prime-time television
                      encourage sexual permissiveness by depicting sex
                      without love in a variety of superficial encounters.

Application 2–4

For each thesis statement in Application 2–3, brainstorm and write
three or four topic statements for individual supporting paragraphs.
Arrange your topic statements in logical order. (Review pages 34–35.)

Example

Thesis statement   Too many movies shown on prime-time television
                      encourage sexual permissiveness by depicting sex
                      without love in a variety of superficial encounters.

First topic statement One of the most common forms of sexual
                      encounter I've seen on television is the "first-date"

	syndrome, in which sex becomes part of the ritual of introduction.
Second topic statement	Other movies recently shown on television depict sex as an educational experience.
Third topic statement	Some films degrade the act of love by showing characters who use sex as a device for obtaining something.
Fourth topic statement	The most demeaning portrayal, however, occurs when sex is treated as casual recreation.

Application 2–5

From Application 2–4, select the most promising set of materials, and write your best essay. Use selected items from your brainstorming list to develop each support paragraph. Outline as necessary. Provide an engaging introduction and a definite conclusion. Use the questions on pages 23–24 as guidelines for revising your essay.

Application 2–6

From this list of broad subjects, select *four* about which you would have something worthwhile to say to your classmates. (Review pages 29–30.)

animals	drinking	life-styles	old age
cars	drugs	love	television
college	ecology	marriage	travel
dating	families	money	sex
death	jobs	nuclear power	war

After limiting these four subjects, compose *one* thesis statement for each. (You may wish to freewrite or to compose a purpose statement beforehand.) Your thesis can be expressed as an opinion, an attitude, an observation, or a suggestion. (Use the questions on pages 40–41 to get started.) Revise each statement until it meets the standards on pages 35–36.

Example

Broad subject	television
Limited subject	certain effects of television commercials
Thesis statement	Television commercials prey on the insecurities of consumers. *[gives an informed opinion]*
Broad subject	marriage
Limited subject	fear of parenthood
Thesis statement	The prospect of becoming a parent in the 1990s frightens me. *[expresses an attitude]*
Broad subject	life-styles
Limited subject	the pace of American life
Thesis statement	Americans everywhere are obsessed with speed. *[shares an observation]*
Broad subject	money
Limited subject	one way to save money
Thesis statement	Becoming a vegetarian is a great way to save money. *[makes a suggestion]*

Application 2–7

From the thesis statements you composed in Application 2–6, select one that seems the best candidate for an essay. List the questions you could expect readers to have about this thesis statement. (Review pages 38–39.)

Example

Thesis statement	Americans everywhere are obsessed with speed.
Readers' questions	Can you show me how?
	Can you give me some examples?
	Says who?

Now, brainstorm for answers to readers' questions. Be sure to delete the items that do not relate directly to your purpose.

Example

Brainstorming list

1. big engines in cars
2. ten-minute oil changes offered by service stations
3. shoes repaired "while you wait"
4. fast-food restaurants are booming
5. jets that can cross the Atlantic in two hours
6. life in the fast lane
7. drive-in church services
8. people gobbling their hamburgers
9. spitting out your prayer and hitting the road

Using your selected brainstorming materials, compose an essay that explains the viewpoint in your thesis statement. Revise until the essay represents your best effort. Use the questions on pages 23–24 as revision guidelines.

Application 2-8

Revise any four of these assertions that do not already meet the following standards. (Review pages 35–36.)

- focus on a limited topic
- establish a definite viewpoint
- express a significant viewpoint
- preview, in order, the supporting ideas*

Mark an *X* next to those that are adequate.

Example

Faulty thesis
Grades are a way of life in college. [*expresses no definite or significant viewpoint and fails to preview the main supporting points*]

---

* For practice, this exercise specifies that each thesis statement include a preview. Remember that many of your own thesis statements will not require a preview.

Revised thesis   Grades are an aid to education because they
                        motivate students, provide an objective measure of
                        performance, and prepare people to compete
                        successfully in their careers.

1. My academic adviser is a new professor.

2. Less than one semester in college has changed my outlook.

3. My last blind date was childish, repulsive, and boring.

4. I would love to spend a year in (name a country).

5. Nuclear power is a controversial issue.

6. I have three great fears.

7. In this essay, I will discuss my attitude toward abortion.

8. Elvis Presley had an amazing career.

9. The Batmobile is a good car because it's inexpensive, fuel efficient, and dependable.

10. I (look forward to, dread) marriage.

11. Education enriches our world.

Application 2–9

Write thesis statements for *five* of these subjects. Include a preview of main supporting points in each, if your instructor so requests. (Review pages 32–34.)

> your opinion of college life
>
> your opinion of today's teenagers
>
> why you like or dislike pets
>
> someone you love
>
> what you would like your life to be like in ten years
>
> what worries you most about the future
>
> why animals should or should not be allowed on campus
>
> why your hometown is a good or bad place to live
>
> what makes a good teacher
>
> why you came to college

an improvement your college needs

why you enjoy a specified activity

your biggest complaint

anything else you can think of

Application 2–10

Collaborative Project: Organize into small groups. Assume your group is preparing a paper titled "The Negative Effects of Strip Mining on the Cumberland Plateau Region of Kentucky." (Review pages 44–47.) This is your thesis:

> Decades of strip mining on the Cumberland Plateau have devastated this region's environment, economy, and social structure.

After brainstorming and research, you all settle on these four major topics:

economic and social effects of strip mining

description of the strip-mining process

environmental effects of strip mining

description of the Cumberland Plateau

Arrange these topics in the most effective sequence.

Now that your topics are arranged, assume that you have written out (as full sentences) these minor topics and subtopics from your brainstorming list:

Contour mining consists of shaving down all ground cover to expose the coal deposits.

Silt dams, designed to trap sediment in ponds rather than downstream, quickly fill and break, causing extensive flood damage and loss of life.

A recent census showed that 19 to 25 percent of the adult population of this region neither could read nor write.

Strip mining is ruining many other areas besides Kentucky.

The Cumberland Plateau was formed approximately 200 million years ago from a plain that had risen from a dried-up inland sea.

One danger of coal as a fuel source is the sulfur dioxide it produces.

This poverty-level existence leaves many families always hungry.

Auger mining employs huge drills that bore through the earth into the coal seam to draw out the coal.

Strip mining scars and pollutes hundreds of acres each week.

Strip-mining processes vary according to the type of terrain.

Using coal for fuel is one way of ending our dependence on imported oil.

Strip mining in the Cumberland Plateau continues to have far-reaching and irreversible effects on the environment.

Strip-mining technology has rendered the skills of farmers and conventional coal miners obsolete, and it has laid waste to a good deal of America's tillable land.

Open-pit mining consists of excavating a terraced, inverted cone into the earth from 100 to 3,000 feet deep; or, this method may employ a series of parallel trenches.

The Cumberland Plateau is a land of jagged hills and narrow, winding valleys covering 10,000 square miles and located 300 miles west of Washington, D.C.

In the Cumberland region of Kentucky and elsewhere in the Appalachians, more than 1 million Americans live in squalor, ignorance, and demoralization.

Soil erosion from strip-mined surfaces occurs at a rate one thousand times greater than that of undisturbed adjacent land.

Air pollution is the terrible price we have to pay for burning coal.

Most of the region's counties show a vast population decrease over the last decade.

Before exploitation, the original plateau held the richest forest on the planet, along with extensive deposits of oil, gas, and coal.

Streams, rivers, and watersheds are polluted by acids and other chemicals, and some become swamps because of mud slides.

Chronic illnesses often result from inadequate diets.

After deleting irrelevant items, arrange the remaining items in order under the appropriate major topics. Concentrate on unity, coherence, and emphasis. To increase your control, use this system of notation:

I. (for a major topic)
    A. (for a minor topic)
        1. (for any subtopics)
        2.
    B.

II.
    A. . . . and so on.

Appoint one group member to present the outline in class.

Application 2–11

Collaborative Project: Organize into small groups. Choose a subject from this list. Then decide on a thesis statement and (*not* necessarily in this order) brainstorm. Identify a specific audience. Group similar items under the same major categories, and develop an outline. When each group completes this procedure, one representative can write the outline on the board for class suggestions about revision. (Review pages 41–47.)

    a description of the ideal classroom

    instructions for surviving the first semester of college

    instructions for surviving a blind date

    suggestions for improving one's college experience

    causes of teenage suicide

    arguments for or against a formal grading system

    an argument for an improvement you think this college needs most

    the qualities of a good parent

    what you expect the world to be like in ten years

    young people's needs that parents often ignore

Application 2–12

Using the Planning Guide on pages 50–51 as a model, do all the planning for an essay on one of these two topics:

Look back on a painful or frightening memory from your child-hood or high school years—some event or experience that left you with a feeling of failure, guilt, anger, rejection, embarrassment, or inadequacy. Maybe you remember making a serious mistake or having incredibly bad luck or trying to make a good impression. Describe for classmates how you tried but failed, how you reacted, and what you learned. Whether you write from a serious or humorous perspective, readers will need enough details to visualize what happened and to identify with your feelings about the event or experience.

As an alternative topic, look back on a pleasant memory, on some event or experience in which you tried and succeeded and which left you with a feeling of triumph or confidence or achievement or satisfaction. Maybe you faced a seemingly impossible challenge or did something courageous. Share this experience with your readers, and tell them what you learned from it.

As your instructor requests, you might move beyond the planning stage and compose your best draft of the essay. Or you might read Chapter 3 before you submit your best draft. Either way, don't be afraid to write one or more *rough* drafts (such as Haley's freewriting on page 14) as part of your planning.

3

Drafting the Essay

Once you have a definite plan, you are ready to draft your essay. Here is where you decide on answers to some tough questions:

How do I begin the essay?

What does my reader need to know first?

What comes after that?

How much is enough?

Am I forgetting anything?

How do I end?

Write at least two drafts, revising until the essay represents your best work. Each writing sample in this book is the product of multiple drafts and revisions. None of these writers expected to get it right the first time—neither should you.

Drafting the Title and Introduction

A title should forecast an essay's subject and approach. Clear titles, such as "A Terrifying Experience," "Let's Shorten the Baseball Season," or

"Instead of Running, Try Walking," help readers plan how to interpret the essay. Phrase your title to attract attention but not to sound like a gimmick. To give an accurate forecast, write your title's final version *after* completing the essay.

THE INTRODUCTORY PARAGRAPH

Your introduction tells readers what they need to know first. An introductory paragraph opens an essay in three ways: it leads into the thesis and main discussion; it arouses readers' interest; and it creates a setting and a tone for the whole essay. Above all, your introduction must be *clear* and *vivid* enough to be inviting. If you lose readers here, chances are you have lost them for good.

Introductory paragraphs differ in shape and size; however, many basic introductory paragraphs seem to have a funnel shape:

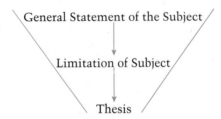

Assume you are continuing your work from Chapter 2 on "Suffering Through Gym Class." To introduce the final draft of your essay, you use a funnel pattern:

Suffering Through Gym Class

General statement (1)
Limitation of subject (2–4)

Thesis (5)

[1]In high school my Monday mornings were awful. [2]Even before the school's front door had slammed behind me, I could sense a nauseating dampness rising up from the locker room, a mist of stale sweat. [3]Monday for me was physical education day. [4]And because I was no athlete, each of my 8:00 a.m. trips downstairs to the gym seemed like a clammy and quivering walk to the guillotine, my heartbeat like a drumbeat, my ego about to suffer its ritual of public execution. [5]For three long years, gym class was my weekly exercise in failure.

This painful account is written for classmates. And so its tone is personal and urgent, created by the first-person *I* and *my, our,* and by images such as "a clammy and quivering walk to the guillotine."

If your only aim were to lead into the main discussion, you might have given this introduction instead:

> I always did poorly in high school gym class.

But this version lacks the vivid images ("nauseating dampness," "a mist of stale sweat") that engage our attention, make us want to read on. And this version is toneless. What kind of attitude is expressed here? We can't possibly tell.

Worse than a lifeless opening is one that exaggerates to attract attention:

> In high school gym class, I had the most incredible experiences of my life, experiences that burned deeply into my soul. Never will I forget those humiliating moments spent trying to be an athlete.

Any introduction for your first draft probably will need revising in your final draft.

PLACING THE THESIS

Where you place your thesis depends on how you want readers to perceive and react to your introduction. Ordinarily, readers expect some background for your thesis, but sometimes they want to know where you stand immediately.

The thesis in a standard essay often appears at the end of the introductory paragraph, as a bridge to the discussion. Also, with the thesis statement at the end, the earlier sentences draw readers into the writer's world. If it had begun flatly with the thesis, the introduction to "Suffering Through Gym Class" would be much less inviting.

Some introductions do call for a thesis statement that leads off the paragraph. For a controversial topic especially, the writer's position might be expressed immediately:

> *Corporal punishment does not belong in our public schools, because it creates a regimented atmosphere that stifles the desire to learn, generates hostility toward the teacher, and causes antisocial behavior.* A school, after all, is not a prison. And among the varied learning experiences school should provide is the opportunity to learn through mistakes.

To evoke an immediate reader response, this writer decided to open with a direct statement of his position. The paragraph then expands the thesis.

Sometimes, even a highly personal piece can open directly with the thesis, especially when the writer is expressing a surprising or controversial viewpoint:

> *I hate summer beaches.* Ocean swimming is impossible; upon conquering a wave, I simply lose to the next, getting pushed back onto the hard-packed, abrasive sand. Booby-traps of bottles, soda cans, toys, and rocks make walking hazardous. Heavy with the stench of suntan lotion, greasy French fries, dead fish, and sweat, the thick, searing air hangs motionless about the scorching sand. Blasting radios and growling hot rods cut the slap-swoosh of the green-gray surf to a weak hiss. People devour a summer beach, gouging the sand with umbrella spikes and gripping it with oiled limbs, leaving only trampled debris at summer's end.

Whenever you wish to be forceful, place your thesis up front.

Keep in mind that, in some essays, the thesis appears later, even near the end (as on page 300). Delaying the thesis is especially useful when the writer's purpose is to tell a story that leads to some larger meaning (for example, "Here is what happened," and then, "Here is what it means").

THE MULTIPLE-PARAGRAPH INTRODUCTION

Some introductions use two or more paragraphs, especially to develop some kind of comparison. In the next introduction the first paragraph offers a view of "primitive" New Guinea, in contrast to the second paragraph's focus on the "modern" aspect of this island nation.

> Poised like an ungainly bird over the north coast of Australia, the island of New Guinea is one of the few remaining "final frontiers" on earth. Hundreds of stone-age tribes survive in the highlands, isolated from each other by massive mountain ranges. Here, in valleys and rain forests still fresh and undiscovered by modern science, live people intimate with the supernatural, skilled in potent sorcery. They are garden people, communing with the land and bound by a complex web of interlocking kinships.
>
> But while the twentieth century is slowly finding its way into these primeval highland villages, it has hurled itself full force on the coastlands. *Port Moresby, New Guinea's capital city, is a symbol of a nation in transition, where the old and the new exist side by side, sometimes in conflict, often in harmony.*

SELECTING AN OPENING STRATEGY

The specific shape and content of your introduction are determined by what you know about your readers and your purpose.

How interested in this topic are my readers likely to be?

How can I make them want to read on?

Are they likely to react defensively?

Is my purpose to describe something, to tell a story, to explain something, to entertain, to change somebody's mind, or what?

The opening strategies that follow serve varied purposes.

Open with an Anecdote   A brief, personal story that makes a point (leads to the thesis*) is a good way to invite readers in.

> Last weekend, I gave a friend's younger brother a ride from the mall. As we drove, I asked him the same old questions about high school, grades, football, and girlfriends. He answered me in one-word sentences and then pulled out a cassette tape. "Wanna hear somethin' cool?" I shrugged and popped it into the tape player. What came pouring through my car speakers made me run a stop sign. The "rap" song spelled out, in elaborate detail, 101 ways to violate a woman's body. Needless to say, it was a long ride across town.
>
> I borrowed the tape and listened to every song, horrified by their recurrent theme of sexual violence and domination. But most horrifying is that a 15-year-old kid actually considers this music "cool."

In this brief but forceful anecdote, the writer's straightforward approach to a troubling issue is sure to make readers take notice.

Open with a Background Story   In an essay that challenges or argues against a popular attitude, telling how and why that attitude became prevalent sometimes helps.

> In 1945, an unearthly blast shook the New Mexico desert. Shortly afterward, the new, awesome force was used, at the cost of hundreds of thousands of lives, to end World War II. Thus began the atomic era, and because of its horrid beginning, it has met with increasing criticism. Now in the 90s the nuclear breeder reactor is our most promising energy alternative, but atomic energy critics have

---

* Many narratives will have no explicit thesis.

> drastically reduced its development and production. *We need the breeder reactor, because it is presently our best long-range source of energy.*

The vivid images here attract our attention. This kind of opening is especially effective in persuasive writing, because it anticipates opposing views and, by acknowledging them, creates a tone of empathy (identification with the reader's attitude).

Open with a Question   A question or series of questions can get readers thinking, especially when you are writing instructions, giving advice, or persuading someone to act.

> What do you do when you find yourself in the produce room cooler with your manager and he nonchalantly wraps his arm around your waist? Or how about when the guys you work with come out with a distasteful remark that makes you seem like a piece of meat? These are just a couple of problems you might face as the only female in a department. *There are, however, ways of dealing with this kind of harassment.*

Any reader who needs this advice would be likely to take it seriously, for the writer clearly has identified with her audience.

Open with a Quotation   Use a quotation summarizing the point you are making or disputing. Always use a *short* quotation, and discuss its significance immediately afterward; don't leave to readers the task of making the connection.

> "The XL Roadster—anything else is just a car," *unless the XL happens to be mine. In that case, it's just a piece of junk.*

Notice how this writer uses the words of the ad ironically to make her point. The abrupt opening reflects her anger and creates a forceful tone.

Open with a Direct Address   Readers generally pay more attention when addressed directly. Using the second-person *you* can be a good way to involve the reader—especially when giving instructions or advice or when writing persuasively.

> Does the thought of artificially preserved, chemically treated food make you lose your appetite? Do limp, tasteless, frozen vegetables leave you cold? *Then you should try your hand at organic gardening.*

This opening combines direct address with questions. Concrete images reinforce the enthusiastic tone. *Caution:* Use *you* only when writing *directly* to the audience—only when the subject is something *about* your audience. Avoid using second person with a subject that calls for third-person point of view. Otherwise, you could make this kind of error:

Incorrect use of *you*	When you are a freshman in college, you soon discover that increased freedom also means increased responsibility for you.
Revised	College freshmen soon discover that increased freedom also means increased responsibility.

Direct address usually works well in ads, popular articles, and brochures—but not in academic reports or most business and technical documents.

Open with a Description   The saying "One picture is worth more than ten thousand words" certainly holds true in writing. A brief, vivid picture is excellent for setting the scene or creating a mood. Instead of including a standard thesis statement in the introduction, some descriptive essays simply have an *orienting sentence* to place readers at the center of things. This next introduction ends with an orienting sentence that leads into the essay:

> The raft bobs gently on the ocean as the four divers help each other with scuba gear. We joke and laugh casually as we struggle in the cramped space; but a restlessness is in the air because we want to be on our way. Finally, everyone is ready, and we split into pairs. I steal a last glance over the blue ocean. I hear the waves slap gently against the boat, the mournful cry of a seagull, and a steady murmur from the crowded beach a mile away. With three splashes my friends jump in. I follow. There is a splash and then silence. The water presses in on me, and all I can hear is the sound of my regulator as I take my first breath. All I see is blue water, yellow light, and endless space. It feels as if we are suspended in time while the world rushes on. *Then my buddy taps me on the shoulder, and we begin a tour of a hidden world.*

Notice how the visual images draw us into the scene and how word choice ("restlessness," "steal a last glance," "finally") contributes to a suspenseful tone.

Although commonly used in narrative and descriptive essays, descriptive openings also can serve in explanatory essays, as with this opening:

> They appear each workday morning from 7:00 to 9:00, role models for millions of career-minded women. Their crisp, clear diction and articulate reporting are second only to their appearance. Slender and lovely, the female co-hosts of "Today" and other morning news shows radiate that businesslike "chic" that networks consider essential in their newswomen. Such perfection is precisely why the networks hire these women as anchors. *Network television rarely tolerates women commentators who are other than young, slim, and attractive.*

Notice the businesslike tone that parallels the topic itself.

Open with Examples   Examples can immediately engage and alert your readers to an issue or problem by enabling them to *visualize* the topic.

> Privacy in America seems to be disappearing. New technologies enable users to unearth the health, credit, and legal records of almost anyone at the punch of a computer key. Beyond these computerized records, our telephones, television sets, and even our trash can be monitored by government agencies, banks, businesses, political groups—or just plain nosy people. *Current United States law does disturbingly little to protect our right to privacy.*

Notice how the list of brief but vivid examples causes us to pay close attention to the thesis.

Open with a Definition   An essay on an abstract subject such as *patriotism* or *courage* almost inevitably requires an opening that defines the abstract term for both writer and reader. This writer begins an essay on abortion by defining the key issue: life.

> What is "life"? A tree is alive, a dog is alive, a fish is alive; yet we willfully eliminate these life forms in favor of building a house, controlling the stray dog population, or catching a fish for dinner. Some of the reasoning behind this form of murder is that these beings lack sophisticated thought processes. They do not question why they are alive; they merely exist. Psychologists claim that without consistent symbols to apply to meanings, there can be no evaluative thoughts on life. In other words, a dog cannot think in an abstract way about why he is a dog or about how being a dog differs from being a cat. He "thinks" in the symbols he knows—hunger, food, pain, or chasing rabbits. But he cannot analyze how he could improve his rabbit chase next time; no symbols are there for him to apply to a time sequence. A human embryo also has no symbols to apply to its growing life form (given the supposition that a developing brain can

partially function). Nothing is there to distinguish "I" from "them" or "life" from "death." The embryo is growing into a complete life form but does not yet have the awareness of a functioning human being. *Is it possible, then, for an embryo to recognize its own existence? And is that embryonic existence more important than the life of a stray dog, if its future will consist of being unwanted in an already overcrowded world?*

These openings have elements in common. Each has some description; several carry a brief background story. Even so, your own introduction might resemble none of these. So much the better—as long as it makes us keep reading.

Some Final Hints

- Many writers consider the introduction the hardest part of an essay and often write its final version *last.* If you do write your introduction first, be sure to revise it later.

- In most college writing, you will want to avoid opening with personal qualifiers such as "it is my opinion that," "I believe that," "I will now discuss," and "in this paper I will."

- Try to let your introduction create some kind of suspense that is resolved by your thesis statement, usually at the end of the paragraph(s).

- Think about the chemistry you want with your reader. If the opening is boring, vague, long-winded, or toneless, readers may give up. Don't waste readers' time with needless background.

Drafting the Body Section

The essay's body reveals the substance and shape of your thinking. Here you deliver on the commitment made in your thesis. Readers always expect a clear line of thought and enough details to convey exact meaning. Readers never expect details that just get in the way, or a jigsaw puzzle they have to unscramble for themselves. Developing the body, therefore, requires decisive answers to these questions:

How much is enough?

How much information or detail should I provide?

How can I stay on track?

What shape will reveal my line of thought?

Decide about the essay's substance (or content). How much is enough? Here is where you discard some material you thought you would keep, and maybe discover additional material. Look hard at everything you've discovered during freewriting, brainstorming, or questioning. Think about your purpose. Stand in the reader's place. Think about unity. Keep whatever belongs, and discard whatever doesn't. Maybe you need to sweat again, until you find what you need.

Decide about the essay's shape. How many support paragraphs will you need? College essays typically have three or more support paragraphs. But three is no magic number. Use as many paragraphs as you need.

Decide how to develop each support paragraph. What order will make the most sense and provide best emphasis?

As illustration of these decisions, let's consider the body section for "Suffering Through Gym Class." Assume you've revised twice, to improve content and organization as well as style. (Chapter 4 traces the steps in revision that created this finished version.) The introductory paragraph from page 63 is included here.

Suffering Through Gym Class

Introductory paragraph

In high school my Monday mornings were awful. Even before the school's front door had slammed behind me, I could sense a nauseating dampness rising up from the locker room, a mist of stale sweat. Monday for me was physical education day. And because I was no athlete, each of my 8:00 a.m. trips downstairs to the gym seemed like a clammy and quivering walk to the guillotine, my heartbeat like a drumbeat, my ego about to suffer

Thesis

its ritual of public execution. *For three long years, gym class was my weekly exercise in failure.*

Topic statement

First body paragraph

Although I respected my gym teacher's focus on excellence, *the standards in this class were beyond my ability.* Everybody was expected to be an athlete—and nothing less would do. Effort was ignored in favor of performance. Winning became all-important, and losing teams were punished with extra laps. The fun in any game quickly disappeared. To make matters worse, some gung ho classmates seemed to mirror our teacher's attitude; in a few short weeks, a kind of caste system had developed: jocks on top, the marginally acceptable in the middle, and klutzes like me—the untouchables—at the very bottom.

Topic statement

Second body
paragraph

Whatever sport we played, I could count on being the loser, even when my team won. In baseball, I was the sure strikeout, the right fielder whose glove had a hole in it. In basketball, I had a hard time hitting the backboard, much less scoring a basket. In soccer, I tripped over my own feet. No less disastrous than team sports were those emphasizing individual performance. Parallel bars, hurdles, broad jumps, or high jumps—all were occasions for my world-class embarrassment. The more pathetic attempts I made, the more I came to feel incompetent and inferior.

Topic statement

Third body paragraph

I was continually reminded of my failures. Whenever players were picked for teams, I was sure to be last—huddled among the few remaining rejects trying to look nonchalant. Bracing myself at home plate for the inevitable swing-and-miss, I could count on hearing a few hisses and groans from teammates, and at least one reassuring "easy out!" from opponents. Even my friends affectionately nicknamed me "the athlete." More charitable than my peers, our teacher simply ignored, for the most part, those of us who qualified as wimps. And, as if to certify my incompetence, my C-minus grade (a gift, I guess, for passing "showers") would destroy an otherwise impressive grade average. At all these indignities I laughed on the outside, but not on the inside.*

This essay is the product of careful decisions about content. The body presents a focused picture, enabling readers to feel what the writer felt. And the picture is unified: nothing gets in the way; everything belongs.

But content alone cannot ensure contact. Thoughts need shaping to help us grasp your experience and appreciate its importance. Each detailed paragraph leads us through your weekly sequence of anxiety, alienation, inadequacy, and then humiliation. Throughout, the shape reveals and reinforces your meaning.

Elements affecting the shape of your writing (unity, coherence, emphasis, and transition) are discussed fully in Chapter 7, "Shaping the Paragraphs." Principles of the individual paragraph are principles as well of the whole essay—or of writing at any length.

---

* The concluding paragraph is on page 73.

Drafting the Conclusion

An essay's conclusion refocuses on the thesis and leaves a final—and lasting—impression on readers. Your conclusion might evaluate the meaning or significance of the body section, restate your position, predict an outcome, offer a solution, request an action, make a recommendation, or pave the way for more exploration. Never just stop, having run out of things to say.

Help readers finish, by summing up, interpreting, evaluating, emphasizing your point. Tell us what we should be thinking or feeling or doing. Should we be angry or curious or supportive, or what? Try to be brief, but give us some perspective.

Avoid conclusions that repeat, apologize, or belabor the obvious:

I have just discussed my reasons for disliking gym class. I never did well at any sport I played. [*repeats*]

Although some readers might be bored reading about my experiences in gym class, they mean a lot to me. [*apologizes*]

Now that you've read my essay, you should have a clear picture of what my gym class was like. [*belabors the obvious*]

Forgettable endings drain the life from any writing. Their biggest flaw is lack of concreteness: nothing about them sticks in the memory. Here, instead, is a forceful conclusion to "Suffering Through Gym Class":

> The whole experience left me feeling defeated. Instead of having fun and gaining self-confidence, I felt blacklisted. Intimidated by a standard of performance impossible for me to achieve, I never gave myself the chance to discover my personal best. Taking fewer and fewer risks, I grew to accept the certainty of failure in sports. Those painful years are now behind me, but I still have trouble playing even a sport as casual as volleyball without feeling self-conscious. Looking back, I can appreciate the value of challenge in any class, but I can't help resenting a system that so relentlessly forces personal shortcomings into public display.

This conclusion explores the meaning of your experience. The first four sentences tell us how repeated failures affected your sense of self-worth. The fifth tells about the lasting effects of such an experience. The final sentence brings everything together by reemphasizing your ambivalence and resentment about an experience that challenges all students but humiliates some.

Readers remember last things best, and this conclusion leaves us with something worth remembering.

SELECTING A CLOSING STRATEGY

This list of strategies is by no means exhaustive, but it samples ways of closing with meaning and emphasis.

Close with an Insightful Look Backward   You might want to pull things together with a concluding insight about your main point, as in the gym class essay above.

Close with a Question   Forcing readers to confront a closing question can be a good way to nail down an argument:

> Overall, the advantages of the breeder reactor strike me as immeasurable. Because it can produce more fuel than it uses, it will theoretically be an infinite source of energy. And efficient use of the fuel it does burn makes it highly desirable in this energy-tight era. What other source promises so much for our long-range energy future?

This closing also summarizes the major points in the body. Summaries are especially effective in argumentative essays.

Close with a Call to Action   Make a specific suggestion for action:

> Just imagine yourself eating a salad of crisp green lettuce, juicy red tomato chunks, firm white slices of cucumber, and crunchy strips of green pepper—all picked fresh from your own garden. If this picture appeals to you, begin planning your summer garden now, and by July the picture of you eating that salad will become a reality. *Bon appétit!*

Direct address, of course, will cause readers to pay more attention to your advice.

Close with a Quotation   If you are writing in response to something you've read, you might close with a relevant quote from the author. This writer quotes from journalist Ellen Goodman's essay, "Blame the Victim."

> I agree with Ellen Goodman's assertion that there is "something malignant about some of the extremists who make a public virtue of their health." The cancer is in the superior attitudes of the "health elite"—an attitude that actually discourages exercise and healthy habits by making average people feel too intimidated and inferior even to begin a fitness program.

Close with an Interpretation or Evaluation   Save readers work by interpreting facts and evaluating evidence.

> A growing array of so-called private information about American citizens is collected daily. And few laws protect one's right to be left alone. In the interest of pursuing criminals, government too often sacrifices the privacy of innocent people, and new technology is making old laws obsolete. Huge collections of data are becoming available to your insurance company, to prospective employers, to companies doing mass mailings, and even to your neighbor. The invasion continues, and no one seems to know how to stop our world from fulfilling the prophecy in George Orwell's *1984*.

Close by Creating a Mood   If you have just told a story or described a place, you may want to leave a final impression that captures the mood. This writer closes her description of New Guinea by sharing with us a tropical sunset.

> Tonight as the sun slips into the Coral Sea, the tropical sky shimmers with pastel shades and then fades to the soft light of the southern constellations. Standing in the twilight on Gabutu Point, you can hear the gecko lizards squabbling in the grass, and farther off, the tide steadily rising against the cliffs, and perhaps farther still, rhythmic drums and voices raised in a tribal song of celebration for a South Pacific night.

These strategies all rely on rich, vivid description. Whichever strategy or combination of strategies you select, be sure that your conclusion is in some way memorable and that it refocuses on your main point without repeating it.

Application 3–1

Plan and draft an essay about something *special* to you; it might be a place, a person, an experience, an activity, or anything else—but it has to be something you are sure is worth writing about. Decide on an audience: your classmates, a friend, readers of the campus paper, or someone close to you. Your purpose here is to *share* your way of seeing, and so be sure your audience comes to understand *why* the thing is special. Let them see it and let them feel your responses to it. Be vivid but not melodramatic. Have a thesis and deliver on it.

Think about a voice that will appeal to your readers. Think about unity so that your writing sticks to the point, and about order and transition so that it sticks together. Have a beginning, a middle, and an ending.

(Use the questions on pages 23–24 for guidance in improving your essay.)

Application 3–2

Now you know more about how to begin, how to develop and shape the middle, and how to end. Return to an essay you wrote earlier (maybe your first, or one your instructor recommends), and write a better draft. List the improvements you make, and be prepared to discuss them.

Application 3–3

Locate a good introduction to a short article in a popular magazine such as *Time, Newsweek,* or *Reader's Digest.* In one paragraph discuss the strategies that make the introduction effective. Bring a copy of the article to class. (Review pages 62–70.)

Application 3–4

Locate a good conclusion to a short article in a popular magazine. In one paragraph discuss the strategies that make the conclusion effective. Bring a copy of the article to class. (Review pages 74–75.)

Application 3–5

Complete the essay you began in Application 2–12.

Application 3–6

Write an essay to next year's incoming students, explaining how to survive the early weeks of college. You might focus on what seems to go wrong, how to avoid some common mistakes, and what students can look forward to—once life settles down to something normal. Be sure your essay supports a clear viewpoint. (Your tone here will be important; you don't want this to sound like a sermon. Give it some personality!)

4
Revising the Essay

The Meaning of Revision • Revision Checklist
• Using the Checklist • Applications

Besides being a battle with impatience, writing is a battle with inertia: once we have rested after writing a draft, we usually want to *continue* resting, too easily satisfied with what we've written. Good writers win the battle by revising as often as needed to make real contact.

For the sake of clarity, earlier chapters have presented a single sequence of steps for composing an essay. To review:

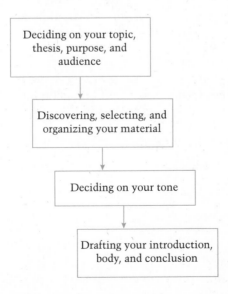

Figure 4.1

But writers rarely follow this exact sequence. Finished essays are achieved in more ways than one. Some writers begin by brainstorming or freewriting. Some come up with a solid thesis immediately, without having to struggle over their purpose. Some outline and then write a thesis. Others use no outline; instead they write and rewrite, using scissors and tape to organize their material. Some even write a whole draft of an essay before coming up with their thesis. Often the best introductions and titles are written last. And so on. The writing process follows no lockstep approach: first do this; then do that. The "process" is a lot more mysterious and unpredictable than that.

No matter what the sequence, a fact of life for any effective writer is *revision*—the one constant in the writing process. When you have finished a first draft, you really have only begun; don't give in to inertia. Take the time to make a poor essay adequate, or an adequate essay excellent. We might say there are no good writers—only good rewriters.

The Meaning of Revision

Revision involves more than proofreading to fix spelling or to insert a comma or to attend to other mechanical details (all covered in the Appendix). Although mechanical correctness is essential, you need to attend, as well, to your essay's *rhetorical* features: worthwhile content, sensible organization, and readable style. Specifically, you might need to cut needless details or add needed ones; to find the exact word or improve coherence; to sharpen the focus, alter the tone, or eliminate wordiness; to improve the organization or eliminate trite expressions. Your instructor might write suggestions on your first draft or might ask you to revise on your own. In any case, revision never means merely *recopying*; it always means *rethinking*.

Before you can improve your draft, you have to decide what in the draft is effective and what is not. Useful revision happens only when you can evaluate accurately what you already have written:

> How does this draft measure up?
>
> Does it achieve what I want it to achieve?
>
> Is it the best I can do?
>
> How can I improve it?

These general questions suggest many more specific questions for evaluating an essay. Nobody can solve problems they cannot identify. You can pretty much pinpoint the problems in any writing by evaluating it for three essential features: content that makes the piece worthwhile; orga-

Revision Checklist

WORTHWHILE CONTENT
The essay's main point is clear and sharply focused.
- ☐ Does the title attract attention and give a forecast? (62)
- ☐ Is the topic limited enough? (29)
- ☐ Do you get to your main point quickly? (64)
- ☐ Is the thesis definite, informative, and easy to find? (35)

The discussion delivers on the promise of your thesis.
- ☐ Will readers learn something new and useful? (37)
- ☐ Do you support every assertion with enough details? (105)
- ☐ Does everything belong, or can anything be cut? (43)
- ☐ Have you used only your *best* material? (108)

SENSIBLE ORGANIZATION
The essay has a definite introduction, body, and conclusion.
- ☐ Will your introduction make readers want to read on? (63)
- ☐ Does each body paragraph develop *one* supporting point? (70)
- ☐ Does the order of body paragraphs reveal a clear line of thought and emphasize what is most important? (71)
- ☐ Does the conclusion give a real sense of an ending? (74)
- ☐ Is everything connected? (131)
- ☐ If you varied this organization, was it for good reason? (216)

Except for paragraphs of transition or special emphasis, each body (or support) paragraph usually is a mini-essay.
- ☐ Does the paragraph have a topic (or orienting) statement? (124)
- ☐ Does the topic statement come at the beginning or end, depending on your emphasis? (134)
- ☐ Does everything stick to the point (unity), and stick together (coherence)? (129)
- ☐ Is the paragraph developed enough to support the point? (113)

READABLE STYLE
Sentences are clear, concise, and fluent.
- ☐ Can each sentence be understood the first time it is read? (155)
- ☐ Is the information expressed in the fewest words? (170)
- ☐ Are sentences put together with enough variety? (179)

Each word does its job.
- ☐ Is a real person speaking, and is the voice likable? (47)
- ☐ Is everything in plain English? (199)
- ☐ Is your meaning precise, concrete, and specific? (193)
- ☐ Is your tone appropriate for this situation and audience? (197)

nization that makes it easy to follow; and style that makes it readable, clear, and engaging. These features are detailed in the Revision Checklist. (Numbers refer to the first page of discussion.)

Using the Checklist

Unless you are writing an in-class essay, your instructor may ask you to revise your first draft before handing in the essay. You can use the Revision Checklist as a guide for rethinking your essay by asking yourself questions such as these:

- Have I conveyed the exact point or feeling I wanted to get across?

- Do vivid details from the event come to mind now that I've finished writing?

- What facts or figures or ideas do I now remember as I read what I've written?

- Can I reorganize anything for greater emphasis or clarity?

- Can I find a better way of saying what I want to?

- Does this draft sound as I wanted it to sound, or is it too corny or detached or arrogant or humble or what?

Eventually you should find that you can revise almost automatically, without following the checklist item by item.

Assume you've written this early draft of "Suffering Through Gym Class":

> Like any other student, I feel that many of my high school experiences were memorable. Few of them, however, were as memorable as my gym class. Every Monday morning, I would feel my anxiety rising as I thought about facing the most hateful part of my week.
>
> In all fairness, I'm sure my gym teacher was kind. But athletic prowess was expected of every student, and nothing less would do. The fun in any game quickly disappeared. The students' effort was ignored in favor of performance. The students seemed to take on the same attitude as the teacher; students with athletic skill were seen as superior to those who lacked athletic skill. The whole thing made me sick. Physical education teachers should learn to control their biases and accept students who lack athletic abilities. The whole system otherwise ends up doing more harm than good.
>
> Whatever sport we played, I could count on being the loser, even when my team won. In both team sports and individual sports, all I

seemed to be able to do in each gym class was to make some kind of pathetic attempt. Some people simply have little or no athletic ability, and I'm one of them. It seemed as if every effort I made resulted in embarrassment. All I could do on these occasions was feel incompetent.

I was always one of the last players picked for teams. As I waited at home plate to swing and miss, I could already hear the hisses and groans from other players on my team, and the "easy-out" chant from members of the opposing team. Even people who were my friends nicknamed me "the athlete." Although these friends were only joking, they nevertheless caused me to suffer emotionally. My teacher seemed to ignore all those students who failed to excel in the achievement of athletic goals. At semester's end, I always received a C-minus grade.

What really are the underlying elements of sports? I would say that the elements are these: rules, teamwork, and tolerance. Combining all these concepts into a grade makes more sense than counting the number of home runs in a semester. Faculty, students, and administrators should work together to improve the system.

We can see that this draft needs a good deal of revision. First, the content leaves lots of reader questions unanswered:

- What, exactly, was the class like?
- What, exactly, did you do that was so bad?
- What was the meaning of this whole experience for you?

And although the organization of this draft hints at an introduction, body, and conclusion, some paragraphs lack topic sentences and clear connections between ideas. Finally, the style has problems: sentences that are too similar in the way they're put together, causing a monotonous tone; other sentences that sound stuffy or too much like a sermon instead of like a person speaking.

On the following pages you will see how the checklist can help you revise to achieve the finished essay shown on pages 71–73. (Notice that this revision treats only the *rhetorical* features: content, organization, and style. A checklist for correcting grammar, punctuation, and mechanics appears on page 536.)

For reference, the paragraphs from the essay are labeled A through E. Specific needed improvements are explained on the facing page. Notice that each suggestion for revision is based on a particular item in the checklist.

Suffering through Gym Class

A

Rewrite introduction to invite readers in

Give more of a forecast in the thesis

~~Like every student, I feel that many of my high school experiences were memorable. Few of them, however, were as memorable as my gym class.~~ Every Tuesday morning, I would feel my anxiety rising as I thought about facing the most hateful part of my week. *Although I respected my gym teacher's commitment to excellence, the standards in this class simply were impossible for me to reach.* ~~In all fairness, I'm sure my gym teacher was kind.~~ *Everybody was expected to be an athlete* ~~But athletic prowess was expected of every student~~, and

B

Sentence variety

More description here

nothing less would do. ⟨The⟩ fun in any game quickly disappeared. ⟨The students'⟩ *E* éffort was ignored in favor of performance. ⟨The⟩ students seemed to take on the same attitude as the teacher; students with athletic skill were seen as superior to those who lacked athletic skill. ⟨The⟩ whole thing made me sick. ~~Physical education teachers should learn to control their biases~~ and ~~accept students who lack athletic abilities.~~ ⟨The⟩ ~~whole system otherwise ends up doing more harm than good.~~

C

give examples

Whatever sport we played, I could count on being the loser, even when my team won. *(parallel bars, hurdles, etc.)* In both team sports and individual sports, all I seemed to be able to do ~~in~~ ~~each gym class~~ was to make some kind of pathetic attempt. *In baseball, I was the sure strike-out, the right-fielder whose glove had a hole in it. In basketball, I had a hard time hitting the backboard, much less scoring a basket. In soccer, I tripped over my own feet.*

Figure 4.2

Paragraph A: The essay lacks a title and the introduction needs more development to give readers an orientation, a clear sense of what they can expect. The opening sentence is so general and obvious as to be meaningless. The second sentence seems to beat around the bush, doing little to advance meaning. Presumably the thesis, the final sentence suggests an attitude, but readers are not sure why gym class was such a hateful experience (because it was boring, too hard, too easy, or what?). The thesis needs to be more definite and informative.

Paragraph B: This first support paragraph needs a topic statement that forecasts the content of the paragraph. Sentences throughout need greater variety, especially to cut down on the many "the" sentence openers that create a monotonous tone. The final two sentences don't really belong; they sound too much like a sermon. And readers need some kind of transition to the paragraph that follows.

Paragraph C: This paragraph contains too many needless words and too few details. Because it merely repeats earlier material, the third sentence can be cut. Concrete and specific details are needed throughout to make meaning clear. What were some of the "pathetic attempts"? To share the writer's embarrassment, readers need to *visualize* what happened.

~~Some people simply have little or no athletic ability,~~

~~and I'm one of them.~~ ~~It seemed as if~~ every effort I
[E] *seemed to*

made ∧resulted in embarrassment. All I could do ~~on~~
—and inferior

~~these occasions~~ was ~~to~~ feel incompetent.
I was continually reminded of my ^failures.

I was always one of the last players picked for
along with the other rejects

teams. As I waited at home plate to swing and miss, I

could already hear the hisses and groans from other

players on my team, and the "easy-out" chant from ~~mem-~~
opponents.

~~bers of the opposing team.~~ Even ~~people who were~~ my
affectionately

friends ∧nicknamed me "the athlete." Although ~~these~~
hurt

~~friends were~~ only joking, they nevertheless ~~caused~~
my feelings

~~me to suffer emotionally.~~ My teacher seemed to ignore
qualified as wimps

all those students who ~~failed to excel in the achieve-~~

~~ment of athletic goals.~~ At semester's end, I always
(a gift for passing "showers" I guess)

received a C-minus grade. *At all these indignities I laughed on the*
outside, but not on the inside.

~~What really are the underlying elements of sports?~~

~~I would say that the elements are these: rules, team-~~

~~work, and tolerance. Combining all these concepts into~~

~~a grade makes more sense than counting the number of~~

~~home runs in a semester. Faculty, students, and admin-~~

~~istrators should work together to improve the system.~~ *The whole experience left me feeling defeated.*

(Loosen the tone)

(Relate the ending directly to the painful memory.)

(show the overall meaning of the experience)

(Talk about this detail)

[D]

[E]

Paragraph D: Although this paragraph seems adequately developed with informative details, it lacks a topic sentence that would give readers a framework for understanding these details. The tone often seems stuffy: "caused me to suffer emotionally" instead of "hurt my feelings." For this kind of personal topic and audience especially, the tone should be more like that of a person speaking. Lightening the tone also would help eliminate many needlessly big or just plain needless words. And some sort of transition to the concluding paragraph is needed.

Paragraph E: This conclusion strays from the essay's purpose: to share with us this painful memory. Instead of giving a real sense of an ending, the paragraph seems more like part of some other essay about how gym classes should be run and evaluated. A good conclusion here would sum up the *meaning* of this experience. Also, the tone seems much too *preachy*, inconsistent with earlier paragraphs.

To give yourself scribbling room as you revise your own work, write longhand drafts on every other line (or, if you type your drafts, use triple spacing).

Although the final version of "Suffering Through Gym Class" (pages 71–73) is not "perfect," it is still a respectable piece of writing. By using the checklist, you have revised to create an essay that makes contact through worthwhile content, sensible organization, and readable style. (For detailed advice on achieving these qualities in any final draft, see Chapters 6–9.)

Application 4–1

Now you know more about what to look for when evaluating an essay—and you have more to think about as well! Using the page 79 Revision Checklist as a guide, return to an essay you have written earlier, and do your best job of revising it.

At this early stage, you are bound to feel a little confused about the finer points of content, organization, and style. But try your best. Later chapters will help improve your skill for diagnosing problems and prescribing cures.

Along with your revised essay, submit an explanation of the improvements you've made, together with the original essay.

Application 4–2

Collaborative Project: Take an essay you have written earlier, and exchange it for a classmate's. Write a detailed evaluation of your classmate's essay, making specific suggestions for revision. Using the page 79 checklist, evaluate all three rhetorical features: content, organization, and style. Use Appendix A to recommend improvements in grammar, punctuation, and mechanics. Do plenty of scribbling on the essay, and sign your evaluation.

Hint: Assume your classmate's essay has been written specifically for *you* as the audience. Do you find it worth reading and easy to follow? Can you understand it easily? Do you like the voice you hear? Does the essay do what it is supposed to do? Why, or why not? The Revision Checklist should help you produce an effective evaluation.

5

Writing About Reading

Throughout college you are asked to write about things you've read. In a psychology assignment you may be asked to summarize a textbook definition of *paranoid schizophrenia* or *superego*. For this type of writing, you read to retrieve and understand the facts. Then you write to demonstrate your knowledge or understanding. To summarize your reading, you write to answer this question:

• What are the main ideas?

Some other assignments require that you go beyond merely retrieving information. You might be asked to read several chapters and articles and to write on this topic: "Explain the role of the id, ego, and superego in human behavior." Here you would write to analyze your reading by answering these questions:

• What are the basic principles?

• What are the parts?

• How do the parts relate?

In this chapter we focus on yet another type of writing about reading—writing to answer questions that are more personal:

- What particular meaning does this reading have for me?
- How do I want to reply?

In this third type of writing, you are more like an active participant in a conversation: reacting to something that was said, you respond with something of your own.

Different Levels of Reading

These different types of writing call for different levels of reading or interacting with the text. To *summarize,* you read to record information. To *analyze,* you read to examine the information. But to *respond,* you read to discover and explore how your own thinking can take shape, or to make up your mind about something, or to get in touch with buried feelings or ideas. As a responding reader, you discover something that makes a difference to you personally, and you *reinvent* it so as to make a difference to readers of your own.

Writing in response to reading, then, can add another way of seeing, another way of expanding and enriching the possibilities for real connection. By helping you discover and explore the things you may want to say, reading can enrich the decisions you make throughout the writing process.

Different Readers, Different Meanings

The connection that writing creates is both public and private. On the one hand, a piece of writing makes a public connection with *all* its readers; on the other hand, the writing makes a private connection with *each* of its readers. Recall, for a moment, "Suffering Through Gym Class" (pages 71–73): Many of us who read this essay can feel the writer's anxiety and alienation and sense of failure. Beyond our common reaction, however, *each* of us has a unique and personal reaction as well—special things that we ended up feeling or remembering or thinking about.

If your whole class were to describe their individual reactions to the gym class essay ("What it means to me"), no two responses would be identical. The essay might cause one reader to remember how competition in high school helped her develop self-confidence; some other reader might remember with regret how he made fun of someone less able. And so on.

You as reader interpret and complete the "private" meaning of the text you read. And, like you, all other readers come away from the same text with a personal meaning of their own. It is this personal meaning that can serve as inspiration for your own writing.

Responding to Reading

This essay by Judy Syfers was published in the very first issue of *Ms.* magazine, in Spring 1972. Even though Syfers seems to write for married readers in particular, in her essay she speaks to anyone who is at all familiar with married people in general. Please read the essay carefully.

Why I Want a Wife

I belong to that classification of people known as wives. I am A Wife. And, not altogether incidentally, I am a mother.

Not too long ago a male friend of mine appeared on the scene fresh from a recent divorce. He had one child, who is, of course, with his ex-wife. He is looking for another wife. As I thought about him while I was ironing one evening, it suddenly occurred to me that I, too, would like to have a wife. Why do I want a wife?

I would like to go back to school so that I can become economically independent, support myself, and, if need be, support those dependent upon me. I want a wife who will work and send me to school. And while I am going to school I want a wife to take care of my children. I want a wife to keep track of the children's doctor and dentist appointments. And to keep track of mine, too. I want a wife to make sure my children eat properly and are kept clean. I want a wife who will wash the children's clothes and keep them mended. I want a wife who is a good nurturant attendant to my children, who arranges for their schooling, makes sure that they have an adequate social life with their peers, takes them to the park, the zoo, etc. I want a wife who takes care of the children when they are sick, a wife who arranges to be around when the children need special care, because, of course, I cannot miss classes at school. My wife must arrange to lose time at work and not lose the job. It may mean a small cut in my wife's income from time to time, but I guess I can tolerate that. Needless to say, my wife will arrange and pay for the care of the children while my wife is working.

I want a wife who will take care of *my* physical needs. I want a wife who will keep my house clean. A wife who will pick up after my children, a wife who will pick up after me. I want a wife who will keep my clothes clean, ironed, mended, replaced when need be, and who will see to it that my personal things are kept in their proper place so that I can find what I need the minute I need it. I want a wife who cooks the meals, a wife who is a *good* cook. I want a wife who will plan the menus, do the necessary grocery shopping, prepare the meals, serve them pleasantly, and then do the cleaning up while I do my studying. I want a wife who will care for me when I am sick and sympathize with my pain and loss of time from school. I want a wife to go along when our family takes a vacation so that someone can continue to care for me and my children when I need a rest and change of scene.

I want a wife who will not bother me with rambling complaints about a wife's duties. But I want a wife who will listen to me when I feel the need to explain a rather difficult point I have come across in my course of studies. And I want a wife who will type my papers for me when I have written them.

I want a wife who will take care of the details of my social life. When my wife and I are invited out by my friends, I want a wife who will take care of the babysitting arrangements. When I meet people at school that I like and want to entertain, I want a wife who will have the house clean, will prepare a special meal, serve it to me and my friends, and not interrupt when I talk about things that interest me and my friends. I want a wife who will have arranged that the children are fed and ready for bed before my guests arrive so that the children do not bother us. I want a wife who takes care of the needs of my guests so that they feel comfortable, who makes sure that they have an ashtray, that they are passed the hors d'oeuvres, that they are offered a second helping of the food, that their wine glasses are replenished when necessary, that their coffee is served to them as they like it. And I want a wife who knows that sometimes I need a night out by myself.

I want a wife who is sensitive to my sexual needs, a wife who makes love passionately and eagerly when I feel like it, a wife who makes sure that I am satisfied. And, of course, I want a wife who will not demand sexual attention when I am not in the mood for it. I want a wife who assumes the complete responsibility for birth control, because I do not want more children. I want a wife who will remain sexually faithful to me so that I do not have to clutter up my intellectual life with jealousies. And I want a wife who understands that *my* sexual needs may entail more than strict adherence to monogamy. I must, after all, be able to relate to people as fully as possible.

If, by chance, I find another person more suitable as a wife than the wife I already have, I want the liberty to replace my present wife with another one. Naturally, I will expect a fresh, new life; my wife will take the children and be solely responsible for them so that I am left free.

When I am through with school and have a job, I want my wife to quit working and remain at home so that my wife can more fully and completely take care of a wife's duties.

My God, who *wouldn't* want a wife?

Now let's examine our reactions to "Why I Want A Wife." We all presumably extract a common meaning from this piece: namely the viewpoint that women in the traditional "wifely" role are overworked and underappreciated. But, beyond its bleak portrait of the "house wife's" destiny, what particular meaning does this essay have for you?

Maybe Syfer's essay makes you feel angry with (1) men, (2) the writer, (3) yourself, or (4) someone else. Or maybe you feel threatened or offended. Or maybe you feel amused or confused about your own attitudes toward gender roles. Or maybe you feel all these things at once—or maybe none. Here are some questions that may help you explore your reactions to the reading:

- How do I feel about this reading? Angry, defensive, supportive, or what?

- Why do I feel this way?

- Does the piece present an accurate picture?

- With which statements do I agree or disagree?

- What is the most striking part of this essay?

- Do I like the way the writing sounds (the tone)?

- Has it reminded me of something, made me aware of something new, or changed my mind about anything?

- What does this essay make me want to think and talk about?

In your answers to these questions, you should be able to discover what you are thinking or feeling or remembering. A good way to explore your reactions and collect your thoughts is by keeping a reading journal in which you record your impressions.

Once you have discovered the particular meaning Syfer's essay has for you, how will you respond? Among all the things you could say, which will be your exact reply? Before you decide, read how two other writers responded.

Here are some of the notes that Jacqueline LeBlanc wrote in her journal after first reading Syfer's essay:

> This essay makes me angry because it reminds me too much of some women in my own generation who seem to want nothing more than a wifely role for themselves. For all we hear about "equal rights," women still feel the pressure to conform to old-fashioned notions. I can really take this essay personally.

After rereading the essay and reviewing her journal entries, Jackie decided to write from the viewpoint that the stereotypical role condemned by Syfers two decades ago continues to be disturbingly evident. Jackie expresses her viewpoint in this thesis statement:

> Although today's "equality-minded" generation presumably sees marriage as more than just an occupation, the wifely stereotype persists.

Here, after several revisions, is the essay that explains Jackie's viewpoint:

A Long Way to Go

Judy Syfers's portrait of a servile wife might appear somewhat dated—until we examine some of today's views about marriage. Syfers defines a wife by the work she does for her husband: she is a secretary, housemaid, babysitter, and sex object. She is, in a word, her husband's employee. Although today's "equality-minded" generation presumably sees marriage as more than an occupation, the wifely stereotype persists.

Among my women friends, I continue to encounter surprisingly traditional attitudes. Last week, for instance, I was discussing my career possibilities with my roommate, who added to the list of my choices by saying, "You can always get married." In her view, becoming a wife seems no different from becoming a teacher or journalist. She implied that marriage is merely another way of making a living. But where do I apply for the position of wife? The notion struck me as absurd. I thought to myself, "Surely, this person is an isolated case. We are, after all, in the nineties. Women no longer get married as a substitute for a job—do they?"

Of course many women do have both job and marriage, but as I look closely at others' attitudes, I find that my roommate's view is not so rare. Before the recent wedding of a female friend, my conversations with the future bride revolved around her meal plans and laundry schedule. To her vows "to love, honor, and cherish" she could have added, "to cook, serve, and clean up." She had been anticipating the first meal she would prepare for her husband. Granted, nothing is wrong with wanting to serve and provide for the one you love—but she spoke of this meal as if it were a pass-or-fail exam given by her employer on her first day on the job. Following the big day of judgment, she was elated to have passed with flying colors.

I couldn't help wondering what would have happened if her meal had been a flop. Would she have lost her marriage as an employee loses a job? As long as my friend retains such a narrow and materialistic view of wifely duties, her marriage is not likely to be anything more than a job.

Not all my friends are obsessed with wifely duties, but some do have a definite sense of husbandly duties. A potential husband must measure up to the qualifications of the position, foremost of which is wealth. One of the first questions about any male is "What does he do?" Engineering majors or premed students usually get highest ranking, and humanities or music majors end up at the bottom. College women are by no means opposed to marriage based on true love, but, as we grow older, the fantasy of a Prince Charming gives way to the reality of an affluent provider. Some women look for high-paying marriages just as they look for high-paying jobs.

Some of my peers may see marriage as one of many career choices, but my parents see it as the *only* choice. To my parents, my not finding a husband is a much more terrifying fate than my not finding a job. In their view, being a wife is no mere occupation, but a natural vocation for all women. But not just any man will do as a husband. My parents have a built-in screening procedure for each man I date. Appearance, money, and general background are the highest qualifications. They ignore domestic traits because they assume that his parents will be screening *me* for such qualifications.

I have always tried to avoid considering male friends simply as prospective husbands; likewise, I never think of myself as filling the stereotypical position of wife. But sometimes I fall into my parents' way of thinking. When I invite a friend to dinner at my house, I suddenly find myself fretting about his hair, his religion, or his job. Will he pass the screening test? Is he the right man for the role of husband? In some ways my attitudes seem no more liberated than those of my peers or parents.

Today's women have made a good deal of progress, but apparently not enough. Allowing the practical implications of marriage to overshadow its emotional implications, a surprising number of us seem to feel that we still have to fit the stereotype that Syfers condemns.

As an active reader, Jackie discovered in Syfers's essay something that made a difference. As the writer, in turn, she responded so as to make a difference to readers of her own.

Our second writer, David Galuski, discovered in the Syfers essay the possibility for humor, summed up in this thesis:

Instead of a wife, I need an assistant.

He uses his response to poke fun at his own inability for coping with an impossibly busy schedule and to discover that (like all of us, at times) he is just looking for a little sympathy.

I Need an Assistant

I am much too busy. Being eighteen takes a lot out of a person—especially anyone who attends college full time, works two part-time jobs, plays sports, and tries to have a social life. I need someone to help me get through the day. Instead of a wife, I need an assistant.

For one thing, my assistant would help with school chores. Although I usually find time to do my homework, it is never without a good deal of pain. My assistant could ease the pain by doing some of my reading, which he could then summarize and explain to me. Maybe he could do some of my research and type the papers I write, as well. Fluent in all subjects, my assistant would be able to transfer his knowledge to me.

Studying is easy—when I have enough time. But keeping up grades while holding down two part-time jobs is another story. I spend twenty hours a week at Max's, a gourmet restaurant, where I am expected to continuously cater to my customers. But when I'm exhausted from studying, I'm likely to be forgetful and irritable. I want an assistant who will stand by me at all times at work. He could help with the work and also cover for any lapses in my patience or attention.

My work as timekeeper for hockey games at the skating rink consumes five hours weekly out of my busy schedule. I need an assistant to cover the games I cannot time because of homework or conflicting hours at the restaurant. My assistant also would stand by my side and take over when I fall asleep because of the late hours at which the games are scheduled. Although I must work at these jobs to pay college expenses, my life isn't all work and studying.

Sports are a big part of my life. I set aside at least one hour every day to run, cycle, or swim. No matter what my other commitments are, without daily exercise I feel I've accomplished nothing. I need an assistant to encourage me to run that extra step or to swim one more pool length. He would push me out the door to exercise in the cold and in the rain. My assistant would compete alongside me in the six triathlons I do each year. He would also be a good hockey player, who would attend practice sessions in my place, leaving the team happy and giving me time to finish homework or earn money.

Besides school, work, and sports, I have other commitments to consider. I try—without much success—to maintain an active social life. I need an assistant to keep me up to date on my friends and girlfriend. I never have time to call them. When I do manage to see them, it is briefly. Even though they understand my obligations, they can't help being annoyed occasionally. My assistant would make my phone calls and arrange dates for me at times when I can squeeze them in.

Dates are something I really can't make with my family. But I see my parents as much as possible. I try to help out at home, but that would be a job for my assistant. He would do my household chores, wash the cars, and mow the lawn. My assistant would make my bed and wash my clothes while I hurry off to some pressing engagement.

> Finally, I need an assistant who will give me emotional support. I want an assistant to whisper in my ear, telling me that everything will turn out all right—one who will sing me to sleep and hold me when I cry. Maybe all I'm looking for after all is a little pity.

Beyond the two samples shown here, the range of possible responses to Syfers's essay is almost infinite. Can you think of other possibilities for your own response?

Suggestions for Reading and Writing

In many later chapters you will be invited to write in response to this or that reading. Some of the readings are professionally written; others are student written. All these readings are selected as enjoyable ways of showing how other writers can connect with you. Besides triggering ideas for your own writing, each reading provides a model of worthwhile content, sensible organization, and readable style.

Here are a few suggestions for reading to respond to the selections assigned throughout the semester:

1. Read the essay at least three times: first, to get a sense of the geography; next, to explore your reactions; finally, to see what you find most striking or important or outrageous.

2. List (or underline) the statements that strike you or set you off.

3. Answer any questions on page 91 that are relevant here.

4. Once you've identified your reaction, think of all the things you would like to say in reply.

5. Settle on the main thing you want to say—your viewpoint.

6. Write out your viewpoint in a thesis statement.

Keep in mind that these are *only* suggestions—not commandments.

Like everything else in the writing process, reading to write calls for an intimate involvement that follows no simple formula. You might read something and want to begin writing immediately, without lists or other helps. Sometimes you won't even have a thesis as you begin, but you will want to write anyway, maybe to tell a story or to describe something personal.

In writing about reading, each of us reinvents a special way of seeing. Maybe, like Jackie LeBlanc, you will respond in a way that sticks closely to what you've read. Or maybe, like David Galuski, you will want to have fun and try something different. Or maybe you will decide to use the reading as a launching toward *new* exploration, as Shirley Haley did after reading this selection from Annie Dillard's prizewinning book, *Pilgrim at Tinker Creek*. (Haley's essay appears on pages 97–99.)

Seeing

It is still the first week in January, and I've got great plans. I've been thinking about seeing. There are lots of things to see, unwrapped gifts and free surprises. The world is fairly studded and strewn with pennies cast broadside from a generous hand. But—and this is the point—who gets excited by a mere penny? If you follow one arrow, if you crouch motionless on a bank to watch a tremulous ripple thrill on the water and are rewarded by the sight of a muskrat kit paddling from its den, will you count that sight a chip of copper only, and go your rueful way? It is dire poverty indeed when a man is so malnourished and fatigued that he won't stoop to pick up a penny. But if you cultivate a healthy poverty and simplicity, so that finding a penny will literally make your day, then, since the world is in fact planted in pennies, you have with your poverty bought a lifetime of days. It is that simple. What you see is what you get.

I used to be able to see flying insects in the air. I'd look ahead and see, not the row of hemlocks across the road, but the air in front of it. My eyes would focus along that column of air, picking out flying insects. But I lost interest, I guess, for I dropped the habit. Now I can see birds. Probably some people can look at the grass at their feet and discover all the crawling creatures. I would like to know grasses and sedges—and care. Then my least journey into the world would be a field trip, a series of happy recognitions. Thoreau, in an expansive mood, exulted, "What a rich book might be made about buds, including, perhaps, sprouts!" It would be nice to think so. I cherish mental images I have of three perfectly happy people. One collects stones. Another—an Englishman, say—watches clouds. The third lives on a coast and collects drops of seawater which he examines microscopically and mounts. But I don't see what the specialist sees, and so I cut myself off, not only from the total picture, but from the various forms of happiness.

Unfortunately, nature is very much a now-you-see-it, now-you-don't affair: A fish flashes, then dissolves in the water before my eyes like so much salt. Deer apparently ascend bodily into heaven; the brightest oriole fades into leaves. These disappearances stun me into stillness and concentration; they say of nature that it conceals with a grand nonchalance, and they say of vision that it is a deliberate gift, the revelation of a dancer who for my eyes only flings away her seven veils. For nature does reveal as well as conceal: now-you-don't-see-it, now-you-do. For a week last September migrating red-winged blackbirds were feeding heavily down by the creek at the back of the house. One day I went out to investigate the racket; I walked up to a tree, an Osage orange, and a hundred birds flew away. They simply materialized out of the tree. I saw a tree, then a whisk of color, then a tree again. I walked closer and another hundred blackbirds took flight. Not a branch, not a twig budged: the birds were apparently weightless as well as invisible. Or, it was as if the leaves of the Osage orange had been freed from a spell in the form of red-winged blackbirds; they flew from the tree, caught my eye in the sky, and vanished. When I looked again at the tree the leaves had reassembled as if nothing had happened. Finally I walked directly to the trunk of the tree and a final hundred, the real diehards, appeared, spread, and vanished. How could so many hide in the tree without my seeing them? The Osage orange, unruffled, looked just as it had looked from the house, when three hundred red-winged blackbirds cried from its crown. I looked downstream where they flew, and they were gone. Searching, I couldn't spot one. I wandered downstream to force them to play their hand, but they'd crossed the creek and scattered. One show to a customer. These appearances catch at my throat; they are the free gifts, the bright coppers at the roots of the trees.

In her response to Annie Dillard, Haley sets out to reinvent the meaning of "Seeing," for herself and her readers. Even though Haley gives us no explicit thesis, her writing clearly enough implies one: Things we truly see outside ourselves sometimes can help ease the pain we feel inside.

Sailboats

On an afternoon in late June I stomped out of the house to walk off the frustration of an argument. White fists jammed into my pockets, I rehearsed what I should have said as I tromped fiercely away from the people, the village, the wharf, and the lifeguarded beaches toward the path. A fringe benefit of putting in town sewage four or five years ago, the path begins with the gravel road to the pumping station and moves on around the deepest curve of the harbor, tracing the old railroad bed. It is by no means private there, but by mutual understanding, speaking is optional, nodding preferable; the illusion of privacy is preserved. It's where I walk when I walk and fancy I'll run when I take up running, and today it was where I was stomping.

Like a child more determined to stay angry the harder you coax and tickle, I was determined to stay hurt. The walk would do no good beyond creating space between me and the house. *Pilgrim at Tinker Creek* lay on the table by my bed, and I was angry at Annie Dillard, too. She makes such work of simply being here: marveling at caterpillar foreheads and all the time refocusing to "see." When I refocus, I see places that need cleaning; better to glance and be happy in my ignorance. I cannot see the universe in a drop of water. Hers is not a gift for seeing; it's a gift for applying imagination. I walked the path that day wanting not to think, or feel or see, wishing to be transformed, melted away like the Little Mermaid into the foam at the tip of a wave.

Not far along the way, the path falls away to brackish water (neither salt nor fresh); on either side, the eel pond. It's only a baby pond on the left connected to the expanse of water on the right by a culvert, a giant corrugated tunnel for boys to hoot into and make echos. The bright sky paled against the vivid blue of the pond. The warming air had freed the scent of beach rose and marsh grass. And across the pond, across the buckskin marsh not yet turned jewel green, was the swans' nest. The swans were there like plastic swans on a wedding cake, one on the giant nest, one swimming near with wings slightly raised in a gesture of vigilance.

The growth of land separating pond and marsh from harbor and beach is called Goodspeed Island. It's not really an island, of course, but it's a good place to pretend and to camp out if you're careful about poison ivy. As the path curves from behind it, dissolving from packed dirt to sand, the harbor opens up on the left. A sandy isthmus between pond and ocean, the path continues; I digressed to my destination. The beach is cluttered with beachy clutter: seaweed, shells, waterlogged wood, and plastic rings from six-packs. Aged quarry stones strewn in odd arrangement make ideal seats for the contemplation of universes, if you're so inclined—or of hurts.

The view is of sailboats, mostly moored; the curve of the shore with houses, shops, wharves, and beaches; and, at the farthest point on the far side, the lighthouse, white. Above, the trees, which from here are a solid green rolling back from the harbor, hiding the village, reach the tips of the steeples, a Congregational Church, white, Center School, yellow, marking the block where I live.

I wonder about the boats sometimes; they never seem to go out. Dangling there at their moorings all summer, they float like vanes into the wind. And when weather comes, and it blows, one always slips its mooring and runs with the storm across the harbor to the rocks. I remember clearly going out like ghouls once in the rain to see such a one, its side torn open, and a lady in a yellow slicker picking up silverware in the dark in the surf.

I stayed a while, nursing my hurts and contemplating boats. Dog walkers passed behind me. A resolute lady strode briskly by in warm-up suit zipped to the chin, and the tide began to change. I headed home by the populated route. Still hurt but no longer angry, I walked quietly, carrying beach roses for the dining-room table. At the wharf a 40-foot wooden sailboat, a mahogany beauty, slid into the water and

then motored to the dock to have her mast and rigging fitted. At
home I took care in arranging my flowers and felt better.

We have seen how three student writers reached deep into their
reading and into themselves to make something happen, to discover a
real connection. Their writing, in turn, makes us part of that connection.

Application 5–1

Respond to any of the essays in this chapter with an essay of your own.
Share with us a new way of seeing.

In planning your response, imagine that you are conversing with
the writer: How would you reply if someone had just spoken what you
have read? In responding to Judy Syfers's essay (pages 89–90), you might
ask yourself questions such as:

- Has anything changed since this essay was written (1972)?

- Is this what my mother is like?

- What do I want for myself in a marriage?

- How do I see my role as a wife or husband?

- What are my expectations?

Ask these questions, those on page 91, and any others that will help
you reach deep into your reading experience.

As you read, record your impressions in a reading journal. In
reviewing these journal entries, you should be able to discover the seeds
that can grow into a truly worthwhile essay.

Application 5–2

People coming of age in different generations tend to be characterized
on the basis of a dominant stereotype. For example, in the 1960s and
early 1970s, young people were known as the "we" generation:
concerned with social, environmental, and political ideals. The late
1970s and 1980s witnessed the so-called "me" generation, focusing on
career success and affluence, and largely indifferent to world problems.
How would you characterize the 1990s generation, in terms of its
values, fears, hopes, goals, and outlook? After reading the essay that
follows, decide how you would respond with a personal portrait of life

in your generation. Use the page 91 questions as a guide for responding to your reading.

Out of College, Out of Work

One of the things my classmates and I were not told at our college graduation four years ago was what papers we would need for a visit to the unemployment office. Luckily, however, in addition to being told that we were the future, etc., we were told to always be prepared. Thus, when I made my first visit a few months ago, all of my papers were in order. I had suspected that getting "processed" would be time consuming, and I was right. But that was OK; I wanted it that way. Like graduation ceremonies and funeral services, applying for unemployment insurance is one of those lengthy rituals whose duration almost seems designed to make one sit and think. It's a valuable time to take stock.

What I was not prepared for was the TV crew facing me as I walked in. The "MacNeil/Lehrer" news team was doing a story on whitecollar unemployment, and they had come to the right place. I had expected the office to be like a great mixing pool, like the Department of Motor Vehicles. But the people in the endless line ahead of me—with their trenchcoats and folded newspapers—looked like the same ones I used to fight with for a seat on the Wall Street–bound subway train every morning when we all had jobs. Like them, I did my indicted-mobster-leaving-the-courthouse imitation, evading the cameras as I inched ahead in line. After finally reaching the front, and giving the clerk evidence of the life and impending death of *Wigwag* magazine, where I was a writer, I was told to sit down in the next room and wait.

The next room looked exactly like a college classroom (when I squeezed into a seat I realized I'd forgotten how uncomfortable school desks are). Looking around me, I was struck by the number of people in the room who were, like me, twentysomething—not the middle-aged crowd I'd expected. But after giving it some thought, it made more sense. I knew that, along with seemingly every other industry, Wall Street and the big law firms were trimming down after the fat years of the 1980s: last hired, first fired, sit down in the next room and wait. So here we were, members of the generation accused by our older siblings of being mercenary and venal, back in the classroom again, only this time having to raise our hands with questions like, "I didn't get the little pink form in my information booklet." Who among us would have guessed it in the heady days of 1986?

In truth, I was never that proud of my generation. I too had been scornful of those who happily graduated to fast, easy money. And although I had rejected that route myself, that suddenly seemed irrelevant. At this perverse reunion I found myself feeling a kinship with my new daylong classmates, squirming in their desks around me, who had embraced the 1980s. Most of these wunderkinder were now counting themselves lucky to have found their little pink forms.

Like most of them, my notions of college and post-college life were formed by watching the 1960s generation. To be young, energetic, and full of conviction seemed important and exciting. The world had listened to them and we looked forward to our turn. There were many of us who would have liked to help stop a war, disrupt political conventions, take over deans' offices, or volunteer in the South for civil rights. We would have welcomed the chance for a few years of world-changing before settling down to more responsible (i.e. lucrative) activities, as so many of the thirtysomething crowd, now with kids and mortgages, had done.

But we had graduated into a different world—one so harsh and competitive that a *Republican* president would soon declare the need for something "kinder and gentler." AIDS, skyrocketing tuition, disappearing federal grants, the lack of so easy a common cause as peace and love (or hating hatred), and a dazzling job market offering salaries that, when offered to people so young with four years of loan indebtedness, left virtually no other choices. We weren't in the 1960s anymore—we never had been. Those who hadn't realized this by graduation quickly found out that student-loan officials don't grant deferments for time spent "finding" oneself.

When comparing themselves to us, members of the 1960s generation, while using their own college years to rationalize their recent, less than idealistic choices, imply that we younger "careerists" didn't pay our dues before joining them in their 20th-story offices. Ironically, though, depending on the severity of the recession, my generation may ultimately come to resemble our grandparents' generation more than the one we always wanted to be a part of. When I talk to my friends about job prospects and we compare our experiences at various unemployment offices (one ex-co-worker had *two* camera crews to dodge), I wonder if we, like our grandparents in the 1930s, will be permanently shaped by these few years. Will we one day say, "Son, when I was your age, in the Great White-Collar Depression, we didn't fool around after college. We took whatever office-temp or bicycle messenger work we could get and we were *grateful.*"

My name was soon called and, along with several others, I filed into another classroom for a 90-minute lecture on how unemployment insurance works—sort of a "Principles of Bureaucracy 101." The last item on my day's agenda was figuring out how to leave while avoiding the only people in the room with jobs: the camera crew. (I began to wonder if their eagerness was due to spending the day with a bunch of former job-holders). When we all finally left the office, most of us had been there for about 3 hours. But we were not the irritated, impatient New York crowd one would expect—we had lots of time on our hands and we were learning how to deal with having even more. We were at last getting the long-awaited "year off," albeit a crueler and less gentle version. Although we can't be quite as free and easy as our counterparts were 20 years ago—we have to mail in our coupons every week, and we've promised to look for work—this may be the only chance for a coming of age my generation will get.

—Stephen Sherrill

SECTION TWO

THE PRODUCT—SUBSTANCE, SHAPE, STYLE

6

Achieving Worthwhile Content

Readers hate to waste time. They want writing worth reading. They expect an insightful thesis backed by solid support. To make contact, writing has to say something worthwhile. If the content is worthless, nothing else matters.

From all the material you develop during planning and drafting, you want to select only what is worthwhile. The first requirement of worthwhile content is *unity:* every word, every detail advances the writer's exact meaning. In addition to unity, three other qualities are essential to worthwhile content: *credibility, informative value,* and *completeness.**

Credibility

How believable and convincing is your draft? Anyone can make assertions; *supporting* the assertion is the real challenge. When you assert an opinion, readers expect it to be *informed.* We all have opinions about political candidates, cars, controversial subjects such as abortion or nuclear energy, and anything else that touches our lives. But sometimes we forget that many of our opinions are *uninformed;* instead of resting

---

* Adapted from James L. Kinneavy's assertion that discourse should be factual, unpredictable, and comprehensive. See James L. Kinneavy, *A Theory of Discourse* (Englewood Cliffs, N.J.: Prentice Hall, 1971).

on *facts*, they lean mostly on a chaotic collection of beliefs repeated around us, notions we've inherited from advertising, things we've read but never checked, and so on.

Uninformed opinions

> Christopher Columbus was a hero.
>
> Christopher Columbus was a villain.
>
> Grindo toothpaste is best for making teeth whiter.
>
> In a democracy, religion deserves a voice in government.

Uninformed opinion is merely a belief that hasn't been verified (shown to be valid).

Informed opinion, in contrast, rests on fact or good sense. Any fact (*my hair is brown; Professor Glum fails more than 50 percent of his students; Americans have more televisions than bathtubs*) can be verified by anyone. A fact might be verified by observation (*I saw Felix murder his friend*); by research (*wood smoke contains the deadly chemical dioxin*); by experience (*I was mugged this morning*); or by measurement (*fewer than 60 percent of our first-year students eventually earn a degree*). Opinions based on these facts would be informed opinions.

Informed opinions

> Felix is guilty of murder.
>
> Homes with woodstoves need good ventilation.
>
> This has been a bad day for me.
>
> College clearly is not for everyone.

To support your opinions, you often must consider a variety of facts. You might be able to support with facts the claim that Grindo toothpaste makes teeth whiter; but a related fact may be that Grindo contains tiny silicone particles—an abrasive that "whitens" by scraping enamel from teeth. The second fact could change your opinion about Grindo.

The Grindo example illustrates that no two facts about *anything* are likely to have equal value. Assume you've asserted this opinion:

> The Diablo Canyon nuclear plant is especially dangerous.

In deciding how to support this opinion, you compare the relative value of each of these facts:

1. The road system is inadequate for rapid evacuation of local residents.

2. Nuclear plants have found no suitable way to dispose of radioactive wastes.

3. The plant is little more than 100 miles from sizable population centers.

4. The plant is built near a major earthquake fault.

Although all these facts support the label *dangerous,* the first three can apply to many nuclear plants. Only the fourth addresses the danger specific to the Diablo Canyon plant—and therefore has most value here. When your space *and* your reader's tolerance are limited—and they usually are—you need to decide which of your facts offer forceful and unified support for your assertion.

Besides unifying your facts, arrange them to reflect vivid and appropriate emphasis. Consider this opening passage:

Passage A

Opening opinion

Child abuse has become our national disgrace. In the past decade, its incidence has increased by an average 20 percent yearly. This year alone, more than 500,000 children (fewer than 20 percent of cases) will be the *reported* victims of physical, sexual, or emotional violence by one or both parents. And among the reported offenders, only *3 percent* are ever convicted. Even more tragic, the pattern of violence is cyclical, with many abused children later becoming abusive parents themselves.

Supporting facts

Notice how the facts are ordered: from the increase in the past decade to the cases this year to the conviction rate to the cyclical pattern; we move from the disquieting numbers to the tragically cyclical process.

Not all opinions can be supported by facts. Take moral or emotional issues (prayer in public schools, the existence of God, the distribution of wealth). Opinions on such issues rest mainly on good sense and insight. Following is a passage supporting the opinion that Americans should do more to help the world's hungry.

Passage B

If we as a nation allow people to starve while we could, through some sacrifice, make more food available to them, what hope can any person have for the future of international relations? If we cannot agree on this most basic of values—feed the hungry—what hopes for the future can we entertain? Technology is imitable and nuclear weaponry certain to proliferate. What appeals to trust and respect can be made if the most rudimentary of moral impulses—feed the hungry—is not strenuously incorporated into national policy?

—James R. Kelly

Although the passage offers no statistics, research data, or observable facts (except that technology can be imitated), the support is credible because of its basis in sensible reasons. Granted, we cannot *prove* the writer's opinion valid by measurement or research, but we can find support for it in our own intuition about our shared humanity.

Informative Value

Relevant facts and sensible insights make writing convincing, but readers don't need every item you can think of. Are you one of those writers who enter college as experts in the art of "stuffing"? The stuffing expert knows how to fill pages by cramming into the essay every thought that will pile up 500 words (or any required total) with minimal pain. Early drafts almost always need radical surgery to trim away the material that serves no purpose.

Readers always expect something *new and useful*; they never want filler that wastes their time. Writing has informative value when it

- shares something new and significant with an audience, or

- reminds the audience about something they know but ignore, or

- offers fresh insight or new perspective about something the audience already knows.

In short, informative writing gives readers exactly what they need.

No matter what the writing situation, you can make certain assumptions about your readers. You know that readers approach your topic with some prior knowledge (or *old* information). These readers don't need a rehash of old information; they can "fill in the blanks" for themselves. But readers may need reminding about something they've ignored or forgotten. On the other hand, readers don't need every bit of *new* information you can think of, either.

How, then, do you zero in on your particular readers' particular information needs? By anticipating their questions. Imagine this situation: You have no formal computer background (only general knowledge); you are debating whether to take an introductory computer course, and I want to offer some information that might help. In this situation, which of these bits of information would you find useful?

a. Interest in computers has grown immensely in the past decade.

b. By 1999, at least 80 percent of businesses will depend on computers.

c. The first digital computer was built by Howard Aiken.

d. Information can be transmitted rapidly by computer.

I can make a good guess about the usefulness of each item by anticipating your questions: "What are the benefits?" and "Why should I?" Item **b** probably would be new to many first-year students, and this fact seems relevant to your needs and my purpose. Item **a,** in contrast, has no informative value here, because it is self-evident to anyone exposed to our media culture. Although **c** is news to anyone with no computer background, the information is not immediately relevant to this situation. (It could be, say, if you already were taking a computer course.) And **d** is a statement everyone would find obvious. Mere facts, then, are not enough; they have to be facts readers can use.

Sometimes a message can have informative value if it reminds us about something familiar or gives us fresh insight into a familiar subject. As a reader of this book, you expect to learn something worthwhile about writing, and my purpose is to help you do that. In this situation, which of these bits of information would you find useful?

a. Writing is hard and frustrating work.

b. Writing is a process of deliberate decisions.

Statement **a** offers no news to anyone who ever has picked up a pencil. But **b** offers a *new* perspective on something familiar. It reminds you that producing good writing can be a lot more painful than we would like. No matter how much you have struggled over decisions about punctuation or spelling or grammar, chances are you haven't viewed writing as entailing the many kinds of deliberate decisions treated in this book. Because **b** offers new insight into a familiar process, then, we can say it has informative value.

Rereading Passages A and B (pages 107–108), we see that each satisfies our criteria for informative value. Passage A offers surprising but convincing evidence about child abuse; Passage B gives fresh insight into the crucial but familiar issue of international relations.

In our previous examples, audience needs were easy to identify. But sometimes we write for a mixed group of readers with varied needs. How, then, can our writing have informative value for each reader?

Imagine you are an ex-jogger and a convert to walking for aerobic exercise. You decide to write an essay explaining to classmates the advantages of walking over running. You can assume a few classmates are runners; others swim, cycle, or do other exercise; some don't do much, but are thinking of starting; and some have no interest in any exercise.

Your problem is to address all these readers (the informed or more interested, and the uninformed or less interested) in one essay that *each* reader will find worthwhile. Specifically, you hope your essay will

- persuade runners and other exercisers to consider walking as an alternative,

- encourage the interested nonexercisers to try walking, and

- create at least a spark of interest among the diehard nonexercisers—and maybe even inspire them to rise up out of their easy chairs and hit the bricks.

To achieve your ambitious purpose, you will need to answer questions shared by all readers:

Why is walking better than running?

How are they similar or different?

What are the benefits in walking?

Can you give examples?

Why should I?

But some readers will have special questions. Nonexercisers might ask, "What exactly is aerobic exercise, anyway?" And the true couch potatoes might ask, "Who cares?" Your essay will have to answer all these questions.

Assume that many hours of planning, drafting, and revising have enabled you to produce this final draft:

Walk but Don't Run

Our bodies gain aerobic benefits when we exercise at a fast enough pace for muscles to demand oxygen-rich blood from the heart and lungs. During effective aerobic exercise, the heart rate increases roughly 80 percent above normal. Besides strengthening muscle groups—especially the heart—aerobic exercise makes blood vessels stronger and larger.

Running, or jogging, has become a most popular form of aerobic exercise. But millions of Americans who began running to get in shape are now limping to their doctors for treatment of running injuries. To keep yourself in one piece as you keep yourself in shape, try walking instead of running.

All the aerobic benefits of running can be yours if you merely take brisk walks. Consider this comparison. For enough aerobic training to increase cardiovascular (heart, lungs, and blood vessels) efficiency, you need to run three times weekly for roughly 30 minutes. (Like any efficient system, an efficient cardiovascular system produces maximum work with minimum effort.) You can gain cardiovascular benefits equivalent to running, however, by taking a brisk walk three times weekly for roughly 60 minutes. Granted, walking takes up more time than running, but it carries fewer risks.

Because of its more controlled and deliberate pace, walking is safer than running. A walker stands far less chance of tripping, stepping in potholes, or slipping and falling. And the slower pace causes less physical trauma. Anyone who has ever run at all knows that a runner's foot strikes the ground with sizable impact. But the shock of this impact travels beyond the foot—to the shins, knees, hips, internal organs, and spine. Walking, of course, creates an impact of its own, but the walker's foot strikes the ground with only half as much force as the runner's foot.

Beyond its apparent physical dangers, running can provoke subtle stress for the devoted exerciser. Because running is generally seen as more competitive than just walking, we too easily can be tempted to push our bodies too far, too fast. Even though we might not compete in races or marathons, we often tend to compete against ourselves—maybe just to keep up with a jock neighbor or to break a personal record. And by ignoring the signals of overexertion and physical stress, we can easily run ourselves into an injury—if not the grave. Slowing to a walk instead is a safe way of leaving the "competition" behind.

—Jeff Leonard

Will this essay have informative value for all your readers? Probably so. It seems to answer all the readers' questions we anticipated on page 110. The uninformed or less interested readers will receive an introduction to aerobic exercise in general and to walking in particular, and some might even be motivated to give walking a try—or at least to learn more about it. And though the better-informed readers will see much here that is familiar, they may also discover some fresh insight—perhaps a new way of looking at their own exercise preferences.

Will all readers become converts? Probably not. Maybe a few will take the advice. Or maybe no one. But each should have something to think about. Rarely can we expect to change everyone's mind, but we usually can cause an audience to recognize that what they've just read was worth their time and effort. In large ways or small, a worthwhile message makes some kind of a difference for its readers—even if it triggers only the slightest insight.

Now let's assume that you had written the walking essay by using the old high school strategy of filling up the page. Your opening paragraph might look like this:

> ### Walk but Don't Run
>
> Medical science has made tremendous breakthroughs in the past few decades. Research has shown that exercise is a good way of staying healthy, beneficial for our bodies and our minds. More people of all ages are exercising today than ever before. Because of its benefits, one popular form of exercise for Americans is aerobic exercise.

This writing lacks informative value because its content is self-evident; no real news or insight is here for anyone. Your readers (in this situation) already know all this.

Even new material can lack informative value when the content is irrelevant:

> To avoid the perils of running, the Chinese attend sessions of T'ai-chi, a dancelike series of stretching routines designed to increase concentration and agility. Although T'ai-chi is less dangerous than running, it fails to provide a truly aerobic workout.

This material might serve in some other essay (say, comparing certain aerobic and nonaerobic exercises). But in this situation, it merely distracts readers from your comparison of walking and running.

Nor would highly technical details have informative value here, as in this example:

> Walking and jogging result in forward motion because you continually fall forward and catch yourself. With each stride, you lift your body, accelerate, and land. You go faster when running because you fall farther, but you also strike the ground harder, and for less time. Your increase in speed and distance fallen combine with the shorter contact period to cause an impact on your body that is more than double the impact from walking.

This material would serve for students of biophysics, exercise physiology, or sports medicine, but it seems too detailed for a mixed audience who need to know only that "the walker's foot strikes the ground with only half the impact of the runner's foot."

Before you write, decide what readers need, and give them just that. While you write, consider whether each particular item advances your meaning. After you write, evaluate your draft to be sure that everything has informative value.

Completeness

Give readers only your best material, but be sure you give them enough.

The completeness of a message is measured by how thoroughly it gets your point across. All writers struggle with this question: How much is enough? (Or, How long should it be?) In answering this question, you face a dual challenge: to give enough information so that your meaning is clear and to include only that which directly advances your meaning.

As a guide to developing complete and unified support, anticipate readers' questions about your thesis. Assume, for instance, that a friend now living in another state is thinking of taking a job similar to one you held last summer. Your friend has written to ask how you liked the job; your response will influence the friend's decision. Here is a passage from your first draft:

> My job last summer as a flagger for a road construction company was boring, tiresome, dirty, and painful. All I did was stand in the road and flag cars. Every day I stood there for hours, getting sore feet. I was always covered with dirt and breathing it in. To make matters worse, the sun, wind, and insects ruined my skin. By the end of summer, I vowed never to do this kind of work again.

This passage *tells* but doesn't *show.* It has only limited informative value because it fails to make the experience vivid for readers. Granted, the opening sentence expresses the main point, and the remaining sentences provide a glimpse of the writer's ordeal; but a glimpse is all we get. The sketchy details fail to answer our obvious questions:

Can you show me what the job was like?

What, exactly, made it boring, tiresome, dirty, and painful?

This revised version (a one-paragraph essay) includes graphic details that *show,* that make readers feel a part of it all:

> My job last summer as a flagger for a road construction company was boring, tiresome, dirty, and painful. With nothing to do but wave a red flag at oncoming traffic, I stood like a robot, the deafening roar

of road machinery at my back, each day dragging by more slowly than the last. My feet would swell, and my legs would ache from standing on the hard-packed earth for as long as fifteen hours a day. And the filth was overwhelming. The fumes, oil, and grime from the heavy machines and the exhaust from passing cars became my second skin. Each breath was filled with dust, clogging my sinuses, irritating my eyes. But the worst part of all was my poor body's exposure to the ravages of the weather. If I was not blistering all over from severe sunburn, or being pounded by hail, my skin was being sandblasted and rubbed raw by windstorms or chewed and bitten by mosquitoes and horseflies. By the end of the summer, I was a mess: swollen feet and ankles, the skin of a leper, and a chronic case of sinusitis. I vowed to starve before taking that kind of job again.

This version is complete; it delivers on the writer's opening promise. Compare these columns to see how the writer made the message more detailed.

First draft	Revision
I stood there for hours.	I stood like a robot, the deafening roar of road machinery at my back, each day dragging by more slowly than the last.
getting sore feet	My feet would swell, and my legs would ache from standing on the hard-packed earth for as long as fifteen hours a day.
I was always covered with road dirt and breathing it in.	The fumes, oil, and grime from the heavy machines and the exhaust from passing cars became my second skin. Each breath was filled with dust, clogging my sinuses, irritating my eyes.
The sun, wind, and insects ruined my skin.	If I was not blistered all over from a severe sunburn, or being pounded by hail, my skin was being sandblasted and rubbed raw by windstorms or chewed and bitten by mosquitoes and horseflies.

By the end of summer, I vowed never to do this kind of work again.

By the end of summer, I was a mess: swollen feet and ankles, the skin of a leper, and a chronic case of sinusitis. I vowed to starve before taking that kind of job again.

The support here can be considered complete and appropriate for this situation. More specific treatment (say, a day-by-day description of every event) only would clutter the message. The reader here needed and *wanted* just enough information to make an informed decision, not a diary of someone's summer on the road. Readers are busy and impatient people; think hard how much your reader can tolerate. Never confuse needless details with legitimate support.

Developing support does not mean merely adding words. Whatever does nothing but fill the page is puffery:

> My job last summer as a flagger for a road construction company was boring, tiresome, dirty, and painful. Day in and day out, I stood ~~on that road~~ for endless hours getting ~~a severe case of~~ sore feet. My face and body were ~~always completely~~ covered with ~~the~~ dust blown up from the ~~passing cars and various other~~ vehicles, and I was forced to breathe in all ~~of~~ this ~~horrible~~ junk ~~day after day. To add to the problems of boredom, fatigue, and dirt~~, the weather did ~~the most~~ horrible things to my skin. ~~Let me tell you that~~ by the time the summer ended, I ~~had~~ made ~~myself~~ a solemn promise never to ~~victimize myself by~~ taking this kind of awful job again.

Although this passage is nearly twice the length of the original (page 113), it adds no meaning; needless words (shown crossed out) offer no real information. Replace puffed-up expressions with sharp details.

Details are writing's lifeblood: facts, ideas, examples, numbers, names, events, dates, or reasons that do the *showing*. Details advance your meaning by answering questions such as these:

Who, what, when, where, and why?

What did you see, feel, hear, taste, smell?

What would a camera record?

What are the dates, numbers, percentages?

Can you compare it to something more familiar?

In the next passage, a noted American writer describes with brutal clarity how a professional boxer was beaten to death during a prizefight. See for yourself how the details here make contact.

The Death of Benny Paret

Paret was a Cuban, a proud club fighter who had become welter-weight champion because of his unusual ability to take a punch. His style of fighting was to take three punches to the head in order to give back two. At the end of ten rounds, he would still be bouncing; his opponent would have a headache. But in the last two years, over the 15 round fights, he had started to take some bad maulings.

This fight had its turns. Griffith won most of the early rounds, but Paret knocked Griffith down in the sixth. Griffith had trouble getting up, but made it, came alive and was dominating Paret again before the round was over. Then Paret began to wilt. In the middle of the eighth round, after a clubbing punch had turned his back to Griffith, Paret walked three disgusted steps away, showing his hindquarters. For a champion, he took much too long to turn back around. It was the first hint of weakness Paret had ever shown, and it must have inspired a particular shame, because he fought the rest of the fight as if he were seeking to demonstrate that he could take more punishment than any man alive. In the twelfth, Griffith caught him. Paret got trapped in a corner. Trying to duck away, his left arm and his head became tangled on the wrong side of the top rope. Griffith was in like a cat ready to rip the life out of a huge boxed rat. He hit him 18 right hands in a row, an act which took perhaps three or four seconds, Griffith making a pent-up whimpering sound all the while he attacked, the right hand whipping like a piston rod which has broken through the crankcase, or like a baseball bat demolishing a pumpkin.

I was sitting in the second row of that corner. They were not ten feet away from me, and like everybody else, I was hypnotized. I had never seen one man hit another so hard and so many times. Over the referee's face came a look of woe as if some spasm had passed its way through him, and then he leaped on Griffith to pull him away. It was the act of a brave man. Griffith was uncontrollable. His trainer leaped into the ring, his manager, his cut man. There were four people holding Griffith, but he was off on an orgy; he had left the garden; he was back on a hoodlum's street. If he had been able to break loose from his handlers and the referee, he would have jumped Paret to the floor and whaled on him there.

And Paret? Paret died on his feet. As he took those 18 punches, something happened to everyone who was in psychic range of the event. Some part of his death reached out to us. One felt it hover in the air. He was still standing in the ropes, trapped as he had been before. He gave some little half-smile of regret, as if he were saying, "I didn't know I was going to die just yet," and then, his head leaning back but still erect, his death came to breathe about him. He began to pass away. As he passed, so his limbs descended beneath him, and he sank slowly to the floor. He went down more slowly than any fighter had ever gone down; he went down like a large ship which turns on end and slides second by second into its grave. As he went down, the sound of Griffith's punches echoed in the mind like a heavy axe in the distance chopping into a wet log.

—Norman Mailer

An illustration of how vivid details advance a writer's meaning, consider this version of Mailer's final paragraph—this one without detailed support:

Paret died on his feet and all the spectators were affected. Standing trapped in the ropes, he almost seemed to smile regretfully, and then sank very slowly to the floor. As he went down, we all remembered the sound of Griffith's punches.

To measure the completeness of your own writing, use these guidelines:

1. The often-stipulated 500 to 1000 words is a realistic length for giving a well-focused topic respectable treatment. Quality, however, is far more important than quantity. Once you have begun the writing process (searching for details, rephrasing in your own words, making connections), you probably will find it harder to *stay within* the limit than to reach it.

2. Your purpose is to make your point—not to show how smart you are. Instead of including every word, fact, and idea that crosses your mind, learn to cut.

3. Write nothing unless your reader needs to know it. If you've written just to get *something* on the page, most of it probably doesn't belong.

4. Sometimes one detail is enough to clarify a point or support an assertion. To make the point about a "boring" job, the passage on page 113 describes the writer standing like a robot, waving a red flag. Some points, however, call for many details. When Norman Mailer shows how "Paret began to wilt," he lays out a gruesome catalog of the events, blow by blow—but nothing is wasted.

"Completeness" doesn't mean using *every* detail, but only those that advance your meaning.

Application 6–1

Each sentence below states either a fact or an opinion. Rewrite all statements of opinion as statements of fact. Remember that a fact can be verified. (Review pages 105–108.)

Example

Opinion   My roommate isn't taking college work seriously.

Fact   My roommate never studies, sleeps through most classes, and has missed every exam.

1. Professor X grades unfairly.

2. My vacation was too short.

3. The salary for this position is $15,000 yearly.

4. This bicycle is reasonably priced.

5. We walked 5 miles last Saturday.

6. He drives recklessly.

7. My motorcycle gets great gas mileage.

8. This course has been very helpful.

9. German shepherds eat more than cocker spaniels do.

10. This apartment is much too small for our family.

Application 6–2

Return to Shirley Haley's essay on pages 18–19. Underline all statements of fact, and circle all statements of opinion. Are all the opinions supported by facts or by good sense? Now, perform the same evaluation on an essay you have written. (Review pages 105–108.)

Application 6–3

Assume you live in the Northeast, and citizens in your state are voting on a solar energy referendum that would channel millions of tax dollars toward solar technology. These two paragraphs are designed to help you, as a voter, make an educated decision. Do both these versions of the same message have informative value? Explain. (Review pages 108–113.)

Solar power offers a realistic solution to the Northeast's energy problems. In recent years the cost of fossil fuels (oil, coal, and natural gas) has risen rapidly while the supply has continued to decline. High prices and short supply will continue to cause a worsening energy crisis. Because solar energy comes directly from the sun, it is an inexhaustible resource. By using this energy to heat and air-condition our buildings, as well as to provide electricity, we could decrease substantially our consumption of fossil fuels. In turn, we would be less dependent on the unstable Middle East for our oil supplies. Clearly, solar power is a good alternative to conventional energy sources.

Solar power offers a realistic solution to the Northeast's energy problems. To begin with, solar power is efficient. Solar collectors installed on fewer than 30 percent of roofs in the Northeast would provide more than 70 percent of the area's heating and air-conditioning needs. Moreover, solar heat collectors are economical, operating for up to 20 years with little or no maintenance. These savings recoup the initial cost of installment within only ten years. Most important, solar power is safe. It can be transformed into electricity through photovoltaic cells (a type of storage battery) noiselessly and with no air pollution—unlike coal, oil, and wood combustion. In sharp contrast to its nuclear counterpart, solar power produces no toxic wastes and poses no catastrophic danger of meltdown. Thus, massive conversion to solar power would ensure abundant energy and a safe, clean environment for future generations.

Application 6–4

We've all had our own experiences—for better or worse—in a competitive society and thus are familiar with the subject of *competition*. The authors of this paragraph explain how the American character is rooted in competition. Are you familiar with experiences like those described here? Does the paragraph have informative value for you? Explain. (Review pages 108–113.)

The drive to compete and to be a "winner" has always been part of the American psyche. Our early ancestors were aggressive and competitive to begin with. They knew they were pitted against amazing odds, but they also felt they were a select and chosen group. They defied their mother country and were successful. Later came the "frontier spirit," the belief in survival of the fittest, and the growing American fetish for figures, statistics, records, and winners. Over 40 years ago, John R. Tunis wrote, in *The American Way in Sport:* "We worship the victors. But why? The Dutch don't especially, nor the Swedes, neither do the Danes, the Swiss, or the English, and they all seem fairly civilized people." We devised an international "score-board" to chart our successes in the Olympics as well as in our wars, an obsession that was tragically reflected in our approach to Vietnam, where both President Johnson and President Nixon vowed that they were not going down in history as "the first American President who lost a war."

—Thomas Tutko and William Bruns

Application 6–5

Collaborative Project: Review a classmate's essay and eliminate all statements that have no informative value (those that offer commonly known, irrelevant, or insignificant material). Be careful *not* to cut material the audience needs in order to understand the essay. (Review pages 108–113.)

Application 6–6

Reread Norman Mailer's essay (pages 116–117) and list the details that do these kinds of *showing:*

1.   Details that help us see. *Example:* Paret began to wilt.

2.   Details that help us feel. *Example:* a clubbing punch.

3.   Numerical details. *Example:* He hit him eighteen right hands in a row.

4.   Vivid comparisons. *Example:* the right hand whipping like a piston rod which has broken through the crankcase.

5.   Details that a camera would record.

6.   A detail that helps us hear.

Application 6–7

Return to one of your earlier essays. Study it carefully, then brainstorm again to sharpen your details. Now write a revised version. (Review pages 41–43.)

Application 6–8

Collaborative Project: Assume that your English teacher has just won $15 million in the state lottery. As a final grand gesture before retiring to a life of sailing, collecting fine wines, and raising polo ponies, your soon-to-be ex-teacher makes this announcement to the class:

> After years of agonizing over ways to motivate my writing students, I've discovered what could be the ultimate solution. I'm going to hold a contest offering $1 million to the student who can write the best essay on this topic: How I Would Spend $1 Million. Essays will be evaluated on the basis of originality, richness of detail, and quality of explanation. The whole class will pick the winner from among the five finalists I select.

Write your essay, revising as often as needed to make it a winner.

Application 6–9

Assume a point of view similar to Norman Mailer's (pages 116–117) and describe something you witnessed and will never forget. Write for your classmates.

Application 6–10

Choose one of the essay options from pages 25–27.

7

Shaping
the Paragraphs

Support Paragraphs as Mini-Essays • Paragraph Function
• Paragraph Length • The Topic Statement
• Structural Variations in Support Paragraphs
• When to Compose Your Topic Statement
• Paragraph Unity • Paragraph Coherence • Applications

Beyond saying something worthwhile, writers must decide how to shape their thinking, to make it *accessible* for readers. For its larger design (introduction, body, conclusion), the essay depends on the smaller design of each paragraph. A paragraph is a place for things that belong together.

Support Paragraphs as Mini-Essays

Paragraphs in an essay have various shapes and purposes. Introductory paragraphs draw us into the writer's reality; concluding paragraphs ease us out; transitional paragraphs help hold things together. But here the subject is *support paragraphs*—those middle blocks of thought, each often a mini-shape of the whole essay. Just as the thesis is sustained by its supporting points, each major supporting point is sustained by its paragraph.

Although part of the essay's larger design, each support paragraph usually can stand alone in meaning and emphasis. Consider this paragraph by a noted psychiatrist:

Introduction (topic statement, 1)

Body (2–9)

¹Crime is everybody's temptation. ²It is easy to look with proud disdain upon "those people" who get caught—the stupid ones, the unlucky ones, the blatant ones. ³But who does not get nervous when a police car follows closely? ⁴We squirm over our income-tax statements and make some "adjustments." ⁵We tell the customs official that we have nothing to declare—well, practically nothing. ⁶Some of us who have never been convicted of any crime picked up over two billion dollars' worth of merchandise last year from the stores we patronize. ⁷Over a billion dollars was embezzled by employees last year. ⁸One hotel in New York lost over seventy-five thousand finger bowls, demitasse spoons, and other objects in its first ten months of operation. ⁹The Claims Bureau of the American Insurance Association estimates that 75 percent of all claims are dishonest in some respect and the amount of overpayment more than $350,000,000 a

Conclusion (10–12)

year. ¹⁰These facts disturb us or should. ¹¹They give us an uneasy feeling that we are all indicted. ¹²"Let him who is without sin cast the first stone."

—Karl Menninger

Menninger's paragraph is part of a much larger design: a chapter in his book *The Crime of Punishment*. But the paragraph's shape is familiar enough: the introduction asserts a definite viewpoint; the body walks us through the writer's reasoning; the conclusion offers perspective on what we've read. As a unit of meaning, Menninger's paragraph is complete.

Paragraph Function

Writers need definite paragraph divisions for *control*; readers need them for *access*.

Paragraphs increase your writing control. Each support paragraph is an idea unit, one distinct space for developing one supporting point. If Menninger begins his paragraph with the point that crime tempts everyone, he can stay on track. He can tailor everything in the paragraph to advance his meaning. And if he ends up talking, say, about neurotic anxiety by the third or fourth sentence, he will know he has strayed from the point. No matter how long your message, you can stay in control by shaping your brainstorming materials into one paragraph at a time. To organize, you look for things that belong together—you think in terms of paragraphs.

Paragraphs also give readers access. Readers look for orientation, for a shape they can recognize; they need to know where they are and where they're going. Paragraphs keep them on the path. By dividing a long piece of writing, paragraphs allow readers to focus on each point. The indention (five spaces) gives a breathing space, a signal that the geography is changing and that it's time to look ahead.

Paragraph Length

Paragraph length depends on the writer's purpose and the reader's capacity for understanding. In writing that carries highly technical information or complex instructions, short paragraphs (perhaps in a list) give readers plenty of breathing space. In a newspaper article, paragraphs of only one or two sentences keep the reader's attention. In writing that explains concepts, attitudes, or viewpoints (as in college essays), support paragraphs generally run from 100 to 300 words.

But word count really means very little. What matters is how *thoroughly* the paragraph makes your point. A flabby paragraph buries readers in needless words and details; but just skin-and-bones leaves readers looking for the meat. Each paragraph requires new decisions.

Try to avoid too much of anything. A clump of short paragraphs can make some writing seem choppy and poorly organized, but a stretch of long ones is tiring. Attract attention with a well-placed short paragraph, sometimes—for special emphasis—just one sentence:

> More than 30 percent of our state's groundwater contains toxic wastes.

Or even just one word:

> Exactly.

Decide on a shape and length for every paragraph; don't just let things happen.

The Topic Statement

A college essay almost always needs a thesis that asserts the main point; and each support paragraph usually needs a topic statement that asserts a supporting point. Sometimes the topic statement comes at the end of the paragraph; sometimes in the middle; but usually it comes first. A paragraph's first sentence should orient readers, tell them what to expect. Without this orientation, readers have no clue.

TOPIC STATEMENT AS READERS' FRAMEWORK

Most paragraphs in college writing begin by telling readers what to look for. Don't write *Some jobs are less stressful than others* when you mean *Mortuary management is an ideal major for anyone craving a stress-free job.* The first topic statement doesn't give a very clear forecast; the second helps us focus, tells us what to expect. Don't write *Summers in Goonville are awful* when you mean *I hate Goonville summers because of the chiggers, ticks, scorpions, and rattlesnakes.* Try not to keep readers guessing.

Avoid creating topic statements that are boring or vague or that lead nowhere. Don't write *In this paragraph, I will discuss whale intelligence.* Announcements like that invite boredom. Don't write *Whales are interesting animals,* thereby sticking readers with the job of figuring out your meaning for *interesting.* And don't close the door before you've opened it by making dead-end statements such as these: *Whales live only in salt water* or *Whales are a species of mammal.* Without a viewpoint, these simple expressions of fact lead nowhere, leave nothing to be explained. Lead your readers in; give them a definite signal about what to expect.

Let your purpose and audience's needs guide your adjustment of focus. Say you're writing an essay about whales for readers you'd like to recruit for the Save-the-Whales movement. First, you need to decide on the exact point about whales that you want to make in this paragraph. Suppose you decide to talk about whale intelligence. What is your *exact* viewpoint?

> Whales seem to exhibit real intelligence.
>
> Whales are measurably intelligent.
>
> Whales are highly intelligent.

You decide that the final version is closest to what you mean. Now you think about ways of making the assertion more informative. Your readers will be asking: "Highly intelligent, relative to what?" Your answer:

> Whales are among the most intelligent of the mammals.

Now you have a clear direction for developing your support. The finished paragraph might look like this:

> *Whales are among the most intelligent of the mammals.*
> Scientists rank whale intelligence with that of higher primates because of whales' sophisticated group behavior. These impressive mammals have been seen teaching and disciplining their young, help-

ing their wounded comrades, engaging in elaborate courtship rituals, and playing in definite gamelike patterns. They are able to coordinate such complex activities through their highly effective communication system of sonar clicks and pings. This remarkable social organization apparently grows out of the almost human devotion that whales seem to have toward one another.

With the framework provided by your topic statement, we can understand your message easily.

Let's imagine other directions your topic statement on whale intelligence might have taken. If your purpose were even *more* specific, you might have come up with this topic statement:

A good indication of whales' intelligence is the way they play in gamelike patterns.

Or, for a different purpose, you might narrow your focus to *one* game:

Like children, a group of whales can spend hours playing tag.

Depending on your purpose and your readers' needs, you can make any topic statement more and more specific by focusing on smaller and smaller parts of it.

TOPIC STATEMENT AS WRITER'S FRAMEWORK

Without a topic statement, readers usually struggle to understand a paragraph, and the writer struggles to shape it—to make it more than a collection of *stuff*. Always take a definite stand; assert something significant.

Imagine that you are a member of Congress, about to vote on abortion legislation. One of your constituents has responded to your request for citizens' viewpoints with a letter that begins like this:

Abortion is a very complex issue. There is a sharp division between those who are for it and those who are against it. Very few people take a neutral stand on this issue. The battle between supporters and opponents has raged for years. This is only one of the serious problems in our society. Every day, things seem to get worse.

Because this writer never identified his purpose, never discovered his own exact meaning, this paragraph merely parrots a number of unrelated thoughts that are all common knowledge. Without a definite topic, the writer had no framework, no place to go. Having ignored some essential early decisions, he was forced to borrow partial meanings from here and there.

If, instead, our writer had refined his meaning by asserting a definite viewpoint, he might have written a worthwhile paragraph. Depending on his purpose, he might have begun with, say:

Abortion laws in our state discriminate against the poor.

or

Abortion is wrong because of the irresponsibility it allows.

Before you can explain yourself, you have to figure out exactly what it is that you mean.

Structural Variations in Support Paragraphs

Some topic statements require two or more sentences. Or your main idea might have several distinct parts, which would result in an excessively long paragraph. You might then break up the paragraph, making your topic statement a brief introductory paragraph that serves the various subparts, which are set off as independent paragraphs for the reader's convenience.

Common types of strip-mining procedures include open-pit mining, contour mining, and auger mining. The specific type employed will depend on the type of terrain covering the coal.

Open-pit mining is employed in the relatively flat lands in western Kentucky, Oklahoma, and Kansas. Here, draglines and scoops operate directly on the coal seams. This process produces long parallel rows of packed spoil banks, 10 to 30 feet high, with steep slopes. Between the spoil banks are large pits that soon fill with water to produce pollution and flood hazards.

Contour mining is most widely practiced in the mountainous terrain of the Cumberland Plateau and eastern Kentucky. Here, bulldozers and explosives cut and blast the earth and rock covering a coal seam. Wide bands are removed from the mountain's circumference to reach the embedded coal beneath. The cutting and blasting result in a shelf along with a jagged cliff some 60 feet high at a right angle to the shelf. The blasted and churned earth is pushed over the shelf to form a massive and unstable spoil bank that creates a danger of mud slides.

Auger mining is employed when the mountain has been cut so thin that it no longer can be stripped. It is also used in other difficult-access terrain. Here, large augers bore parallel rows of holes into the hidden coal seams to extract the embedded coal. Among the three strip-mining processes, auger mining causes least damage to the surrounding landscape.

As you can see, each paragraph begins with a clear statement of the subtopic discussed in it.

Countless other variations are possible. Topic statements aren't always the first sentences. And some paragraphs have no explicit conclusion. Any such variations, however, should be based on good reason.

When to Compose Your Topic Statement

A writer's thinking hardly ever is neat. You won't always be able to think *first* of the right topic statement, and *then* of your support. Your actual framework might not appear until you've done some freewriting or brainstorming. Say you're writing about the dangers of acid rain in your state. To help make one supporting point, you've isolated and arranged from your brainstorming materials these details:

1. Acid rain carries toxic metals.

2. It also leaches other materials from the soil.

3. Mercury and other toxins invade surface water and build up in fish tissues.

4. People or animals who drink the water or eat the fish risk heavy-metal poisoning.

5. Acidified water releases lead, copper, and other toxins from metal plumbing, thus making even tap water hazardous.

Let's say that in another paragraph you've discussed how acid rain is killing lakes and forests and damaging buildings, statues, and almost anything else it falls on. But your list of details suggests its own larger meaning: namely, that *acid rain threatens human health.* Now you can sharpen your meaning: acid rain doesn't directly harm the people it falls on (at least as far as we know), but its threat to humans is *indirect.* Now you've discovered your exact meaning. With the organizing viewpoint provided by the topic statement, you can write a sensible paragraph.

> *Acid rain indirectly threatens human health.* Besides bearing several toxic metals, it percolates through the soil, leaching out natu-

rally present metals. Pollutants such as mercury invade surface water, accumulating in fish tissues. Any organism eating the fish—or drinking the water—in turn faces the risk of heavy-metal poisoning. Moreover, acidified water can release heavy concentrations of lead, copper, and aluminum from metal plumbing, making ordinary tap water hazardous.

You might come up with a topic statement, then your support, or vice versa. The sequence is unimportant—as long as the finished paragraph offers a definite framework and solid support.

Paragraph Unity

Each paragraph in an essay requires *external unity* and *internal unity*. A paragraph has external unity when (as on pages 71–72) it belongs with all the other paragraphs in an essay. But each paragraph requires internal unity as well: everything in the paragraph should belong there.

Internal unity occurs when all the material in a paragraph directly supports the topic statement. Imagine that you're composing a paragraph beginning with this topic statement:

Chemical pesticides and herbicides are both ineffective and hazardous.

The words that signal the meaning here are *ineffective* and *hazardous;* everything in the paragraph should directly advance that meaning. Here is the unified paragraph:

A unified paragraph

Chemical pesticides and herbicides are both ineffective and hazardous. Because none of these chemicals has permanent effects, pest populations invariably recover and need to be resprayed. Repeated applications cause pests to develop immunity to the chemicals. Furthermore, most pesticides and herbicides attack species other than the intended pest, killing off its natural predators, thus actually increasing the pest population. Above all, chemical residues survive in the environment (and in living tissue) for years and often are carried hundreds of miles by wind and water. This toxic legacy includes such biological effects as birth deformities, reproductive failures, brain damage, and cancer. Although intended to control pest populations, these chemicals ironically threaten to make the human population their ultimate victims.

One way to destroy unity in the paragraph above would be to discuss the cost of the chemicals or their unpleasant odor or the number of people who oppose their use. Although those matters do broadly relate to the pesticide and herbicide issue, none directly advances the meaning of *ineffective* and *hazardous*.

Every topic statement has a signal term, a key word or phrase that announces the viewpoint. In the whale paragraph (page 125), the signal term is *intelligent*, causing readers to expect material about whale intelligence. Anything that fails to advance the meaning of *intelligence* throws the paragraph—and the reader—off track:

A disunified paragraph

> *Whales are among the most intelligent of all mammals.* Scientists rank whale intelligence with that of higher primates because of whales' sophisticated group behavior. These impressive mammals have been seen teaching and disciplining their young, helping their wounded comrades, engaging in elaborate courtship rituals, and playing in definite gamelike patterns. *Whales continually need to search for food in order to survive. Their search for krill and other sea organisms can cause them to migrate thousands of miles yearly.*

The shift from intelligence to food problems frustrates the reader's expectations.

Disunity often results when a writer neglects to brainstorm or settles for a foggy topic statement. Lacking either enough material or a definite purpose, writers are tempted to throw in anything—even material that really might not belong. Here's what can happen when the topic statement lacks a definite signal of the writer's viewpoint:

A disunified paragraph

> *Divorce rates have been climbing for the last decade.* People are deciding they want individual freedom after they are married. In the United States, divorces are easy to obtain, and not only young couples are getting divorced. There are many middle-aged people who find themselves unhappy in their situations and who change them. Statistics show that divorce rates are higher for couples who marry young. The breakup of a marriage will always affect children. But children themselves now are growing up with the same view of marriage that their parents have: if it doesn't work, get a divorce.

Without an exact viewpoint to work from, the writer skipped from one half-formed idea to another. Only when you're sure of what you want to say can you decide whether something really belongs.

Paragraph Coherence

In a unified paragraph, everything belongs. In a coherent paragraph, everything sticks together: topic statement and support form a connected line of thought, like links in a chain. To convey exact meaning, a paragraph must be unified. To be readable, a paragraph must be coherent, as well.

This paragraph (written by a track team veteran addressing new runners) is both unified and coherent: everything relates to the topic in a continuous line of thinking.

> [1]To be among the first out of the starting blocks in any race, follow these instructions. [2]First, when the starter says "Into your blocks," make sure you are the last runner down. [3]Take your sweet time; make all the others wait for you. [4]You take your time for three good reasons: one, you get a little more stretching than your competitors do; two, they are down in the blocks getting cold and nervous while you're still warm and relaxed from stretching; and three, your deliberate manner tends to weaken other runners' confidence. [5]The second step is to lean forward over your shoulders, in the "set" position. [6]This way, you will come out of the blocks forward and low, meeting less wind resistance. [7]The third and final step is to pump your arms as fast as you can when you come off the blocks. [8]The faster your arms pump, the faster your legs will move. [9]By concentrating on each of these steps, you can expect your quickest possible start.

The material in this paragraph seems easy enough to follow. Here's how the thinking goes:

1.   The topic statement sets a clear direction.

2.   The first step is introduced.

3–4. The importance of "taking your time" is emphasized and explained.

5–6. The second step is introduced and its importance explained.

7–8. The third step is introduced and its importance explained.

9.   The conclusion sums up.

Within this line of thinking, each sentence follows logically from the one before it. Because the material follows a logical order (in this case, chronological), readers know exactly where they are at any place in the paragraph. And because everything is connected (by parallelism, repetition of key words, pronouns, and transitions), the whole paragraph sticks together. Let's now examine specific ways of achieving coherence.

ORDERING IDEAS FOR COHERENCE

The mind works in structured ways to sort out, arrange, and make sense of its many perceptions. If you decide you like a class (a general observation), you then identify your particular reasons (friendly atmosphere, interesting subject, dynamic teacher, and so on); your thinking has followed a *general-to-specific order.* Or, if you tell a friend about your terrific weekend, you follow the order of events, how things happened over the weekend; your thinking has followed a *chronological order.* These are just two of several ordering patterns the mind uses to filter out that which is not immediately important and to create a sensible sequence of information. Here are the most common ordering patterns that help us think and write clearly.

- general-to-specific order
- specific-to-general order
- emphatic order
- spatial order
- chronological order

Of course, thinking and writing do not always fall neatly into one of these categories. On the whole, though, these ordering patterns can help you sort out your ideas and answer these questions:

What comes first?

What comes next?

Does the subject have any features that suggest an order?

Answers will be based on your subject and purpose. In a letter describing your new car (subject) to a friend, you might decide to move from outside to inside in a spatial order, as one would first see the car. A description that skipped around (say, from hubcaps to seats to tires to carpeting) would be confusing. Or, if you decided to concentrate on the car's computerized dashboard (subject), you might move from left to right (as one would see it from the driver's seat). If, instead, you were trying to persuade someone to stay in school or to quit smoking, you probably would present your reasons in an emphatic order, from least to most important or vice versa. Choosing the appropriate order makes your message easy to follow.

As we will see, some kinds of order call for your topic statement to come last instead of first. Even then, your opening sentence should tell readers what to expect. Before considering those variations, however, let's begin with the standard ordering pattern: general to specific.

General-to-Specific Order   The commonest way of arranging a paragraph is general to specific: a general topic statement supported by specific details. Most sample paragraphs we've seen so far follow a general-to-specific order, as this one does:

General assertion (topic statement, 1)	[1]Americans everywhere are obsessed with speed. [2]The airlines think it's so important that they've developed jets that can cross the ocean in a few hours. [3]Despite energy shortages, Detroit often makes the speed of a car and the power of its engine a focal point of its advertising campaign. [4]Ads for oil companies boast of ten-minute oil changes at their gas stations. [5]Even pedestrians aren't spared: some shoemakers will put soles and heels on shoes "while you wait." [6]Fast-food restaurants prosper as increasing millions gobble increasing billions of "all-beef" hamburgers and guzzle their Cokes in seconds flat. [7]And the Day of Rest, too, has given way to the stopwatch as more and more churches offer brief evening services or customize their offerings to suit "people on the go." [8]Some churches even offer drive-in ceremonies— pay your money, spit out your prayer, and hit the road, streaking toward salvation with Ronald McDonald. [9]These days, even the road to eternity has a fast lane.
Specific support (2–8)	
Conclusion (9)	

Paragraphs of general-to-specific order are the workhorses of virtually all nonfiction writing: first, the big picture; then, the close-ups—everything sticking together.

Specific-to-General Order   For some purposes, instead of narrowing and restricting your meaning, you will generalize and extend it. Thus, your support will come first, and your topic statement last. A specific-to-general order is especially useful for showing how pieces of evidence add up to a convincing conclusion, as in this paragraph.

Orienting statements (1–2)	[1]For thousands of years, the single species *Homo sapiens*, to which you and I have the dubious honor of belonging, has been increasing in numbers. [2]In the past couple of centuries, the rate of increase has itself increased explosively. [3]At the time of Julius Caesar, when Earth's human popula-
Specific details (3–4)	

General conclusion
(topic statement, 5)

tion is estimated to have been 150 million, that population was increasing at a rate such that it would double in 1,000 years if that rate remained steady. [4]Today, with Earth's population estimated at about 4,000 million (26 times what it was in Caesar's time), it is increasing at a rate which, if steady, will cause it to double in 35 years. [5]The present rate of increase of Earth's swarming human population qualifies *Homo sapiens* as an ecological cancer, which will destroy the ecology just as sure as any ordinary cancer would destroy an organism.

—Isaac Asimov

Even though the topic statement is saved for last, the opening statements give readers a forecast of the paragraph. Whenever you decide to delay your topic sentence, be sure the paragraph's opening sentence gives readers enough orientation for them to know what's going on.

A specific-to-general order works well for supporting a position that some readers might disagree with, as in this example:

Specific observation
in orienting
statement (1)

Specific arguments
(2–7)

General conclusion
(topic statement, 8)

[1]Strange that so few ever come to the woods to see how the pine lives and grows and spires, lifting its evergreen arms to the light—to see its perfect success; but most are content to behold it in the shape of many broad boards brought to market, and deem *that* its true success! [2]But the pine is no more lumber than man is, and to be made into boards and houses is no more its true and highest use than the truest use of a man is to be cut down and made into manure. [3]There is a higher law affecting our relations to pine as well as to men. [4]A pine cut down, a dead pine, is no more a pine than a dead human carcass is a man. [5]Can he who has discovered only some of the values of whalebone and whale oil be said to have discovered the true use of the whale? [6]Can he who slays the elephant for his ivory be said to have "seen the elephant"? [7]These are petty and accidental uses; just as if a stronger race were to kill us in order to make buttons and flutes of our bones; for everything may serve a lower as well as a higher use. [8]Every creature is better alive than dead, men and moose and pine trees, and he who understands it correctly will rather preserve its life than destroy it.

—Henry David Thoreau

Some readers (especially those in the paper and lumber industry, as well as hunters) would find Thoreau's main point harder to accept if it were placed at the beginning, without the full paragraph lead-in. By moving from the specific to the general, Thoreau presents his evidence before drawing his conclusion. Also, things that come last (last word in a sentence, last sentence in a paragraph, last paragraph in an essay) are the things readers remember best. The order of Thoreau's material increases its persuasiveness.

Emphatic Order   In earlier chapters, we've seen how emphasis can make important things stand out, become easier to remember. Writers achieve emphasis within paragraphs by positioning material in two common ways: (1) from least to most important or serious or dramatic, and (2) vice versa. The next paragraph is from an essay analyzing television advertisements for toys of violence. Joe Bolton offers dramatic support for his opening assertion by saving his strongest example for last.

Topic statement (1–2)	[1]Too many toys advertised during television programs for children are of what I call the "death and destruction" variety: toys that stimulate the killing of humans by humans. [2]Such toys make children's "war games" seem far too real. [3]During the pre-Christmas season, children are bombarded with ads promoting all the new weapons: guns, tanks, boats, subs, jets, helicopters, lasers, and more. [4]One new warplane is described as "the wickedest weapon yet," and a new satellite resembles an old "Nike" missile and is designed to be moved around on railroad tracks to avoid an enemy strike. [5]One of the enemy dolls is even dubbed a "paranoid schizophrenic killer" and advertised as such on the side of the box.
Examples in increasing order of importance (3–5)	

Because last things are best remembered, the end position of Bolton's most dramatic example fixes it in the reader's mind.

   In another paragraph from the same essay, Bolton reverses the emphasis: he begins with his most serious material (a statement of the problem) and then proposes a solution that becomes increasingly far-fetched.

Topic statement (1)	[1]Today, as always, children learn about killing before they understand the concept of death. [2]Seeing we still are a violent, warlike species, maybe we should try a new approach. [3]Children might be less likely to enjoy playing
Support in decreasing order of seriousness (2–4)	

"war" if they could first be shown how guns blow holes in their targets; then they could be made to understand that, when the targets are *people*, those bloody holes cause pain and death. [4]If toy manufacturers introduced a "sounds and smells of death" accessory for their toys of violence, for instance, more parents and children might object to the nature of the "game" these toys simulate.

The increasingly grotesque solution is meant not to be taken seriously, but only to focus attention on the problem asserted in the topic statement.

Spatial Order   Sometimes, instead of explaining something, you will want to describe it with a word picture. You treat the parts of your subject in the same order that readers would follow if they actually were looking at it. In this paragraph, the writer describes a missing friend to the police.

Topic statement

A gradually
narrowing focus

My missing friend should be easy to recognize. When I last saw Roger, he was wearing dark blue jeans, a pair of dark brown hunting boots with red laces, and a light blue cableknit sweater with a turtleneck; he was carrying a red daypack with black trim filled with books. He stands about 6 feet 4 inches, has broad, slouching shoulders, and carries roughly 190 pounds on a medium frame. He walks in excessively long strides, like a cowboy. His hair is sunstreaked, sandy blond, cut just below his ears and feathered back on the sides. He has deep purple eyes framed by dark brown eyelashes and brows set into a clear, tanned complexion. The bridge of his nose carries a half-inch scar in the shape of an inverted crescent. His right front tooth has a small chip in the left corner.

Notice the writer's decisions in organizing this piece, based on her knowledge of the readers' needs: she begins with Roger's clothing and accessories and moves to his height, posture, weight, body build, stride and finally his facial features, from hair down to mouth. This sequence follows the order of features readers would recognize in approaching Roger: first, from a distance, by his clothing, size, posture, and stride; next, from a closer view—the hair, eye color, and so on; and, finally, from right up close—the scar on his nose and the chip on his tooth. The earlier details, visible from a distance, would alert readers, and the later ones would confirm their early impression as they moved up close. The details here were selected to answer these reader questions:

What does he look like?

How could we recognize him?

Whenever we describe something, we have to make these decisions about content and organization, about the kinds and sequence of details that will be clearest. The writer above decided to take the angle of a movie camera gradually closing in.

Many descriptive paragraphs begin with no topic statement at all. Instead, the opening sentence puts us immediately in the writer's place, as in this sample:

> The tarpaulin is down, and a midafternoon rain is falling steadily. Play has been halted. The lights are on, and the wet, pale-green tarp throws off wiggly, reptilian gleams. The players are back in their locker rooms, and both dugouts are empty. A few fans have stayed in their seats, huddling under big, brightly colored golf umbrellas, but almost everybody else has moved back under the shelter of the upper decks, standing there quietly, watching the rain. The huge park, the countless rows of shiny-blue wet seats, the long emerald outfield— all stand silent and waiting. By the look of it, this shower may hold things up for a good half-hour or more. Time for a few baseball stories.
>
> —Roger Angell

This paragraph places us in a setting, *showing* the scene as the writer saw and felt it. Because the paragraph is designed to create a dominant impression of the whole ballpark in the rain, the details are presented from an elevated angle of vision—like that of a television camera scanning the park from up in the press box.

Chronological Order   Another common order in a paragraph follows time. A chronological paragraph follows the natural order in which something happens. Writers use chronological order to give instructions (how to be first out of the starting blocks), to explain how something works (how the heart pumps blood), or to show how something happened. This paragraph from George Orwell's "Shooting an Elephant" shows how something brutal happened. As with many paragraphs that tell a story, this one has no topic statement. Instead, the opening sentence places us in the middle of the action.

Orienting statement
(1–2)

¹When I pulled the trigger I did not hear the bang or feel the kick—one never does when a shot goes home—but I heard the devilish roar of glee that went up from the crowd. ²In that instant, in too short a time, one would have thought, even for the bullet to get there, a mysterious, terrible change had come over the elephant. ³He neither stirred nor fell, but every line on his body had altered. ⁴He looked suddenly stricken, shrunken, immensely old, as though the frightful impact of the bullet had paralyzed him without knocking him down. ⁵At last, after what seemed like a long time—it might have been five seconds, I dare say—he sagged flabbily to his knees. ⁶His mouth slobbered. ⁷An enormous senility seemed to have settled upon him. ⁸One could have imagined him thousands of years old. ⁹I fired again into the same spot. ¹⁰At the second shot he did not collapse but climbed with desperate slowness to his feet and stood weakly upright, with legs sagging and head drooping. ¹¹I fired a third time. ¹²That was the shot that did it for him. ¹³You could see the agony of it jolt his whole body and knock the last remnant of strength from his legs. ¹⁴But in falling he seemed for a moment to rise, for as his hind legs collapsed beneath him he seemed to tower upwards like a huge rock toppling, his trunk reaching skywards like a tree. ¹⁵He trumpeted, for the first and only time. ¹⁶And then down he came, his belly towards me, with a crash that seemed to shake the ground even where I lay.

Besides a series of events ordered in time, Orwell's paragraph contains the writer's *impressions* of what happened at various moments. The actual chronology is simple enough:

1. With the first shot, the elephant falls to its knees.

2. With the second shot, instead of collapsing, the elephant drags itself up.

3. With the third shot, the elephant falls, rises, and then falls for good.

If narrating these events in order were the writer's only purpose, the paragraph might look like this:

> When I pulled the trigger, a change came over the elephant. He neither stirred nor fell, but every line on his body had altered as if the impact of the bullet had paralyzed him without knocking him down. At last, he sagged to his knees. His mouth slobbered. I fired again into the same spot. At the second shot, he did not collapse but climbed slowly to his feet and stood with legs sagging and head drooping. I fired a third time. That was the shot that did it for him. But in falling he seemed for a moment to rise. And then, down he came, with his belly towards me, with a crash that shook the ground.

This paragraph lists the details a camera would record. It lacks the strength of the original, where personal comments create a vivid angle of vision. The author's purpose is not simply to narrate the shooting of an elephant; it is to express horror over his actions, to record the animal's dignity in dying, to make us confront the senseless brutality of this kind of slaughter. Yet despite these digressions in the original version, we are able to follow the events because they are narrated in chronological order. And despite the absence of a topic statement, the author's attitude toward his actions is clearly implied.

Keep in mind that paragraph order is just another device to help writer and reader stay on track. Any specific order or combination of orders will depend on your subject and purpose. Writers don't begin by saying, "I've decided to write a spatial paragraph, and so now I need to find a subject that will fit that order." Instead, they say, "I want to discuss *X*; therefore, I need to select the most logical order to make my message sensible." Granted, in the exercises here you are asked to follow this or that specific order in writing a paragraph, but only to give you practice in improving coherence. In all later writing, you will make such decisions for yourself.

COMBINED TYPES OF ORDER

Often your subject and purpose will call for combining types of order. This paragraph combines general-to-specific and chronological order.

> [1]Television is the most effective brainwashing medium ever invented by man. [2]Advertisers know this to be true. [3]Children are affected by television in ways we scarcely understand. [4]In the fall of 1973 I was assigned a story involving a young white woman living on the fringe of Boston's black ghetto. [5]Her car had run out of gas. [6]She had gone to a filling station with a can and was returning to her car when she was trapped in an alley by a gang of black youths. [7]The gang poured gasoline over her and set fire to her. [8]She died of her burns. [9]It was later established that some of the youths involved had, on the night before the killing, watched on television a rerun of an old movie

in which a drifter is set on fire by an adolescent gang. [10]There is some kind of strange reductive process at work here. [11]To see something on television robs it of its reality, and then when the same thing is acted out, it is like the reenactment of something unreal. [12]In other words, when the gang set fire to the girl, they were imitating what they had seen on a screen, as if they themselves were on a screen, and in a story. [13]I don't think we have even begun to realize how powerful a medium television is.

—Ted Morgan

The overall order of this paragraph is general to specific. In the topic statement the author expresses a general viewpoint about television. The remaining sentences provide supporting points and a detailed example. But the example itself (sentences 4 to 9) follows chronological order.

PARALLELISM

Along with paragraph order, several other devices are useful for increasing coherence. The first is parallelism—similar grammatical structures and word order for similar items, or for items of equal importance. Note how parallelism is employed in this paragraph:

[1]What is the *shape* of my life? [2]The *shape* of my life today starts with a family. [3]I *have* a husband, five children, and a home just beyond the suburbs of New York. [4]I *have* also a craft, writing, and therefore work I want to pursue. [5]The *shape* of my life is, of course, determined by many other things: my *background and* childhood, *my mind and* its education, *my conscience and* its pressures, *my heart and* its desires. [6]I want *to give and take* from my children and husband, *to share* with friends and community, *to carry out* my obligations *to man* and *to the world, as a woman, as an artist, as a citizen.* [emphasis added]

—Anne Morrow Lindbergh

This writer uses parallelism between as well as within sentences. Sentences 2 and 5 open with identical structures ("The shape of my life . . . ") to show that in both sentences she will treat the same subject. Sentences 3 and 4, too, have parallel openings ("I have a husband . . . I have also a craft . . . ") to reflect their close relationship. Sentence 5 has four parallel phrases ("my background and . . . my mind and . . . , my conscience and . . . , my heart and . . . "). Sentence 6 has three sets of parallel phrases: (1) "to give and take . . . to share . . . to carry out . . . ," (2) "to man . . . to the world. . . ," and (3) "as a woman, as an artist, as a citizen." These similar structures emphasize similarity between ideas, thereby tying the paragraph together. See pages 160–161 for further discussion of parallelism.

REPETITION, RESTATEMENT, AND VARIATION

Repeating key words or phrases or rephrasing them in different ways helps link ideas, as in this paragraph (emphasis added):

> [1]The ultimate threat posed by nuclear *weapons* is not only *death* but *meaninglessness:* an unknown *death* by an unimaginable weapon. [2]War with such *weapons* is no longer heroic; *death* from such *weapons* is without valor. [3]*Meaninglessness* has become almost a stereotyped characterization of twentieth-century *life,* a central theme in modern art, theater, and politics. [4]The roots of this *meaninglessness* are many. [5]But crucial, we believe, is the anxiety deriving from the sense that all forms of human associations are perhaps *pointless* because subject to sudden *irrational* ends. [6]Cultural *life* thus becomes still more *formless.* [7]No one form, no single *meaning* or style, appears to have any ultimate claim. [8]The psychological implications of this *formlessness* are not fully clear; while there seem to be more *life* choices available, fewer are inwardly compelling.
>
> —Robert J. Lifton and Eric Olson

The signal word *meaninglessness* in the topic statement is repeated in sentences 3, 4, and 7 (its variant: *meaning*). *Formless* (or its variants), here treated as a symptom of meaninglessness, is used in 5, 6, 7, and 8. Repetition of these two key words helps tie the paragraph together. In 5, *pointless* and *irrational* serve as synonyms (different words with similar meaning) for the idea of meaninglessness that dominates the paragraph. And, throughout, the antonyms (words with opposite senses) *life* and *death* seem to clash, each uncertain of ultimate victory. Both clauses in 2 have parallel structure ("War with such weapons is . . . ; death from such weapons is . . . "). The similar structure reflects the similarity of ideas, linking them neatly. And, of course, the repetition of *weapon* from 1 further clarifies the connection. Such repetition and restatement help keep our attention where it belongs: on the writer's view of a world threatened with annihilation.

Needless repetition, of course, makes writing seem tedious, juvenile, and annoying to read. For a clear distinction between effective and ineffective repetition, see page 171.

PRONOUNS FOR COHERENCE

Instead of repeating certain nouns, it is sometimes more natural to use pronouns that refer to an earlier key noun. Pronouns improve coherence by relating sentences, clauses, and phrases to one another. This paragraph uses pronouns to avoid repeating *the bull fighters.*

> The bull fighters march in across the sand to the president's box. *They* march with easy professional stride, swinging along, not in the

least theatrical except for *their* clothes. *They* all have the easy grace and slight slouch of the professional athlete. From *their* faces *they* might be major league ball players. *They* salute the president's box then spread out along the barrera, exchanging *their* heavy brocaded capes for the fighting capes that have been laid along the red fence by the attendants. [emphasis added]

—Ernest Hemingway

Without the pronouns *they* and *their,* the writer would have to repeat *the bull fighters* as many as seven times. Such repetition in this short paragraph would be awkward and excessive. The pronouns in this paragraph clearly refer to *the bull fighters.* When you do use pronouns, be sure they refer clearly to the appropriate nouns. See page 158 for a full discussion of pronoun-antecedent agreement.

CONSISTENCY FOR COHERENCE

Underlying all these strategies for coherence is the need for consistent tense, point of view, and number. Do not shift from past to present tense, from third- to first-person point of view, or from singular to plural nouns or pronouns—unless your meaning requires you to do so. See Appendix A for a discussion of shifts that destroy coherence.

TRANSITIONS

The devices we have studied for achieving coherence (order, parallelism, repetition and restatement, pronouns) *suggest* specific relations between ideas. Transitional expressions, on the other hand, *state* those relations. These are words and phrases that work like bridges between thoughts. Here are a few transitional phrases that give readers definite signals: *for example, meanwhile, however, moreover, thus.* Each transition indicates a definite relation between ideas. Each has a definite meaning—even without a specific context—as shown below.

Transition	Relation
X; meanwhile, *Y*	*X* and *Y* are occurring at the same time.
X; however, *Y*	*Y* is in contrast or exception to *X.*
X; moreover, *Y*	*Y* is in addition to *X.*
X; thus, *Y*	*Y* is a result of *X.*

Here is a paragraph in which these transitions are used to clarify the writer's line of thinking:

Psychological and social problems of aging too often are aggravated by the final humiliation: poverty. One of every three older Americans lives near or below the poverty level. *Meanwhile,* only one of every nine younger people lives in poverty. The American public assumes that Social Security and Medicare provide adequate support for the aged. These benefits alone, *however,* rarely are enough to raise an older person's living standards above the poverty level. *Moreover,* older people are the only group living in poverty whose population recently has increased rather than decreased. More and more of our aging citizens *thus* confront the horror of poverty.

Transitions help make your meaning clear. They announce that you are in a specific time or place, or that you are giving an example, showing a contrast, concluding your discussion, or shifting gears. Here are some common transitions and the relations they indicate.

An addition: *moreover, in addition, and, also*

I am majoring in naval architecture; *furthermore,* I spent three years crewing on a racing yawl.

Results: *thus, hence, therefore, accordingly, thereupon, as a result, and so, as a consequence*

Mary enjoyed all her courses; *therefore,* she worked especially hard last semester.

An example or illustration: *for instance, to illustrate, namely, specifically*

Competition for part-time jobs is fierce; *for example,* 80 students applied for the clerk's job at Sears.

An explanation: *in other words, simply stated, in fact*

She had a terrible semester; *in fact,* she flunked four courses.

A summary or conclusion: *in closing, to conclude, to summarize, in brief, in summary, to sum up, all in all, on the whole, in retrospect, in conclusion*

Our credit is destroyed, our bank account is overdrawn, and our debts are piling up; *in short,* we are bankrupt.

Time: *first, next, second, then, meanwhile, at length, later, now, the next day, in the meantime, in turn, subsequently*

Mow the ball field this morning; *afterwards,* clean the dugouts.

A comparison: *likewise, in the same way, in comparison*

Our reservoir is drying up because of the drought; *similarly,* water supplies in neighboring towns are dangerously low.

A contrast or alternative: *however, nevertheless, yet, still, in contrast, otherwise, but, on the other hand, to the contrary, notwithstanding, conversely*

Felix worked hard *yet* received poor grades.

Note: Transitional expressions should be a limited option for improving coherence. Use them sparingly, and only when a relationship is not already made clear by the devices discussed earlier.

Besides the transitional expressions that increase coherence *within* a paragraph, whole sentences serve as transitions *between* paragraphs. Here is a transitional sentence that could end one paragraph, begin another, or stand alone for emphasis as a single-sentence paragraph:

> Because the AKS amplifier increases bass range by 15 percent, our company should install it as a standard item in all our stereo speakers.

This kind of transitional sentence both looks back and looks ahead, providing a clear direction for following the discussion.

Sometimes a whole paragraph can serve as a transition between sections of writing. Assume that you have a summer job as a marketing intern for a manufacturer of stereo components. You have just completed a section of a memo on the advantages of the new AKS amplifier and are now moving to a section on selling the idea to consumers. Here is a paragraph that might link the two sections:

> Because the AKS amplifier increases bass range by 15 percent, it should be installed as a standard item in all our stereo speakers. Tooling and installation adjustments, however, will add roughly $50 to the list price of each model. We must, therefore, explain the cartridge's long-range advantages to consumers. Let's consider ways of explaining these advantages.

Notice that this paragraph *contains* transitional expressions as well.

ALL DEVICES FOR ACHIEVING COHERENCE COMBINED

Devices for achieving coherence include logical order, parallelism, repetition and restatement, pronouns, and transitional expressions. Most paragraphs employ some combination of devices; not every paragraph employs them all. The next paragraph contains a variety of transitional devices. How many can you identify?

> [1]*In a society based on self-reliance and free will, the institutionalization of life scares me.* [2]Today, America has government-funded

programs to treat all society's ills. [3]We have day-care centers for the young, nursing homes for the old, psychologists in schools who use mental health as an instrument of discipline, and mental hospitals for those whose behavior does not conform to the norm. [4]We have drug-abuse programs, methadone-maintenance programs, alcohol programs, vocational programs, rehabilitation programs, learning-how-to-cope-with-death-for-the-terminally-ill programs, make-friends-with-your-neighborhood-policeman programs, helping-emotionally-dis-turbed-children programs, and how-to-accept-divorce programs. [5]Unemployment benefits and welfare are programs designed to insti-tutionalize a growing body of citizens whose purpose in life is the avoidance of work. [6]They are dependent on the state for their liveli-hood. [7]We can't even let people die in peace. [8]We put them in hospi-tals for the dying, so that they can be programmed into dying cor-rectly. [9]They don't need to be hospitalized; they would be better off with their families, dying with dignity instead of in these macabre halfway houses. [10]All this is a displacement of confidence from the individual to the program. [11]We can't rely on people to take care of themselves anymore so we have to funnel them into programs. [12]This is a self-perpetuating thing, for the more programs we make available, the more people will become accustomed to seeking help from the government. [emphasis added]

—Ted Morgan

Application 7–1

This essay is shown without proper paragraph divisions. Mark the spot where each new paragraph should begin. *Hint:* Here is a rough (six-paragraph) outline: (1) introduction, (2) description of the plant, (3) a typical night shift, (4) the writer's specific job, (5) overview, (6) concluding story. Material that belongs together—and not length—should dictate specific paragraph divisions. (Review pages 123–124.)

Swing Shift

Have you ever worked in a factory? Have you ever worked swing shift? Can you stand to function like a machine in 95-degree heat or more? Let alone stand it—can you work in it for eight hours of end-less repetition and mindless labor? I did, for more than eight years. The Acme Tire and Rubber Company, about 5 miles east of our cam-pus, resembles a prison. (Look for a massive and forbidding three-story building occupying two city blocks on Orchard Street.) The plant was built 50 years ago, and its windows, coated by the soot and grit of a half-century, admit no light, no hope of seeing in or out. Add to this dismal picture the drab red bricks and the stench of burned rubber. This is what I faced five nights a week at 10:00 P.M. when I reported for work. A worker's life inside the plant is arranged so as not to tax the mind. At exactly 10:00 P.M. a loud bell rings. Get to work. The bell has to be loud in order to be heard over the roar of machinery and hissing steam escaping from the high-pressure lines. In time you don't even notice the noise. It took me about two weeks. At midnight the bell rings again: a ten-minute break. At 2:00 A.M. it rings again: lunch, 20 minutes. Two hours later, it rings for the last break of the night. At 6:00 A.M. the final bell announces that the long night is over; it's time to go home. My dreary job was stocking tires. (I say "was" because I quit the job last year.) I had to load push trucks, the kind you see in railroad depots. I picked the tires up from the curing presses. A curing press is an 8-foot-high by 6-foot-wide by 6-foot-deep pressure cooker. There are 18 curing presses all in a row, and the temperature around them is over 100 degrees. Clouds of steam hang just below the 20-foot ceiling. By the time I had worked for ten minutes, my clothes were drenched with sweat and reeked with the acrid stench of steamed rubber. Once the truck was full, I'd push it to the shipping department on the other side of the plant. It's quiet there; they ship only during the day. And it's much cooler. I'd feel chilled even though the temperature was around 75 degrees. Here I would leave the full truck, look for an empty one, push it back, and start again. It was the same routine every night: endless truckloads of tires, five nights a week—every week. Nothing ever changed except the workers; they got older and worn out. I wasn't surprised to hear that a worker had hanged himself there a few weeks ago. He was a friend of mine. Another friend told me that the work went on anyway. The police said to leave the body hanging until the medical examiner could clear it—like so much meat hanging on a hook. Someone put a blanket around the hanging body. They had to move around it. The work went on.

—Glenn Silverberg

Application 7–2

The following topic statements are inadequate in some way. Some fail to focus on a limited subject; others express no definite viewpoint; others fail to say anything significant. Identify the deficiencies, and revise the statements to sharpen their meaning. (Review pages 125–127.)

Examples

| Inadequate | My town has a population of 10,000. [*no viewpoint*] |

Revised	Growing up in a small town has given me a sense of "belonging."
Inadequate	Boa constrictors are fascinating pets. [*subject not sufficiently limited*]
Revised	My boa Tyrone is a friend, a protector, and a companion.
Inadequate	Grades are a controversial subject. [*obvious, therefore not significant*]
Revised	Grades encourage excellence.

1. Women have changed radically over the years.

2. My best friend's name is Sally.

3. A part-time job really cuts down on a student's study time.

4. My college enrolls more men than women.

5. Cross-country skiing is a popular sport.

6. I have strong feelings about television.

7. College is a complex experience.

8. Some college requirements are silly.

Application 7–3

Your assignment is to assume a situation in which you would write a paragraph about some limited aspect of college life for a specific audience who will use your information for a definite purpose. Here are some possible situations.

1. The Student Senate has published a request in the school newspaper for nominations for the Teacher of the Year award. This request stipulates that all nominations be accompanied by a paragraph of 200 words or fewer, showing why that teacher should be nominated. After several weeks of delightful and informative classes with Professor X, you decide to nominate him or her. Write a paragraph.

2. You've decided to apply for a scholarship offered by your college. Among other application materials requested by the Scholarship Committee is a paragraph explaining your reasons for attending this college. Write the paragraph.
    Before composing your paragraph, read the material below carefully. The topic statements (in italics) limit the subject *college*

life so that the writer's viewpoint can be supported in one paragraph. The first paragraph is written to a friend who cares especially about personal identity, and thus about attending a college that will appreciate each student as an individual.

> *Because you're a person who hates the idea of being lost in the crowd, I know you would like Grunter College.* In a school such as this one, with limited enrollment and small classes, it's easy to make friends and to get to know your professors well. In no time you will find that all the faces look familiar and that everyone is on a first-name basis. Also, there will be lots of people asking you to join various organizations and activities. You can count on being welcomed here, on having a real sense of belonging, on making a difference. So why not give it a try? You won't be sorry.

The writer of the next paragraph had a different purpose. Helping to write a college brochure, she wanted to emphasize the varied activities and organizations at Grunter College. Because the focus of her topic statement is narrower than in the first paragraph, the details themselves are more specific.

> *Whether your interests are social, political, artistic, or athletic, you'll find many ways to keep busy at Grunter College.* In addition to our eight sororities and seven fraternities, we have a social club that sponsors dances, parties, concerts, and whatever else might be needed to liven up even the dreariest weekend. If you like politics, run for the Student Senate or join the Visitors' Council, which brings social and political celebrities to campus. If you're musically inclined, join the marching band, chamber orchestra, or rock group. Also, the various clubs for painters, writers, and dancers are always looking for new talent. To stay in shape, try out for varsity baseball, soccer, or track (all have both men's and women's teams), or join an intramural team. In short, if you seek involvement and challenge, Grunter College is for you.

Depending on the writer's purpose and the audience's needs, a topic statement about college life might be narrowed even further—say, for a paragraph describing a sorority or fraternity or the activities of the Visitors' Council.

Application 7–4

Identify the subject and the signal term in each of these sentences. (Review pages 129–130.)

Example

The pressures of the sexual revolution are everywhere.
—Joyce Maynard

Subject   pressures of the sexual revolution

Signal term   everywhere

1. High voltage from utility transmission lines can cause bizarre human and animal behavior.

2. Nuclear power plants need stricter supervision.

3. Producers of television commercials have created a loathsome gallery of men and women patterned, presumably, on Mr. and Mrs. America.
—Marya Mannes

4. From the very beginning of school, we make books and reading a constant source of possible failure and possible humiliation.
—John Holt

5. High interest rates cripple the auto and housing industries.

6. America's population centers inevitably are shifting to the Sunbelt states.

Application 7–5

This paragraph is an early draft of part of an open letter to the governor published in a college newspaper. Read it carefully, and answer the questions that follow.

[1]Conditions in the state mental hospital are shameful. [2]The big brick building is two miles from the main highway, and many people do not even know that there is such a place. [3]It is surrounded by spacious grounds. [4]Hundreds of patients are left in filthy conditions, never receiving the care they desperately need. [5]When my sociology class toured the hospital, we spent the entire morning walking through the wards and talking to the attendants. [6]Because the windows are kept tightly closed, the air is damp and musty. [7]Geraniums and African violets in small flowerpots are growing on the windowsills. [8]Patients lie for long hours staring vacantly at the dirty ceiling. [9]Some of them listen to the radio or watch television hour after hour. [10]The food is too cold and is always unappetizing. [11]Some people are ashamed when a relative must go to the hospital, but mental illness is no disgrace. [12]The hospital has only four physicians for more

than 500 patients. [13]A doctor in a mental institution should be a trained psychiatrist. [14]Straitjackets, ropes, and leather straps are used to tie down violent patients. [15]Sedatives, soothing baths, occupational therapy, and individual counseling rarely are used, because the hospital cannot afford them. [16]Patients who are recovering are allowed to work outdoors, and most of them seem to enjoy gardening. [17]But, on the whole, anyone who tours the mental hospital feels ashamed of this state.

1. What is the subject of the paragraph?

2. What is the signal term?

3. Which sentences do not relate to the main idea? (List the numbers.)

Application 7–6

Think about a place in your town or on campus that needs improvement. Describe the problem in one paragraph to a specified audience who will use your information as a basis for action.

Application 7–7

The paragraph below is unified but not coherent, because the sentences are not in logical order. Rearrange the sentences so that the line of thinking is clear. Be prepared to discuss reasons for your order.

[1]The Supreme Court's ruling against sex discrimination has touched all parts of American life—even the doll industry. [2]For example, Mattel, a large manufacturer of dolls, decided to change its ways—and make a little profit as well. [3]Now, little girl mommies might not have realized the significance of this arrival had it not been for the television announcement that "No family is complete without a tender Baby Brother." [4]Where would they find that little boy before Christmas? [5]In short, the doll was one small step for Mattel, but one giant leap for man. [6]Thus sexism died, and a new doll was born: Mattel's Baby Brother Tender Love, a soft, lovable doll complete with boy parts. [7]Not only did it give children a dose of sex education, but it also made men grin with satisfaction upon having invaded the doll industry. [8]As a consequence, parents quivered with anxiety that they would be unable to meet the demands of little mothers. [9]Yes, Baby Brother Tender Love was Mattel's gift to society that year.

Application 7–8

Select one of these assignments, and write a paragraph organized from the general to the specific.

1. Study the paragraph about America's obsession with speed, on page 133. Then compose your own paragraph about some other obsession you have witnessed among friends, students, coworkers, family, or others. Give plenty of examples.

2. Select a writing situation from this list, or make up one of your own.

    •   Picture the ideal summer job. Explain to an employer why you would like the job.

    •   Assume that it's time for end-of-semester student evaluations of courses. Write a one-paragraph evaluation of your favorite course to be read by the professor's department chairperson.

    •   Explain your views on video games. Write for your classmates.

    •   Describe the job outlook in your chosen field. Write for a high-school senior interested in your major.

Application 7–9

Identify someone who you think undervalues something, as in these possibilities:

•   a sibling who fails to appreciate your parents' sacrifices

•   a neighbor who is cutting down his trees for firewood

•   a roommate who doesn't appreciate the social or educational opportunities offered by your college

•   a friend who dislikes another friend

•   a friend who wants to drop out of school

•   someone close who needs more exercise

•   any other situation

Using Thoreau's paragraph (page 135) as a model, write a paragraph alerting your reader to the importance of X. Save your main point for last, with your support leading up to it. Be sure your opening sentence provides an orientation.

Application 7–10

Identify a problem in a group to which you belong (such as family, club, sorority). Or select a topic from the list, or make up one of your own. With the paragraphs on pages 135–136 as models, write your own emphatic paragraph.

- advice to an entering freshman about surviving in college
- your life goal, to your academic adviser, who is recommending you for a scholarship
- your reasons for wanting to live off campus, to the dean of students

Application 7–11

Using Angell's paragraph (page 137) as a model, describe to your classmates a memorable scene. Include details about *who, what, when, where,* and *why,* as well as any details that will help readers *see, feel, hear, taste,* or *smell.* Decide on the best angle of vision (such as outside to inside, near to far, right to left) to provide the clearest possible picture.

As an alternate assignment, choose a situation from this list, or make up one of your own.

- Show your classmates that a room in which you spend much of your time is pleasant or depressing.
- Show the local animal officer how to recognize your lost pet.
- Show a friend that the view from a favorite spot is worth the trip.

Your paragraph may or may not have a topic statement. But be sure your opening sentence (or sentences) provides a clear orientation.

Application 7–12

Using Orwell's paragraph (page 138) as a model, tell your classmates of a striking event in which you were involved. Use sharp details to make the scene vivid. Including your *impressions* will create a definite angle of vision. Instead of beginning with a topic statement, you might begin with an orienting statement that places readers immediately in the action. You might conclude with a topic statement or let the details of your story imply your main point. Be sure, though, that your story conveys a definite point.

As an alternate assignment, select a situation from this list, or make up one of your own. Write for your classmates.

1. Tell about the worst (or best) hour of your life.

2. Tell about how you said good-bye to someone close to you.

3. Tell about something frightening that happened in your childhood.

Application 7–13

In a logically ordered paragraph addressed to someone whose child watches television constantly, discuss one major effect television has had on you or someone you know. Use Morgan's paragraph (page 139) as a model.

Application 7–14

Supply the transitional expression that best connects each pair of sentences or clauses. (Review pages 142–144.)

An addition

1. Most elderly people wish to preserve their skills and possessions; _____ they wish to maintain their sense of freedom and prestige in the family, group, and community.

Time

2. Between ages 60 and 70, one feels the physical effects of aging; _____, retirement causes changes in an older person's social status, income, and self-concept.

A comparison

3. Minorities in America often are treated as people who must be tolerated but who ought to stay out of the way. The elderly, _____, often suffer discrimination and stereotyping and are thought to have little social worth.

A contrast or alternative

4. Old age should be a time of comfort and leisure for those who are still healthy; _____, society's indifference toward the elderly often breeds depression and dependency.

A result

5. Our society values what is young and beautiful but discards what is old and unattractive. It is, _____, no surprise that we find ways to ignore the fact that people age and die.

An example

6. Active community support can make a great difference in the quality of life for the elderly; _____, clubs, community centers, public housing, and other services can help ease the burden of aging.

An explanation

7. By segregating the aged through neglect, society itself suffers great losses; _____, the loss of purchasing power, taxes, and talent can often outweigh the cost of providing services to the aged.

Application 7–15

Reread Morgan's paragraph (page 139), and identify the features that help make it coherent.

1. Identify the topic statement.

2. What is the ordering pattern?

3. Identify all examples of parallel structure.

4. Identify the key words that are repeated, and explain how this repetition helps clarify the author's meaning.

5. Identify the synonyms in the paragraph.

6. Do the pronouns all refer to the same noun?

7. Identify any transitional expressions, and briefly explain the relationship signaled by each. Should there be any transitions in this paragraph?

Application 7–16

Select the best paragraph or essay you have written thus far (or one that your instructor suggests). Using the strategies in this chapter, revise the paragraph or essay for improved coherence. After revising, list the specific strategies you employed (logical order, parallelism, repetition of key terms, restatement, pronouns, transitions).

8

Writing Effective Sentences

Every bit as important as *what* you have to say is *how* you say it. No matter how vital your content and how sensible your organization, your message will mean little unless it is easy to understand—in a word, *readable.* Any paragraph can be only as readable as the sentences that form it. And a readable sentence is one that can be understood in a *single* reading.

One requirement for readable sentences, of course, is that they have correct grammar, punctuation, and mechanics. Basic errors, such as fragments and comma splices (all covered in Appendix A), distract readers. But "correctness" alone is no guarantee that a sentence will be readable. Readers also can be distracted by sentences that are hard to interpret, that take too long to make the point, or that seem choppy. Besides being grammatical, effective sentences emphasize relationships, waste no words, and make for smooth reading. In short, effective sentences are *clear, concise,* and *fluent.*

Before working with this section, you may wish to review some basic grammatical terms (clauses, phrases, and the like) in Appendix A.

Making Sentences Clear

A clear sentence conveys the writer's meaning on the first reading. It signals relationships among its parts, and it emphasizes the main idea. These guidelines will help you write clear sentences.

155

AVOID FAULTY MODIFIERS

Modifiers explain, define, or add detail to other words or ideas. Prepositional phrases usually define or limit adjacent words:

> the foundation **with the cracked wall**
>
> the repair job **on the old Ford**
>
> the journey **to the moon**

Phrases with "-ing" verb forms limit:

> the student **painting the portrait**
>
> **Opening the door,** we entered quietly.

Phrases with "to + verb" form limit:

> **To succeed,** one must work hard.

Some clauses limit:

> the man **who came to dinner**
>
> the job **that I recently accepted**

If a modifier is too far from the words it modifies, the message can be ambiguous.

Misplaced modifier   At our campsite, **devouring the bacon,** I saw a huge bear.

Was it *I* who was devouring the bacon? Of course not. But placing the modifier *devouring the bacon* next to *I* conveys that message. Moving the modifier next to *bear* clarifies the sentence:

Revised   At our campsite, I saw a huge bear **devouring the bacon.**

The order of adjectives and adverbs in a sentence is as important as the order of modifying phrases and clauses. Notice how changing word order affects the meaning of these sentences:

> **I often** remind myself to balance my checkbook.
>
> I remind myself to balance my checkbook **often.**

Be sure that modifiers and the words they modify follow an order that reflects your meaning.

Misplaced modifier	She read a report on using nonchemical pesticides **in our conference room.** [*Are the pesticides to be used in the conference room?*]
Revised	In our conference room, she read a report on using nonchemical pesticides.
Misplaced modifier	*Only* press the red button in an emergency. (Does **only** modify **press** or **emergency?**)
Revised	Press **only** the red button in an emergency. *or* Press the red button in an emergency **only.**
Misplaced modifier	Nonsmokers are harmed by tobacco smoke **as well as smokers.** [*Do smokers harm nonsmokers?*]
Revised	Nonsmokers **as well as smokers** are harmed by tobacco smoke.

Another problem with word order occurs when a modifying phrase begins a sentence and has no word to modify.

Dangling modifier	**Answering the telephone,** the cat ran out the door.

The cat obviously did not answer the telephone. But because the modifier **Answering the telephone** has no word to modify, the word order suggests that the noun beginning the main clause (**cat**) names the one who answered the phone. Without any word to join itself to, the modifier *dangles.* By inserting a subject, we can repair this absurd message.

Revised	**As Mary answered the telephone,** the cat ran out the door.

A dangling modifier also can obscure your meaning.

Dangling modifier	**After completing the student financial aid application form,** the Financial Aid Office will forward it to the appropriate state agency.

Who completes the form—the student or the financial aid office?

Here are some other dangling modifiers that make the message confusing, inaccurate, or downright absurd:

Dangling modifier	**While walking,** a cold chill ran through my body.
Revised	While **I** walked, a cold chill ran through my body.
Dangling modifier	**By planting different varieties of crops,** the pests were unable to adapt.
Revised	By planting different varieties of crops, **farmers** prevented the pests from adapting.
Dangling modifier	**An an expert in this field,** I'm sure your advice will help.
Revised	**Because you are an expert in this field,** I'm sure your advice will help.

KEEP YOUR PRONOUN REFERENCES CLEAR

A pronoun takes the place of a noun. Any pronoun (**she, it, his, their,** and so on) must refer to one clearly identified noun. If the pronoun's referent (or antecedent) is vague, readers will be confused.

| Vague referent | Our patients are enjoying the warm days while **they** last. [*Are the patients or the warm days on the way out?*] |

Depending on whether the referent for **they** is **days** or **patients,** the sentence can be clarified:

| Clear referent | While these warm days last, our patients are enjoying them.
or
Our terminal patients are enjoying the warm days. |

Be sure readers can identify the noun your pronoun replaces.

| Ambiguous | **Sally** told **Sarah** that **she was obsessed** with her job. |

Does **she** refer to **Sally** or **Sarah?** Many interpretations are possible.

| Revised | Sally told Sarah, "I'm obsessed with my job."

Sally told Sarah, "I'm obsessed with your job."

Sally told Sarah, "You're obsessed with [your, my] job."

Sally told Sarah, "She's obsessed with [her, my, your] job." |

Avoid using **this, that,** or **it**—especially to begin a sentence—unless the pronoun refers to a specific antecedent (referent).

Vague	As he drove away from his menial **job,** boring **lifestyle,** and damp **apartment,** he was happy to be leaving it behind.
Revised	As he drove away, he was happy to be leaving his menial job, boring life-style, and damp apartment behind.
Vague	The problem with our **defective machinery** is only compounded by the new **operator's incompetence.** This annoys me!
Revised	I am annoyed by the problem with our defective machinery as well as by the new operator's incompetence.
Inaccurate	Increased blood pressure is caused by narrowing of the blood vessels, making the pressure higher as it flows through the blood vessels.

Here, **it** seems to refer to **pressure,** which is absurd.

Revised	Increased blood pressure is caused by narrowing of the blood vessels, which makes the pressure higher as the blood flows through the vessels.

AVOID OVERSTUFFING

A sentence that crams in too many ideas forces the reader to struggle over its meaning.

Overstuffed	A smoke-filled room causes not only teary eyes and runny noses but also can alter people's hearing and vision, as well as creating dangerous levels of carbon monoxide, especially for people with heart and lung ailments, whose health is particularly threatened by "second-hand" smoke.

Clear things up by sorting out the relationships:

Revised	Besides causing teary eyes and runny noses, a smoke-filled room can alter people's hearing and vision. One of "second-hand" smoke's biggest dangers, however, is high levels of carbon monoxide, a particular health threat for people with heart and lung ailments.

KEEP EQUAL ITEMS PARALLEL

To reflect relationships among items of equal importance, express them in identical grammatical form (see also page 140).

Correct   We here highly resolve . . . that government **of the people, by the people, for the people** shall not perish from the earth.

This statement describes the government with three modifiers of equal importance. Because the first modifier is a prepositional phrase, the others must be also. Otherwise, the message would be garbled, like this:

Faulty   We here highly resolve . . . that government **of the people, which the people created and maintain, serving the people** shall not perish from the earth.

If you begin the series with a noun, use nouns throughout the series; likewise for adjectives, adverbs, and specific types of clauses and phrases.

Faulty   The new tutor is **enthusiastic, skilled,** and **you can depend on her.**

Revised   The new tutor is **enthusiastic, skilled,** and **dependable.** [*all subjective complements*]

Faulty   In his new job he felt **lonely** and **without a friend.**

Revised   In his new job he felt **lonely** and **friendless.** [*both adjectives*]

Faulty   She plans **to study** all this month and **on scoring well** in her licensing examination.

Revised   She plans **to study** all this month and **to score** well in her licensing examination. [*both infinitive phrases*]

Faulty   She **sleeps well** and jogs daily, **as well as eating** high-protein foods.

Revised   She **sleeps** well, **jogs** daily, and **eats** high-protein foods. [*all verbs*]

To improve coherence in long sentences, repeat words that introduce parallel expressions:

Faulty   Before buying this property, you should decide whether you plan to settle down and raise a family, travel for a few years, or pursue a graduate degree.

Revised

Before buying this property, you should decide whether you plan **to settle** down and raise a family, **to travel** for a few years, or **to pursue** a graduate degree.

ARRANGE WORDS FOR COHERENCE AND EMPHASIS

In coherent writing, everything sticks together; each sentence builds on the preceding sentence and looks ahead to the following sentence. Sentences generally work best when the beginning looks back at familiar information and the end provides the new (or unfamiliar) information.

Familiar		Unfamiliar
My dog	has	fleas.
Our boss	just won	the lottery.
This company	is planning	a merger.

Besides helping a message stick together, the familiar-to-unfamiliar structure emphasizes the new information. Just as every paragraph has a key sentence, every sentence has a key word or phrase that sums up the new information. That key word or phrase usually is emphasized best at the end of the sentence.

Faulty emphasis

We expect a **refund** because of your error in our shipment.

Correct

Because of your error in our shipment, we expect a **refund.**

Faulty emphasis

After your awful behavior, an **apology** is something I expect. But I'll probably get an excuse.

Correct

After your awful behavior, I expect an **apology.** But I'll probably get an excuse.

One exception to placing key words last occurs with *instructions.* Each step in a list of instructions should contain an action verb (**insert, open, close, turn, remove, press**). To provide readers with a forecast, place the verb in that instruction at the beginning.

Correct

Insert the diskette before activating the system.

Remove the protective seal.

With the key word at the beginning of the instruction, readers know immediately the action they need to take.

USE PROPER COORDINATION

Give equal emphasis to ideas of equal importance by joining them, within simple or compound sentences, with coordinating conjunctions: **and, but, or, nor, for, so,** and **yet.**

Correct	This course is difficult, **but** it is worthwhile.
	My horse is old **and** gray.
	We must decide to support **or** reject the dean's plan.

But do not confound your meaning by coordinating excessively.

Excessive coordination	The climax in jogging comes after a few miles **and** I can no longer feel stride after stride **and** it seems as if I am floating **and** jogging becomes almost a reflex **and** my arms **and** legs continue to move **and** my mind no longer has to control their actions.
Revised	The climax in jogging comes after a few miles, when I can no longer feel stride after stride. By then I am jogging almost by reflex, nearly floating, my arms and legs still moving, my mind no longer having to control their actions.

Notice how the meaning becomes clear when the less important ideas (**nearly floating, arms and legs still moving, my mind no longer having**) are shown as dependent on, rather than equal to, the most important idea (**jogging almost by reflex**)—the idea that contains the lesser ones.

Avoid coordinating ideas that cannot be sensibly connected:

Faulty	I was late for work and wrecked my car.
Revised	Late for work, I backed out of the driveway too quickly, hit a truck, and wrecked my car.

In the faulty sentences above, the **and** is made to do too much work.

Instead of **try and,** use **try to.**

Faulty	I will try and help you.
Revised	I will try to help you.

USE PROPER SUBORDINATION

Proper subordination shows that a less important idea is dependent on a more important idea. By using subordination, you can combine related simple sentences into complex sentences and emphasize the most important idea. Consider these complete ideas:

Joe studies diligently. He has a learning disability.

Because these ideas are expressed as simple sentences, they appear coordinate (equal in importance). But if you wanted to indicate your opinion of Joe's chances of succeeding, you would need a third sentence: **His handicap probably will prevent him from succeeding** or **His willpower will help him succeed** or some such. To communicate the intended meaning concisely, combine the two ideas and subordinate the one that deserves less emphasis:

Despite his learning disability [*subordinate idea*], Joe studies diligently [*independent idea*].

This first version suggests that Joe will succeed. Below, subordination is used to suggest the opposite meaning:

Despite his diligent study [*subordinate idea*], Joe is unlikely to overcome his learning disability.

A dependent (or subordinate) clause in a sentence is signaled by a subordinating conjunction: **because, so that, if, unless, after, until, since, while, as,** and **although.** Be sure to place the idea you want emphasized in the independent (main) clause; do not write

Although Alfred is receiving excellent medical treatment, he is seriously ill.

if you mean to suggest that Alfred has a good chance of recovering.
    Do not coordinate when you should subordinate:

Faulty   Television viewers can relate to a person they idolize, and they feel obliged to buy the product endorsed by their hero.

Of the two ideas in this sentence, one is the cause, the other the effect. Emphasize this relationship through subordination.

Revised   Because television viewers can relate to a person
                           they idolize, they feel obliged to buy the product
                           endorsed by their hero.

When combining several ideas within a sentence, decide which is the
most important, and make the other ideas subordinate to it.

Faulty   This employee is often late for work, and he writes
                           illogical reports, and he is a poor manager, and he
                           should be fired.

Revised   Because this employee is often late for work,
                           writes illogical reports, and is a poor manager, **he
                           should be fired.** [*The last clause is independent.*]

Do not overstuff sentences by subordinating excessively:

Faulty   This job, which I took when I graduated from
                           college, while I waited for a better one to come
                           along, which is boring, in which I've gained no
                           useful experience, makes me eager to quit.

Revised   Upon college graduation, I took this job while
                           waiting for a better one to come along. Because I
                           find it boring and have gained no useful experience,
                           I am eager to quit.

USE ACTIVE VOICE OFTEN, PASSIVE VOICE SELECTIVELY

The active voice (**I did it**) is more direct, concise, and forceful than the
passive voice (**It was done by me**). In the active voice, the agent performing the action serves as subject:

	Agent	**Action**	**Recipient**
Active	Joe	lost	your report.
	Subject	**Verb**	**Object**

The passive voice reverses the pattern, making the recipient of an action
serve as subject:

	Recipient	**Action**	**Agent**
Passive	Your report	was lost	by Joe.
	Subject	**Verb**	**Prepositional phrase**

Sometimes the passive eliminates the agent altogether:

Passive   Your report was lost. [*Who lost it?*]

Some writers mistakenly rely on the passive voice because they think it sounds more objective and important. But the passive voice often makes writing seem merely wordy or evasive. Consider the effect when an active statement is recast in the passive voice:

Concise and direct   I underestimated expenses for this semester.
(active)   [*7 words*]

Wordy and indirect   Expenses for this semester were underestimated by
(passive)   me. [*9 words*]

Evasive (passive)   Expenses for this semester were underestimated.

For economy, directness, and clarity, use the active voice in most of your writing.

Do not evade responsibility by hiding behind the passive voice:

Passive   **A mistake was made** in your shipment. [*By
"irresponsibles"*   whom?*]

                            It was decided not to hire you. [*Who decided?*]

                            A layoff is recommended. [*By whom?*]

Acknowledge responsibility for your actions:

Active   **I made** a mistake in your shipment.

                            I decided not to hire you.

                            Our committee recommends a layoff.

In reporting errors or bad news, use the active voice. Readers appreciate clarity and sincerity.

But do use the passive voice if the person behind the action has reason for being protected:

Correct passive   The criminal was identified.

                            The embezzlement scheme was exposed.

Here, the passive protects the innocent person who identified the criminal or who exposed the scheme.

Use the passive only when your audience does not need to know the agent:

Correct passive	Mr. Jones was brought to the emergency room.
	The bank failure was publicized statewide.

Readers do not need to know *who* brought Mr. Jones or *who* publicized the bank failure. Notice again how the passive voice focuses on the *recipient* rather than the *agent.*

Use the passive voice to focus on events or results when the agent is unknown, unapparent, or unimportant:

Correct passive	The victim was asked to testify.
	Mary's article was published last week.

The information that will interest readers here is *that* the victim was asked to testify or *that* Fred's article was published.

Prefer the passive when you deliberately wish to be indirect or inoffensive (as in requesting the customer's payment or the employee's cooperation, or to avoid blaming anyone):

Active but offensive	**You** have not paid your bill.
	You need to overhaul our filing system.
Inoffensive passive	**This bill** has not been paid.
	Our filing system needs overhauling.

By focusing on the recipient rather than the agent, these passive versions help retain the audience's goodwill.

The passive voice is weaker than the active voice and creates an impersonal tone:

Weak and impersonal	An invitation will be sent next week.
Strong and personal	We will send you an invitation next week.

Use the active voice when you want action. Otherwise, your statement will have no power:

Weak passive	If my claim is not settled by May 15, the Better Business Bureau will be contacted, and their advice on legal action will be taken.

This passive and tentative statement is unlikely to move readers to action: *Who* is making the claim? *Who* should settle the claim? *Who* will contact the Bureau? *Who* will take action? Nobody is here! Following is a more direct, concise, and forceful version, in the active voice:

Strong active	If you do not settle my claim by May 15, I will contact the Better Business Bureau for advice on legal action.

Notice how this active version emphasizes the new and significant information by placing it at the end.

Ordinarily, use the active voice for giving instructions.

Faulty passive	The door to the cobra's cage should be closed.
	Care should be taken with the dynamite.
Correct active	**Close** the door to the cobra's cage.
	Be careful with the dynamite.

Avoid shifts from active to passive voice in the same sentence:

Faulty shift	During the meeting, project members spoke and presentations were given.
Correct	During the meeting, project members spoke and gave presentations.

By using the active voice, you direct the reader's attention to the subject of your sentence. Unless you have a deliberate reason for choosing the passive voice, prefer the *active* voice in most of your writing.

Application 8–1

These sentences are unclear because of faulty modification, unclear pronoun reference, or overstuffing. Revise them so that their meaning is clear. For sentences suggesting two meanings, write separate versions—one for each meaning intended. (Review pages 156–159.)

1. Bill told Fred that he was wrong.

2. I bought a house from a real estate agent full of termites.

3. Only use this phone in a red alert.

4. Making the shelves look neater was another of my tasks at X-Mart that is very important to a store's business because if the merchandise is not always neatly arranged, customers will not have a good impression, whereas if it is neat they probably will return.

5. Wearing high boots, the snake could not hurt me.

6. Having more than an hour left to travel, the weather kept getting worse.

7. When my ninth-grade teacher caught daydreamers, she would jab them in the shoulder with gritted teeth and a fierce eye.

8. While they eat dead fish, our students enjoy watching the alligators.

9. After being late for work twice in one week, my boss is annoyed with me.

Application 8–2

These sentences are unclear because of faulty parallelism or key words buried in midsentence. Revise them so that their meaning is clear. (Review pages 160–162.)

1. Education enables us to recognize excellence and to achieve it.

2. Student nurses are required to identify diseases and how to treat them.

3. My car needs an oil change, a grease job, and the carburetor should be adjusted.

4. In a business relationship, trust makes it work.

5. I have a critical need for financial aid.

6. In all writing, revision is required.

Application 8–3

Use coordination or subordination as appropriate to clarify relationships in these sentences. (Review pages 162–164.)

1. Martha loves John. She also loves Bruno.

2. You will succeed. Work hard.

3. I worked hard in calculus and flunked the course.

4. Now I have no privacy. My cousin moved into my room.

5. I will try and get a refund on my defective watch.

6. The instructor entered the classroom. Some students were asleep.

Application 8–4

These sentences are wordy, weak, or evasive because of passive voice. Revise each sentence as a concise, forceful, and direct expression in the active voice, in order to identify the person or agent performing the action. (Review pages 164–167.)

1. The evaluation was performed by us.

2. The essay was written by me.

3. Unless you pay me within three days, my lawyer will be contacted.

4. Hard hats should be worn at all times.

5. It was decided to decline your invitation.

6. Gasoline was spilled on your Ferrari's leather seats.

7. The manager was kissed.

Application 8–5

These sentences lack proper emphasis because of active voice. Revise each ineffective active as an appropriate passive, emphasizing the recipient rather than the agent. (Review pages 164–167.)

1. Joe's company fired him.

2. A rockslide buried the mine entrance.

3. Someone on the maintenance crew has just discovered a crack in the nuclear-core containment unit.

4. A power surge destroyed more than 2000 lines of our new computer program.

5. Your essay confused me.

6. You are paying inadequate attention to students' safety.

7. You are checking temperatures too infrequently.

Making Sentences Concise

Writing can suffer from two kinds of wordiness: one kind occurs when readers are given information they don't need. (See Chapter 6, or watch a typical weather report on local television news.) The other kind of wordiness occurs when too many words are used conveying information readers *do* need (as in saying **a great deal of potential for the future** instead of **great potential**). A concise sentence conveys most information in fewest words. It gets right to the point without clutter; however, conciseness does not mean omitting specific details necessary for clarity. A brief but vague message is useless.

| Brief but vague | Clarence's grades for last semester were poor. |
| Brief but informative | Last semester Clarence received one **C**, two **D's**, and two **F's**. |

Be sure your information is adequate, but use fewer words whenever fewer will do.

| Cluttered | At this point in time I must say that I need a vacation. |
| Concise | I need a vacation **now**. |

First drafts rarely are concise. Always revise parts that are wordy, repetitious, or vague. Trim the fat by getting rid of anything that adds no meaning.

AVOID NEEDLESS PHRASES

Don't use a whole phrase when one word will do. Instead of **in this day and age,** write **today.** Each needless phrase here can be reduced to one word—without loss in meaning.

at this point in time	= now
has the ability to	= can
aware of the fact that	= know
due to the fact that	= because
dislike very much	= hate
athletic person	= athlete
the majority of	= most

being in good health	= healthy
on a daily basis	= daily
in close proximity to	= near

ELIMINATE REDUNDANCY

A redundant expression says the same thing twice, in different words, as in **fellow classmates.** Each bracketed word or phrase below merely adds clutter, because its meaning is included in the other word.

a [dead] corpse	enter [into]
the reason [why]	[totally] monopolize
the [final] conclusion	[totally] oblivious
[utmost] perfection	[very] vital
[mental] awareness	[past] experience
[the month of] August	correct [amount of] change
[mutual] cooperation	[future] prospects
mix [together]	[valuable] asset
[viable] alternative	[free] gift

AVOID NEEDLESS REPETITION

Unnecessary repetition clutters writing and dilutes meaning.

Repetitious
> In trauma victims, breathing is restored by **artificial respiration.** Techniques of **artificial respiration** include mouth-to-mouth **respiration** and mouth-to-nose **respiration.**

Repetition in that passage disappears when sentences are combined.

Concise
> In trauma victims, breathing is restored by artificial respiration, either mouth-to-mouth or mouth-to-nose.

Repetition, of course, can be useful. Don't hesitate to repeat, or at least rephrase, material (even whole paragraphs in a longer piece) if you feel that readers need reminders.

AVOID *THERE* SENTENCE OPENERS

Save words, add force, and improve your emphasis by not using **there is** and **there are** to begin sentences—whenever your intended meaning allows.

Faulty	There are several good reasons why Boris dropped out of school.*
Concise	Boris dropped out of school for several good reasons.
Faulty	There is a serious fire danger created by your smoking in bed.
Concise	Your smoking in bed creates danger of fire.

Dropping these openers places the key words at the end of the sentence, where they are best emphasized.

AVOID SOME *IT* SENTENCE OPENERS

Try not to begin a sentence with **It**—unless the **It** clearly refers to a specific referent in the preceding sentence.

Wordy	[It was] his negative attitude [that] caused him to fail.
Wordy	It gives me great pleasure to introduce our speaker.
Concise	I am pleased to introduce our speaker.

AVOID WEAK VERBS

Prefer verbs that express a definite action: **open, close, move, continue, begin.** These strong verbs advance your meaning. Avoid verbs that express no specific action: **is, was, are, has, give, make, come, take.** These weak verbs add words without advancing your meaning. All forms of the verb **to be** are weak. This sentence achieves conciseness because of the strong verb **consider:**

Concise	Please **consider** my application.

---

* Of course, in some contexts, proper emphasis would call for a **There** opener.

Correct   People often have wondered about the rationale behind Boris's sudden decision. Actually, there are several good reasons for his dropping out of school.

Most often, however, **There** openers are best dropped.

Here is what happens with a weak verb in the same sentence:

Weak and wordy   Please **take into consideration** my application.

Don't disappear behind weak verbs and their baggage of needless nouns and prepositions.

Weak   My recommendation **is** for a larger budget.

Strong   I **recommend** a larger budget.

Strong verbs, or action verbs, suggest an assertive, positive, and confident writer. Here are some weak verbs converted to strong:

give a summary of	= summarize
make an assumption	= assume
come to the conclusion	= conclude
take action	= act
make a decision	= decide
come to the realization	= realize

DELETE NEEDLESS *TO BE* CONSTRUCTIONS

The preceding section showed that all forms of the verb **to be (is, was, are,** and so on) are weak. Sometimes the **to be** form itself mistakenly appears behind such verbs as **appears, seems,** and **find.**

Wordy   She seems [to be] upset.

Wordy   I find some of my classmates [to be] brilliant.

Eliminating **to be** in these examples saves words while preserving meaning.

AVOID EXCESSIVE PREPOSITIONS

Needless prepositions (especially **of**) interfere with a writer's meaning.

Wordy   Some of the members of the committee made
                        these recommendations.

Concise   Some committee members made these
                        recommendations.

| Wordy | I gave the money to Sarah. |
| Concise | I gave Sarah the money. |

USE *THAT* AND *WHICH* SPARINGLY

Excessive use of **is** often drags along a needless **that** or **which.**

Wordy	The Batmobile is a car [that is] worth buying.
Wordy	This [is a] math problem [that] is impossible to solve.
Wordy	The book[, which is] about Hemingway[,] is fascinating.

FIGHT NOUN ADDICTION

Nouns manufactured from verbs (nominalizations) make sentences weak and wordy. Nominalizations often accompany weak verbs and needless propositions.

Weak and wordy	We ask for the **cooperation** of all students.
Strong and concise	We ask that all students **cooperate.**
Weak and wordy	Give **consideration** to the possibility of a career change.
Strong and concise	**Consider** a career change.

Besides causing wordiness, nominalizations can be vague—by hiding the agent of an action.

| Wordy and vague | A **need for immediate action exists.** [*Who should take the action? We can't tell.*] |
| Precise | **We must act** immediately. |

Here are nominalizations restored to their verb forms:

conduct an investigation of	= investigate
provide a description of	= describe
conduct a test of	= test
engage in the preparation of	= prepare
make a discovery of	= discover

Along with weak verbs and needless prepositions, nominalizations drain the life from your style. In cheering for your favorite team, you wouldn't say

> Blocking of that kick is a necessity!
> *instead of*
> Block that kick!

Write as you would speak—but avoid slang or overuse of colloquialisms (page 49).

MAKE NEGATIVES POSITIVE

A positive expression is more easily understood than a negative one. As writing expert Joseph Williams points out, "To understand the negative, we have to translate it into an affirmative, because the negative only implies what we should do by telling us what we shouldn't do. The affirmative states it directly."

Indirect and wordy	I did not gain anything from this course.
Direct and concise	I gained nothing from this course.

Readers have to work even harder to translate sentences with two or more negative expressions:

Confusing and wordy	Do **not** distribute this memo to employees who have **not** received security clearance.
Clear and concise	Distribute this memo only to employees who have received security clearance.

Besides the directly negative words (**no, not, never**), some words are indirectly negative (**except, forget, mistake, lose, uncooperative**). When these indirectly negative words combine with directly negative words, readers are forced to translate.

Confusing and wordy	**Do not neglect** to activate the alarm system.
	My conclusion was **not inaccurate.**

The second example above shows how multiple negatives can make the writer seem evasive.

Clear and concise	**Be sure** to activate the alarm system.
	My conclusion was **accurate.**

Some negative expressions, of course, are perfectly correct, as in expressing disagreement.

Correct negatives	This is **not** the best plan.
	Your offer is **unacceptable.**
	This project **never** will succeed.

Prefer positives to negatives, however, whenever your meaning allows. Here are negative expressions translated into positive versions:

did not succeed	= failed
does not have	= lacks
did not prevent	= allowed
not unless	= only if
not until	= only when
not absent	= present

CLEAR OUT CLUTTER WORDS

Clutter words stretch a message without adding meaning. Here are some of the commonest: **very, definitely, quite, extremely, rather, somewhat, really, actually, situation, aspect, factor.**

Cluttered	**Actually,** one **aspect** of a marriage **situation** that could **definitely** make me **very** happy would be to have a **somewhat** adventurous partner who **really** shared my **extreme** love of traveling.
Concise	I'd like to marry an adventurous person who loves traveling.

Use such words only when they **actually** advance your meaning.

DELETE NEEDLESS PREFACES

Don't keep readers waiting for the new information in your sentence. Get right to the point.

Wordy	[I am writing this letter because] I wish to apply for the position of dorm counselor.
Wordy	[The conclusion we can draw is that] writing is hard work.

DELETE NEEDLESS QUALIFIERS

Qualifiers such as **I feel, it would seem, I believe, in my opinion,** and **I think** soften the tone and impact of a statement. Use qualifiers to express uncertainty.

Appropriate qualifiers   Despite Frank's poor academic performance last semester, he will, **I think,** do well in college.

Your product **seems to be** what I need.

But when you are certain, eliminate the qualifier so as not to seem tentative or evasive.

Needless qualifiers   [It seems that] I've wrecked the family car.

[It would appear that] I've lost your credit card.

[In my opinion,] you've done a good job.

Application 8–6

Make these sentences more concise by eliminating redundancies and needless repetition. (Review pages 170–171.)

1.   She is a woman who works hard.

2.   This book is the best book I've read in months.

3.   I am aware of the fact that Sam is a trustworthy person.

4.   The college is imposing a curfew due to the fact that several students have been mugged.

5.   On previous occasions we have worked together.

6.   Albert's outlook on life is optimistic.

7.   Clarence completed his assignment in a short period of time.

8.   Bruno has a stocky build.

9.   Sally is a close friend of mine.

10.   I've been able to rely on my parents in the past.

Application 8–7

Make these sentences more concise by eliminating **There is** and **There are** sentence openers, and the needless use of **it, to be, is, of, that,** and **which.** (Review pages 172–174.)

1. I consider Martha to be a good friend.

2. Our summer house, which is located on Cape Cod, is for sale.

3. The static electricity that is generated by the human body is measurable.

4. Writing must be practiced in order for it to become effective.

5. Another reason the job is attractive is because the salary is excellent.

6. There are many activities and sports that I enjoy very much, but the one that stands out in my mind is the sport of jogging.

7. Friendship is something that people should be honest about.

8. Smoking of cigarettes is considered by many people to be the worst habit of all habits of human beings.

9. There are many students who are immature.

10. It is necessary for me to leave immediately.

Application 8–8

Revise each wordy and vague sentence to eliminate weak verbs. (Review pages 172–173.)

1. I have a preference for Ferraris.

2. Please make a decision today.

3. We need to have a discussion about the problem.

4. I have just come to the realization that I was mistaken.

5. We certainly can make use of this information.

6. Your conclusion is in agreement with mine.

Application 8–9

Make these sentences more concise by replacing nouns with verbs, by changing negatives to positives, and by clearing out clutter words, needless prefatory expressions, and needless qualifiers. (Review pages 174–176.)

1. We request the formation of a committee of students for the review of grading discrepancies.

2. I am not unappreciative of your help.

3. Actually, I am very definitely in love with you.

4. I find Susan to be an industrious and competent employee.

5. Bill made the suggestion that we get an additional roommate.

6. It seems that I've made a mistake in your order.

7. My mother's quick wit is an extremely impressive aspect of her personality.

8. Igor does not have any friends at this school.

9. In my opinion, winter is an awful season.

10. As this academic year comes upon us, I realize that I will have trouble commuting to school this semester.

11. There is an undergraduate student attrition causes study needed at our school.

12. A need for your caution exists.

13. Never fail to attend classes.

14. Our acceptance of the offer is a necessity.

Making Sentences Fluent

Fluent sentences are easy to read because of clear connections, variety, and emphasis. Their varied length and word order eliminate choppiness and monotony. Fluent sentences enhance *clarity*, allowing readers to see ideas that are most important, with no struggle to sort out relationships. Fluent sentences enhance *conciseness*, often replacing several short, repetitious sentences with one longer, more economical sentence. The strategies discussed here will help you write fluent sentences.

COMBINE RELATED IDEAS

A series of short, disconnected sentences is not only choppy and wordy, but unclear as well.

Disconnected	Jogging can be healthful. You need the right equipment. Most necessary are well-fitting shoes. Without this equipment you take the chance of injuring your legs. Your knees are especially prone to injury. [5 *sentences*]

Clear, concise, and
fluent

Jogging can be healthful if you have the right equipment. Shoes that fit well are most necessary because they prevent injury to your legs, especially your knees. [2 *sentences*]

Never force readers to figure out connections for themselves.

Most sets of information can be combined in different relationships depending on what you want to emphasize. Imagine that this set of facts describes an applicant for a ski instructor's position:

- Sarah James has been skiing since age 3.

- She has no experience teaching skiing.

- She has won several slalom competitions.

Assume that you are Snow Mountain Ski Area's head instructor, writing to the manager to convey your impression of this candidate. To convey a negative impression, you might combine the facts in this way:

Strongly negative
emphasis

Although Sarah James has been skiing since age 3 and has won several slalom competitions, **she has no experience teaching skiing.**

The *independent* idea (in boldface) receives the emphasis. Earlier ideas are made dependent on (or subordinate to) the independent idea by the subordinating word **although.** When a sentence has two or more ideas of unequal importance, the less important idea is signaled by a subordinating word such as **often, as, because, if, unless, until,** or **while.**

Let's continue with our Sarah James example. If you are undecided but leaning in a negative direction, you might combine the information in this way:

Slightly negative
emphasis

Sarah James has been skiing since age 3 and has won several slalom competitions, **but** she has no experience teaching skiing.

In the sentence above, the ideas before and after **but** are both independent. These independent ideas are joined by the coordinating word **but,** which suggests that both sides of the issue are equally important (or "coordinate"). Placing the negative idea last, however, gives it slight emphasis. When a sentence has two or more ideas equal in importance, their equality is signaled by coordinating words such as **and, but, for, nor, or, so,** or **yet.**

Consider once again our Sarah James example. To emphasize strong support for the candidate, you could use this combination:

Positive emphasis   Although Sarah James has no experience teaching
                           skiing, **she has been skiing since age 3 and has won
                           several slalom competitions.**

In the version above, the earlier idea is subordinated by **although,** leaving the two final ideas independent.

Readers interpret our meaning not only by what we say, but by how we put our sentences together. The following sentences, excerpted from a student pilot's description of "Taking Off," further illustrate that fluent sentences are both more readable and meaningful.

First draft   My mind's eye is locked on the runway's center
                           line. My eyes flash from the windshield to the
                           instruments. They read and calculate, and they
                           miss nothing.

Because these actions took place at the same time, the writer decided to emphasize that relationship by combining her information in one sentence:

More fluent   My mind's eye is locked on the runway's center
                           line, while my eyes flash from the windshield to
                           instruments, reading, calculating, missing nothing.

The revised version captures the mood that the writer set out to convey: one of immediacy, of excitement, of all things happening at once.

Here, from the same writer, is another illustration of how sentence structure can be revised to emphasize a particular meaning.

First draft   Gravity pulls at us. It insists that we are bound to
                           the earth. It makes us slaves of its laws. This
                           vibrating second seems like an eternity.

Because the idea of pulling deserves most emphasis here, the writer combines her information to reflect that sense:

More fluent   Gravity pulls at us, insisting that we are bound to
                           the earth, slaves of its laws, this vibrating second
                           like an eternity.

The lead verb, **pulls,** is placed in an independent clause, and the three subsequent ideas are subordinated—pulled along by the first clause.

Caution: Combine sentences only to advance your meaning, to ease the reader's task. A sentence with too much information and too many connections can be impossible for readers to sort out.

Overstuffed   The night supervisor's orders from upper
                                   management to repair the overheated circuit were
                                   misunderstood by Harvey Kidd, who gave the
                                   wrong instructions to the emergency crew, thereby
                                   causing the fire.

Notice how many times you have to read the following overstuffed instruction in order to understand what to do.

Overstuffed   In developing less than a tankful of film, be sure to
                                   put in enough empty reels to fill all the space in
                                   the tank so that the film-loaded reels won't slide
                                   around when the tank is agitated.

Readability is affected less by the number of words in a sentence than by the amount of information. Even relatively short sentences can be unreadable if they carry too many details:

Overstuffed   Send three copies of Form 17-e to all six
                                   departments, unless Departments A or B or both
                                   request Form 16-w.

Although effective combining *enhances* and *streamlines* meaning, over-combining makes meaning impenetrable.

VARY SENTENCE CONSTRUCTION AND LENGTH

Long and short sentences each have their purpose: to express ideas logically or forcefully.* We have just seen how related ideas often need to be linked in one sentence so that readers can grasp the connections:

Disconnected   The nuclear core reached critical temperature. The
                                   loss-of-coolant alarm was triggered. The operator
                                   shut down the reactor.

Connected   As the nuclear core reached critical temperature,
                                   triggering the loss-of-coolant alarm, the operator
                                   shut down the reactor.

The ideas above have been combined to show that one action resulted from another. But an idea that should stand alone for emphasis needs a whole sentence of its own:

---

* My thanks to Professor Edith K. Weinstein, University of Akron, for suggesting this distinction.

Correct   Core meltdown seemed inevitable.

Too much of anything loses effect. An unbroken string of long or short sentences can bore and confuse readers; so too can a series with identical openings:

Dreary   There are some drawbacks about diesel engines. They are difficult to start in cold weather. They cause vibration. They also give off an unpleasant odor. They cause sulfur dioxide pollution.

Varied   Diesel engines have some drawbacks. Most obvious are their noisiness, cold-weather starting difficulties, vibration, odor, and sulfur dioxide emission.

Opening sentences repeatedly with **The, This, He, She,** or **I** creates monotony. When you write in the first person, overusing **I** makes you appear self-centered.

Do not, however, avoid personal pronouns if they make the writing more readable (say, by eliminating passive constructions). Instead, to avoid repetitious openings, combine ideas and shift word order.

USE SHORT SENTENCES FOR SPECIAL EMPHASIS

With all this talk about combining ideas, one might conclude that short sentences have no place in good writing. Wrong. Short sentences (even one-word sentences) provide vivid emphasis. Consider another part of the student pilot's description (page 181) of taking off:

Our airspeed increases. The plane vibrates. We reach the point where the battle begins.

Instead, the student might have written: **As our airspeed increases, the plane vibrates, and we reach the point where the battle begins.** However, she wanted to emphasize three discrete instances here: (1) the acceleration, (2) the vibration, and (3) the critical point of lifting off the ground.

Whereas long sentences combine ideas to clarify relationships, short sentences isolate a thought for special emphasis. They drive home a crucial point. They stick in a reader's mind.

Application 8–10

Combine each set of sentences into one fluent sentence.

1. John was in love.
    He was in love with Martha.

He walked with her through the night.
He was holding Martha's hand.

2. The Red Sox are an exciting team.
   The Red Sox are supported by loyal fans.
   The Red Sox sometimes win the pennant.
   The Red Sox have not won the World Series in decades.

3. On summer nights the breeze from the lake cools the bedroom of
   our cabin.
   It helps us forget the sweltering nights in the city.
   It makes us curl up under warm blankets.
   It lulls us to sleep.

4. Boats with excessive horsepower should be banned from our lakes
   and ponds.
   This would be one way to decrease noise and water pollution.
   It also could save precious fuel.

5. I was employed by the Food Mart supermarket.
   I held the position of service clerk.
   It was my job to operate a cash register.
   I priced items and stocked shelves.

Application 8–11

Improve fluency in the next paragraph by combining related ideas; by
varying sentence structure, openings, and length; and by using short
sentences for special emphasis. (*Note:* When rephrasing to achieve
conciseness, be sure to preserve the meaning of the original.)

Each summer, semitropical fish appear in New England salt
ponds. They are carried northward by the Gulf Stream. The Gulf
Stream is a warm ocean current. It flows like a river through the cold
Atlantic. It originates in the Caribbean. It winds through the Florida
straits. It meanders northward along the eastern coast of the United
States. Off the shore of Cape Hatteras, North Carolina, the Gulf
Stream's northerly course veers. It veers slightly eastward. This veer-
ing moves the stream and its warming influence farther from the
coast. Semitropical fish are swept into the Gulf Stream from their
breeding ground. The breeding ground is south of Cape Hatteras. The
fish are carried northward. The strong current carries them. The current is often 20 degrees warmer than adjacent waters. Some of these
fish are trapped in eddies. Eddies are pools of warm water that split
from the Gulf Stream. These pools drift shoreward. By midsummer
the ocean water off the New England coast is warm. It is warm
enough to attract some fish out of the eddies and nearer to shore. In
turn, even warmer water flows from the salt ponds. It flows to the

ocean. It attracts these warm-water fish. They are attracted into the ponds. Here they spend the rest of the summer. They die off in the fall. The ponds cool in the fall.

Application 8–12

The sentence sets below lack fluency because they are disconnected, have no variety, or have no emphasis. Combine each set into one or two fluent sentences.

Choppy	The world's forests are now disappearing. The rate of disappearance is 18 to 20 million hectares a year (an area half the size of California). Most of this loss occurs in humid tropical forests. These forests are in Asia, Africa, and South America.
Revised	The world's forests are now disappearing at the rate of 18 to 20 million hectares a year (an area half the size of California). Most of this loss is occurring in the humid tropical forests of Africa, Asia, and South America.*

1. The world's population will grow.
   It will grow from 4 billion in 1975.
   It will reach 6.5 billion in 2000.
   This will be an increase of more than 50 percent.

2. In sheer numbers, population will be growing.
   It will be growing faster in 2000 than it is today.
   It will add 100 million people each year.
   This figure compares with 75 million in 1975.

3. Energy prices are expected to increase.
   Many less-developed countries will have increasing difficulty.
   Their difficulty will be in meeting energy needs.

4. One-quarter of humanity depends primarily on wood.
   They depend on wood for fuel.
   For them, the outlook is bleak.

5. The world has finite fuel resources.
   These include coal, oil, gas, oil shale, and uranium.
   These resources, theoretically, are sufficient for centuries.
   These resources are not evenly distributed.

---

* Sample sentences are adapted from *Global Year 2000 Report to the President: Entering the 21st Century* (Washington: GPO, 1980)

6. Already the populations in parts of Africa and Asia have exceeded the carrying capacity of the immediate area.
This overpopulation has triggered erosion.
This erosion has reduced the land's capacity to support life.

Application 8–13

Combine each set of sentences below into one or two fluent sentences that provide the requested emphasis.

Sentence set	John is a loyal employee.
	John is a motivated employee.
	John is short-tempered with his colleagues.
Combined for positive emphasis	Even though John is short-tempered with his colleagues, he is a loyal and motivated employee.
Sentence set	This word processor has many excellent features.
	It includes a spelling checker.
	It includes a thesaurus.
	It includes a grammar checker.
Combined to emphasize the thesaurus	Among its many excellent features, such as spelling and grammar checkers, this word processor includes a thesaurus.

1. The job offers an attractive salary.
It demands long work hours.
Promotions are rapid.
(Combine for negative emphasis.)

2. The job offers an attractive salary.
It demands long work hours.
Promotions are rapid.
(Combine for positive emphasis.)

3. Company X gave us the lowest bid.
Company Y has an excellent reputation.
(Combine to emphasize Company Y.)

4. Superinsulated homes are energy efficient.
Superinsulated homes create a danger of indoor air pollution.
The toxic substances include radon gas and urea formaldehyde.
(Combine for negative emphasis.)

5. Computers cannot *think* for the writer.
Computers eliminate many mechanical writing tasks.
They speed the flow of information.
(Combine to emphasize the first assertion.)

9

Choosing
the Right Words

Word choice ultimately determines the quality of your writing. After all, any sentence is only as effective as the words it contains. The range of what we see, think, and feel is infinite, and finding words to label these experiences is not easy. The following suggestions will, however, help you choose words that are convincing, precise, informative, and engaging.

Making Your Message Convincing

Our underlying purpose in all writing is to convince readers that a message is original, sensible, and sincere. Readers will consider worthless any message that is trite, slang-ridden, overstated, or devious. Observe the suggestions here to make your writing more convincing.

AVOID TRITENESS

Writers who rely on tired old phrases (clichés) come across as too lazy or too careless to find convincing or exact ways to say what they mean. Here are just a few of the countless expressions worn out by overuse.

first and foremost	tough as nails
in the final analysis	holding the bag
needless to say	up the creek
work like a dog	over the hill
last but not least	bite the bullet
dry as a bone	fly off the handle
victim of circumstance	get on the stick

If it sounds like a "catchy phrase" you've heard before, don't use it.

AVOID OVERSTATEMENT

When they exaggerate to make a point, writers lose credibility. Be cautious when using words such as **best, biggest, brightest, most,** and **worst.**

Overstated | If you try skiing, you will find it to be one of the most memorable experiences of your life.

Revised | If you try skiing, you will enjoy it.

Overstated | If you hire me, I will be the best worker you have ever had.

Revised | If you hire me, I will do a good job.

AVOID UNSUPPORTABLE GENERALIZATIONS

Unsupported or sweeping generalizations (see also page 368) harm your credibility because they have no way of being proved.

Sweeping | Television is rotting everyone's brain.

Revised | Many authorities argue that television is one cause of declining literacy.

Sweeping | Democracy in America is collapsing.

Revised | American democracy is threatened by fanatical groups—both from the left and from the right.

Be sure your conclusions are based on adequate evidence.

Unsupported generalization | In 1983, 21 murderers were executed, and the murder rate dropped 8.1 percent for that year. These figures prove that the death penalty should be reinstated.

This isolated piece of evidence does not justify such a sweeping generalization.

Reasonable generalization	In 1983, 21 murderers were executed, and the murder rate dropped 8.1 percent for that year. These figures suggest that the death penalty may deter violent crimes.

Be aware of the vast differences in meaning among these words:

few	never
some	rarely
many	sometimes
most	often
all	always

Unless you specify **few, some, many,** or **most,** readers can interpret your statement as meaning **all.**

Misleading	Classmates are doing shabby work.

Unless you mean **all** classmates, be sure to qualify your generalization with **some, most,** or another limiting word.

AVOID MISLEADING EUPHEMISMS

Euphemisms are expressions that are aimed at politeness or at making unpleasant subjects seem less offensive. Thus, we **powder our nose** or **use the boys' room** instead of **using the bathroom;** we **pass away** or **meet our Maker** instead of **dying.** Euphemisms make the truth seem less painful.

When euphemisms avoid offending or embarrassing our audience, they are perfectly legitimate. Instead of telling a job applicant that he or she is **unqualified,** we might say, **Your background doesn't meet our needs.** There are times when friendliness and diplomacy stand a better chance of being preserved with writing that is not too abrupt, blunt, bold, or emphatic.

Euphemisms, however, are unethical if they understate the truth when only the truth will serve. In the sugar-coated world of misleading euphemisms, bad news disappears:

- Instead of being **laid off** or **fired,** workers are **surplused** or **deselected,** or the company is **downsized.**

- Instead of **lying** to the public, the government **engages in a policy of disinformation.**

- Instead of **wars** and **civilian casualties,** we have **conflicts** and **collateral damage.**

Plain talk is always better than deception. If someone offers you a job **with limited opportunity for promotion,** expect a **dead-end job.**

Application 9–1

Revise these sentences to eliminate triteness, overstatements, sweeping generalizations, and euphemisms.

1. This course gives me a pain in the neck.

2. We'll have to swallow our pride and admit our mistake.

3. There is never a dull moment in my dorm.

4. Last night's party was out of sight.

5. When it comes to neatness, my roommate is a hopeless case.

6. I was less than candid.

7. This student is poorly motivated.

8. You are the world's most beautiful person.

9. Marriage in America is a dying institution.

10. She expropriated company funds.

11. When the grenade exploded, his arm was traumatically amputated.

12. I love you more than life itself.

13. We have decided to terminate your employment.

14. People of our generation are all selfish.

Making Your Language Precise

Be sure that what you say is what you mean. A word used carelessly can offend readers. Even words listed as synonyms can carry different shades of meaning. Do you mean to say "I'm slender; you're slim; he's lean; and she's scrawny"? The wrong choice could be disastrous. Did you **walk,**

stroll, shuffle, or **amble** into the party? No two words mean exactly the same thing; don't use one word when you mean another. Don't write to apply for college admission with a statement like this:

Another attractive feature of the college is its **adequate** track program.

The writer later explained his choice of **adequate:** the program, he said, wasn't highly ranked, and so he tried to choose a word that would be sincere.

While **adequate** might convey honestly the writer's meaning, the word seems inappropriate in this context (i.e., an applicant expressing a judgment about a program). Although the program may not have been highly ranked, our writer could have used any of several alternatives (**solid, promising, growing**—or no modifier at all) without overstating the point or being offensive.

Be especially aware of similar words with dissimilar meanings, as in these examples:

affect/effect	farther/further
all ready/already	fewer/less
almost dead/dying	healthy/healthful
among/between	imply/infer
continual/continuous	invariably/inevitably
eager/anxious	uninterested/disinterested
fearful/fearsome	worse/worst

Do not write **Skiing is healthy** when you mean that skiing promotes good health (is healthful). **Healthy** means to be in a state of health. **Healthful** things help keep you healthy.

Be on the lookout for imprecise (and therefore illogical) comparisons:

Faulty

Your bank's interest rate is higher than the First National Bank. [*Can an interest rate be higher than a bank?*]

Revised

Your bank's interest rate is higher than the First National Bank's.

Finally, be sure your phrasing is not ambiguous. A statement suggesting more than one meaning will confuse readers. For instance, is **send us more personal information** a request for more information that is personal or for information that is more personal?

Ambiguous

I cannot recommend Professor Harvey too highly. [*Is the writer recommending or not?*]

Revised   Professor Harvey has my highest recommendation.
                            or
                            I cannot highly recommend Professor Harvey.

   Precision is essential above all to the informative value of your writing. Imprecise language can be misleading. Consider how meanings differ in these sentences:

Differing meanings   Include **less** technical details in your essay.

                            Include **fewer** technical details in your essay.

   Precision ultimately enhances conciseness, when one *exact* word replaces multiple inexact words.

Wordy and less exact   I have **put together** all the financial information.

                            Keep doing this exercise for ten seconds.

                            It occurred to me that I had had the same problem earlier.

Concise and more   I have **assembled** all the financial information.
exact
                            Continue this exercise for ten seconds.

                            I **remembered** having the same problem earlier.

Application 9–2

Revise these sentences to make them precise.

1. Our outlet does more business than San Francisco.

2. Low-fat foods are healthy.

3. Fred quickly got used to college life.

4. Anaerobic fermentation is used in this report.

5. Her license is for driving an automatic car only.

6. My mind became alive when I saw my drawing completed.

7. To perfect the sport of jogging, develop good breathing habits.

8. It's the final two minutes; my eyes are glaring at the scoreboard.

9. This is the worse course I've taken.

10. Sarah's cold is getting worst.

11. Unlike many other children, her home life was good.

12. State law requires that restaurant personnel serve food with a sanitation certificate.

13. It looks like they will be married in June.

Making Your Writing Concrete and Specific

General words name broad classes of things, such as **job, car,** or **person.** Such terms usually need to be clarified by more *specific* ones:

> job = senior accountant for Rockford Press
>
> car = red, four-door, Ford Escort station wagon
>
> person = male Caucasian, with red hair, blue eyes (and so on)

The more specific your words, the sharper your meaning:

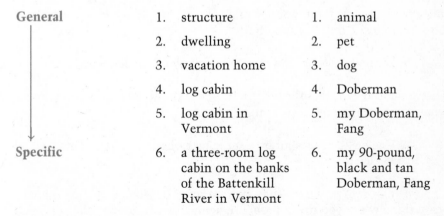

General		
	1. structure	1. animal
	2. dwelling	2. pet
	3. vacation home	3. dog
	4. log cabin	4. Doberman
	5. log cabin in Vermont	5. my Doberman, Fang
Specific	6. a three-room log cabin on the banks of the Battenkill River in Vermont	6. my 90-pound, black and tan Doberman, Fang

Notice how the picture becomes more vivid as we move to lower levels of generality. A word such as **pain** is general—it only **tells;** a phrase such as **a throbbing in my temples** is more specific—it *shows.* To understand your way of seeing and your exact meaning, readers need specifics.

Abstract words name qualities, concepts, or feelings (**beauty, luxury, depression**) whose exact meaning has to be nailed down by *concrete* words—words that name things we can know through our five senses:

> a beautiful view = snowcapped mountains, a wilderness lake, pink granite ledge, and 90-foot blue spruce trees

> a luxury condominium = redwood hot tub, hand-painted Mexican tile counters, floor-to-ceiling glass walls, oriental rugs

> a depressed person = suicidal urge, feeling of worthlessness, no hope for improvement, insomnia

A word such as **terrible** is abstract—it only **tells.** Instead of telling that yesterday's weather was terrible, **show** how it was terrible:

> Yesterday was another of those terrible January days, with a gray sky, freezing rain, icy winds, and not one ray of sunshine.

Just as your subject must be limited enough to be treated in one paragraph, your discussion must be concrete and specific enough to provide clear and convincing support. Let's say that your topic statement is this one:

> Pedestrians crossing the street in front of my house place their lives in danger.

In supporting your main point you need to *show* with concrete and specific examples. Don't say merely:

> For example, a **person** was **injured** there by a **vehicle recently.**

The boldfaced words only tell; they don't show. Readers won't know what you mean. Instead, you might write:

> My Uncle Albert was hit by a speeding garbage truck last Tuesday and had his leg broken.

Choose informative words that express *exactly* what you mean. Don't write **thing** when you mean **problem, pencil,** or **gift.** Revise **she is a swell person** to **she is kind, loving, and generous.** Instead of evaluating a coworker as **nice, great,** or **terrific,** use terms that are more concrete, such as **reliable, skillful,** and **competent** or **dishonest, irritable,** and **awkward**—further clarified by examples (**never late for work,** and the like). Words such as **great** reveal your attitude but nothing about the person.

Keep in mind that *general* and *specific* are relative terms. Thus, **football player** is more specific than **athlete** but more general than **quarterback,** which in turn is more general than **Miami quarterback, Dan**

Marino. The more you move from a general class to a particular member of that class, the more specific you become.

> teacher → college professor → brilliant sociology professor → Dr. Gomez, with the photographic memory

Your level of generality for any message depends on your purpose and audience.

In some instances, of course, you may wish to generalize for the sake of diplomacy. Instead of writing **Bill, Mary, and Sam have been tying up the office phones with personal calls,** you might prefer to generalize: **Some employees have been tying up.** . . . The second version allows you to get your message across without pointing the finger.

Most good writing has both general and specific information. The more general material is in the topic statement and sometimes in the conclusion because these parts, respectively, set the paragraph's direction and summarize its content. Informative writing invariably has a balance of *telling* and *showing.* Abstract and general expressions tell, and concrete and specific expressions show. But if the telling or showing is too abstract or general, the writing will be useless. Consider these expressions:

Meaningless abstraction	Professor Able's office is a sight to behold. [*What does "a sight to behold" mean?*]
Meaningless generalization	Pollution is affecting our environment. [*What kind of pollution? What kind of effect? What part of our environment?*]

Neither statement gives any useful information. Here are more concrete and specific versions:

Informative abstraction	Professor Able's office looks like a dump.
Informative generalization	Industrial emissions are causing lakes to die.

Now, the telling in these statements needs clarification through concrete and specific showing:

Concrete showing	The office has a floor strewn with books, a desk buried beneath a mountain of uncorrected papers, and ashtrays overflowing with ripe cigar butts.
Specific showing	Sulfur dioxide emissions from coal-burning plants combine with atmospheric water to produce

sulfuric acid. The resultant "acid rain" increases the acidity of lakes until they no longer can support life.

The showing should be as concrete and specific as necessary to make the point. Consider this general point:

Telling   A 55-mile-per-hour speed limit makes highways safer.

Here is a general explanation of the point:

General   In 1972, thousands of people were killed or injured on America's highways. Many families had at least one relative who was a casualty. After the speed limit was lowered to 55 miles per hour in 1973, the death toll began to drop.

Although the explanation offers some information, it would be more effective if amplified with valid numbers and statistics that get the original point across.

Specific   In 1972, 56,000 people died on America's highways; 200,000 were injured; 15,000 children were orphaned. In that year, if you were a member of a family of five, chances are that someone related to you by blood or law was killed or injured in an auto accident. After the speed limit was lowered to 55 miles per hour in 1973, the death toll dropped steadily to 41,000 deaths in 1975.

Concrete and specific expressions are not only more informative; they are more persuasive as well.

Application 9–3

In each set of terms, identify the most abstract or general and the most concrete or specific. Be prepared to give reasons for your choices.

1. a presidential candidate, a U.S. senator, Edward Kennedy, a politician

2. a favorite spot, a beautiful place, an island in the Bahamas, a hideaway

3. woman, surgeon, person, professional, individual

4. an awful person, a cruel and dishonest person, a nasty person

5. a competitor, a downhill racer, an athlete, a skier, a talented amateur

6. violence, assassination, terrorism, political action

Making the Tone Appropriate

Your tone is your personal stamp—the personality that takes shape between the lines. The tone you create in any writing depends on (1) the distance you impose between yourself and the reader, and (2) the attitude you show toward the subject.

Assume that a friend is going to take over a job you've held. You've decided to write your friend instructions for parts of the job. Here is your first sentence:

> Now that you've arrived in the glamorous world of office work, put on your track shoes; this is no ordinary clerical job.

What is the tone in that sentence? First, we notice that the sentence imposes little distance between the writer and the reader (it uses the direct address, **you,** and the humorous suggestion to **put on your track shoes**). And the ironic use of **glamorous** suggests that the writer means just the opposite, that the job holds little glamour.

For a different reader (let's say the recipient of a company training manual) the writer would have chosen some other way to open:

> As an office assistant with this company, you will spend little of your day seated at your desk.

The tone now is serious, no longer intimate, and the writer expresses no distinct attitude toward the job. For yet another audience (say, those who will read a company pamphlet for all new office assistants), the writer again might have altered the tone:

> Office assistants in our company are responsible for duties that extend far beyond desk work.

Here, the businesslike tone imposes greater distance between writer and audience, especially through the shift from second- to third-person address. This tone seems too impersonal for any writing addressed to the trainees themselves.

Your tone changes in response to the situation and the audience, even if the subject remains the same. Letters to your professor, your grandmother, and your friend, each about a disputed grade, would have noticeably different tones:

1. Dear Professor Snapjaws:
   I am convinced that my failing grade in calculus did not reflect a fair evaluation of my work over the semester . . . [*a formal tone*]

2. Dear Grandma,
   Thanks for your letter. I'm doing well in school, except for the failing grade I unjustly received in calculus . . . [*semiformal tone*]

3. Dear Carol,
   Boy, have I been shafted! That old turkey, Snapjaws, gave me an F in calculus . . . [*informal tone*]

In each version the writer expresses disapproval. But as the distance between writer and audience decreases, the tone becomes more informal: (1) **did not reflect a fair evaluation;** (2) **I unjustly received;** (3) **Have I been shafted!** Clearly the intimate tone and attitude of outrage in the letter to Carol would be inappropriate for the letter to Professor Snapjaws, in which the writer settles for firm disapproval. So too would the attitude of polite disapproval in the letter to Grandma be inappropriate for the letter to Carol or the professor.

ESTABLISH AN APPROPRIATE DISTANCE

We already know how tone works in speaking. When you meet someone new, you respond in a tone that defines your relationship.

Honored to make your acquaintance. [*formal tone—greatest distance*]

How do you do? [*formal*]

Nice to meet you. [*semiformal—medium distance*]

Hello. [*semiformal*]

Hi. [*informal—least distance*]

Hey. [*informal*]

What's happening? [*informal*]

Your greeting (and tone) will depend on how much distance you decide is appropriate; and, in turn, the tone will determine how you come across. Each of these responses is appropriate in specific situations, inappropriate in others. **What's happening?** might be okay when you meet another student, but not the college president. Just as different types of dress fit different situations (cut-offs for the beach, a suit for a job interview), so also do different tones of writing and speaking.

To decide on an appropriate distance from which to address a particular audience, follow these guidelines:

- Use a formal or semiformal tone in writing for superiors, professionals, or academics (depending on what you think the reader expects).

- Use a semiformal or informal tone in essays and letters (depending on how close you feel to your reader).

- Use an informal tone when you want your writing to be conversational, or when you want to sound like a person talking.

Whichever tone you decide on, be consistent throughout your message.

Inconsistent tone	My dorm room isn't fit for a pig [*too informal*]; it is ungraciously unattractive [*too formal*].
Revised	My dilapidated dorm room is unfit to live in.

In general, lean toward an informal tone without falling into slang. Make your writing conversational by following these suggestions:

1. Keep the language simple.
2. Use an occasional contraction.
3. Address readers directly, when appropriate.
4. Don't be afraid to use **I**, when appropriate.
5. Prefer active to passive voice.
6. Emphasize the positive.

Keep the Language Simple   Say it in plain English. Try not to use a three-syllable word when one syllable will do. Trade for less:

utilize	= use
to be cognizant	= to know
to endeavor	= to try
endeavor	= effort
to secure employment	= to find a job

multiplicity of	= many
effectuate	= do
terminate	= end
component	= part

Count the syllables. Trim whenever you can. But, most important, choose words that you hear and use in everyday speaking—words that are universally familiar.

Don't write **I deem** when you mean **I think,** or **Keep me apprised** instead of **Keep me informed,** or **I concur** instead of **I agree,** or **securing employment** instead of **finding a job,** or **it is cost prohibitive** instead of **we can't afford it.** Experiments have shown that readers have to spend extra time on passages with unfamiliar or less familiar words. Don't write like the author of a report from the Federal Aviation Administration who suggested that manufacturers of the DC-10 be directed to **reevaluate the design of the entire pylon assembly to minimize design factors which are resulting in sensitive and/or critical maintenance and inspection procedures** (25 words, 50 syllables). Here is a plain-English translation: **Redesign the pylons so they are easier to maintain and inspect** (11 words, 18 syllables). Here is another case of inflated language:

Inflated   Upgrade your present employment situation. [*5 words, 12 syllables*]

Revised   Get a better job. [*4 words, 5 syllables*]

These are examples of the worst kind of puffery: too many words, and words bigger than needed. Here are more:

Inflated   I am thoroughly convinced that Sam is a trustworthy individual.

Revised   I trust Sam.

Inflated   Make an improvement in the clerical situation.

Revised   Hire more secretaries.
or
Hire better secretaries. (*Inflated language also can be ambiguous!*)

Words chosen to impress readers too often confuse them instead. Of course, now and then the fancier or more impressive word is best—if it expresses your exact meaning. For instance, we would not substitute **end** for **terminate** in referring to something with an established limit.

Correct	Our lease terminates this month.

Also, if one bigger word can replace a handful of simpler words and can sharpen your meaning, use the bigger word.

Weak	Six loops around the outside edges of the dome tent are needed for the pegs to fit into.
Informative and precise	Six loops around the dome tent's **perimeter accommodate** the pegs.
Weak	Upper management has **taken over for themselves** our authority as decision makers.
Informative and precise	Upper management has **usurped** our authority as decision makers.
Weak	Sexist language **contributes to the ongoing prevalence of** gender stereotypes.
Forceful and Precise	Sexist language **perpetuates** gender stereotypes.

Never seek simplicity at the cost of clarity; make every word count. Use the fancy word *only* when your meaning and your audience demand it.

Use an Occasional Contraction   Unless you have reason to be formal, use (but do not overuse) contractions to loosen up the tone. Balance an **I am** with an **I'm**, a **you are** with a **you're**, an **it is** with an **it's**, and so on (as we've done throughout this book).

Generally, use contractions only with pronouns—not with nouns or proper nouns (names). Otherwise, the constructions are awkward or ambiguous.

Awkward contractions	Barbara'll be here soon.
	She could've come earlier.
	Health's important.
	Love'll make you happy.
Ambiguous contractions	The dog's barking.
	Bill's skiing.
	The baby's crying.

These ambiguous contractions easily can be confused with possessive constructions (page 569).

Address Readers Directly   Use the personal pronouns **you** and **your** to connect with readers. Otherwise, your writing sounds impersonal.

Impersonal tone

A writer should use **you** and **your** generously to create contact with his or her readers.

Notice how distance *and* words increase. Direct address creates a more personal tone.

Impersonal tone

Students at our college will find the faculty always willing to help.

Personal tone

As a student at our college, **you** will find the faculty always willing to help.

Research shows that readers relate better to something addressed to them directly.

Caution: Use **you** and **your** only to correspond *directly* with the reader, as in a letter, memo, instructions, or some form of advice, encouragement, or persuasion. By using **you** and **your** when your subject and purpose call for first or third person, you might write something wordy and awkward such as this:

Wordy and awkward

When **you** are in northern Ontario, **you** can see wilderness lakes everywhere around **you.**

Appropriate

Wilderness lakes are everywhere in Northern Ontario.

Use *I* and *we* When Appropriate   Don't disappear behind your writing. Use **I** when referring to yourself.

Distant

This writer would like a refund.

Revised

I would like a refund.

Distant

The fear was awful until the police arrived.

Revised

I was terrified until the police arrived.

Avoid, of course, opening too many sentences with **I.** Combine ideas and shift word order instead (page 179).

Prefer the Active Voice Because the active voice is more direct and economical than the passive voice, it generally creates a less formal tone. Review pages 164–167 for use of active and passive voice.

Emphasize the Positive We all respond more favorably to encouragement than to criticism. Whenever you offer advice, suggestions, or recommendations, try to emphasize benefits rather than flaws.

Critical tone	Study harder and you might not flunk out.
Encouraging tone	As soon as I began studying one extra hour each day, my grades improved. Why not give it a try?

EXPRESS A CLEAR AND APPROPRIATE ATTITUDE

Another problem with tone occurs when you suggest an unclear or inappropriate attitude toward the subject. Let readers know where you stand. Don't force them to translate. Say **I enjoyed the course** instead of **My attitude toward the course was one of high approval.** Say **Let's liven up our dull relationship** instead of **We should inject some rejuvenation into our lifeless and dull liaison.**

Don't be afraid to inject personal commentary when it's called for. Consider how the message below increases in force and effectiveness with the boldfaced commentary:

> In 1972, 56,000 people died on America's highways; 200,000 were injured; 15,000 children were orphaned. In that year, if you were a member of a family of five, chances are that someone related to you, by blood or law, was killed or injured by **one of the most violent forms of self-elimination ever devised by humanity**—an auto accident.

If, however, your job is to report objectively, try to suppress any bias you might have; do not volunteer your attitude. Biased people make judgments without examining the facts. Even controversial subjects deserve objective treatment.

Imagine you are a reporter for your campus newspaper. You have been sent to investigate the causes of a confrontation between female faculty and the administration. Your initial report, written for tomorrow's edition, is intended simply to describe what happened. Here is how an unbiased description might read:

> At 10:00 A.M. on Wednesday, October 24, 80 women faculty members set up picket lines around the college's administration building, bringing business to a halt. The group issued a formal protest, claiming that their working conditions were repressive, their

salary scale unfair, and their promotional opportunities limited. The women demanded affirmative action, insisting that the college's hiring and promotional policies and wage scales be revised. The demonstration ended when Glenn Tarullo, vice-president in charge of personnel, promised to appoint a committee to investigate the group's claims and to correct any inequities.

Notice the absence of implied judgments; the facts are presented objectively. A less impartial version of the event, from a protester's point of view, might read like this:

Last Wednesday, sisters struck another blow against male supremacy when 80 women faculty members paralyzed the college's repressive and sexist administration for more than six hours. The timely and articulate protest was aimed against degrading working conditions, unfair salary scales, and lack of promotional opportunities for women. Stunned administrators watched helplessly as the group organized their picket lines, determined to continue their protest until their demands for equal rights were met. An embarrassed vice-president quickly agreed to study the group's demands and to revise the college's discriminatory policies. The success of this long-overdue confrontation serves as an inspiration to oppressed women employees everywhere.

Judgmental words (**male supremacy, degrading, paralyzed, articulate, stunned, discriminatory**) inject the writer's attitude, even though it isn't called for. In contrast to this bias, the following version patronizingly defends the status quo:

Our administration building was the scene of an amusing battle of the sexes last Wednesday, when a group of irate faculty feminists, 80 strong, set up picket lines for six hours. The protest was lodged against supposed inequities in hiring, wages, working conditions, and promotion for women faculty at our college. The libbers threatened to continue their protest until their demands for "equal rights" were met. A bemused vice-president responded to this carnival demonstration with patience and dignity, assuring the militants that their claims and demands—however inaccurate and immoderate—would receive just consideration.

Again, loaded words and superlatives slant the tone. Let your facts speak for themselves.

Writing teacher Marshall Kremers reminds us that being unbiased, of course, doesn't mean burying your head—and your values—in the sand.* Remaining "neutral" about something you know to be wrong or dangerous is unethical. You have an ethical responsibility to weigh the facts and to make your views known. If, for instance, you conclude that the college protest was clearly justified, don't hesitate to say so.

AVOID SEXIST USAGE

The way we as a culture use language reflects the way we think about ourselves. Usage that gives people in general a male identity allows no room for females. In fact, females become virtually invisible in a world of **policemen, congressmen, firemen, foremen, selectmen, and aldermen.**

Sexist usage refers to doctors, lawyers, and other professionals as **he** or **him** while referring to nurses, secretaries, and homemakers as **she** or **her.** In this traditional stereotype, males do the jobs that really matter (and that pay higher wages), whereas females serve only as support and decoration. And when the odd pretenders do invade traditional "male" roles, we might express our surprise at their boldness by calling them **female executives** or **female sportscasters** or **female surgeons** or **female hockey players.** Likewise, to demean males who have settled for "female" roles, we refer to **male secretaries** or **male nurses** or **male flight attendants** or **male models.**

In the biased reality of sexist usage, the title **Mr.** protects the privacy of a male who might be married or unmarried, whereas **Mrs.** and **Miss** announce a female's marital status to the world. Moreover, an unmarried male is fondly referred to as a **bachelor,** although his female counterpart is stigmatized as an **old maid** or a **spinster.**

Besides being misleading and demeaning, sexist usage is offensive. Instead of bringing writer and readers closer together, sexist usage severs any human connection our writing otherwise might achieve.

To eliminate sexism from your writing, follow these guidelines:

* Use neutral expressions:

chair, or **chairperson**	rather than	**chairman**
businessperson	rather than	**businessman**
supervisor	rather than	**foreman**
police officer	rather than	**policeman**
letter carrier	rather than	**postman**

---

* See *IEEE Transactions on Professional Communication* 32.2 (1989):58–61.

homemaker	rather than	**housewife**
humanity	rather than	**mankind**
actor	rather than	**actor vs. actress**

- Rephrase to eliminate the pronoun, if you can do so without altering your original meaning.

| **Sexist** | A writer will succeed if **he** revises. |
| **Revised** | A writer who revises succeeds. |

- Use plural forms. Instead of **Each doctor . . . he,** use **All doctors . . . they** (but *not* **Each doctor . . . they**).

| **Sexist** | A writer will succeed if **he** revises. |
| **Revised** | Writers will succeed if **they** revise. (but *not* A writer will succeed if **they** revise.) |

Note: When using a plural form, don't create an error in pronoun-referent agreement by having the *plural* pronoun **they** or **their** refer to a *singular* referent, as in "**Each writer** should do **their** best."

- When possible (as in direct address) use **you:** "**You** will succeed if **you** revise." But use this form *only* when addressing someone directly. (See page 202 for discussion.)

- Use occasional pairings (**him or her, she or he, his or hers, he/she**): "A writer will succeed if **she or he** revises."

Note: Overuse of such pairings can be awkward. A writer should do **his or her** best to make sure that **she or he** connects with **his or her** readers.

- Use feminine and masculine pronouns alternately: "An effective writer always focuses on **her** audience. The writer strives to connect with all **his** readers."

- Drop diminutive endings such as **-ess** and **-ette** used to denote females (**poetess, drum majorette, actress,** etc.). Such endings seem to perpetuate an image of **the little woman.**

- Use **Ms.** instead of **Mrs.** or **Miss,** unless you know that the person prefers one of the traditional titles. Or omit titles completely: **Jane Kelly** and **Roger Smith; Kelly** and **Smith.**

Not only do the words you choose reveal your way of seeing, but they also influence your reader's way of seeing. Sexist language carries built-in judgments, and, as the renowned linguist S. I. Hayakawa reminds us: "Judgment stops thought." In the world defined by sexist language, everyone remains frozen in her and his place.

Application 9–4

Rewrite these statments in plain English, with special attention to tone.

1. This writer desires to be considered for a position with your company.

2. My attitude toward your behavior is one of disapproval.

3. Please refund my full purchase expenditure in view of the fact that this radio is defective.

4. I can wish you no better luck than that you find this job to be as enjoyable as I have.

5. Prior to this time I have never failed an exam.

6. In relation to your job, I would like to say that we no longer can offer you employment.

7. A good writer is cognizant of how to utilize grammar in correct fashion.

8. Replacement of the weak battery should be effectuated.

9. Considering the length of the present school day, it is my opinion that the day is excessive lengthwise for most elementary pupils.

10. Make an improvement in your studying situation.

Application 9–5

In this letter, a student has written to the registrar, asking that his deadline for paying tuition be extended and explaining why he needs the extra time. Rewrite the letter in plain English.

Dear Mr. Jones:

Pursuant to your notice of September 6, advising me that my tuition was overdue, I regret to advise you that my tuition payment will be delayed until September 21, when my scholarship is received.

I humbly request you to be cognizant of the fact that this writer's tuition for all five prior semesters has been paid on time. At the present time, my first, and hopefully last, late payment is due to the fact that a computer breakdown in the NDEA offices has occasioned a delay in the processing of all scholarship renewal applications for a period of time roughly approximating two weeks. Enclosed please find a copy of a recent NDEA notice to this effect.

I am in hopes that you will be kind enough to grant me an extension of my tuition-due date for this brief period of time. Thanking you in anticipation of your kind cooperation, I remain

Gratefully yours,
Charles Smith
Student

Application 9–6

Collaborative Project: A version of this letter was published in a local newspaper. Working in small groups, rewrite it in plain English.

In the absence of definitive studies regarding the optimum length of the school day, I can only state my personal opinion based upon observations made by me and upon teacher observations that have been conveyed to me. Considering the length of the present school day, it is my opinion that the school day is excessive length-wise for most elementary pupils, certainly for almost all of the primary children.

To find the answer to the problem requires consideration of two ways in which the problem may be viewed. One way focuses upon the needs of the children, while the other focuses upon logistics, scheduling, transportation, and other limits imposed by the educational system. If it is necessary to prioritize these two ideas, it would seem most reasonable to give the first consideration to the primary and fundamental reason for the very existence of the system itself, i.e., to meet the educational needs of the children the system is trying to serve.

Application 9–7

Rewrite these statements to eliminate sexist expressions—without altering the meaning.

1. Each student should select his courses early.

2. An employee in our organization can be sure he will be treated fairly.

3. Almost every child dreams of being a fireman.

4. The average man is a good citizen.

5. The future of mankind is uncertain.

6. Being a stewardess is not as glamorous as it may seem.

7. Everyone has the right to his opinion.

8. Every married surgeon depends on his spouse for emotional support.

9. Our female carpenter is also a poetess.

10. Dr. Marcia White is not only a female professor, but also chairman of the English department.

Application 9–8

Find a piece of writing that expresses a sexist bias. Rewrite one or more paragraphs to eliminate sexist usage without altering the original meaning. Attach a copy of your original to your rewrite, and be prepared to discuss the rewrite in class.

Find a piece of writing that refers to both sexes without lapsing into sexist usage, and bring it to class for analysis and discussion.

Application 9–9

Collaborative Project: How would you respond to someone who claimed that our concern with sexist language is just another fad? Working in small groups, brainstorm for material, and then draft a short essay that supports your group's viewpoint convincingly. Begin your essay with a clear thesis statement.

Each group can then discuss its essay with the whole class.

Avoiding Reliance on Automated Tools

Many of the strategies in Chapters 8 and 9 could be executed rapidly with word-processing software. By using the *global search-and-replace func-*

tion in some programs, you can command the computer to search for ambiguous pronoun references, overuse of passive voice, **to be** verbs, **There** and **It** sentence openers, negative constructions, clutter words, needless prefatory expressions and qualifiers, sexist language, and so on. With an on-line dictionary or thesaurus, you can check definitions or see a list of synonyms for a word you have used in your writing.

Despite the increasing sophistication of style checkers, diction checkers, and other editing aids, automation can be extremely imprecise. No amount of automation is likely to eliminate the writer's burden of *choice*. None of the "rules" or advice offered in Chapters 8 and 9 applies universally. Our language confronts us with almost infinite choices that cannot be programmed into a computer. Ultimately it is the informed writer's sensitivity to meaning, emphasis, and tone—the human contact—that determines the effectiveness of any message.

SECTION THREE

ESSAYS FOR VARIOUS GOALS

Introduction

Earlier chapters have stressed the importance of identifying a *goal* and of refining the goal into a *purpose* (goal plus plan). This section will show you how to focus on your purpose more sharply to achieve a variety of writing goals.

Three Major Goals of Writing

The bulk of your writing in college and beyond can be categorized according to three major goals: *expressive, referential,* and *persuasive.* Let's consider each of these categories separately.

Expressive writing is mostly about *you,* the writer (your feelings, experiences, impressions, personality). Its goal is to help readers understand something about you or about your way of seeing things. Here are a few writing situations with an expressive goal:

> You write to cheer up a sick friend with a tale about your latest blind date.
>
> You write a Dear John (or Jane) letter.
>
> You describe for your classmates a special relationship.
>
> You write to your parents, explaining why you've been feeling down-in-the-dumps.

In each writing your goal is to share something about yourself with your audience.

Referential (or *explanatory*) *writing* is mostly about your view (your opinion, attitude, observation, or suggestion) on some *outside* subject. The goal is not so much to express emotions; it is to provide readers with information that explains your viewpoint or position. Most of your writing has a referential goal. Here are examples of referential writing situations:

> You write to describe the exterior of your dorm so that your parents can find it.

> You define *condominium* for your business law class.

> You report on the effects of budget cuts at your college for the campus newspaper.

> You write instructions for your classmates on how to obtain autographs of famous people by mail.

> You write an essay for your psychology professor on why people gossip.

The focus in each of these situations is not you or your reader, but rather on a subject that interests you both.

Persuasive writing is mostly about your *audience*. Beyond merely informing readers, your goal is to motivate them to change their thinking or take some action on a controversial issue. Persuasive writing is designed to appeal to the audience's reason, and sometimes to their emotions as well. Here are examples of persuasive-writing situations:

> You write an editorial for the campus newspaper, calling for a stricter alcohol policy in the dorms.

> You write a diplomatic note to your obnoxious neighbor, asking him to keep his dogs quiet.

> You write to ask a professor on sabbatical to reconsider the low grade you were given in history.

> You write to persuade citizens in your country to vote against a proposal for a toxic-waste dump.

The focus in each of these situations is on your reader's way of thinking.

These three categories (expressive, referential or explanatory, and persuasive) often overlap in your writing. In writing to *persuade* the dean to beef up campus security, you might discuss your personal fears (expressive goal) and explain how some students have been attacked (ref-

erential goal). But your *primary* goal will be persuasive. Most writing situations have *one* primary goal. And by keeping that goal sharply in focus,
you can decide on the best strategies for getting the job done.

Major Development Strategies

A development strategy is simply a *plan* for achieving a goal. Specifically,
it is a plan for coming up with the details, events, examples, explanations, and reasons that enable readers to grasp your exact meaning—a
way of answering readers' questions. Depending on your writing situation, you can choose from four major strategies for developing a message:
description, narration, exposition, and *argument.*

   Description creates a word picture. It is either objective or subjective; that is, it provides a factual picture of something (referential goal),
or it shares an impression or feeling (expressive goal). If your goal were to
describe the geology of the Lady Evelyn Wilderness in northern Ontario
for an environmental impact statement, you would use objective description. But if you wished to share with an interested friend your sensations
while camping there, you would use subjective description.

   Narration tells a story or depicts a series of related events, usually
in chronological order. In essay writing, a narrative almost always makes
a clear and definite point. Narration relies heavily on descriptive details
to make the events vivid. If your goal were to tell about being stalked by
a black bear while traveling through Ontario's Lady Evelyn Wilderness,
you would use the strategy of narration.

   Exposition is the commonest strategy for developing a message.
Although exposition relies on description and, sometimes, narration,
exposition does more than paint a picture or tell a story: this strategy
explains the writer's viewpoint. Strategies of exposition can be divided
into more specific plans: illustration, classification, process analysis,
cause-effect analysis, comparison/contrast, and definition. For one paragraph or a whole essay, a writer decides on the strategy that best explains
the main point. Although an essay often embodies some combination of
these strategies, it usually will have one *primary* strategy. If your goal
were to explain how sulfur dioxide pollution from industries in the
Midwest threatens the waters of the Lady Evelyn Wilderness, you might
use several expository strategies to make your point, but your primary
strategy would be cause-effect analysis.

   With *argument,* we strive to persuade readers that our stand on an
issue is valid. Whereas the main point in exposition can be *shown* to be
true or valid, the main point in an argument is debatable—capable of
being argued by reasonable people on either side of the issue. Thus, if
your goal were to persuade readers that logging companies should not be

allowed to operate in the Lady Evelyn Wilderness, you would argue that logging would destroy this natural refuge. Opponents, however, might argue that logging would create jobs for local residents, thereby improving the economy. But neither side ever could *prove* that its position is the right one. The stronger argument, then, would be the one that makes the more convincing case. Although argument follows its own specified patterns of reasoning, it also relies on the strategies of description, narration, and exposition.

Just as writing may have overlapping goals, writing may employ overlapping strategies for development. Many of your essays, though, will employ one or another primary strategy; that is, a particular essay will be primarily descriptive, narrative, expository, or argumentative. The chapters in Section Three will help you spell out your purpose according to your goals and your strategies for achieving those goals. Sample essays and study questions precede the assignments. Careful analysis of these essays should help you compose your responses to the assignments. Some of these are professional essays; some are versions of essays by students. And, though not all of them can be considered "perfect," they do represent the kind of imaginative, engaging, and fluent responses that make writing make a difference. Each essay has been revised often enough to ensure worthwhile content, sensible arrangement, and a clear, readable style.

Note: Keep in mind that none of these development strategies is an end in itself. In other words, we don't write merely for the sake of contrasting or of discussing causes and effects. Instead, we contrast or discuss causes and effects because we've decided that this particular approach seems the best way to connect with readers on this particular topic. Each strategy is merely one way of looking at something—another option for approaching the countless writing situations we face throughout our lives and careers.

A Word About Structural Variations

Most sample essays in earlier chapters are basic examples of an introduction-body-conclusion structure: a one-paragraph introduction that leads into the thesis; several supporting paragraphs, each developed around a topic statement that treats one part of the thesis; and a one-paragraph conclusion that relates to the main point. But a quick glance at published writing—including these very paragraphs—shows that not all writing rigidly follows this one formula. Within this three-part structure are many variations. Some topics might call for several introductory paragraphs; a complicated supporting point may require that one topic statement serve two or more body paragraphs; some conclusions may take up more than one paragraph. On the other hand, you often will see single-sentence paragraphs opening, supporting, or closing an essay.

Furthermore, the thesis is not always the final sentence in the introduction. The thesis can be the first sentence of the essay, or it may be saved for the conclusion or not stated at all—*though it is always unmistakably implied.*

Sometimes the body paragraphs vary greatly in length or are interrupted by digressions (interpretations, personal remarks, flashbacks, and so on). This structure is acceptable if the connection between digressions and the main discussion is clear.

Still other essays have neither introductory nor concluding paragraphs. Instead, the opening or closing is incorporated into the main discussion.

Such choices about structural variation are all part of a writer's deliberate decisions—decisions that determine the ultimate quality of the message. But regardless of the type and extent of its variations, a good essay *always* reveals a distinct beginning, middle, and ending—and a clear line of thought.

Many of the essays in the following chapters embody one or more of these variations. Use them as inspiration for your own writing, whenever such variations can help sharpen your meaning.

10
Developing a Description

Because it creates a word picture—a clear image in readers' minds—description is the common denominator in all writing. Specifically, description answers these questions:

What is it?

What does it look like?

How could I recognize it?

What is it made of?

What does it do?

How does it work?

What is your impression of it?

How does it make you feel?

Although itself one of the four basic strategies for development (along with narration, exposition, and argument), description most often supports these other strategies by helping readers visualize details. Before discussing description as an exclusive strategy (*pure description*), let's consider its supporting role in writing developed through other strategies.

219

Description as a Support Strategy

Whether telling a story, explaining something, or arguing a point, writers rely on the *showing power* of description to enrich their discussions. Consider this topic statement about the physical complexities of New York City:

It is a miracle that New York works at all.

Now that we've been told, we need to be shown so that we can see for ourselves. The author enables us to share his impression of New York in this way:

> ¹It is a miracle that New York works at all. ²The whole thing is implausible. ³Every time the residents brush their teeth, millions of gallons of water must be drawn from the Catskills and the hills of Westchester. ⁴When a young man in Manhattan writes a letter to his girl in Brooklyn, the love message gets blown to her through a pneumatic tube—*pfft*—just like that. ⁵The subterranean system of telephone cables, power lines, steam pipes, gas mains, and sewer pipes is reason enough to abandon the island to the gods and the weevils. ⁶Every time an incision is made in the pavement, the noisy surgeons expose ganglia that are tangled beyond belief. ⁷By rights New York should have destroyed itself long ago, from panic or fire or rioting or failure of some vital supply line in its circulatory system or from some deep labyrinthine short circuit. ⁸Long ago the city should have experienced an insoluble traffic snarl at some impossible bottleneck. ⁹It should have perished of hunger when food lines failed for a few days. ¹⁰It should have been wiped out by a plague starting in its slums or carried in by ships' rats. ¹¹It should have been overwhelmed by the sea that licks at it on every side. ¹²The workers in its myriad cells should have succumbed to nerves, from the fearful pall of smoke-fog that drifts over every few days from Jersey, blotting out all light at noon and leaving the high offices suspended, [people] groping and depressed, and the sense of world's end. ¹³It should have been touched in the head by the August heat and gone off its rocker.
>
> —E. B. White

To support his key term of *implausible,* White uses the primary development strategy of cause-and-effect analysis. But vivid description carries much of the burden here.

Because any subject can be viewed in countless ways, decisions about descriptive details must consider the writer's purpose and the reader's needs. The purpose of the paragraph above is not to describe New York as a tourist brochure would; instead, it is to share the writer's dominant impression of the city as a huge, impossibly complex, living organism. He thus decides to communicate his impression through examples of the causes and effects of New York's problems—examples enriched and clarified by precise and vivid description.

White's paragraph has two types of descriptive details: (1) objective, which include precise images that a camera would record (people brushing their teeth, water flowing by the riversful), and (2) subjective, which include the vivid images that are filtered through the author's personal way of seeing ("incision," "ganglia," "myriad cells"). Objective details make the picture clear; subjective details make it vivid. The two types complement each other.

Finally, the level of details in White's paragraph provides enough solid images for the reader to understand the main point. Imagine if the paragraph had been developed at a higher level of generality:

Abstract and general	Concrete and specific
water must be drawn from great distances	millions of gallons of water must be drawn from the Catskills and the hills of Westchester [*sentence 3*]
the subterranean system of utilities	the subterranean system of telephone cables, power lines, steam pipes, gas mains, and sewer pipes [*sentence 5*]

To ensure coherence, White orders his details logically (in this case, from underground to ground level to sky). This spatial order creates a clear and distinct angle of vision, saving the major emphasis (the dehumanizing effect of this environmental chaos on the workers in skyscrapers) for last. The supporting description makes White's paragraph come to life for us.

Description as a Primary Strategy

So-called pure description does not mean describing merely for the sake of describing. Any pure description has one or both of these goals:

1. To provide factual information about something for someone who will use it, buy it, or assemble it, or who needs to know more about it for some good reason (objective description)

2. To create a mood or impression in the reader's mind or to share a feeling (subjective description)

A strictly objective description has a referential goal. It includes facts about the thing itself, without the writer's personal comments:

Objective description	All day we had temperatures of 30 degrees F and heavy rains driven by winds of 35–45 mph.

This is the type of description commonly found in business and technical reports.

Subjective description has an expressive goal. It emphasizes the writer's impressions about the thing:

Subjective description	All day the weather was dismal.

Many of your own descriptions will include both observable facts and your personal impressions:

Combined description	The freezing rain and gale-force winds made our first day of vacation dismal.

For illustration, however, objective description and subjective description are treated separately in this chapter.

OBJECTIVE DESCRIPTION

Objective description filters out—as much as appropriate—personal impressions, and focuses on observable details.* Objective description records *exactly* what the writer sees, which should be what anyone else would see from the writer's vantage point. Readers of an objective description expect only the facts. If your tape deck has been stolen, the police will need a description that includes the brand name, serial number, model, color, size, shape, identifying marks or scratches, and so on. For this audience, a subjective description (that the tape deck was a handsome addition to your car; that its sound quality was superb; that it made driving a pleasure) would be useless. These details describe only your feelings, not the object itself.

Here is a purely objective description:

Orienting sentence (1)	[1]The 2-acre site (lot 7) for my proposed log cabin is on the northern shore of Moosehead Lake, roughly 1000 feet east of the Seboomook Point

---

* "Pure objectivity" is, of course, humanly impossible. Each writer has a unique perspective on the facts and their meaning, and chooses what to put in and what to leave out.

View from the water (2–5)	camping area. ²It is marked by a granite ledge, 30 feet long and 15 feet high. ³The ledge faces due south and slopes gradually east. ⁴A rock shoal along the westerly frontage extends about 30 feet from the shoreline. ⁵On the easterly end of the frontage is a landing area on a small gravel beach immediately to the right of the ledge. ⁶Lot boundaries are marked by yellow stakes a few feet from the shoreline. ⁷Lot numbers are carved on yellow-marked trees adjacent to the yellow stakes.
View from the shoreline (6–7)	

This paragraph, written to help a soil engineer find the property by boat, answers these questions:

What is it?

What does it look like?

How could I recognize it?

The answers follow a spatial order, moving from whole to parts—the same order in which we would actually view the property.

Notice that the opening sentence is not a standard topic statement but a statement of fact. It does, however, provide an orientation, giving us a definite sense of what to expect in the discussion. Descriptions often have no topic statement, but they nonetheless begin with an orienting statement.

Because the writer's goal is referential, the passage includes only factual information, without personal impressions. Details are limited to the recognizable characteristics of the property. And because the writer simply wants to *introduce* the subject, description is restricted to a brief but specific catalog of the lot's major features. For some other situation, the description naturally would be more specific. For instance, the soil engineer's evaluation report of the building site would be read by the health officials who approve building permits. That report therefore would carry details of this kind:

Hand-dug test holes revealed a well-draining, granular material, with a depth of at least 48 inches to bedrock.

The quantity of detail in a description is always keyed to the writer's purpose and the audience's needs.

Objective description serves many uses in college writing. In describing a lab experiment or a field trip or a fire hazard in the dorm, you would focus on the facts, not on your feelings.

In the workplace, you might use objective description to inform customers about a new product or service. If you apply for a business loan, the bank will require a description of the property or venture. As an architect or engineer you would describe your proposed building on paper before construction begins. As a medical professional, you would write detailed records of a patient's condition and treatment. Whenever readers need to visualize *the thing itself*, objective description is essential.

SUBJECTIVE DESCRIPTION

Strictly speaking, no useful description can be completely subjective; to get the picture, readers need at least some observable details. For our purposes, we can define subjective description as that which has objective details colored by personal impressions. The usual goal of subjective description is to create a mood or to share a feeling, as shown in the italicized expressions:

> One of my own favorite approaches to a rocky seacoast is by a rough path through an evergreen forest that has its own peculiar enchantment. It is usually an early morning tide that takes me along the forest path, so that the light is still pale and the fog drifts in from the sea beyond. *It is almost a ghost forest,* for among the living spruce and balsam are many dead trees—some still erect, some sagging earthward, some lying on the floor of the forest. All the trees, the living and the dead, are *clothed* with green and silver crusts of lichens. Tufts of the bearded lichen or old man's beard hang from the branches *like bits of sea mist* tangled there. Green woodland mosses and a *yielding carpet* of reindeer moss cover the ground. In the quiet of that place even the *voice of the surf* is reduced to a *whispered echo* and the sounds of the forest are but the *ghosts of sound*—the *faint sighing* of evergreen needles in the moving air; the creaks and heavier groans of half-fallen trees *resting against their neighbors* and rubbing bark against bark; the *light rattling fall* of a dead branch broken under the feet of a squirrel and sent bouncing and ricocheting earthward. [emphasis added]
>
> —Rachel L. Carson

This paragraph blends objective and subjective description to answer these questions:

Objective   What is it?

                          What does it look like?

                          What is it made of?

Subjective   What is your impression of it?

                                        How does it make you feel?

The paragraph is developed to help us understand what the writer means by a forest with "its own peculiar enchantment." Concrete and specific details are those any reader could visualize:

the early morning light and fog

the many dead trees among the living ones

the lichens that coat the trees and hang from the branches

the mossy forest floor

the eerie sounds

But these details alone would not cause readers to share the writer's dominant impression of "peculiar enchantment." To create that special mood, the writer had to insert subjective details (in italics) as well. She had to filter the facts through her own feelings and impressions.

The observable details are arranged in the same order (general to specific) that we would follow in noticing things if we were in the writer's place: first location, then atmosphere, trees, algae on the trees, ground cover, sounds. Thus, we are able to perceive things in the same sequence as the writer perceived them.

Beyond creating a mood or sharing a feeling, subjective description can serve practical purposes. The following writer uses personal impressions to make a persuasive point.

> Close your eyes for a moment, and picture a professional base-ball game. You probably see something like this: a hot summer afternoon, complete with sizzling bats, fans clad in the reds and yellows and pastels of summer, and short-sleeved vendors yelling "ICE CREAM HEEERE!" If you recall some recent World Series, though, you might envision a scene more like this: a c-c-cold starlit night highlighted by players in Thinsulate gloves and turtlenecks, fans in ski hats instead of baseball caps, and vendors hurriedly hawking coffee. This "football-like" image suggests that baseball season is just plain too long!
>
> —Mike Cabral

This paragraph creates contrasting moods in order to win readers' support for its conclusion—a subjective view addresses a practical matter.

Other such subjective appeals to readers' feelings can have persuasive value as well. A colorful description of your messy dorm or apartment might encourage fellow residents to clean up their act. Or a nauseating catalog of greasy food served in the college dining hall might move school officials to improve the menu. Even the most subjective writing can cause readers to see things as you do.

In this next selection, a noted Mexican-American author combines objective and subjective details to document the hardships of Mexicans immigrating to the United States.

To the Border

You stand around. You smoke. You spit. You are wearing your two shirts, two pants, two underpants. Jesús says if they chase you, throw that bag down. Your plastic bag is your mama, all you have left: the yellow cheese she wrapped has formed a translucent rind; the laminated scapular of the Sacred Heart nestles flame in its cleft. Put it in your pocket. Inside. Put it in your underneath pants' pocket. The last hour of Mexico is twilight, the shuffling of feet. Jesús says they are able to see in the dark. They have X rays and helicopters and searchlights. Jesús says wait, just wait, till he says. Though most of the men have started to move. You feel the hand of Jesús clamp your shoulder, fingers cold as ice. *Venga, corre.** You run. All the rest happens without words. Your feet are tearing dry grass, your heart is lashed like a mare. You trip, you fall. You are now in the United States of America. You are a boy from a Mexican village. You have come into the country on your knees with your head down. You are a man.

Papa, what was it like?

I am his second son, his favorite child, his confidant. After we have polished the De Soto, we sit in the car and talk. I am sixteen years old. I fiddle with the knobs of the radio. He is fifty.

He will never say. He was an orphan there. He had no mother, he remembered none. He lived in a village by the ocean. He wanted books and he had none.

You are lucky, boy.

In the Fifties, Mexican men were contracted to work in America as *braceros*, farm workers. I saw them downtown in Sacramento. I saw men my age drunk in Plaza Park on Sundays, on their backs on the grass. I was a boy at sixteen, but I was an American. At sixteen, I wrote a gossip column, "The Watchful Eye," for my school paper.

Or they would come into town on Monday nights for the wrestling matches or on Tuesdays for boxing. They worked over in Yolo County. They were men without women. They were Mexicans without Mexico.

---

* Go, run.

On Saturdays, they came into town to the Western Union office where they sent money—money turned into humming wire and then turned back into money—all the way down into Mexico. They were husbands, fathers, sons. They kept themselves poor for Mexico.

Much that I would come to think, the best I would think about male Mexico, came as much from those chaste, lonely men as from my own father who made false teeth and who—after thirty years in America—owned a yellow stucco house on the east side of town.

The male is responsible. The male is serious. A man remembers.

Fidel, the janitor at church, lived over the garage at the rectory. Fidel spoke Spanish and was Mexican. He had a wife down there, people said; some said he had grown children. But too many years had passed and he didn't go back. Fidel had to do for himself. Fidel had a clean piece of linoleum on the floor, he had an iron bed, he had a table and a chair. He had a coffeepot and a frying pan and a knife and a fork and a spoon, I guess. And everything else Fidel sent back to Mexico. Sometimes, on summer nights, I would see his head through the bars of the little window over the garage at the rectory.

The migration of Mexico is not only international, south to north. The epic migration of Mexico, and throughout Latin America, is from the village to the city. And throughout Latin America, the city has ripened, swollen with the century. Lima, Caracas, Mexico City. So the journey to Los Angeles is much more than a journey from Spanish to English. It is the journey from *tú*—the familiar, the erotic, the intimate pronoun—to the repellent *usted* of strangers' eyes.

—Richard Rodriguez

Instead of stating a thesis directly, this author describes people and places and circumstances through a series of sketches that create a dominant impression. Can you sum up the dominant impression here in your own words?

Guidelines for Description

Whether paragraphs or essays, all descriptions are developed according to these guidelines:

1.   *Although some descriptions have no topic (or thesis) statement, they often begin with some type of orienting statement.* Objective descriptions in particular rarely call for a standard topic or thesis statement, because the goal of such descriptions is merely to catalog the details of a subject so that readers can visualize it.

2. *The choice of details in a description depends precisely on the writer's purpose and the reader's needs.* Brainstorming yields more details than a writer can use. Select only those that advance your meaning. Use objective details to provide a clear and exact picture and subjective details to convey a dominant impression.

3. *All details are at a level that is concrete and specific enough to convey an unmistakable picture.* Most often description works best at the lowest levels of abstraction and generality.

Vague	Exact
at high speed	80 miles an hour
a tiny office	an 8-by-12-foot office
some workers	the accounting staff
a high salary	$50,000 per year
impressive gas mileage	40 mpg, city; 50, highway

4. *The details are ordered in a clear sequence.* Descriptions generally follow a spatial or general-to-specific order—whichever parallels the angle of vision readers would have if viewing the item. Or the details are arranged according to the dominant impression desired.

Application 10–1

PARAGRAPH WARM-UP: OBJECTIVE DESCRIPTION

Assume that a close friend has been missing for two days. The police have been called in. Because you know this person well, the police have asked you for a written description. Write an *objective description* that would help the police identify this person. To create a clear picture, stick to details any observer could recognize. If possible, include one or more *unique* identifying features (scar, mannerisms, and so on). Leave out personal comments, and give only objective details. Refer to "Guidelines for Developing a Description," above. Use the paragraph on page 136 as a model.

Application 10–2

PARAGRAPH WARM-UP: SUBJECTIVE DESCRIPTION

Assume that your college newspaper runs a weekly column titled "Memorable Characters." You have been asked to submit a brief sketch of a person you find striking in some way. Create a word portrait of this person in one paragraph. Your description should focus on a dominant impression, blending objective details and subjective commentary. Be sure to focus on personal characteristics that support your dominant impression. Develop your description according to the guidelines above.

Application 10–3

ESSAY PRACTICE

Read this selection and answer the questions that follow it.

Cruelty at Tinker Creek

[1]A couple of summers ago I was walking along the edge of the island to see what I could see in the water, and mainly to scare frogs. Frogs have an inelegant way of taking off from invisible positions on the bank just ahead of your feet, in dire panic, emitting a froggy "Yike!" and splashing into the water. Incredibly, this amused me, and incredibly, it amuses me still. As I walked along the grassy edge of the island, I got better and better at seeing frogs both in and out of the water. I learned to recognize, slowing down, the difference in texture of the light reflecting from mudbank, water, grass, or frog. Frogs were flying all around me. At the end of the island I noticed a small green frog. He was exactly half in and half out of the water, looking like a schematic diagram of an amphibian, and he didn't jump.

[2]He didn't jump; I crept closer. At last I knelt on the island's winter-killed grass, lost, dumbstruck, staring at the frog in the creek just four feet away. He was a very small frog with wide, dull eyes. And just as I looked at him, he slowly crumpled and began to sag. The spirit vanished from his eyes as if snuffed. His skin emptied and drooped; his very skull seemed to collapse and settle like a kicked tent. He was shrinking before my eyes like a deflating football. I watched the taut, glistening skin on his shoulders ruck, and rumple, and fall. Soon, part of his skin, formless as a pricked balloon, lay in floating folds like bright scum on top of the water; it was a monstrous and terrifying thing. I gaped bewildered, appalled. An oval shadow hung in the water behind the drained frog; then the shadow glided away. The frog skin bag started to sink.

[3]I had read about the giant water bug, but never seen one. "Giant water bug" is really the name of the creature, which is an enormous, heavy-bodied brown beetle. It eats insects, tadpoles, fish, and frogs. Its grasping forelegs are mighty and hooked inward. It seizes a victim with these legs, hugs it tight, and paralyzes it with enzymes injected during a vicious bite. That one bite is the only bite it ever takes.

Through the puncture shoot the poisons that dissolve the victim's muscles and bones and organs—all but the skin—and through it the giant water bug sucks out the victim's body, reduced to a juice. This event is quite common in warm fresh water. The frog I saw was being sucked by a giant water bug. I had been kneeling on the island grass; when the unrecognizable flap of frog skin settled on the creek bottom, swaying, I stood up and brushed the knees of my pants. I couldn't catch my breath.

⁴Of course, many carnivorous animals devour their prey alive. The usual method seems to be to subdue the victim by drowning it or grasping it so it can't flee, then eating it whole or in a series of bloody bites. Frogs eat everything whole, stuffing prey into their mouths with their thumbs. People have seen frogs with their wide jaws so full of live dragonflies they couldn't close them. Ants don't even have to catch their prey: in the spring they swarm over newly hatched, featherless birds in the nest and eat them tiny bite by bite.

—Annie Dillard

Questions About Content

1. What is the implied thesis in this description? State it in your own words.

2. List five objective and five subjective details in the essay.

3. What is the dominant impression created by this description?

4. Name three features that make this essay interesting.

Questions About Organization

1. Is the introductory paragraph adequately developed? Explain.

2. Which paragraph has the most subjective description? Why are the other paragraphs more objective?

3. How does the writer order her details in the first two paragraphs? Trace the movement of the description.

4. Should the writer have explained about the beetle before describing the event? Why or why not?

5. Does each paragraph begin with an adequate orienting sentence? In your own words, state the main point of each paragraph.

6. Does the conclusion create a sense of completeness? Does it relate back to the introduction? Explain how it reinforces the implied thesis.

7. How does each paragraph deliver on the promise implied in its orienting sentence? Be specific.

8. What are four major devices that lend coherence to this selection? Give an example of each.

Questions About Style

1. Identify one sentence that relies on subordination for combining related thoughts. How does this structure reinforce the meaning of the sentence?

2. Identify one sentence that relies on coordination for combining related thoughts. How does this structure reinforce the meaning of that sentence?

3. Which seems the most emphatic short sentence in the selection?

4. What is the writer's attitude toward what she witnessed? How do you know? What are the signals?

5. Describe the tone that emerges from this essay. What kind of person does the author seem to be? How do you know?

RESPONDING TO YOUR READING

Explore your reactions to "To the Border" (pages 226–227) by using the questions on page 91. Then respond with an essay of your own.

Perhaps you or someone you know has been forced to abandon something comfortably familiar (a place, a lifestyle, a relationship, a culture) for something unfamiliar or alien. Or perhaps you can describe a decision that involved great promise, risk, and personal cost. As you reread the Rodriguez essay, think of all the things you would like to say in reply, and then settle on the main thing you want to say.

Or perhaps you were struck more profoundly by something in Annie Dillard's essay (pages 229–230). If so, you might respond to that one instead.

OPTIONS FOR ESSAY WRITING

1. In an essay for your classmates, describe a memorable scene— something that left a deep impression. Like Annie Dillard, blend objective and subjective details to convey a dominant impression. For precision and vividness, make your details specific and concrete.

2.   In an essay for your classmates, describe a place that is special. Give a clear picture of both the place and your feelings about it. Be sure your audience comes to understand why the place is special.

3.   Do you have a hero or villain? Describe this person in an essay for your classmates. Provide enough descriptive details for your audience to understand why you admire or despise this person. Focus on a dominant impression and on at least *three* characteristics that support your impression. To provide the intimate details that will make your description vivid, choose someone about whom you know a good deal.

4.   Describe for your classmates an automobile. It can be a luxuriously appointed or high-performance dream car or the basic transportation you drive to school. Give your audience the feel of the car, its "personality." Make them feel as if they are riding in it with you.

5.   Describe what you like or dislike about your neighborhood.

6.   Describe yourself to someone who doesn't know you. Choose at least three features that give the most accurate picture of who you are.

7.   Describe a place that frightens you. Allow readers to share your fright.

8.   What do you expect from your old age? Picture yourself as a senior citizen, and describe a day in your life.

11

Developing a Narrative

Narration That Merely Reports • **Narration That Makes a Point**
• **Guidelines for Narration** • **Applications**

Like description, narration creates a word picture. But description tells about things as they *appear* (in space), whereas narration tells about events as they *happen* (in time). Of course, narration relies on descriptive details to make the story vivid. But the main function of narration is to enable readers to follow events by answering these questions:

What happened?

Who was involved?

When did it happen?

Where did it happen?

Why did it happen?

Narration sometimes answers these questions as well:

What were your impressions of it?

How did it make you feel?

Narration can play a number of roles: in a novel or fictional story, it stimulates our imagination and entertains us; in a newspaper story, it reports newsworthy events objectively; in essays, it makes a definite point. Our interest here, however, is not in stories for entertainment; instead, we will discuss narration designed merely to report and narration designed to make a point.

Narration That Merely Reports

Some narratives simply give a picture of what happened, without stating—or even implying—any particular viewpoint. Some newspaper stories or courtroom testimonies offer only the bare facts. Because its goal is simply to re-create the events, this objective reporting does not answer these questions:

> What were your impressions of it?
>
> How did it make you feel?

In this paragraph the writer's job is simply to describe the events without inserting personal impressions:

The climactic scene (1)

A related detail (2)

Background (3–9)

Conclusion (10–11)

[1]Two [suspects] hobbled into Federal Court in Brooklyn on crutches yesterday, each with a leg missing and each charged with smuggling cocaine and marijuana stored in the hollowed-out parts of their confiscated artificial limbs. [2]A third suspect, a . . . woman, was also accused of taking part in the smuggling of $1 million worth of cocaine from Bogota to Kennedy International Airport. [3]Acting on confidential information, customs agents took the three into custody Monday night. [4]The agents took one of the suspects, William Ochoa, 25 years old, to St. Vincent's Hospital in Manhattan, where physicians removed his plastic leg. [5]Inside, they said, they found one kilo (2.2 pounds) of cocaine wrapped in plastic bags. [6]The suspect told them he had lost his leg during a guerilla uprising in Colombia two years ago. [7]Agents said they found six ounces of marijuana in the artificial right limb worn by Jaime Zapata-Reyes, another suspect. [8]The woman, identified as Mrs. Lenore Jaramillo, 34, was allegedly found to be wearing three girdles, each concealing quantities of plastic-wrapped cocaine totaling one kilo. [9]Agents reported that each suspect had more than $400 and return tickets to Bogota. [10]United States Magistrate Vincent A. Catoggio held each in $100,000 bail.

[11]Expressing concern over the missing artificial limbs, which had been described as damaged, he directed that customs agents return them in good condition. . . .

—The New York Times

This paragraph implies no main point—no insertion of the writer's feelings or impressions. Because the focus is on a bizarre smuggling practice, we simply are given the details that clarify the opening (and climatic) scene of smugglers hobbling into court. Explanations of how the smugglers were caught are left out, because they are not relevant to this story.

To attract readers' interest, the writer juggles the sequence of events. The first two sentences place us at the story's climax. Then the background details follow strict chronological order so that we can keep track of events leading to the courtroom scene. To help us follow the story, the author consistently uses past tense and third-person point of view.

Narrative reports serve many purposes. In college, you might report on experiments or investigations in chemistry, biology, or psychology. Or you might retrace the events leading up to the American Revolution or the 1929 stock market crash. In the workplace, you might report on the events that led up to an accident on the assembly line. Or you might write daily accounts of your crew's progress on a construction project. Whenever readers need to understand *what happened,* narrative reporting is essential.

Narration That Makes a Point

Many of your narratives will be designed to make or support some definite viewpoint or thesis. When you recount last night's date, your purpose usually is to explain some viewpoint: that some people can be fickle, that first dates can be disastrous, or the like. Narratives of this type focus on some aspect of the subject that deserves our attention. In this story of a scene witnessed from a commuter train, our attention is focused on how urban dwellers can become desensitized to tragedy.

Orienting sentence

[1]One afternoon in late August, as the summer's sun streamed into the car and made little jumping shadows on the windows, I sat gazing out at the tenement-dwellers, who were themselves looking out of their windows from the gray crumbling buildings along the tracks of upper Manhattan. [2]As we crossed into the Bronx, the

train unexpectedly slowed down for a few miles. [3]Suddenly from out of my window I saw a large crowd near the tracks, held back by two policemen. [4]Then, on the other side, from my window, I saw a sight I would never be able to forget: a little boy almost severed in halves, lying at an incredible angle near the track. [5]The ground was covered with blood, and the boy's eyes were opened wide, strained and disbelieving in his sudden oblivion. [6]A policeman stood next to him, his arms folded, staring straight at the windows of our train. [7]In the orange glow of late afternoon, the policeman, the crowd, the corpse of the boy were for a brief moment immobile, motionless, a small tableau to violence and death in the city. [8]Behind me, in the next row of seats, was a game of bridge. [9]I heard one of the four men say as he looked out at the sight, "God, that's horrible." [10]Another said in a whisper, "Terrible, terrible." [11]There was a momentary silence, punctuated only by the clicking of the wheels on the track. [12]Then, after a pause, I heard the first man say: "Two hearts."

—Willie Morris

In this narrative, the author filters the events through his own feelings. Although the awful facts of this story are colored only slightly by the author's own impressions (sentences 4, 5, and 7), the point implied is all too clear. Sometimes, narration can be the best form of *showing*.

We are kept on track in the paragraph by the author's consistent use of past tense and first-person point of view (the author tells of *his* experience). An alternative point of view for narration is the third person (telling of someone else's experience). Whichever point of view you select, be consistent; avoid shifting from one to another.

Narratives also can serve a persuasive purpose, by causing readers to change their attitudes or take some sort of action. You might tell about a boating accident as a way of encouraging voters' support for tougher boating laws. On the job, you might recount the details of a disruptive conflict among employees as a way of persuading your employer to finance stress-management workshops. By telling the story, you can help readers see things your way.

This next narrative helps persuade us not to smoke by telling what it's like for a young person to confront the possibility of early death.

I entered college at 17 and began taking classes with some 25- and 30-year-old students. Such an age difference made me feel much luckier than these older people. What were they doing in a freshman class, anyway? Compared to them, I had unlimited time to succeed— or so I thought. Soon after my eighteenth birthday, the horrid piece of lung tissue I coughed into the sink gave a whole new meaning to my notion of "youth." Five years of inhaling hot smoke, carbon monoxide, nicotine, and tobacco pesticides finally had produced enough coughing and sickness to terrify me. "Oh, my god, I'm going to die young; I'm going to die before all those 30-year-olds." For years, I had heard my mother tell me that I was committing suicide on the installment plan. Now I seemed to be running out of installments.

—Chris Adey

By letting the story make the point, Chris's narrative seems far more persuasive than the usual sermons that begin with something like, "Smoking is bad for you."

The viewpoint in a narrative might be expressed as a topic or thesis statement at the beginning or end of the story. Or, as in the two narratives above, the main point might not be stated at all, but only implied by the story. Many stories from the Bible make a definite point without ever stating it directly. But even when its point is saved for last or just implied, the story almost always opens with some statement that orients readers to the events.

The following narrative, "Back At the Ranch," recalls how a dreadful moment during the writer's adolescence changed his own perception of "manhood."

Back At the Ranch

A young boy molts. Tender skin falls off, or gets scraped off, and is replaced by a tougher, more permanent crust. The transition happens in moments, in events. All of a sudden, something is gone and something else is in its place. I made a change like that standing in the back of a pick-up truck when I was 15.

It was 1967 and I had a summer job at a camp in Wyoming. It was beautiful there, high-pasture country with a postcard view of the Tetons. As an apprentice counselor I straddled the worlds of boys and men, breathing the high air, watching over kids, hanging out with cowboys. The cowboys wrangled the horses for the camp and were mostly an itinerant group, living in summer cabins below the barn, and they tolerated my loitering down there. I hitched up my jeans just like them, braided my lasso like them, smoked and cursed and slouched like them.

On the day it happened, I was standing with a group of cowboys by the ranch office. We heard the sound of a big engine coming in the long driveway, and after a while a red Corvette Sting Ray convertible, of all things, motored up in front of us. Conversation stopped. In the driver's seat was a hippie. His hair fell straight down his back and a bandanna was tied around his head. His style may have been standard for somewhere, but not for Jackson, Wyo.

The guy was decked out with beads and earrings and dressed in fantastic colors, and next to him his girlfriend, just as exotic, with perfect blond hair, looked up at us over little square glasses with a distracted, angelic expression. All in a red Corvette.

I was fascinated, mesmerized. I looked around me with a big grin and realized that I was alone in this feeling. The cowboys all had hard stares, cold eyes. I adjusted, a traitor to myself, and blanked out my expression in kind.

The hippie opened up a big smile, and said: "I went to camp here when I was a kid . . . came by to say hi. Is Weenie around?"

In that moment, Weenie, the owner of the place, having heard the throb of the engine, appeared in the ranch office door and walked toward us with a bowlegged stride, his big belt buckle coming first. He walked right up to the driver and looked down on him.

"Get out." Weenie didn't say hi. "Get out of here now."

"What? Wait a minute. I came to say hi. I went to camp here. I just came to say hi."

"Get the hell off this ranch. *Now.*" And staring at the hippie, Weenie kicked some dust up on the side of the Corvette.

"What's wrong with you, man?"

"You're what's wrong with me, son."

I noticed the cowboys were nodding. I nodded. Weenie's right. The guy should leave. He doesn't belong here.

"But you sent me a Christmas card!" By this time, the hippie had choked up a little. "I don't believe it. You sent me a goddamn Christmas card!"

The group of us closed in a little around the car. We-don't-like-that-kind-of-talk-from-a-hippie was the feeling I was getting. Thumbs came out of belt-loops. Jaws began to work.

"Looks like the little girlie's cryin'," said one of the cowboys, a tough one named Hondu. He spoke with his lips turned down on one side as if he was mouthing a cigarette. "Maybe so," said another, with mock consideration.

The notion rested in the air peacefully for a moment, then, in a sudden whipping motion, Hondu's jackknife was out, open and raised. With his other hand, he reached down and grabbed a fat bunch of the hippie's hair and pulled it toward him. Smiling grimly, he hacked it off and held it up for us to see.

During this, I looked down at the hippie's face, which was lifted up and sideways in such a way that he was looking right at me. Involuntarily, my head tilted just like his and we froze like that for a second.

"There now, that's better, ain't it?" asked Hondu.

The hippie, stunned, turned to his girlfriend, whose eyes and mouth had been wide open as long as he had been sitting there. Then he turned back to us, his face contorted, helpless. And then he went wild. He threw open his door and tried to jump up from the seat, but forgot that his seat belt was fastened and it held him in place. He struggled against it, screaming, swinging his arms like a bar fighter trying to shrug off his buddies restraining him. It was funny. Like a cartoon.

I looked around. We were all laughing. Our group closed up a little more, and came toward the car. The air bristled. He was the one who started the trouble. Well, he would get what he was looking for, all right.

The hippie stopped struggling, threw the Vette into gear, and fishtailed in the dust. We all jumped out of the way, but the open door of the car bumped into Weenie's favorite dog, a Rhodesian Ridgeback, an inside-out-looking animal that gave a wild yelp and ran straight into a willow thicket. We could hear his yips over the sound of the big engine as the hippie gunned it and took off.

That settled it. The hippie hit the dog.

Without hesitation, we jumped into one of the trucks. Rifles were drawn from the rack in the cab. Other weapons were thrown up into the bed of the pickup. I was standing there and caught one.

We took off, and because the rough road slowed down the Corvette, we were gaining. I was filled with a terrible, frightening righteousness. I was holding a rifle, chasing a man and a woman with a rifle in my hand. I looked around at my partners in the truck, and the air came out of me. We meant harm. We didn't care. I wondered who I was exactly. I needed to know. And in that moment, it happened: I switched sides and never said a word about it.

We hit the asphalt road and floored it, but we couldn't catch the Corvette. No way. The smoke from its exhaust settled around us like fog in the valley.

Still, 23 years later, I can see the two of us clearly, chosen by the same moment. Memory cuts back and forth between our faces. The wind pulls tears from the hippie's eyes; his long hair waves behind him in his fiery convertible rocketing down Route 191 under the Tetons. I with my short hair stand in the back of a pickup truck watching after him, chasing after him, following, facing the same wind.

—Jay Allison

What is the implied thesis in this essay? Can you sum up the thesis in your own words?

Sometimes a narrative can be a good way of recording our confusion or ambivalence about something. Some experiences or events might leave us with all kinds of conflicting feelings that are impossible to sort out. At times such as these, we simply *don't* know how we feel about what has happened. But even though we can't distill one dominant impression from the experience, we know the story deserves telling. The next narrative, "A Funeral in Manitoba," records several impressions simultaneously; in the events she witnesses, the author sees all at once comedy, sadness, grotesque preoccupation with funeral rituals, but also a shared sense of faith and respect.

A Funeral in Manitoba

When Nick Wiebe, the undertaker, arrives with the body, the lobby is jammed and a small respectful crowd is gathered in the yard. Pulling the casket on a dolly, Nick elbows his way through the mob and clears a path to the main aisle; the crowd reforms like an honor guard on either side. Word of the deceased's arrival crackles through the congregation; heads turn and crane to catch a glimpse. The dead man's relatives march down the aisle in a procession and take their seats at the front; heads turn slowly to follow them. Nick trundles the casket down the aisle, places it in the center of a circle of observers, and opens it.

The funeral is very cheerful. It's an old-fashioned service, mostly in German. The church is stark and bare and the hymns are droned unaccompanied. The young minister wears a black suit and a black silk shirt with no collar. He is flanked by the church deacons who, seated all in a row like six ravens, lead the singing. The sermon is simple and quietly spoken. The minister describes the dead man floating in an azure sky surrounded by a joyful host of departed friends and relatives. He speaks with such calm reassurance and such conviction that on this sunny summer afternoon he almost compels belief in a radiant eternal life. Death is the beginning, not the end; the funeral is a celebration. The crux of the service is the obituary. Read by the minister, it is a lengthy, detailed account of the dead man's accomplishments, his baptism and marriage, the highlights to his career, the strengths of his character, his love for his family and for God, and his last thoughts before he died; it includes a history of his last illness, minutely chronicling the time, nature, and extent of all his operations as the agony of the cancer took hold. Crude and direct, the obituary is very powerful; for a few moments it gives the dead man mythic stature. Lying up there in his coffin, he is the focus of all eyes and his character is the subject of all thoughts; the church becomes a theatre for the tiny human drama of which he is the star.

The service is very long, over an hour. The air in the church becomes foetid, and people begin to fan themselves with their hymn books, waving them like so many small white wings. At the end everyone files out past the open coffin; the line winds round and round the church and reaches down into the basement where people have been listening on the intercom. The corpse looks very yellow and waxy. Turning back towards the congregation, I can see that people's glistening faces are beatific; it's been a good service.

Funerals are Winkler's most popular mass entertainment. They are advertised all over southern Manitoba on radio CFAM, a Mennonite station partly owned by the Kroekers which specializes in religious broadcasts, classical music, and commercials. Hundreds of people come 30 and 40 miles to attend the funeral of someone they didn't know. Most funerals are spectaculars requiring a cast of thousands, and the lunch of coffee and buns served in the basement later parallels the parable of the loaves and the fishes. Winkler shuts up tight during a funeral; an eerie silence descends on the town and the streets are deserted. The only clue to everyone's whereabouts is the mass of cars around the church. A particularly grotesque suicide or a gruesome accident will draw an especially big crowd.

"I had a young couple once who were killed in a car accident shortly after they were married," says Nick Wiebe. "We laid her out in her wedding dress. It was very sad. I figure between 4,000 and 5,000 people went through the funeral home on the weekend, just to look. They made a complete shambles of the place."

An especially long and impressive funeral is a symbol of community status. "I remember when a minister died," smiles Nick. "The funeral lasted three hours. Thirteen ministers spoke. They went on so long it got dark. We ran into a blizzard on our way to the cemetery and had to turn back. On Sunday we had another service at the little country church by the cemetery. That service lasted three hours. It got so dark by the time we buried him we had to turn on the lights of the hearse to light the grave."

—Heather Robertson

Although it never is stated, Robertson's implied viewpoint might be summed up like this: *This kind of ritual is in one way amusing, but in another way touching as well.* On the one hand, we get the impression of a carnival atmosphere, of funerals as "spectaculars requiring a cast of thousands." But beyond its appeal as "mass entertainment," the ritual suggests a deeper meaning: "Crude and direct, the obituary is very powerful; for a few moments it gives the dead man mythic stature." The narrator invites us to discover the significance of the event for ourselves. Can you find other phrases that reveal the narrator's mixed feelings of condescension and respect and empathy?

Guidelines for Narration

As paragraphs or essays, all narratives are developed according to these guidelines:

1. *Whether stated or implied, the viewpoint (or main point) is clearly conveyed by the narrative details.* When the main point is stated, the topic or thesis statement is often at the end of the narrative. (A narrative that simply reports, of course, has no main point.) The narrative always begins with a clear orienting statement that places readers at the center of the action. By helping us analyze and evaluate an experience, complex narratives such as "Back At the Ranch" or "A Funeral in Manitoba" make some point about a larger issue.

2. *The choice of details in a narrative depends specifically on the writer's purpose and the reader's needs.* Because your brainstorming is likely to yield more details than you can use, select only those that directly advance your meaning. Focus on the important details, but don't leave out the lesser details that hold the story together. Whenever appropriate, filter the facts through your own impressions.

3. *All details are at a level that is concrete and specific enough to convey a clear picture of what happened.* Narration is most effective at the lowest levels of abstraction and generality. Whenever you can, show people talking.

4. *The details are ordered in a clear sequence.* Chronological ordering often works best in a narrative, because it enables readers to follow the events as they occurred. But for special emphasis, the sequence sometimes can be revised (as in the paragraph from Willie Morris, pages 235–236).

5. *The coherence of a narrative depends mostly on the writer's use of consistent tense and point of view and on the use of transitions as time and sequence markers.* Instead of past tense, you might use present tense, to create a greater sense of immediacy, making readers feel like actual participants (as in "A Funeral in Manitoba"). Also, decide whether you are writing from the point of view of a spectator (as in "A Funeral in Manitoba") or a participant (as in "For My Indian Daughter," pages 243–246), and stick to that one point of view. Review pages 142–144 for use of transitions.

Application 11–1

PARAGRAPH WARM-UPS: NARRATION THAT SIMPLY REPORTS

1. Think of an event you've witnessed that would interest your classmates. Using the paragraph on page 234 as a model, write an

objective narrative reporting the story. Begin with an orienting sentence that places readers at the center of the action.

2. Assume that you have recently witnessed an event or accident in which someone has been accused of an offense. Because you are an objective witness, the authorities have asked you to write a short report, telling *exactly* what you saw. Your report will be used as evidence. Tell what happened without injecting personal impressions or interpretations.

Application 11–2

PARAGRAPH WARM-UPS: NARRATION THAT MAKES A POINT

1. Using George Orwell's paragraph on page 138 as a model, write a narrative about something you did that you instantly regretted. Allow your readers to *see* the event and to *share* your immediate feelings. If you decide not to state your point directly, be sure it is implied by the details of the story.

2. Tell about a recent experience or incident you witnessed that left a strong impression on you. Write for your classmates, and be sure to include the facts of the incident as well as your emotional reaction to it. In other words, give your audience enough details so that they will understand your reaction. Use Willie Morris's or Chris Adey's paragraph as a model, letting the details of the story imply your main point.

Application 11–3

In the following narrative, a Native American traces events that led to his own cultural awakening. After reading the essay, answer the questions that follow it.

For My Indian Daughter

My little girl is singing herself to sleep upstairs, her voice mingling with the sounds of the birds outside in the old maple trees. She is two and I am nearly 50, and I am very taken with her. She came along late in my life, unexpected and unbidden, a startling gift.

Today at the beach my chubby-legged, brown-skinned daughter ran laughing into the water as fast as she could. My wife and I laughed watching her, until we heard behind us a low guttural curse and then an unpleasant voice raised in an imitation war whoop.

I turned to see a fat man in a bathing suit, white and soft as a grub, as he covered his mouth and prepared to make the Indian war cry again. He was middle-aged, younger than I, and had three little children lined up next to him, grinning foolishly. My wife suggested we leave the beach, and I agreed.

I knew the man was not unusual in his feelings against Indians. His beach behavior might have been socially unacceptable to more civilized whites, but his basic view of Indians is expressed daily in our small town, frequently on the editorial pages of the county newspaper, as white people speak out against Indian fishing rights and land rights, saying in essence, "Those Indians are taking our fish, our land." It doesn't matter to them that we were here first, that the U.S. Supreme Court has ruled in our favor. It matters to them that we have something they want, and they hate us for it. Backlash is the common explanation of the attacks on Indians, the bumper stickers that say, "Spear an Indian, Save a Fish," but I know better. The hatred of Indians goes back to the beginning when white people came to this country. For me it goes back to my childhood in Harbor Springs, Michigan.

Theft

Harbor Springs is now a summer resort for the very affluent, but a hundred years ago it was the Indian village of my Ottawa ancestors. My grandmother, Anna Showanessy, and other Indians like her, had their land there taken by treaty, by fraud, by violence, by theft. They remembered how whites had burned down the village at Burt Lake in 1900 and pushed the Indians out. These were the stories in my family.

When I was a boy my mother told me to walk down the alleys in Harbor Springs and not to wear my orange football sweater out of the house. This way I would not stand out, not be noticed, and not be a target.

I wore my orange sweater anyway and deliberately avoided the alleys. I was the biggest person I knew and wasn't really afraid. But I met my comeuppance when I enlisted in the U.S. Army. One night all the men in my barracks gathered together and, gang-fashion, pulled me into the shower and scrubbed me down with rough brushes used for floors, saying, "We won't have any dirty Indians in our outfit." It is a point of irony that I was cleaner than any of them. Later in Korea I learned how to kill, how to bully, how to hate Koreans. I came out of the war tougher than ever and, strangely, white.

I went to college, got married, lived in La Porte, Indiana, worked as a surveyor and raised three boys. I headed Boy Scout groups, never thinking it odd when the Scouts did imitation Indian dances, imitation Indian lore.

One day when I was 35 or thereabouts I heard about an Indian powwow. My father used to attend them and so with great curiosity and a strange joy at discovering a part of my heritage, I decided the thing to do to get ready for this big event was to have my friend make me a spear in his forge. The steel was fine and blue and iridescent. The feathers on the shaft were bright and proud.

In a dusty state fairground in southern Indiana, I found white people dressed as Indians. I learned they were "hobbyists," that is, it was their hobby and leisure pastime to masquerade as Indians on weekends. I felt ridiculous with my spear, and I left.

It was years before I could tell anyone of the embarrassment of this weekend and see any humor in it. But in a way it was that weekend, for all its silliness, that was my awakening. I realized I didn't know who I was. I didn't have an Indian name. I didn't speak the Indian language. I didn't know the Indian customs. Dimly I remembered the Ottawa word for dog, but it was a baby word, *kahgee*, not the full word, *muhkahgee*, which I was later to learn. Even more hazily I remembered a naming ceremony (my own). I remembered legs dancing around me, dust. Where had that been? Who had I been? "Suwaukquat," my mother told me when I asked, "where the tree begins to grow."

That was 1968, and I was not the only Indian in the country who was feeling the need to remember who he or she was. There were others. They had powwows, real ones, and eventually I found them. Together we researched our past, a search that for me culminated in the Longest Walk, a march on Washington in 1978. Maybe because I now know what it means to be Indian, it surprises me that others don't. Of course there aren't very many of us left. The chances of an average person knowing an average Indian in an average lifetime are pretty slim.

Circle

Still, I was amused one day when my small, four-year-old neighbor looked at me as I was hoeing in my garden and said, "You aren't a real Indian, are you?" Scotty is little, talkative, likable. Finally I said, "I'm a real Indian." He looked at me for a moment and then said, squinting into the sun, "Then where's your horse and feathers?" The child was simply a smaller, whiter version of my own ignorant self years before. We'd both seen too much TV, that's all. He was not to be blamed. And so, in a way the moronic man on the beach today is blameless. We come full circle to realize other people are like ourselves, as discomfiting as that may be sometimes.

As I sit in my old chair on my porch, in a light that is fading so the leaves are barely distinguishable against the sky, I can picture my girl asleep upstairs. I would like to prepare her for what's to come, take her each step of the way saying, there's a place to avoid, here's what I know about this, but much of what's before her she must go through alone. She must pass through pain and joy and solitude and community to discover her own inner self that is unlike any other and come through that passage to the place where she sees all people are one, and in so seeing may live her life in a brighter future.

—Lewis P. Johnson

Questions About Content

1. For whom, besides his daughter, does Johnson appear to be writing?

2. What are Johnson's assumptions about his audience's knowledge and attitudes? Are these assumptions accurate? Why or why not?

3. What does Johnson want his audience to be thinking or feeling after reading this piece?

4. Does the essay achieve its purpose? If so, how?

5. What and where is the thesis? Why does it appear at that point in the essay? Is this placement effective? Explain.

6. Does this essay have credibility (opinions and assertions supported by fair and reasonable assessment of the facts)? Explain and give examples.

7. Does this essay have informative value (new information, fresh insights, unusual perspectives)? Explain and give examples.

8. Does this essay seem complete (enough support to achieve its purpose; details that help us see, feel, understand)? Explain and give examples.

Questions About Organization

1. What opening strategy or combination of strategies is used to create immediate interest?

2. In what sequence are the major events presented? Trace the chronology in a brief outline.

3. Is the chronology effective? Explain.

4. Is the conclusion supported by the facts presented? Explain.

5. What are the major devices that lend coherence to this essay? Give an example of each.

Questions About Style

1. What are at least two outstanding style features of this essay? Explain and give examples.

2. What is the writer's attitude toward his subject? Toward his audience? How do we know? What are the signals?

3. How would you characterize the tone that emerges from this essay? Give examples of word choice and sentence structure that contribute to the tone.

4. Is the tone appropriate for this writer's audience and purpose? Explain.

RESPONDING TO YOUR READING

1. Explore your reactions to "A Funeral in Manitoba" (pages 240–241) by using the questions on page 91. Then respond with your own narrative essay. You might share with readers some ritual or ceremony in your family or community, a ritual that you consider particularly meaningful or meaningless. Or you might want to tell about a ceremony you attended that changed your way of thinking or feeling about something. Or you might tell about an initiation ceremony for some organization.

   Perhaps you will want your narrative to show that the ceremony or ritual has a place in human experience, or is merely silly or destructive. Or perhaps your viewpoint will be less definite, and you will want to show how the event left you feeling confused or ambivalent. You might then let readers discover for themselves the significance of the event.

   Whether you settle on one definite impression about the event ("This is dumb" or "This is important" or some such) or are left struggling with conflicting impressions, be sure your narrative states or clearly implies a viewpoint.

2. Explore your reactions to "For My Indian Daughter" by using the page 91 questions. What are the major issues here? How has this essay affected your thinking about these issues? As you reread the essay, try to think of a story you might be able to tell about your own ethnic or cultural or social background. Ideally your experiences have led to some new awareness or "awakening" on your part. Perhaps you have wrestled with issues of personal identity in relation to your background. Perhaps certain experiences caused you to discover a sense of alienation or a sense of belonging. Perhaps something made you appreciate your background or made you realize you were "different." Perhaps you struggled to meet certain cultural expectations or to overcome a sense of inferiority. Identify your intended audience, and decide what you want readers to be thinking or feeling or doing after reading your essay.

Your narrative should make a definite point—whether stated directly or merely implied. Describe the events and your reactions in enough detail for readers to understand how you arrived at your insight or realization—the larger meaning *beyond* the narrative details. To increase interest, begin with the action, saving the main point for later.

3. "Back At the Ranch" (pages 237–239) proves that an essay about "What I Did Last Summer" can be much more than a tired list of worn-out images and travel clichés—that telling our own story *can* make a difference.

    Explore your reactions to this essay by using the page 91 questions. Then respond with your own narrative about an event that has made a difference in your life. Work to recapture for us the force of the event and its impact on you. Tell us all about what happened, but be sure to let us know what *meaning* the event ultimately had for you.

OPTIONS FOR ESSAY WRITING

1. Assume that you are applying for your first professional job after college. Respond to the following request from the job application:

    Each of us has been confronted by an "impossible situation"—a job that appeared too big to complete, a situation that seemed too awkward to handle, or a problem that felt too complex to deal with. Describe such a situation and how you dealt with it. Your narrative should make a point about the situation, problem solving, or yourself.

2. Use Norman Mailer's essay (page 116) as a model for a narrative/descriptive essay about an unforgettable event.

3. Tell about the most disillusioning experience of your life and how it has affected you.

4. Tell about the event that has caused you the greatest guilt and how you have dealt with that guilt.

12
Explaining Through Examples: Illustration

Examples are among the most powerful tools for explaining what you mean. We can see how examples work by looking at this next example. Assume that you've expressed this viewpoint:

Topic or Thesis Statement   Commercial television is not all bad.

You can anticipate that your readers will respond with questions such as these:

Reader's Questions   What makes you think so?

Can you give me examples I can grasp?

Your readers, in other words, expect definite and specific instances of what they could accept as "good commercial television." Examples give the evidence that enables readers to understand and accept your viewpoint.

Uses and Types of Examples

The backbone of explanation, examples are concrete and specific instances of a writer's main point. The best way to explain what you mean by an "inspiring teacher" is to use one of your professors as an

249

example. You might illustrate this professor's qualities by describing several of her teaching strategies. Or you might give an extended example (say, how she helped you develop confidence). Either way, you have made the abstract notion "inspiring teacher" concrete and thus understandable—you have made your meaning clear. (Notice how the main point in *this* paragraph is clarified by the professor example.)

In your school and workplace writing, you will use examples time and time again. For a psychology course, you might give examples of paranoid behavior among world leaders; for an ecology course, of tree species threatened by acid rain—and so on. In the workplace, you might give examples of how the software developed by your company can be used for medical diagnosis, of how your community can provide a favorable economic climate for new industry, or the like. Whenever readers need evidence to understand or accept an assertion, examples are essential.

Examples do more than clarify meaning. They also make writing more interesting and convincing. Here is a paragraph without examples:

> ¹The irony of the emphasis being placed on careers is that nothing is more valuable for anyone who has had a professional or vocational education than to be able to deal with abstractions or complexities, or to feel comfortable with subtleties of thought or language, or to think sequentially. ²People who have such skills will have a major advantage in just about any career. ³In all these respects, the liberal arts have much to offer. ⁴Just in terms of career preparation, therefore, a student is shortchanging himself or herself by shortcutting the humanities.

The writer of this paragraph fails to persuade us that a liberal arts education is vital, because the paragraph never gets below the highest level of generality—all *telling*, no *showing*. Sentences 2 and 3 provide no information to clarify and support the opening and closing points. Any reader will be left with unanswered questions.

> What do you mean by "abstractions or complexities," "subtleties of thought or language," or "to think sequentially"?
>
> How, exactly, do students "shortchange" themselves by shortcutting the humanities?
>
> Can you show me how a liberal arts education is useful in one's career?

Here is a version of the same paragraph, this time developed with examples (in italics) that answer readers' questions:

Main point (1)

Examples (2–5)

Summary of
examples (6)
Concluding point (7)

¹The irony of the emphasis being placed on careers is that nothing is more valuable for anyone who has had a professional or vocational education than to be able to deal with abstractions or complexities, or to feel comfortable with subtleties of thought or language, or to think sequentially. ²*The doctor* who knows only disease is at a disadvantage alongside the doctor who knows at least as much about people as [he or she] does about pathological organisms. ³*The lawyer* who argues in court from a narrow legal base is no match for the lawyer who can connect legal precedents to historical experience and who employs wide-ranging intellectual resources. ⁴*The business executive* whose competence in general management is bolstered by an artistic ability to deal with people is of prime value to [her] company. ⁵For *the technologist*, the engineering of consent can be just as important as the engineering of moving parts. ⁶In all these respects, the liberal arts have much to offer. ⁷Just in terms of career preparation, therefore, a student is short-changing himself by shortcutting the humanities. *[emphasis added]*

—Norman Cousins

The first version only *tells*, whereas the second *shows* as well. The examples convince us that the author has a valid point.

In developing his paragraph, the author had to answer questions of his own:

How much should I say?

Which details will best clarify my meaning?

How can I be sure that I don't say too much?

By anticipating readers' questions about his main point, the writer was able to put himself in their place. From this perspective he could decide on kinds and number of examples. He chose examples from four major fields (medicine, law, business, and technology), deciding that these four would be enough to get his point across. Additional (or less familiar) examples might only have confused or overwhelmed readers. Seeing things from a reader's perspective is a writer's best guidance for developing any type of message.

In contrast to the humanities paragraph, with its series of brief examples, here is a paragraph developed through an extended example:

Main point (1)
Extended example of
the problem (2–6)

¹This seems to be an era of gratuitous inventions and negative improvements. ²Consider the beer can. ³It was beautiful—as beautiful as the clothespin, as inevitable as the wine bottle, as dignified and reassuring as the fire hydrant. ⁴A tranquil cylinder of delightfully resonant metal, it could be opened in an instant, requiring only the application of a hand gadget freely dispensed by any grocer. ⁵Who can forget the small, symmetrical thrill of these two triangular punctures, the dainty *pfff*, the little crest of suds that foamed eagerly in the exultation of release? ⁶Now we are given, instead, a top beetling with an ugly, shmoo-shaped "tab," which, after fiercely resisting the tugging, bleeding fingers of the thirsty [person], threatens [the] lips with a dangerous and hideous hole.

Extended example of
the solution (8–11)

⁷However, we have discovered a way to thwart Progress, usually so unthwartable. ⁸*Turn the beer can upside down and open the bottom.* ⁹The bottom is still the way the top used to be. ¹⁰True, this operation gives the beer an unsettling jolt, and the sight of a consistently inverted beer can might make people edgy, not to say queasy. ¹¹But the latter difficulty could be eliminated if manufacturers would design cans that looked the same whichever end was up, like playing cards. ¹²What we need is Progress with an escape hatch.

Conclusion (12)

—John Updike

To support his main point about "gratuitous inventions and negative improvements," the author selects the beer can as a familiar example. His purpose, however, is not only to point out the problem but to offer a solution, as well. Thus the two extended examples follow a logical order: from *problem* to *solution*.

A narrative also can serve as an extended example. The sample paragraph on page 139 uses a brief narrative to illustrate the point that television is a potent brainwashing medium.

Good examples have persuasive value; they give readers something to hold on to, a way of understanding even the most surprising or unlikely assertion. This next essay relies on well-chosen examples to justify a new way of looking at old junk—to explain why the writer "saves" things she no longer needs.

My Time Capsule

I always seem to be searching for the right change at checkout counters. The situation is familiar enough: my purchase totals something that involves a few extra pennies, so I open my little brown purse and begin digging for the correct coins. After a few minutes of rummaging through assorted junk, I come up red-faced and empty-handed. But despite my repeated frustrations, I just can't bring myself to clean that purse. I guess I hang on to things I don't need because some of my worst junk holds vivid memories. If someone were to find the purse, they would have a record of my recent life—a kind of time capsule.

For instance, in my purse is an old car key. It belonged to my '73 Chevy, a car that rarely started on cold mornings. I still remember the hours I spent huddled on that frosty front seat, flicking the ignition key on and off, pumping the accelerator, and muttering various pro-fanities every time the engine refused to turn over. Even though I junked the car last year, I still (Who knows why?) keep the key in my so-called change purse.

Whenever I dig for coins, I always encounter the torn half-ticket I've been saving for several years, a ticket to the Broadway musical *The King and I*. The famous Yul Brynner was outstanding in his vin-tage role as the King of Siam. Unfortunately, though, I had to miss a good part of the show simply because I needed to use the bathroom at the same time as half the audience. And much of what I did see was obscured by the green, porcupine hairdo on the guy in front of me. From my view behind Mr. Porcupine, the actors looked like they were in the woods. But because of Yul, I guess, I keep my ticket stub—in my purse, of course.

Somewhere near the key and the ticket sits another artifact: the coat button that came undone earlier this year (the same button I always initially mistake for a coin). The button helps me remember the day I wore not only a turtleneck sweater, but also two scarves for one of last winter's coldest days. Like a fool, I tried tying my coat col-lar around what had now become a 20-inch neck. Naturally, the but-ton popped off, and naturally, it got thrown into my purse.

For weeks I've been buying "micro-rays-of-hope" toward mil-lionaire-hood in the state's lottery game. I can't resist playing my usual six numbers on Wednesdays and Saturdays—even though I always lose. *Not winning* poses no real problem for me, but kissing my obsolete ticket good-bye does. Somehow the act of throwing away even a losing ticket symbolizes admitting defeat. It means the state's racket has caught another sucker. It means my latest tangible flash of financial hope must sit among the soggy potato skins in my garbage pail. So I "temporarily" save my defunct tickets by folding them neatly away in my purse. Every time I see them, I'm reminded of the many times I COULD have become a millionaire.

I'm convinced that the passing of time is directly related to the bloatedness of my change purse because it's forever expanding. In fact, if I opened it right now, I'd find many more memories than the few I've mentioned. I'd see the semi-wrapped sourball I almost ate, until I realized it was lime green. I'd find the three unmated earrings, each with its own life history. I'd rediscover the safety pin that once saved me from awful embarrassment. And my old pen cap (minus the pen), a golf tee, a packet of sugar, and a few expired coupons would all be in there, all with legends of their own.

Even though I'm a slow learner, I know now that metal money belongs not in a purse but in a piggy bank. I'll never have to worry about a coin in my time capsule again—unless, of course, it's my old Susan B. Anthony quarter. But that's another story.

—Gina Ciolfi

Ciolfi challenges our assumptions about the value of junk-filled purses by giving us a catalog of her buried treasures. Her explanation relies on an engaging array of extended examples, followed by a series of brief examples (next-to-last paragraph).

Guidelines for Using Examples

All illustrations, whether paragraphs or essays, are developed according to these guidelines:

1. *All examples serve the writer's purpose and the readers' needs.* An effective example fits the point it is designed to illustrate. Also, the example is familiar and forceful enough for readers to recognize and remember.

2. *The example is always more specific and concrete than the point it illustrates.* Most vivid examples are at the lowest level of generality and abstraction.

3. *Examples in a series are arranged in an accessible order.* If your illustration is a narrative or some historical catalog, the examples are ordered chronologically. Otherwise, a "least-to-most" (least-to-most-dramatic or important or useful, and so on) order works well. Placing the most striking example last ensures greatest effect.

4. *Effective writers know "how much is enough."* Overexplaining is a good way to insult a reader's intelligence.

Application 12–1

PARAGRAPH WARM-UP: EXPLAINING THROUGH ILLUSTRATION

Assume your campus newspaper is inviting contributions for a new section called "Insights," a weekly collection of one-paragraph essays by students. This new section has two goals:

1.   to provide a forum for fresh points of view

2.   to raise readers' consciousness, helping them think more incisively about the world

Each paragraph in this section should be designed to share a specific insight the writer has gained by close observation of campus life, American values, habits, or the like. Using the paragraph by Cousins or Updike as a model, write such a paragraph for the newspaper.

Application 12–2

ESSAY PRACTICE

The following essay appeared in *Newsweek* magazine. Read this essay, and answer the questions that follow it. Then select one of the essay assignments.

A Case of "Severe Bias"

¹This is who I am not. I am not a crack addict. I am not a welfare mother. I am not illiterate. I am not a prostitute. I have never been in jail. My children are not in gangs. My husband doesn't beat me. My home is not a tenement. None of these things defines who I am, nor do they describe the other black people I've known and worked with and loved and befriended over these 40 years of my life.

²Nor does it describe most of black America, period.

³Yet in the eyes of the American news media, this is what black America is: poor, criminal, addicted and dysfunctional. Indeed, media coverage of black America is so one-sided, so imbalanced that the most victimized and hurting segment of the black community—a small segment, at best—is presented not as the exception but as the norm. It is an insidious practice, all the uglier for its blatancy.

⁴In recent months, oftentimes in this very magazine, I have observed a steady offering of media reports on crack babies, gang warfare, violent youth, poverty and homelessness—and in most cases, the people featured in the photos and stories were black. At the same time, articles that discuss other aspects of American life—from home buying to medicine to technology to nutrition—rarely, if ever, show blacks playing a positive role, or for that matter, any role at all.

⁵Day after day, week after week, this message—that black America is dysfunctional and unwhole—gets transmitted across the American landscape. Sadly, as a result, America never learns the truth about what is actually a wonderful, vibrant, creative community of people.

⁶Most black Americans are *not* poor. Most black teenagers are

not crack addicts. Most black mothers are *not* on welfare. Indeed, in sheer numbers, more *white* Americans are poor and on welfare than are black. Yet one never would deduce that by watching television or reading American newspapers and magazines.

[7]Why does the American media insist on playing this myopic, inaccurate picture game? In this game, white America is always whole and lovely and healthy while black America is usually sick and pathetic and deficient. Rarely, indeed, is black America ever depicted in the media as functional and self-sufficient. The free press, indeed, as the main interpreter of American culture and American experience, holds the mirror on American reality—so much so that what the media says *is*, even if it's not that way at all. The media is guilty of a severe bias and the problem screams out for correction. It is worse than simply lazy journalism, which is bad enough; it is inaccurate journalism.

[8]For black Americans like myself, this isn't just an issue of vanity—of wanting to be seen in a good light. Nor is it a matter of closing one's eyes to the very real problems of the urban underclass—which undeniably is disproportionately black. To be sure, problems besetting the black underclass deserve the utmost attention of the media, as well as the understanding and concern of the rest of American society.

[9]But if their problems consistently are presented as the *only* reality for blacks, any other experience known to the black community ceases to have validity, or to be real. In this scenario, millions of blacks are relegated to a sort of twilight zone, where who we are and what we are isn't based on fact but on image and perception. That's what it feels like to be a black American whose lifestyle is outside of the aberrant behavior that the media presents as the norm.

[10]For many of us, life is a curious series of encounters with white people who want to know why we are "different" from other blacks—when, in fact, most of us are only "different" from the now common negative images of black life. So pervasive are these images that they aren't just perceived as the norm; they're *accepted* as the norm.

[11]I am reminded, for example, of the controversial Spike Lee film, "Do the Right Thing," and the criticism by some movie reviewers that the film's ghetto neighborhood isn't populated by addicts and drug pushers—and thus is not a true depiction.

[12]In fact, millions of black Americans live in neighborhoods where the most common sights are children playing and couples walking their dogs. In my own inner-city neighborhood in Denver—an area that the local press consistently describes as "gang territory"—I have yet to see a recognizable "gang" member or any "gang" activity (drug dealing or drive-by shootings), nor have I been the victim of "gang violence."

[13]Yet to students of American culture—in the case of Spike Lee's film, the movie reviewers—a black, inner-city neighborhood can only be one thing to be real: drug-infested and dysfunctioning. Is this my ego talking? In part, yes. For the millions of black people like myself—ordinary, hard-working, law-abiding, tax-paying Americans—the media's blindness to the fact that we even exist, let alone to our contributions to American society, is a bitter cup to drink. And as self-reliant as most black Americans are—because we've had to be self-reliant—even the strongest among us still crave affirmation.

[14]I want that. I want it for my children. I want it for all the beautiful, healthy, funny, smart black Americans I have known and loved over the years.

[15]And I want it for the rest of America, too.

[16]I want America to know us—all of us—for who we really are. To see us in all our complexity, our subtleness, our artfulness, our enterprise, our specialness, our loveliness, our American-ness. That is the real portrait of black America—that we're strong people, surviving people, capable people. That may be the best-kept secret in America. If so, it's time to let the truth be known.

—Patricia Raybon

Questions About Content

1. Where is the thesis? Why does it come at that point in the essay? Is this an effective placement of the thesis? Explain.

2. Is this essay convincing? Does it adequately support the thesis? Explain.

3. Identify one paragraph developed through an extended example and one through a series of brief examples.

4. Should the examples be more specific? Why, or why not?

Questions About Organization

1. Is Raybon's opening effective? Explain.

2. Are the two single-sentence paragraphs appropriate? Explain.

3. Is this essay organized to provide the best emphasis? Explain.

Questions About Style

1. Name an outstanding style feature of this essay. Explain, and give examples.

2. How would you characterize the tone of this essay? Is it appropriate for the audience and purpose? Explain, and give examples.

RESPONDING TO YOUR READING

1. Explore your reactions to "My Time Capsule" (pages 252–254) by using the questions on page 91. Then respond with an essay of your own, relying on examples to support your viewpoint.

    You might show readers the worth you perceive in things that seem unimportant to most people. Maybe you keep some childhood toys, or clothes that no longer fit, or "junk" that holds special meaning for you only.

    Or you might challenge readers' assumptions by asserting a surprising or unorthodox viewpoint: that some "natural" foods can be hazardous, that television game shows can be truly educational, that "growing up" is something to be dreaded, that exercise can be bad for health, or that so-called advances in medical science or electronics make us worse off.

    Or maybe you want to talk about examples of things that make you angry or sad or happy or frightened, or things too many of us take for granted. Whatever your topic, be sure your examples illustrate and explain a definite viewpoint.

2. Explore your reactions to "A Case of Severe Bias" by using the questions on page 91. Then respond with an essay of your own, using powerful examples to make your point.

    Perhaps someone has misjudged or stereotyped you or a group to which you belong. If so, set the record straight in a forceful essay to a specified audience. Or perhaps you can think of other types of media messages that seem to present a distorted or inaccurate view (say, certain commercials or sports reporting or war movies, and so on). For instance, do certain movies or TV programs give the wrong message? Give your readers examples they can recognize and remember.

OPTIONS FOR ESSAY WRITING

1. Write a human interest article for your campus newspaper in which you discuss some feature of our society that you find humorous, depressing, contemptible, or admirable. Subjects might include our eating habits, our consumer habits, our suburban living habits, our idea of a vacation, the cars we drive, how we show our patriotism, how we exercise, how we follow fads, how we dress, how we ignore the elderly, how we exploit minorities, how we create heroes, how we exercise our freedom of speech, or our obsession with gadgets. Provide at least three well-developed examples to support your thesis.

2. What pleases or disappoints you most about college life? Illustrate the causes to your parents (or some other specific audience) with at least three examples.

3. Suppose you were a filmmaker for a group that wanted to explain American life as honestly as possible to a small nation whose people know little about us. Your assignment is to make three five-minute movies, each about a feature of American life, the three together intended to give a typical view of America. What would be the subjects of your three segments? Indicate why you chose each subject. Write a description of each movie.

4. Assume that, as a first-year student, you've been assigned a faculty adviser, a caring sociology professor who likes to know as much as possible about her advisees. She asks each student to write an essay on this topic:

    Is your hometown (city, section of a city) a good or bad place for a young adult to live?

    Notice that the professor has not asked you to write about yourself directly (as you might in a personal narrative); rather, she has solicited your judgment. Support your response with specific and concrete examples that will convince the reader of your sound judgment.

5. "Clothes make the person." Assess the validity of this statement, supporting your thesis with examples.

6. What makes a good friend? Cite examples to back up your thesis.

7. What would you take with you in a catastrophe? Give detailed examples, and explain your choices.

8. Pierre, a French teenager who plans to attend an American university, has asked what the typical American college student is like. He has inquired about interests, values, leisure activities, attitudes, and tastes. Selecting several characteristics *you* think typify American college students, write a response to Pierre.

9. How are groups of people (women, minorities, young or old people) stereotyped by the media? Select a group, and give detailed examples of their portrayal by the media.

10. Assume you have been commissioned to write a magazine article predicting how something in society will have changed by the year 2010. Focus on *one* area (life-styles, science, education, transportation, space travel, medicine, politics, the environment,

our diet, or something else), and describe how that area will differ in 2010.

11. Besides your family, who or what has influenced you most? Give specific examples to show how you have been influenced.

12. Serials and series have become a very popular type of television program. Weekly or daily shows such as "Days of Our Lives," "L.A. Law," "Northern Exposure," and "General Hospital" attract faithful viewers who enjoy episodes in the lives of a group of fictional characters.

    Select a series that you particularly enjoyed at some time during the last few years, and write an essay in which you discuss the elements in the show that made it interesting or appealing.

    If you never have tuned in regularly to a series, write about the appeal of some other leisure activity you enjoyed while others were watching television.

13. Americans generally consider themselves thrifty and efficient. Yet wastefulness is rampant in the American life-style: machines are built to be obsolete within five years; usable clothes are discarded; disposable items clog our landfills; energy and natural resources are wasted.

    Are the above statements justified? If so, what do they tell us about ourselves? Explain and defend your answer, using examples from your reading, study, or observation.

13
Explaining Parts and Categories: Division and Classification

Sometimes we divide one thing into parts to make sense of it; at other times we group an assortment of things into categories to sort them out. Division and classification are the two strategies for sorting things out. Although these two activities often go hand-in-hand, each serves a distinct purpose. *Division* deals with *one* thing. Its purpose is to separate that thing into parts, pieces, sections, or categories (say, a paragraph or essay divided into introduction, body, and conclusion). *Classification* has to do with an *assortment* of things that have some similarities. Its purpose is to group these things systematically (say, a record collection sorted into categories—jazz, rock, country and western, classical, and pop).

We use division and classification almost every day. Assume that you are shopping for a refrigerator. If you are mechanically inclined, you will probably begin by thinking about the major parts that make up a refrigerator: storage compartment, cooling element, motor, insulation, and exterior casing. With individual parts identified, you can now ask questions about them to determine the efficiency or quality of each part in different kinds of refrigerators. You have divided the refrigerator into its components.

261

You then shop at five stores and come home with a list of 20 refrigerators that seem to be built from high-quality parts. You now try to make sense out of your list by grouping items according to selected characteristics. First, you divide your list into three classes according to size in cubic feet of capacity: small refrigerators, middle-sized refrigerators, and large refrigerators. But size is not the only criterion. You want economy, too, and so you group the refrigerators according to cost. Or you might classify them according to color, weight, energy efficiency, and so on, depending on your purpose. Here is how division and classification are related:

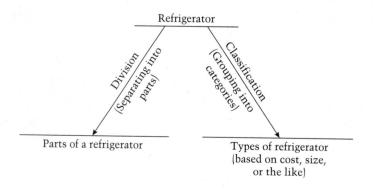

These two ways of sorting also can be used for more abstract items. You might divide a day into daytime and nighttime or into morning, afternoon, and evening. Or, for other purposes, you may want to classify days, sorting them as good days and bad days, or profitable days and unprofitable days, and so on.

Whether you choose to apply division or classification can depend on your purpose. An architect called upon to design a library will think almost entirely of division. Once she has defined the large enclosed area that is needed, she must identify the parts into which that space must be divided: the reference area, reading areas, storage areas, checkout facilities, and office space. In some kinds of libraries she might consider providing space for special groups of users (such as reading areas for children). In very large libraries she might need to carry the division further into specialized kinds of space (such as highly secure areas for rare manuscripts or special collections, or areas with special acoustic provisions for listening to recorded materials). But however simple or complex her problem, she is thinking now only about the appropriate division of *space*. She does not have to worry about how the library will classify its books and other material.

But classification is one of the library staff's main problems. The purpose of a library is not only to store books and other forms of information, but above all to make the information retrievable. In order for us to find a book or item, the thousands or millions of books stored in the library must be arranged in logical categories. That arrangement becomes possible only if the books are carefully classified.

Combined Strategies

Taken from a university's *Career Handbook,* this essay incorporates both classification and division as ways of explaining the major career specialties in computer science.

Computer Scientists: A Classification

Computer scientists deal with the software (programming) end of computer technology. They hold B.S. degrees from accredited schools, with majors in software engineering or computer science. The curriculum focuses on the logic and language of programming, and, briefly, on the hardware of the machine. (Programming is the process of instructing computers to perform various applications. A program defines in complete and minute detail just what the computer is to do in particular circumstances.)

Computer scientists play major roles in science, government, and business. Their programs might be used for guiding satellites, developing federal and state budgets, controlling inventories, making and confirming reservations, or grading examinations—among countless other uses. This broad demand for programs creates a diversity of job opportunities. The major specialties within computer science can be grouped into three categories: systems programming, applications programming, and systems analysis.

Systems programmers write programs that run the computer equipment itself. These programs act as an interface (connector) between the machines and the users' programs. Examples of systems programs include those that control the computer's operating system, monitor, printer, and interpreter. Much systems programming is done in machine language (using a binary-number system: 0's and 1's).

The job of the applications programmer overlaps with that of the systems programmer in that both entail the same type of programming logic, but for different purposes and in different codes (languages). Applications programs put the computer to work on specific jobs such as keeping track of accounts in banks and insurance companies. These programs act as an interface between the systems program and the user. Applications programs usually are written in high-level languages (COBOL, Pascal, BASIC, FORTRAN, etc.).

Systems analysts are the organizers. They monitor the systems and applications programs, and are responsible for eliminating any bugs (program failures). Instead of actually writing the programs, systems analysts update those written by systems programmers, as required. They may also analyze an organization's particular needs, and write specifications for a computer system. These specifications are then given to a programmer. Systems analysts require several years of experience as programmers.

In any role, computer scientists are responsible for analyzing a problem, and then reducing it to the sequence of small, deliberate steps the computer can use to solve the problem.

—Armand Dumont

This essayist groups the career specialties into three individual categories and, in the final paragraph, divides the collective specialties into the major tasks they have in common. Whenever readers need help sorting things out, division and classification are indispensable.

Using Division

As a development strategy, division answers these questions for readers:

What are its parts?

What is it made of?

In this paragraph, the author uses division to explain his view of the ideal education.

Lead-in to main point (1–3)	¹It is perhaps idle to wonder what, from my present point of view, would have been an ideal education. ²If I could provide such a curriculum for my children they, in their turn, might find it all a bore. ³But the fantasy of what I would have liked to learn as a child may be revealing, since I feel unequipped by education for problems that lie outside the cloistered, literary domain in which I am
Main point (4)	competent and at home. ⁴Looking back, then, I would have arranged for myself to be taught survival techniques for both natural and urban wilder-
Parts of the "ideal education" (5)	nesses. ⁵I would want to have been instructed in self-hypnosis, in aikido (the esoteric and purely self-defensive style of judo), in elementary medicine, in sexual hygiene, in vegetable gardening, in astronomy, navigation, and sailing; in cookery and

clothesmaking, in metalwork and carpentry, in drawing and painting, in printing and typography, in botany and biology, in optics and acoustics, in semantics and psychology, in mysticism and yoga, in electronics and mathematical fantasy, in drama and dancing, in singing and in playing an instrument by ear; in wandering, in advanced daydreaming, in prestidigitation, in techniques of escape from bondage, in disguise, in conversation with birds and beasts, in ventriloquism, in French and German conversation, in planetary history, in morphology,*

Most important part (6)

and in Classical Chinese. 6Actually, the main thing left out of my education was a proper love for my own body, because one feared to cherish anything so obviously mortal and prone to sickness.

—Alan Watts

Moving on from a topic statement that *tells*, the author *shows* by dividing the *ideal education* into specific kinds of instruction. In developing his message, the author followed the guidelines listed here.

Guidelines for Division

1. *The division is applied to a singular subject.* Only one thing at a time can be divided (*ideal education*; not *ideal education* and *ideal career*).

2. *The division is consistent with the writer's purpose.* The author could have divided education in countless ways: into primary, secondary, and higher education; into vocational and liberal education; into social sciences, humanities, sciences, and mathematics—and so on. But his purpose was to explain a view that goes beyond traditional categories. And we are given the "parts" of an education that we may not yet have considered.

3. *The division is complete in serving the writer's purpose.* Only 100 percent of something can be divided, and the parts, in turn, should add up to 100 percent. If a part is omitted, the writer should say so ("*some* of the parts of an ideal education"). For his purposes, the author above includes all the parts.

4. *The subject is subdivided as far as needed to make the point.* The author's first division is into survival techniques for (a) natural

---

* The structure of organisms.

and (b) urban wildernesses. He then subdivides each of these into the specific parts listed in sentences 5 and 6. If he had stopped after the first division, he would not have made his point.

5. *The division follows a logical order.* In sentence 5 the parts of an ideal education range from practical to recreational to intellectual skills. In sentence 6 the most important part is saved for last—to provide emphasis.

Using Classification

Whereas division identifies the parts of one thing, classification sorts a group of related things into categories, thereby answering the readers' question:

In what categories do *X, Y,* and *Z* belong?

You ask this same question in looking through the college catalog for courses that fulfill specific requirements.

The next paragraph uses classification to explain how television commercials distort and degrade the image of American women. (Both men and women are mentioned in the topic statement because this paragraph is part of an essay discussing images of men as well as of women. One main idea can serve more than one paragraph.)

Main point (1

Supporting point (2)

Categories of women in television commercials (3)

Supporting points and lead-in to final classification (4–5)

Categories of women not shown in commercials (6)

¹In the guise of what they consider comedy, the producers of television commercials have created a loathsome gallery of men and women patterned, presumably, on Mr. and Mrs. America. ²Women liberationists have a major target in the commercial image of women flashed hourly and daily to the vast majority. ³There are, indeed, only four kinds of females in this relentless sales procession: the gorgeous teen-age swinger with bouncing locks; the young mother teaching her baby girl the right soap for skin care; the middle-aged housewife with a voice like a power saw; and the old lady with dentures and irregularity. ⁴All these women, to be sure, exist. ⁵But between the swinging sex object and the constipated granny there are millions of females never shown in commercials. ⁶These are—married or single—intelligent, sensitive women who bring charm to their homes, who work at jobs as well as lend grace to their marriage,

who support themselves, who have talents or hobbies or commitments, or who are skilled at their
professions.

—Marya Mannes

In developing her message, the author followed guidelines that govern any classification.

Guidelines for Classification

1. *The classification is applied to a plural subject.* Here, the subject
    is American women.

2. *The basis of the classification is consistent with the writer's
    purpose.* To make her point, this author used two bases: first, she
    classified women by their roles in television commercials; next, by
    the many other actual roles that women fill. For a different
    purpose, she might have classified women by occupation or level
    of education or political persuasion, and so on.

3. *The classification is complete (according to its basis).* Because
    television commercials only pretend to provide enough role
    categories to account for all women, the author completes the
    classification with her own categories in sentence 6.

4. *The categories are arranged in logical order.* The advertisers'
    categories move from youth to old age. The author's categories
    come last, to provide the best emphasis for her point.

5. *The categories do not overlap.* If the author had added the category
    of *mindless female* to the four stereotypes that she identifies in
    television commercials, her classification would overlap, because
    all four categories could be included in the stereotype *mindless
    female.*
        As further illustration of overlapping categories, suppose a
    supermarket classified its meats as *pork, beef, ham,* and *lamb.*
    This classification would overlap because ham is a product of pork
    meat rather than an exclusive category.

Application 13–1

PARAGRAPH WARM-UPS: DIVISION

1. Assume that your social life is less than desirable because you are
    new in town, are shy, and haven't met many people. You decide to

contact a dating service for professional help in meeting a companion. Among the forms you are given to complete is this statement: "In one paragraph, describe the qualities you desire in an ideal companion." Write the paragraph according to the "Guidelines for Division" on page 265.

2.   Using the paragraph on pages 264–265 as a model, write a paragraph for the college curriculum committee, explaining your idea of an ideal education.

Application 13–2

PARAGRAPH WARM-UP OR ESSAY PRACTICE: CLASSIFICATION

As a work-study student, you are helping prepare the orientation for next year's incoming freshmen. Your supervisor asks you to write a paragraph (or essay, if your instructor requires) outlining the jobs available to graduates in your major. Your piece will be published in a career pamphlet for new students. Write the piece. (You may need to do some library research for this assignment. A good source would be *The Occupational Outlook Handbook.*)

Application 13–3

ESSAY PRACTICE

Read this essay, and answer the questions that follow it. Then select one of the essay assignments.

> *Friends, Good Friends—and Such Good Friends*
>
> Women are friends, I once would have said, when they   1
> totally love and support and trust each other, and bare to each
> other the secrets of their souls, and run—no questions asked—to
> help each other, and tell harsh truths to each other (no, you
> can't wear that dress unless you lose ten pounds first) when
> harsh truths must be told.
>
> Women are friends, I once would have said, when they   2
> share the same affection for Ingmar Bergman, plus train rides,
> cats, warm rain, charades, Camus, and hate with equal ardor
> Newark and Brussels sprouts and Lawrence Welk and camping.
>
> In other words, I once would have said that a friend is a   3
> friend all the way, but now I believe that's a narrow point of
> view. For the friendships I have and the friendships I see are con-
> ducted at many levels of intensity, serve many different func-

tions, meet different needs and range from those as all-the-way as the friendship of the soul sisters mentioned above to that of the most nonchalant and casual playmates.

Consider these varieties of friendship: 4

1. Convenience friends. These are the women with whom,   5
if our paths weren't crossing all the time, we'd have no particular reason to be friends: a next-door neighbor, a woman in our car pool, the mother of one of our children's closest friends or maybe some mommy with whom we serve juice and cookies each week at the Glenwood Co-op Nursery.

Convenience friends are convenient indeed. They'll lend us   6
their cups and silverware for a party. They'll drive our kids to soccer when we're sick. They'll take us to pick up our car when we need a lift to the garage. They'll even take our cats when we go on vacation. As we will for them.

But we don't, with convenience friends, ever come too   7
close or tell too much; we maintain our public face and emotional distance. "Which means," says Elaine, "that I'll talk about being overweight but not about being depressed. Which means I'll admit being mad but not blind with rage. Which means I might say that we're pinched this month but never that I'm worried sick over money."

But which doesn't mean that there isn't sufficient value to   8
be found in these friendships of mutual aid, in convenience friends.

2. Special-interest friends. These friendships aren't inti-   9
mate, and they needn't involve kids or silverware or cats. Their value lies in some interest jointly shared. And so we may have an office friend or a yoga friend or a tennis friend or a friend from the Women's Democratic Club.

"I've got one woman friend," says Joyce, "who likes, as I   10
do, to take psychology courses. Which makes it nice for me—and nice for her. It's fun to go with someone you know and it's fun to discuss what you've learned, driving back from the classes." And for the most part, she says, that's all they discuss.

"I'd say that what we're doing is *doing* together, not being   11
together," Suzanne says of her Tuesday-doubles friends. "It's mainly a tennis relationship, but we play together well. And I guess we all need to have a couple of playmates."

I agree.   12

My playmate is a shopping friend, a woman of marvelous   13
taste, a woman who knows exactly *where* to buy *what,* and furthermore is a woman who always knows beyond a doubt what one ought to be buying. I don't have the time to keep up with what's new in eyeshadow, hemlines and shoes and whether the

smock look is in or finished already. But since (oh, shame!) I care a lot about eyeshadow, hemlines and shoes, and since I don't *want* to wear smocks if the smock look is finished, I'm very glad to have a shopping friend.

3. Historical friends. We all have a friend who knew us when . . . maybe way back in Miss Meltzer's second grade, when our family lived in that three-room flat in Brooklyn, when our dad was out of work for seven months, when our brother Allie got in that fight where they had to call the police, when our sister married the endodontist from Yonkers and when, the morning after we lost our virginity, she was the first, the only, friend we told.   14

The years have gone by and we've gone separate ways and we've little in common now, but we're still an intimate part of each other's past. And so whenever we go to Detroit we always go to visit this friend of our girlhood. Who knows how we looked before our teeth were straightened. Who knows how we talked before our voice got un-Brooklyned. Who knows what we ate before we learned about artichokes. And who, by her presence, puts us in touch with an earlier part of ourself, a part of ourself it's important never to lose.   15

"What this friend means to me and what I mean to her," says Grace, "is having a sister without sibling rivalry. We know the texture of each other's lives. She remembers my grandmother's cabbage soup. I remember the way her uncle played the piano. There's simply no other friend who remembers those things."   16

4. Crossroads friends. Like historical friends, our crossroads friends are important for *what was*—for the friendship we shared at a crucial, now past, time of life. A time, perhaps, when we roomed in college together; or worked as eager young singles in the Big City together; or went together, as my friend Elizabeth and I did through pregnancy, birth and that scary first year of new motherhood.   17

Crossroads friends forge powerful links, links strong enough to endure with not much more contact than once-a-year letters at Christmas. And out of respect for those crossroads years, for those dramas and dreams we once shared, we will always be friends.   18

5. Cross-generational friends. Historical friends and crossroads friends seem to maintain a special kind of intimacy—dormant but always ready to be revived—and though we may rarely meet, whenever we do connect, it's personal and intense. Another kind of intimacy exists in the friendships that form across generations in what one woman calls her daughter-mother and her mother-daughter relationships.   19

Evelyn's friend is her mother's age—"but I share so much
more than I ever could with my mother"—a woman she talks to
of music, of books and of life. "What I get from her is the benefit
of her experience. What she gets—and enjoys—from me is a
youthful perspective. It's a pleasure for both of us."

I have in my own life a precious friend, a woman of 65
who has lived very hard, who is wise, who listens well; who has
been where I am and can help me understand it; and who represents not only an ultimate ideal mother to me but also the person I'd like to be when I grow up.

In our daughter role we tend to do more than our share of
self-revelation; in our mother role we tend to receive what's
revealed. It's another kind of pleasure—playing wise mother to a
questing younger person. It's another very lovely kind of friendship.

6. Part-of-a-couple friends. Some of the women we call our
friends we never see alone—we see them as part of a couple at
couples' parties. And though we share interests in many things
and respect each other's views, we aren't moved to deepen the
relationship. Whatever the reason, a lack of time or—and this is
more likely—a lack of chemistry, our friendship remains in the
context of a group. But the fact that our feeling on seeing each
other is always, "I'm *so* glad she's here" and the fact that we
spend half the evening talking together says that this too, in its
own way, counts as a friendship.

(Other part-of-a-couple friends are the friends that came
with the marriage, and some of these are friends we could live
without. But sometimes, alas, she married our husband's best
friend; and sometimes, alas, she *is* our husband's best friend.
And so we find ourself dealing with her, somewhat against our
will, in a spirit of what I'll call *reluctant* friendship.)

7. Men who are friends. I wanted to write just of women
friends, but the women I've talked to won't let me—they say I
must mention man-woman friendships too. For these friendships can be just as close and as dear as those that we form with
women. Listen to Lucy's description of one such friendship:

"We've found we have things to talk about that are different from what he talks about with my husband and different
from what I talk about with his wife. So sometimes we call on
the phone or meet for lunch. There are similar intellectual interests—we always pass on to each other the books that we love—
but there's also something tender and caring too."

In a couple of crises, Lucy says, "he offered himself, for
talking and for helping. And when someone died in his family
he wanted me there. The sexual, flirty part of our friendship is
very small, but *some*—just enough to make it fun and different."

She thinks—and I agree—that the sexual part, though small is always *some*, is always there when a man and a woman are friends.

It's only in the past few years that I've made friends with   28
men, in the sense of a friendship that's *mine*, not just part of two couples. And achieving with them the ease and the trust I've found with women friends has value indeed. Under the dryer at home last week, putting on mascara and rouge, I comfortably sat and talked with a fellow named Peter. Peter, I finally decided, could handle the shock of me minus mascara under the dryer. Because we care for each other. Because we're friends.

8. There are medium friends, and pretty friends, and very   29
good friends indeed, and these friendships are defined by their level of intimacy. And what we'll reveal at each of these levels of intimacy is calibrated with care. We might tell a medium friend, for example, that yesterday we had a fight with our husband. And we might tell a pretty good friend that this fight with our husband made us so mad that we slept on the couch. And we might tell a very good friend that the reason we got so mad in that fight that we slept on the couch had something to do with that girl who works in his office. But it's only to our very best friends that we're willing to tell all, to tell what's going on with that girl in his office.

The best of friends, I still believe, totally love and support   30
and trust each other, and bare to each other the secrets of their souls, and run—no questions asked—to help each other, and tell harsh truths to each other when they must be told.

But we needn't agree about everything (only 12-year-old   31
girl friends agree about *everything*) to tolerate each other's point of view. To accept without judgment. To give and to take without ever keeping score. And to *be* there, as I am for them and as they are for me, to comfort our sorrows, to celebrate our joys.

—Judith Viorst

Questions About Content

1.   Is the title effective? Explain.

2.   Where is the thesis? Is it effective? Why?

3.   How many bases can you identify in the above classification? Are these bases consistent with the writer's purpose? Explain.

4.   What specific reader questions are answered in the body?

Questions About Organization

1. How many paragraphs make up the introduction? Is the introduction effective? Explain.

2. Does the arrangement of supporting paragraphs provide the best emphasis for the thesis? Explain.

3. Are the many short paragraphs appropriate to the writer's purpose? Explain. What effect do these short paragraphs have on the readers?

4. Is the conclusion effective? Explain.

Questions About Style

1. What is an outstanding style feature of this essay? Give examples.

2. Characterize the tone of this essay. Identify four expressions contributing to that tone.

3. Are the sentence fragments acceptable and effective here? (See page 544.)

RESPONDING TO YOUR READING

Explore your reactions to Viorst's "Friends, Good Friends—and Such Good Friends" by using the questions on page 91. Then respond with an essay of your own that uses classification to support some particular point about different types of friends. Or you might write about different types of dates you've had or other different types of people in your life. Whether your approach is humorous or serious, be sure your classification supports a definite viewpoint.

OPTIONS FOR ESSAY WRITING

1. Differences among members are the details that make any group of people interesting. Male college freshmen may be sorted into categories according to majors, socioeconomic backgrounds, political preferences, racial backgrounds, religious backgrounds, driving habits, attitudes toward studies, attitudes toward marriage, styles of dress, or countless other characteristics. We could do the same for any other group: teachers, parents, employers, athletes, people we see at the beach. Your basis for sorting will depend on the point you want to make about the group.

   Identify a group that you find interesting. Sort that group into at least three categories. Write for your classmates, and make sure your classification has a point. (Review "Guidelines for Classification" on page 267 for a discussion of the features that make a classification effective.)

2. Television seems to invade every part of our lives. It can influence our buying habits, our political views, our literacy, and our attitudes about sex, marriage, family, and violence. Identify a group of commercials, sitcoms, talk shows, sports shows, or the like that have a bad (or good) influence on viewers. Sort the group according to a clear basis, using at least three categories for your classification.

14
Explaining Each Step or Stage: Process Analysis

Explaining How to Do Something • **Guidelines for Instructions**
• **Explaining How Something Happens** • **Applications**

A process is a sequence of actions or changes leading to a product or result.

People and things interact in different ways to produce different results. Each interaction is a process. In the manufacturing process, people interact with machines and materials to produce finished goods. In the natural process, earth, air, sunlight, and water interact to produce plant life. In a chemical process, air and fuel interact in an engine's carburetor to produce a combustible vapor. Most process analyses you will write in college and afterward are designed to answer one of these two questions for readers:

How do I do it?

How does it happen?

In school you might give instructions to a classmate for dissecting a frog or solving a physics problem. At work you might tell a colleague or customer how to achieve a result: how to analyze a soil sample; how to program a computer; how to swing a golf club.

Besides showing how to do something, you often have to explain how things happen: how the United States became involved in World War I; how a digital computer works; how economic inflation occurs. The type of explanation will depend on your writing situation.

Explaining How to Do Something

Almost anyone with a responsible job writes instructions. And everyone reads some sort of instructions. The new employee needs instructions for operating the office machines; the employee going on vacation writes instructions for the person filling in. An owner of a new car reads the manual for service and operating instructions. Readers of instructions have these questions:

How do I do it?

Why do I do it?

What materials or equipment will I need?

Where do I begin?

What do I do next?

Are there any precautions?

Instructions *emphasize the reader's role,* explaining each step in enough detail for readers to complete the task safely and efficiently. Here is a paragraph of instructions aimed at inexperienced joggers:

Main point (1)	[1]Instead of breaking into a jog too quickly and risking injury, take a relaxed and deliberate approach.
First step (2)	[2]Before taking a step, spend at least ten minutes stretching and warming up, using any exercises you
Supporting detail (3)	find comfortable. [3](After your first week, consult a
Second step (4)	jogging book for specialized exercises.) [4]When you've completed your warm-up, set a brisk pace walking.
Supporting detail (5)	[5]Exaggerate the distance between steps, taking long strides and swinging your arms briskly and loosely.
Transitional sentence (6)	[6]After roughly 100 yards at this brisk pace, you should feel ready to jog. [7]Immediately break into a
Third step (7–8)	very slow trot: lean your torso forward and let one foot fall in front of the other (one foot barely leaving the ground while the other is on the pavement).
Precaution (9–10)	[8]Maintain the slowest pace possible, just above a walk. [8]*Do not bolt like a sprinter!* [10]The biggest mis-
Supporting details (11–15)	take is to start fast and injure yourself. [11]While jogging, relax your body. [12]Keep your shoulders straight and your head up, and enjoy the scenery—after all, it is one of the joys of jogging. [13]Keep your arms low and slightly bent at your sides. [14]Move your legs freely from the hips in an action that is easy, not forced. [15]Make your feet perform a heel-to-toe action: land on the heel; rock forward; take off from the toe.

In developing this selection, the writer followed guidelines that govern all instructions.

Guidelines for Instructions

1. *The instructions are informed.* The instruction writer has to know the process, down to the smallest detail. Unless you have performed the task, do not try to write instructions for it.

2. *The instructions are complete but not excessive.* The material answers all questions a reader has about how to carry out the procedure. Each step is spelled out *and* clarified by precautions, supporting points, and details as needed.

   It is easy to assume that other people know more than they really do about a procedure, especially when you can perform the task almost automatically. Think about when someone was teaching you to drive a car; or perhaps you have tried to teach someone else. When you write instructions, remember that the reader knows less than you. On the one hand, you need to include enough details for your reader to understand and perform the task successfully. On the other hand, you should omit general information that the average reader can be expected to know. Excessive details get in the way.

   The jogging instructions are clear and uncluttered because the writer has assessed correctly the general reader's needs. Terms such as **long stride, torso,** and **sprinter** should be clear to the general reader without definitions or illustrations. In contrast, *a slow trot* is explained in detail, because different readers might have differing interpretations of this term. When in doubt about the need for details, you are safer to overexplain than to underexplain.

3. *The instructions are logically organized.* Instructions almost always are arranged in chronological order, with warnings and precautions inserted for specific steps.

4. *The instructions are immediately readable.* Instructions must be understood upon *first* reading, because readers usually take immediate action. Because they emphasize the *reader's role*, instructions are written in the *second person*, as direct address.

   All steps are in the *active voice* (**move your legs** versus **your legs should be moved**) and the *imperative mood* ("rock forward" versus "you should rock forward"). In this way, each step begins with an *action verb* (**lean, relax, keep**) that gives an immediate signal about the specific actions to be taken.

Generally, sentences are shorter in instructions than in other kinds of writing: use one sentence for one step, so that readers can perform one step at a time.

Finally, transitional expressions (**while, after, next**) improve readability by marking time and sequence.

Explaining How Something Happens

When you explain how steps or stages lead to completion of a process, you answer these readers' questions:

How does it happen? (or, How is it made?)

When and where does it happen?

What happens first, next, and so on?

What is the result?

In an essay exam you may have to explain how salt water can be converted to fresh water, or how a color television image is transmitted. Colleagues and clients need to know such things as how stock and bond prices are governed, how your bank reviews a mortgage application, how your town decided on its zoning laws, and so on. This type of explanation *emphasizes the process itself*—instead of the reader's or writer's role—as shown here.

Main point (1–3)	¹The most alarming of all man's assaults upon the environment is the contamination of air, earth, rivers, and sea with dangerous and even lethal materials. ²This pollution is for the most part irrecoverable; the chain of evil it initiates not only in the world that must support life but in living tissues is for the most part irreversible. ³In this now universal contamination of the environment, chemicals are the sinister and little-recognized partners of radiation in changing the very nature of
Details of the process and its results (4–6)	the world—the very nature of its life. ⁴Strontium 90, released through nuclear explosions into the air, comes to earth in rain or drifts down as fallout, lodges in soil, enters into the grass or wheat or corn grown there, and in time takes up its abode in the bones of a human being, there to remain until his [or her] death. ⁵Similarly, chemicals sprayed on croplands or forest or gardens lie long in soil, entering into living organisms, passing from one to the

other in a chain of poisoning and death. 6Or they pass mysteriously by underground streams until they emerge and, through the alchemy of air and sunlight, combine into new forms that kill vegetation, sicken cattle, and work unknown harm on

Conclusion (7)   those who drink from once pure wells. 7As Albert Schweitzer has said, "Man can hardly even recognize the devils of his own creation."

—Rachel Carson

Carson's explanation suits her purpose and her audience's needs. The paragraph is part of a book for general readers; therefore, the author needed to decide on her level of detail. Without the clarifying details, the paragraph would be vague—only telling, not showing. But even more specific and technical details, such as chemical formulas or the half-life of strontium, would have confused the audience. The author knew that, as nonspecialists, we would use her information simply for a broad understanding of dangers to our environment. Her goal was to make us aware of the problems, not to write a textbook on chemical pollution. Of course, an audience of chemistry or ecology majors would require more technical details. In various situations, the subject, purpose, and audience differ; therefore, paragraphs vary in their mixture of general and specific.

Like a set of instructions, an explanation of how something happens must be factual and objective as well as clear and detailed enough to allow readers to follow the process step by step. Because this type of analysis emphasizes the process itself, rather than the reader's role, it ordinarily is written in the third person.

Processes occur in our personal experiences as well—for example, our stages of maturation, of emotional growth and development, of intellectual awareness, and so on. The following essay traces a personal process some readers might consider horrifying: the stages of learning to live by scavenging through garbage. As you read, think about how the factual and "objective" style paints a gruesome portrait of survival at the margin of American affluence.

Dumpster Diving*

I began Dumpster diving about a year before I became homeless.

I prefer the term *scavenging.* I have heard people, evidently meaning to be polite, use the word *foraging,* but I prefer to reserve that word for gathering nuts and berries and such, which I also do, according to the season and opportunity.

---

* Lars Eighner, "Dumpster Diving," *Utne Reader,* March/April 1992. Originally appeared in *The Threepenny Review,* Fall 1991. Reprinted by permission of the author.

I like the frankness of the word *scavenging*. I live from the refuse of others. I am a scavenger. I think it a sound and honorable niche, although if I could I would naturally prefer to live the comfortable consumer life, perhaps—and only perhaps—as a slightly less wasteful consumer owing to what I have learned as a scavenger.

Except for jeans, all my clothes come from Dumpsters. Boom boxes, candles, bedding, toilet paper, medicine, books, a typewriter, a virgin male love doll, coins sometimes amounting to many dollars: all came from Dumpsters. And, yes, I eat from Dumpsters, too.

There is a predictable series of stages that a person goes through in learning to scavenge. At first the new scavenger is filled with disgust and self-loathing. He [or she] is ashamed of being seen.

This stage passes with experience. The scavenger finds a pair of running shoes that fit and look and smell brand-new. He finds a pocket calculator in perfect working order. He finds pristine ice cream, still frozen, more than he can eat or keep. He begins to understand: people do throw away perfectly good stuff, a lot of perfectly good stuff.

At this stage he may become lost and never recover. All the Dumpster divers I have known come to the point of trying to acquire everything they touch. Why not take it, they reason, it is all free. This is, of course, hopeless, and most divers come to realize that they must restrict themselves to items of relatively immediate utility.

The finding of objects is becoming something of an urban art. Even respectable, employed people will sometimes find something tempting sticking out of a Dumpster or standing beside one. Quite a number of people, not all of them of the bohemian type, are willing to brag that they found this or that piece in the trash.

But eating from Dumpsters is the thing that separates the dilettanti from the professionals. Eating safely involves three principles: using the senses and common sense to evaluate the condition of the found materials; knowing the Dumpsters of a given area and checking them regularly; and seeking always to answer the question "Why was this discarded?"

Yet perfectly good food can be found in Dumpsters. Canned goods, for example, turn up fairly often in the Dumpsters I frequent. I also have few qualms about dry foods such as crackers, cookies, cereal, chips, and pasta if they are free of visible contaminants and still dry and crisp. Raw fruits and vegetables with intact skins seem perfectly safe to me, excluding, of course, the obviously rotten. Many are discarded for minor imperfections that can be pared away.

A typical discard is a half jar of peanut butter—though nonorganic peanut butter does not require refrigeration and is unlikely to spoil in any reasonable time. One of my favorite finds is yogurt—often discarded, still sealed, when the expiration date has passed—because it will keep for several days, even in warm weather.

No matter how careful I am I still get dysentery at least once a month, oftener in warm weather. I do not want to paint too romantic a picture. Dumpster diving has serious drawbacks as a way of life.

I find from the experience of scavenging two rather deep lessons. The first is to take what I can use and let the rest go. I have come to think that there is no value in the abstract. A thing I cannot use or make useful, perhaps by trading, has no value, however fine or rare it may be.

The second lesson is the transience of material being. I do not suppose that ideas are immortal, but certainly they are longer-lived than material objects.

The things I find in Dumpsters, the love letters and rag dolls of so many lives, remind me of this lesson. Now I hardly pick up a thing without envisioning the time I will cast it away. This, I think, is a healthy state of mind. Almost everything I have now has already been cast out at least once, proving that what I own is valueless to someone.

I find that my desire to grab for the gaudy bauble has been largely sated. I think this is an attitude I share with the very wealthy—we both know there is plenty more wherever we have come from. Between us are the rat-race millions who have confounded their selves with the objects they grasp and who nightly scavenge the cable channels for they know not what.

I am sorry for them.

—Lars Eighner

Eighner lets the facts of his experience do the showing, without self-pity or melodrama. Despite his outrageous circumstances, he avoids sounding like a victim; he maintains instead a kind of detachment that makes his troubling perspective on our throw-away society all the more forceful.

Much of your writing in college term papers and essay exams is designed to explain how things happen. Your audience is the professor, who is evaluating what you have learned. Because this informed reader knows *more* than you do about the subject, you often need to discuss only the main points, omitting some details.

But explaining the stages of a process for readers who know *less* than you is the real challenge. Here you have to translate specialized information for people unable to fill in the blanks; thus, you become the teacher, and uninformed readers become the students.

Application 14–1

PARAGRAPH WARM-UP: GIVING INSTRUCTIONS

Choose some activity you perform well. Think of a situation requiring you to write instructions for that activity. Single out a major step within the process (such as pitching a baseball or adjusting ski bindings for safe release). Provide enough details from the reader to perform that step safely and efficiently.

Application 14–2

PARAGRAPH WARM-UP: EXPLAINING HOW SOMETHING HAPPENS

Select a simple but specialized process that you understand well (how gum disease develops, how the heart pumps blood, how steel is made, how electricity is generated, how a corporation is formed, how a verdict is appealed to a higher court, and so on). Write a paragraph giving an uninformed classmate a general but clear understanding of the process.

Application 14–3

ESSAY PRACTICE: GIVING INSTRUCTIONS

Read this essay, and answer the questions following it. Then select one of the essay assignments.

The writer of these instructions is a counselor at the North American Survival School, which offers courses ranging from mountaineering to desert survival. Besides being a certified Emergency Medical Technician, this writer has extensive experience hiking and camping in snake country. The school is preparing a survival manual for distribution to all its students. This writer's contribution is a set of instructions on dealing with snakebites. Many of the readers will have no experience with snakes (or first aid), and so the writer decides to be brief and simple, for quick, easy reading as needed.

How to Deal with Snakebites

[1]Too often, a pleasant weekend outdoors can become a nightmare. Every year, thousands of Americans are injured—sometimes fatally—by poisonous snakebites. Fewer than one percent of poisonous snakebites are fatal. But many of the injuries and virtually all fatalities can be avoided as long as you are alert and cautious and follow a few simple instructions.

[2]First, remember that although most snakes can bite, in the United States only rattlesnakes, copperheads, coral snakes, and water moccasins are poisonous. All these snakes are most dangerous in early spring, when venom sacs are full from winter hibernation. Rattlers are found in most of the United States, while copperheads are only in the

East. Coral snakes range throughout the South, while water moccasins live in Southern lowlands and swampy areas. You might disturb a venomous snake by pushing over a log or stone, walking through tall grass, stumbling over one sunning on a rock, or bumping into one while swimming. You could even wake up after a cold night to find one sharing your tent or sleeping bag.

³Some simple precautions can help you avoid snakebites. Since most bites occur around the ankles, wear long, thick pants and high boots of heavy rubber or leather. Also, watch where you walk, swim, or sleep. As you walk, watch where you put your feet, and be especially careful climbing over fallen tress or stone walls. In moccasin country, swim only where the water is moving and the shoreline is free of heavy vegetation. If you cannot sleep in a closed tent with a snakeproof floor, place your sleeping bag on a high, dry, open spot, and keep it zipped tightly. When you do encounter a snake, stop dead! Then move backwards *very* slowly, making no moves that will frighten the snake. Above all, carry a snakebite kit in your pack, just in case the precautions fail.

⁴A poisonous snakebite is easy enough to recognize. Within minutes the wound will swell and turn bright red. You will feel a throbbing pain that radiates from the bite. The swelling, redness, and pain will spread gradually and steadily. (Bites from nonvenemous snakes, in contrast, resemble mere pinpricks.) You may experience nausea and/or hot flashes. In any case, if you are not sure whether the bite is poisonous, play it safe and treat it as if it were poisonous.

⁵If you have been bitten, *do nothing that could hasten the spread of the poison.* Above all, don't panic. Resist the temptation to walk, run, or move quickly. And stay away from stimulants such as coffee, tea, cola, alcohol, or aspirin. In fact, avoid ingesting anything except perhaps for a few sips of water. Begin by taking a minute to think calmly about what you *should* do.

⁶To ensure your safety, follow these suggestions. Remain calm and move as little as possible. Keep the wound lower than the rest of your body so that the poison will remain localized. Have companions get you to a hospital as quickly as possible, without causing you needless exertion. If the hospital is more than an hour away, you might apply an icepack to retard the spread of the poison, or a tourniquet (snugly enough to step venous flow but not so tight as to stop arterial flow—and loosened briefly every five minutes). If you have no snakebite kit, you might cut a small X about $1/_4$-inch deep at the point of greatest swelling on the wound to suck out and spit out some poison. Perform this last procedure *only* if you have no oral cuts or injuries and there is no chance of getting medical treatment for several hours.

⁷By taking precautions and remaining alert, you should not have to fear snakebites. But if you are bitten, your best bet is to remain calm.

—Frank White

Questions About Content

1. Is there a thesis sentence? If so, where?

2. What opening strategy is used to create interest?

3. Is the first body paragraph necessary? Explain.

4. Is the information adequate and appropriate for the stated audience and purpose? Explain.

5. What specific readers' questions are answered in the body?

Questions About Organization

1. What is the order of the body paragraphs? Is this the most effective order? Explain.

2. Is the conclusion adequate and appropriate? Explain.

Questions About Style

1. What is the outstanding stylistic feature of this piece?

2. Is the tone of these instructions too "bossy"? Explain.

ESSAY ASSIGNMENT

Assume a specific situation and audience (like those for snakebite procedures), and write instructions for one of the following procedures, or for anything that you can do well (no recipes, please). Be sure you know the process down to the smallest detail. Narrow your subject (perhaps to one complex activity within a longer procedure) so you can cover it fully. Avoid day-to-day procedures that college readers would already know (brushing teeth, washing hair, and other such elementary activities). Here are some possibilities:

how to portage a canoe

how to care for a down sleeping bag

how to avoid hypothermia

how to select a used car

how to snowplow on skis

how to jump-start a car

how to housebreak a puppy

how to survive the first semester in college

how to overcome insomnia

how to apply the Heimlich Maneuver

how to sprout new plants from clippings

how to defend oneself from a mugger

how to study for finals

how to deal with sexual harassment

Application 14–4

ESSAY PRACTICE: EXPLAINING HOW SOMETHING HAPPENS

This essay, written by a biology major for a pamphlet on environmental pollution, is aimed at an uniformed audience. Read it, and answer the study questions that follow. Then select one of the essay assignments.

How Acid Rain Develops, Spreads, and Destroys

[1]Acid rain is environmentally damaging rainfall that occurs after fossil fuels burn and release nitrogen and sulfur oxides into the atmosphere. Acid rain, simply stated, increases the acidity level of waterways, because these nitrogen and sulfur oxides combine with the air's normal moisture. The resulting rainfall is far more acidic than normal rainfall. Acid rain is a silent threat because its effects, although slow, are cumulative. This analysis explains the cause, the distribution cycle, and the effects of acid rain.

[2]Most research shows that power plants burning oil or coal are the primary cause of acid rain. Fossil fuels contain a number of elements that are released during combustion. Two of these, sulfur oxide and nitrogen oxide, combine with normal moisture to produce sulfuric acid and nitric acid. The released gases undergo a chemical change as they combine with atmospheric ozone and water vapor. The resulting rain or snowfall is more acid than normal precipitation.

[3]Acid level is measured by pH readings. The pH scale runs from 0 through 14; a pH of 7 is considered neutral. (Distilled water has a pH of 7.) Numbers above 7 indicate increasing degrees of alkalinity. (Household ammonia has a pH of 11.) Numbers below 7 indicate increasing acidity. Movement in either direction on the pH scale, however, means multiplying by 10. Lemon juice, which has a pH value of 2, is 10 times more acidic than apples, which have a pH of 3, and 1000 times more acidic than carrots, which have a pH of 5.

[4]Because of carbon dioxide (an acid substance) normally present in air, unaffected rainfall has a pH of 5.6. At this time, the pH of precipitation in the northeastern United States and Canada is between

4.5 and 4. In Massachusetts, rain and snowfall have an average pH reading of 4.1. A pH reading below 5 is considered to be abnormally acidic, and therefore a threat to aquatic populations.

[5]Although it might seem that areas containing power plants would be most severely affected, acid rain can in fact travel thousands of miles from its source. Stack gases escape and drift with the wind currents. The sulfur and nitrogen oxides thus are able to travel great distances before they return to earth as acid rain.

[6]For an average of two to five days after emission, the gases follow the prevailing winds far from the point of origin. Estimates show that about 50 percent of the acid rain that affects Canada originates in the United States; at the same time, 15 to 25 percent of the U.S. acid rain problem originates in Canada.

[7]The tendency of stack gases to drift makes acid rain a widespread menace. More than 200 lakes in the Adirondacks, hundreds of miles from any industrial center, are unable to support life because their water has become so acidic.

[8]Acid rain causes damage wherever it falls. It erodes various types of building rock, such as limestone, marble, and mortar, which are gradually eaten away by the constant bathing in acid. Damage to buildings, houses, monuments, statues, and cars is widespread. Some priceless monuments and carvings already have been destroyed, and even trees of some varieties are dying in large numbers.

[9]More important, however, is acid rain damage to waterways in the affected areas. Because of its high acidity, acid rain dramatically lowers the pH in lakes and streams. Although its effect is not immediate, acid rain eventually can make a waterway so acidic it dies. In areas with natural acid-buffering elements such as limestone, the dilute acid has less effect. The northeastern United States and Canada, however, lack this natural protection, and so are continually vulnerable.

[10]The pH level in an affected waterway drops so low that some species cease to reproduce. In fact, a pH level of 5.1 to 5.4 means that fisheries are threatened; once a waterway reaches a pH level of 4.5, no fish reproduction occurs. Because each creature is part of the overall food chain, loss of one element in the chain disrupts the whole cycle.

[11]In the northeastern United States and Canada, the acidity problem is compounded by the runoff from acid snow. During the cold winter months, acid snow sits with little melting, so that by spring thaw, the acid released is greatly concentrated. Aluminum and other heavy metals normally present in soil also are released by acid rain and runoff. These toxic substances leach into waterways in heavy concentrations, affecting fish in all stages of development.

—Bill Kelly

Questions About Content

1. Is the title too long? Explain.

2. Is the information appropriate for the intended audience (uninformed readers)? Explain.

3. What specific readers' questions are answered in the body?

Questions About Organization

1. Are the body paragraphs arranged in the best order for readers to follow the process? Explain.

2. What is the purpose of so many short paragraphs?

3. Why does this essay have no specific conclusion?

Questions About Style

1. What is the outstanding style feature of this essay? Give an example.

2. Give one example of each of the following sentence constructions, and explain briefly how each reinforces the writer's meaning: passive construction, subordination, short sentence.

RESPONDING TO YOUR READING

Explore your reactions to "Dumpster Diving" (pages 279–281) by using the page 91 questions. What point is Eighner making about values? What are the main issues here? How has this essay affected your thinking about these issues? As you reread the essay, try to recall some process that has played a role for you personally or for someone close to you. Perhaps you want to focus on the process of achievement (say, preparing for academic or athletic or career competition). Perhaps you have experienced or witnessed the process of giving in to human frailty (say, addiction to drugs, tobacco, alcohol, or food). Perhaps you know something about the process of enduring and recovering from personal loss or misfortune or disappointment. Identify your audience, and decide what you want these readers to be doing or thinking or feeling after reading your essay. Do you want readers to appreciate this process, to try it themselves, to avoid it, or what?

Describe the process in enough detail for readers to visualize what happened and what resulted. But whatever you write about—college or high school or family life or city streets—try to make a definite point about the *larger meaning* beyond the details of the process itself, about the values involved.

You may want to emulate Eighner's level of detachment—for a tone that avoids whining, complaining, boasting, or casting you in the role of the victim or the hero.

ESSAY ASSIGNMENT

Select a specialized process that you understand well (from your major or an area of interest) and explain that process to uninformed readers. Choose a process that has several distinct steps. Write so that members of your composition class will gain detailed understanding. Topics might include these:

how the body metabolizes alcohol

how industrial pollution is killing our lakes

how economic inflation occurs

how a lake or pond becomes a swamp

how a volcanic eruption occurs

how cigarettes cause heart and lung disease

how exposure to the sun causes skin cancer

Do not merely generalize. Get down to specifics.

15

Explaining Why It Happened or What Will Happen: Cause-and-Effect Analysis

Reasoning from Effect to Cause
- **Guidelines for Effect-to-Cause Analysis**
- **Reasoning from Cause to Effect**
- **Guidelines for Cause-to-Effect Analysis** • **Applications**

Whereas a process analysis explains *how* something is done or how something works, a cause-and-effect analysis explains *why* something happened or what happens as a result of something.

We use cause-and-effect analysis daily. If you awoke this morning with a sore shoulder (effect), you might recall exerting yourself yesterday at the college Frisbee olympics (cause). In turn, you may take aspirin, hoping for relief (effect). If the aspirin works, it will have *caused* you to feel better. But some causes and effects are not so easy to identify, because their relationships are more complex. Consider these cause-and-effect statements:

     [*cause*]   [*effect*]
1. I tripped over a chair and broke my nose.

     [*effect*]   [*cause*]
2. I never studied because I slept too much.

One might argue that other causes or effects could be identified for each
of the statements above.

> [effect]   [cause]
> I tripped over the chair because the lights in my apartment were
> out.

> [effect]   [cause]
> The lights were out because the power had been shut off.

> [effect]   [cause]
> The power was shut off because my roommate forgot to pay the
> electric bill.

or

> [cause]   [effect]
> Because I slept too much, my grades were awful.

> [effect]   [effect]
> Because my grades were awful, I hated college.

> [effect]   [effect]
> Because I hated college, I dropped out.

> [cause]   [effect]
> Because I dropped out of college, I lost my scholarship.

As we analyze a situation, some effects can, in turn, become causes
of other effects, or vice versa. As our reasoning proceeds in the examples
above, the causes or effects become more *distant*. The *immediate* cause
of 1, however—the one most closely related to the effect—is that the
writer tripped over the chair. Likewise, the *immediate* effect of 2 is that
the writer did no studying. Thus, even with apparently simple events,
the challenge in a causal analysis is to distinguish between *immediate*
causes or effects and *distant* ones. And when we set out to explain cause-
and-effect relationships, we need to make our reasoning clear to readers.
Otherwise, we might confuse readers with such illogical statements:

> [cause]   [effect]
> Because my roommate forgot to pay the electric bill, I broke my
> nose.

> [effect]   [cause]
> I lost my scholarship because I slept too much.

To understand the writer's meaning, readers need a step-by-step breakdown of the process.

A writer also must distinguish among *probable, possible,* and *definite* causes. Sometimes a definite cause is apparent ("The engine's overheating is caused by a faulty radiator cap"); but usually much searching and thought are needed to isolate a specific cause.

Suppose you want to answer this question: "Why are there no children's day-care facilities on our state college campus?" A brainstorming session might yield these possible causes:

lack of need among students

lack of interest among students, faculty, and staff

high cost of liability insurance

lack of space and facilities on campus

lack of trained personnel

prohibition by state law

lack of legislative funding for such a project

Say you proceed with interviews, questionnaires, and research into state laws, insurance rates, and availability of personnel. You begin to rule out some items, and others appear as probable causes. Specifically, you find a need among students, high campus interest, an abundance of qualified people for staffing, and no state laws prohibiting such a project. Three probable causes remain: lack of funding, high insurance rates, and lack of space. Further inquiry shows that lack of funding and high insurance rates *are* issues. These causes, however, could be eliminated through new sources of revenue: charging a fee for each child, soliciting donations, diverting funds from other campus organizations, and so on. Finally, after examining available campus space and speaking with school officials, you arrive at one definite cause: lack of space and facilities.*

Early in your analysis you might have based your conclusions hastily on insufficient evidence (say, an opinion expressed in a newspaper editorial that the campus was apathetic). Now you can base your conclusions on solid, factual evidence. You have moved from a wide range of possible causes to a narrower range of probable causes, and finally to a definite cause. Anything but the simplest effect is likely to have more than one cause. By narrowing the field, you can focus on the real issues.

The fact that one event occurs just before another is no proof that the first caused the second. You might have walked under a ladder in the

---

* Of course, one could argue that the lack of space and facilities somehow is related to funding. And the college's inability to find funds or space may be related to student need, which is not sufficiently acute or interest sufficiently high to exert real pressure. Lack of space and facilities, however, appears to be the *immediate* cause.

hallway an hour before flunking your chemistry exam—but you would not be able to argue convincingly that the one event had caused the other.

Cause-and-effect analysis serves countless uses in college writing. In a research paper, you might explore the causes of the Israeli-Palestinian conflict or the effects of stress on college students or the prime causes of small-business failure. In a report for the Dean of Students, you might explain the causes of students' disinterest in campus activities or the effect of a ban on smoking in public buildings.

In your workplace problem solving, you might analyze the high rates of absenteeism among your company's employees or the causes of low morale. You might explore the cause(s) of a decrease in company profits or the malfunction of a piece of equipment. Perhaps local citizens will need to know how air quality will be affected by your power plant's proposed change from coal to oil. Or perhaps you will need to predict for assembly line workers the effects of robotics technology on their jobs within ten years. Whenever readers want to understand why something happened or what will happen next, cause-and-effect analysis is essential.

For all its *practical* value, cause-effect analysis also can make a *personal* difference. In this next essay, Al Andrade remembers the cause of a turning point in his own awareness.

The Old Guy

The workout was progressing as it usually does. My father and I took turns grunting the weights up and down off our chests. Our pectorals, shoulders, and arms were shaking. Throughout the one-hour session, we encouraged and coached one another. Fortunately, weight lifting demands short breaks after every set. Without these breaks, our workout might last only two minutes. The time spent preparing for the next set (or recovering from the last one) is important, not because I'm lazy, but because it gives me a chance to catch up on things with Dad. Since we don't get to see each other very often, the latest news, gossip, and philosophies get aired in the weight room.

While I was changing the weight on the barbell for our next set, Dad was hanging around the exercise room. We'd been talking about the possibility of building an apartment on the lot next door. This discussion led to one about real estate, which led to one about the stock market, which led to one about his retirement. Lately, Dad has been complaining about his company's lousy retirement plan. I figured he was just a practical guy planning for a more comfortable retirement. Then he looked up from behind the squat rack and said, "You know, Al, if I'm lucky, I only have 20 or 25 years left, and I don't want to be eating dog food when I retire." I snickered at the dog food remark. He's always overstating things for emphasis. The other part of his remark—the part about having only 20 or 25 years left—also seemed a bit melodramatic. At first, Dad's comment rolled off me like a bead of sweat, until I began doing some personal arithmetic of my own.

Our workout moved from the bench press to the chinning bar. I went first. Then I watched while Dad strained to pull himself up for the tenth repetition. "Not bad for an old guy," he said after he jumped down off the bar. I looked at him and thought he really wasn't bad. (For an old guy.) Aside from a minor middle-aged belly, he is more powerful now than ever. He routinely dead lifts 450 pounds. And even with a bad shoulder, Dad can still bench press over 250 pounds. Not bad for an old guy is right. (Or a young guy, for that matter.) This time, however, the reference to his age wasn't as easy for me to shrug off.

No longer concentrating on the weights, I thought about aging. The thought of Dad aging didn't overly distress me. I mean, the man was healthy, strong, and sweating just a few feet away. But then I pictured myself getting old, considering what I'll be doing and saying in 25 years. Would I be grousing about retirement plans? Would I be working out twice as hard with the notion that I might live a little longer?

Most likely I'd be doing the same things Dad is doing now. A 45-year-old family man counting the years he has left. I'd be a man who's too busy making a living to ever make enough money. Instead of counting up the years, I'd be counting them down: 10 years before my retirement, 15 years before I won't be penalized for withdrawing money from my I.R.A., and 2 years before my son's twenty-fifth birthday. The cycle will be complete. I will replace my father, and a son will replace me.

I understand how "life goes on" and how "we're not getting any younger." But now I worried about the inevitability of middle age. I couldn't help putting myself in the old guy's place—of retirement worries and declining chin-ups. Twenty-three-year-old people aren't supposed to worry about retirement, or even middle age. Brilliant careers and healthy, productive lives lie ahead for us, right? We've got everything to look forward to. We think about raising families, achieving goals, and becoming a success, not about our own mortality. But we all eventually reach a time when thoughts of our own old age and death become an everyday reality.

Dad wrapped his hands around the chinning bar for his last set. He struggled to get six repetitions this time. I jabbed him from behind and jokingly scolded "What's the matter with you?" He turned, and shook his finger at me, and said, "We'll see what you can do at 45 years old." I told him I could wait.

—Al Andrade

Using vivid description and narration, Andrade shows us what happened and why it happened. As readers we are allowed to experience that inevitable moment when a young person first confronts the reality of aging. Andrade gives us no explicit thesis. But what thesis does his essay seem to imply? Can you express his implied thesis in one sentence?

In the following essay, an African American explores how a black man can cause paranoia among people who react to a racial stereotype. As you read, think about how the writer's analysis compels the audience to examine their biases.

Black Men and Public Space*

My first victim was a woman—white, well dressed, probably in her early twenties. I came upon her late one evening on a deserted street in Hyde Park, a relatively affluent neighborhood in an otherwise mean, impoverished section of Chicago. As I swung onto the avenue behind her, there seemed to be a discreet, uninflammatory distance between us. Not so. She cast back a worried glance. To her, the youngish black man—a broad six feet two inches with a beard and billowing hair, both hands shoved into the pockets of a bulky military jacket—seemed menacingly close. After a few more quick glimpses, she picked up her pace and was soon running in earnest. Within seconds she disappeared into a cross street.

That was more than a decade ago. I was twenty-two years old, a graduate student newly arrived at the University of Chicago. It was in the echo of that terrified woman's footfalls that I first began to know the unwieldy inheritance I'd come into—the ability to alter public space in ugly ways. It was clear that she thought herself the quarry of a mugger, a rapist, or worse. Suffering a bout of insomnia, however, I was stalking sleep, not defenseless wayfarers. As a softy who is scarcely able to take a knife to a raw chicken—let alone hold one to a person's throat—I was surprised, embarrassed, and dismayed all at once. Her flight made me feel like an accomplice in tyranny. It also made it clear that I was indistinguishable from the muggers who occasionally seeped into the area from the surrounding ghetto. That first encounter, and those that followed, signified that a vast, unnerving gulf lay between nighttime pedestrians—particularly women—and me. And I soon gathered that being perceived as dangerous is a hazard in itself. I only needed to turn a corner into a dicey situation, or crowd some frightened, armed person in a foyer somewhere, or make an errant move after being pulled over by a policeman. Where fear and

---

* Brent Staples, "Black Men and Public Space." From *Ms.*, September 1986 and *Harper's*, December 1986. Copyright © 1986 by Brent Staples. Reprinted by permission of the author.

weapons meet—and they often do in urban America—there is always the possibility of death.

In that first year, my first away from my hometown, I was to become thoroughly familiar with the language of fear. At dark, shadowy intersections, I could cross in front of a car stopped at a traffic light and elicit the *thunk, thunk, thunk, thunk* of the driver—black, white, male, or female—hammering down the door locks. On less traveled streets after dark, I grew accustomed to but never comfortable with people crossing to the other side of the street rather than pass me. Then there were the standard unpleasantries with policemen, doormen, bouncers, cabdrivers, and others whose business it is to screen out troublesome individuals *before* there is any nastiness.

I moved to New York nearly two years ago and I have remained an avid night walker. In central Manhattan, the near-constant crowd cover minimizes tense one-on-one street encounters. Elsewhere—in SoHo, for example, where sidewalks are narrow and tightly spaced buildings shut out the sky—things can get very taut indeed.

After dark, on the warrenlike streets of Brooklyn where I live, I often see women who fear the worst from me. They seem to have set their faces on neutral, and with their purse straps strung across their chests bandolier-style, they forge ahead as though bracing themselves against being tackled. I understand, of course, that the danger they perceive is not a hallucination. Women are particularly vulnerable to street violence, and young black males are drastically overrepresented among the perpetrators of that violence. Yet these truths are no solace against the kind of alienation that comes of being ever the suspect, a fearsome entity with whom pedestrians avoid making eye contact.

It is not altogether clear to me how I reached the ripe old age of twenty-two without being conscious of the lethality nighttime pedestrians attributed to me. Perhaps it was because in Chester, Pennsylvania, the small, angry industrial town where I came of age in the 1960s, I was scarcely noticeable against a backdrop of gang warfare, street knifings, and murders. I grew up one of the good boys, had perhaps a half-dozen fistfights. In retrospect, my shyness of combat has clear sources.

As a boy, I saw countless tough guys locked away; I have since buried several, too. They were babies, really—a teenage cousin, a brother of twenty-two, a childhood friend in his mid-twenties—all gone down in episodes of bravado played out in the streets. I came to doubt the virtues of intimidation early on. I chose, perhaps unconsciously, to remain a shadow—timid, but a survivor.

The fearsomeness mistakenly attributed to me in public places often has a perilous flavor. The most frightening of these confusions occurred in the late 1970s and early 1980s, when I worked as a journalist in Chicago. One day, rushing into the office of a magazine I was writing for with a deadline story in hand, I was mistaken for a burglar. The office manager called security and, with an ad hoc posse, pursued me through the labyrinthine halls, nearly to my editor's door. I had no way of proving who I was. I could only move briskly toward the company of someone who knew me.

Another time I was on assignment for a local paper and killing time before an interview. I entered a jewelry store on the city's affluent Near North Side. The proprietor excused herself and returned with an enormous red Doberman pinscher straining at the end of a leash. She stood, the dog extended toward me, silent to my questions, her eyes bulging nearly out of her head. I took a cursory look around, nodded, and bade her good night.

Relatively speaking, however, I never fared as badly as another black male journalist. He went to nearby Waukegan, Illinois, a couple of summers ago to work on a story about a murderer who was born there. Mistaking the reporter for the killer, police officers hauled him from his car at gunpoint and but for his press credentials would probably have tried to book him. Such episodes are not uncommon. Black men trade tales like this all the time.

Over the years, I learned to smother the rage I felt at so often being taken for a criminal. Not to do so would surely have led to madness. I now take precautions to make myself less threatening. I move about with care, particularly late in the evening. I give a wide berth to nervous people on subway platforms during the wee hours, particularly when I have exchanged business clothes for jeans. If I happen to be entering a building behind some people who appear skittish, I may walk by, letting them clear the lobby before I return, so as not to seem to be following them. I have been calm and extremely congenial on those rare occasions when I've been pulled over by the police.

And on late-evening constitutionals I employ what has proved to be an excellent tension-reducing measure: I whistle melodies from Beethoven and Vivaldi and the more popular classical composers. Even steely New Yorkers hunching toward nighttime destinations seem to relax, and occasionally they even join in the tune. Virtually everybody seems to sense that a mugger wouldn't be warbling bright, sunny selections from Vivaldi's *Four Seasons*. It is my equivalent of the cowbell that hikers wear when they know they are in bear country.

—Brent Staples

Staples shows that a racial stereotype has a double effect: in narrowing the perceptions for those who *impose* the stereotype, and in narrowing the choices for those who *endure* the stereotype. Instead of resorting to sermons or accusations, this essay makes its point through a dispassionate analysis of facts and events.

Reasoning from Effect to Cause

By reasoning from effect to cause, you answer these readers' questions:

Why did it happen?

What caused it?

Here is an effect-to-cause paragraph:

Effect (main point) (1) Distant cause and examples (2) Examples (3–4) Evidence (5) Immediate cause (6–7)	[1]In the right situation, a perfectly sane person can hallucinate. [2]It is most likely to happen when [he or she] is in a place that provides little stimulation to [the] senses, such as a barren, unbroken landscape or a quiet, dimly lit room. [3]Hallucinations are an occupational hazard of truck drivers, radar scanners, and pilots. [4]These occupations have in common long periods of monotony: lengthy stretches of straight highway, the regular rhythms of radar patterns, the droning hum of engines. [5]A. L. Mosely of the Harvard School of Public Health found that every one of 33 long-distance truck drivers he surveyed could recall having at least one hallucination. [6]Monotony means that the brain gets fewer sensory messages from the outside. [7]As external stimulation drops off, the brain responds more to messages from inside itself.

—Daniel Goleman

Guidelines for Effect-to-Cause Analysis

In developing the paragraph above, the author followed guidelines that govern any causal analysis.

1. *The support shows that the cause fits the effect.* To clarify his main point, the author shows varied examples of "right" situations and of "sane" persons. Research evidence from Harvard is included to provide convincing support.

2. *The links between effect and cause are clear.* The author's reasoning goes like this:

| [*distant cause*] | | [*immediate cause*] | | [*effect*] |
| nonstimulating places | $\rightarrow$ | monotony | $\rightarrow$ | hallucination |

The distant cause is discussed first so that the immediate cause will make sense. Because readers need to see connections, the author had to organize his paragraph carefully.

Reasoning from Cause to Effect

When you reason from cause to effect, you answer these readers' questions:

What are its effects?

What will happen if it is done?

A cause-effect analysis must distinguish between ultimate (or distant) and immediate effects or among possible, probable, and definite effects. Here is a cause-to-effect paragraph:

> ¹What has the telephone done to us, or for us, in the hundred years of its existence? ²A few effects suggest themselves at once. ³It has saved lives by getting rapid word of illness, injury, or famine from remote places. ⁴By joining with the elevator to make possible the multistory residence or office building, it has made possible—for better or worse—the modern city. ⁵By bringing about a quantum leap in the speed and ease with which information moves from place to place, it has greatly accelerated the rate of scientific and technological change and growth in industry. ⁶Beyond doubt it has crippled if not killed the ancient art of letter writing. ⁷It has made living alone possible for persons with normal social impulses; by so doing, it has played a role in one of the greatest social changes of this century, the breakup of the multigenerational household. ⁸It has made the waging of war chillingly more efficient than formerly. ⁹Perhaps (though not probably) it has prevented wars that might have arisen out of international misunderstanding caused by written communications. ¹⁰Or perhaps—again not probably—by magnifying and extending irrational personal conflicts based on voice contact, it has caused wars. ¹¹Certainly it has extended the scope of human conflicts, since it impartially disseminates the useful knowledge of scientists and the babble of bores, the affection of the affectionate and the malice of the malicious.
>
> —John Brooks

Guidelines for Cause-to-Effect Analysis

The previous paragraph conforms to these guidelines:

1. *The support shows that the effects fit the cause.* To clarify and support his main point, the author shows the telephone's effects on familiar aspects of modern life. Because his purpose is to discuss effects in general (not only *positive* effects), the author balances his development with both positive and negative effects.

2. *The links between cause and effects are clear.* The reasoning goes like this:

   [cause]   *[immediate effect]*   *[ultimate effects]*
   telephone → created rapid communication → saved lives, led to the
                                                                modern city, and so on

   [cause]   *[immediate effect]*   *[ultimate effect]*
   telephone → enabled people to live alone → led to breakup of multi-
                                                                generational household

Without the link provided by the immediate effects, the ultimate effects would make no sense to readers:

> The telephone has saved lives. [*Why?*]
>
> It has made possible the modern city. [*Why?*]
>
> It perhaps has caused wars. [*Why?*]

For further linking, the paragraph groups *definite effects* (3–8), and then *possible effects* (9–10), with a conclusion that ties the discussion together.

Application 15–1

PARAGRAPH WARM-UP: FROM EFFECT TO CAUSE

Identify a problem that affects you, your community, family, school, dorm, or other group ("The library is an awful place to study because ———"). You might wish to phrase your topic statement as a question. In a paragraph, analyze the causes of this problem. Choose a subject you know about or one you can research to get the facts. Identify clearly the situation, the audience, and your purpose. Here are some possible subjects:

why I did poorly in a course

why a friendship was destroyed

why I am so deeply in debt

why I quit my job

Application 15–2

PARAGRAPH WARM-UP: FROM CAUSE TO EFFECT

Think of a major change you have made or would like to make in your life (moving off campus, changing majors, studying more seriously, or the like). Write a paragraph discussing the effects of this change, for a stipulated audience and purpose.

As an alternate assignment, discuss the good or bad effects of a recent friendship or relationship. Write directly to the person affected.

Application 15–3

ESSAY PRACTICE: ANALYZING CAUSES

After reading this essay, answer the study questions. Then select one of the essay assignments.

Fear of Dearth

[1]I hate jogging. Every dawn as I thud around New York City's Central Park reservoir, I am reminded of how much I hate it. It's so tedious. Some claim jogging is thought-conducive; others insist the scenery relieves the monotony. For me, the pace is wrong for contemplation of either ideas or vistas. While jogging, all I can think about is jogging—or nothing. One advantage of jogging around a reservoir is that there's no dry shortcut home.

[2]From the listless look of some fellow trotters, I gather I am not alone in my unenthusiasm: Bill-paying, it seems, would be about as diverting. Nonetheless, we continue to jog; more, we continue to *choose* to jog. From a practically infinite array of opportunities, we select one that we don't enjoy and can't wait to have done with. Why?

[3]For any trend, there are as many reasons as there are participants. This person runs to lower [her] blood pressure. That person runs to escape the telephone or a cranky spouse or a filthy household. Another person runs to avoid doing anything else, to dodge a decision about how to lead his life or a realization that his life is leading nowhere. Each of us has [her] own carrot and stick. In my case, the

stick is my slackening physical condition, which keeps me from beating opponents at tennis whom I overwhelmed two years ago. My carrot is to win.

⁴Beyond these disparate reasons, however, lies a deeper cause. It is no accident that now, in the last third of the 20th century, personal fitness and health have suddenly become a popular obsession. True, modern [people] like to feel good, but that hardly distinguishes [us] from [our] predecessors.

⁵With zany myopia, economists like to claim that the deeper cause of everything is economic. Delightfully, there seems no marketplace explanation for jogging. True, jogging is cheap, but then not jogging is cheaper. And the scant and skimpy equipment which jogging demands must make it a marketer's least favored form of recreation.

⁶Some scout-masterish philosophers argue that the appeal of jogging and other body-maintenance programs is the discipline they afford. We live in a world in which individuals have fewer and fewer obligations. The work week has shrunk. Weekend worship is less compulsory. Technology gives us more free time. Satisfactorily filling free time requires imagination and effort. Freedom is a wide and risky river; it can drown the person who does not know how to swim across it. The more obligations one takes on, the more time one occupies, the less threat freedom poses. Jogging can become an instant obligation. For a portion of his day, the jogger is not his own [person]; he is obedient to a regimen he has accepted.

⁷Theologists may take the argument one step further. It is our modern irreligion, our lack of confidence in any hereafter, that makes us anxious to stretch our mortal stay as long as possible. We run, as the saying goes, for our lives, hounded by the suspicion that these are the only lives we are likely to enjoy.

⁸All of these theorists seem to me more or less right. As the growth of cults and charismatic religions and the resurgence of enthusiasm for the military draft suggest, we do crave commitment. And who can doubt, watching so many middle-aged and older persons torturing themselves in the name of fitness, that we are unreconciled to death, more so perhaps than any generation in modern memory?

⁹But I have a hunch there's a further explanation of our obsession with exercise. I suspect that what motivates us even more than a fear of death is a fear of dearth. Our era is the first to anticipate the eventual depletion of all natural resources. We see wilderness shrinking; rivers losing their capacity to sustain life; the air, even the stratosphere, being loaded with potentially deadly junk. We see the irreplaceable being squandered, and in the depths of our consciousness we are fearful that we are creating an uninhabitable world. We feel more or less helpless and yet, at the same time, desirous to protect what resources we can. We recycle soda bottles and restore old buildings and protect our nearest natural resource—our physical health—in

the almost superstitious hope that such small gestures will help save an earth that we are blighting. Jogging becomes a sort of penance for our sins of gluttony, greed, and waste. Like a hairshirt or a bed of nails, the more one hates it, the more virtuous it makes one feel.

[10]That is why *we* jog. Why *I* jog is to win at tennis.

—Carrl Tucker

Questions About Content

1. Is the title appropriate for this essay? Explain.

2. In your own words, restate the main point (or thesis) of the essay in a complete sentence.

3. Why would readers find the content of this essay interesting?

4. Is this essay convincing? Explain.

5. What specific readers' questions are answered in the body?

Questions About Organization

1. Why do you suppose the writer used two paragraphs for his introduction? Explain the function of each.

2. What combination of opening strategies is used in the introduction?

3. Are the body paragraphs arranged in an order (such as general-to-specific) that emphasizes the thesis? If so, what is that order?

4. In a brief outline, list the major topic of each body paragraph.

5. Underline each topic statement. Does each paragraph have a topic statement?

6. Which topic statement in the body serves four individual paragraphs? Is this an effective arrangement? Explain.

7. The body paragraphs vary greatly in length; is this variation justified? Explain.

8. Which two reasons, among those offered to explain the jogging craze, does the author find least credible? Why are these reasons discussed at that place in the essay?

9. Is the brief, two-sentence conclusion effective? Explain.

Questions About Style

1. Identify one sentence that relies on subordination for combining related thoughts. Explain why this structure reinforces the meaning of that sentence.

2. Identify one sentence that relies on coordination for combining related thoughts. How does this coordinate structure reinforce the meaning of that sentence?

3. What is the most notable feature of sentence style throughout this essay? Comment on the effectiveness of this feature.

4. In the second sentence, is **thud** the best word the writer could have chosen? Explain.

5. Characterize the tone of Tucker's essay. Explain briefly how word choice and sentence structure contribute to this tone.

Note: The introduction to Section Three mentions that many published essays break the mold of the "formula essay." Tucker's essay is a good example of structural variation. After reviewing pages 216–217, reread Tucker's essay to identify specific ways (not covered in the questions above) in which he has broken the mold. Try to incorporate some of these variations into your own essay. At this stage of your writing, you should be ready to take some chances!

RESPONDING TO YOUR READING

1. Explore your reactions to "Fear of Dearth" by using the questions on page 91. Then respond with an essay of your own, analyzing a cause or causes.

   You might write about some activity or behavior (harmful or beneficial, pleasurable or painful) that takes up much of your (and other people's) time. Beginning with that as an effect, analyze its cause(s). Like Tucker, you might want to generalize (as justified by your experience and observation) about why that activity has become so popular. Here are activities or behaviors whose causes you could analyze:

   • Why do I (or we) spend so much time watching football games (or some other sport)?

   • Why am I so obsessed with exercise, fashion, or diet?

   • Why am I a soap opera fan?

   • Why are we such party animals?

   Be sure that your analysis supports a definite thesis about the cause(s) of the thing. Feel free to inject some humor.

2. Explore your reactions to "The Old Guy" (pages 292–293) by using the page 91 questions. Then respond with an essay about something that worries or scares you, something you usually try not to

think about. Maybe it's a person or a place, a situation or an event. Maybe, as with Andrade, it's something about growing up. Or maybe you worry about having to face some kind of change or about losing something or about having to confront something you've preferred to ignore or deny.

Analyze the cause(s) of your feelings in enough detail so that we can stand in your place. Show us what is happening and why it's happening and what it means for you. Be sure your analysis supports a definite thesis—whether you state the thesis or merely imply it.

OPTIONS FOR ESSAY WRITING

1. Write an essay on the causes of human cruelty.

2. Why are many Americans afraid of old age?

3. Think about people you know who enjoy (or dislike) their work. What do you think explains that enjoyment (or dislike)?

4. Why do people gossip? What human need does gossip satisfy, and how? Be sure that your essay makes some definite point about human nature.

5. Most young people do not need to be told to enjoy life. They do. Personal growth and social experiences provide teenagers with what adults often label as the "best years of one's life." For some teenagers, however, problems are overwhelming; recent statistics show an alarming increase in teenage suicide. What do you think are some major causes of teenage suicide? Explain in an essay.

Application 15–4

ESSAY PRACTICE: ANALYZING EFFECTS

In this essay, the writer shows that a type of weather can dramatically exemplify how our lives are ruled by forces beyond our control. Read the essay carefully, and answer the questions that follow. Then select one of the essay assignments.

Close to the Edge*

[1]There is something uneasy in the Los Angeles air this afternoon, some unnatural stillness, some tension. What it means is that tonight a Santa Ana will begin to blow, a hot wind from the northeast

---

* Title added.

whining down through the Cajon and San Gorgonio Passes, blowing up sandstorms out along Route 66, drying the hills and the nerves to the flash point. For a few days now we will see smoke back in the canyons, and hear sirens in the night. I have neither heard nor read that a Santa Ana is due, but I know it, and almost everyone I have seen today knows it too. We know it because we feel it. The baby frets. The maid sulks. I rekindle a waning argument with the telephone company, then cut my losses and lie down, given over to whatever it is in the air. To live with the Santa Ana is to accept consciously or unconsciously, a deeply mechanistic* view of human behavior.

²I recall being told, when I first moved to Los Angeles and was living on an isolated beach, that the Indians would throw themselves into the sea when the bad wind blew. I could see why. The Pacific turned ominously glossy during a Santa Ana period, and one woke in the night troubled not only by the peacocks screaming in the olive trees but by the eerie absence of surf. The heat was surreal. The sky had a yellow cast, the kind of light sometimes called "earthquake weather." My only neighbor would not come out of her house for days, and there were no lights at night, and her husband roamed the place with a machete. One day he would tell me that he had heard a trespasser, the next a rattlesnake.

³"On nights like that," Raymond Chandler once wrote about the Santa Ana, "every booze party ends in a fight. Meek little wives feel the edge of the carving knife and study their husbands' necks. Anything can happen." That was the kind of wind it was. I did not know then that there was any basis for the effect it had on all of us, but it turns out to be another of those cases in which science bears out folk wisdom. The Santa Ana, which is named for one of the canyons it rushes through, is a *foehn* wind, like the *foehn* of Austria and Switzerland and the *hamsin* of Israel. There are a number of persistent malevolent winds, perhaps the best known of which are the *mistral* of France and the Mediterranean *sirocco*, but a *foehn* wind has distinct characteristics: it occurs on the leeward slope of a mountain range and, although the air begins as a cold mass, it is warmed as it comes down the mountain and appears finally as a hot dry wind. Whenever and wherever a *foehn* blows, doctors hear about headaches and nausea and allergies, about "nervousness," about "depression." In Los Angeles some teachers do not attempt to conduct formal classes during a Santa Ana, because the children become unmanageable. In Switzerland the suicide rate goes up during the *foehn*, and in the courts of some Swiss cantons the wind is considered a mitigating circumstance for crime. Surgeons are said to watch the wind because the blood does not clot normally during a *foehn*. A few years ago an Israeli physicist discovered that not only during such winds, but for

---

* *Mechanistic:* having purely physical or biological causes.

the ten or twelve hours which precede them, the air carries an unusually high ratio of positive to negative ions. No one seems to know exactly why that should be; some talk about friction, others suggest solar disturbances. In any case, the positive ions are there, and what an excess of positive ions does, in the simplest terms, is make people unhappy. One cannot get much more mechanistic than that.

[4]Easterners commonly complain that there is no "weather" at all in Southern California, that the days and the seasons slip by relentlessly, numbingly bland. That is quite misleading. In fact the climate is characterized by infrequent but violent extremes: two periods of torrential subtropical rains which continue for weeks and wash out the hills and send subdivisions sliding toward the sea; about twenty scattered days a year of the Santa Ana, which, with its incendiary dryness, invariably means fire. At the first prediction of a Santa Ana, the Forest Service flies men and equipment from northern California into the Southern forests, and the Los Angeles Fire Department cancels its ordinary non-firefighting routines. The Santa Ana caused Malibu to burn the way it did in 1956, and Bel Air in 1961, and Santa Barbara in 1964. In the winter of 1966–1967 eleven men were killed fighting a Santa Ana fire that spread through the San Gabriel mountains.

[5]Just to watch the front-page news out of Los Angeles during a Santa Ana is to get very close to what it is about the place. The longest single Santa Ana period in recent years was in 1957, and it lasted not the usual three or four days but fourteen days, from November 21 until December 4. On the first day 25,000 acres of the San Gabriel mountains were burning, with gusts reaching 100 miles an hour. In town, the wind reached Force 12, or hurricane force, on the Beaufort Scale; oil derricks were toppled and people ordered off the downtown streets to avoid injury from flying objects. On November 22 the fire in the San Gabriels was out of control. On November 24 six people were killed in automobile accidents, and by the end of the week the Los Angeles *Times* was keeping a box score of traffic deaths. On November 26 a prominent Pasadena attorney, depressed about money, shot and killed his wife, their two sons, and himself. On November 27 a South Gate divorcee, twenty-two, was murdered and thrown from a moving car. On November 30 the San Gabriel fire was still out of control, and the wind in town was blowing eighty miles an hour. On the first day of December four people died violently, and on the third the wind began to break.

[6]It is hard for people who have not lived in Los Angeles to realize how radically the Santa Ana figures in the local imagination. The city burning is Los Angeles's deepest image of itself: Nathaniel West perceived that, in *The Day of the Locust*; and at the time of the 1965 Watts riots what struck the imagination most indelibly was the fires. For days one could drive the Harbor Freeway and see the city on fire, just as we had always known it would be in the end. Los Angeles

weather is the weather of catastrophe, of apocalypse, and, just as the reliably long and bitter winters of New England determine the way life is lived there, so the violence and the unpredictability of the Santa Ana affect the entire quality of life in Los Angeles, accentuate its impermanence, its unreliability. The wind shows us how close to the edge we are.

—Joan Didion

Questions About the Content

1. Is the title effective? Explain briefly.

2. In your own words, restate the main point of the essay in a complete sentence.

3. Does the thesis statement clearly express the writer's attitude toward the wind? If so, how would you characterize her attitude?

4. Is Didion's essay credible? Are you convinced that this writer knows what she is talking about? Explain.

5. Identify three statements of opinion and three statements of fact.

6. Does the essay have informative value? Explain.

7. What did you like or dislike about Didion's essay? Make your answer as specific as possible.

Questions About Organization

1. In Didion's introduction identify (a) two sentences that provide background and (b) two sentences that create suspense.

2. Which order (general-to-specific, chronological, and so on) do the combined body paragraphs follow?

3. Identify four devices that increase the coherence of Didion's essay, and give examples of each.

4. Explain the purpose served by the mention of New England weather in the conclusion.

5. Does Didion's conclusion sum up the main points, or does it interpret and evaluate material in the body? Explain your answer.

Questions About Style

1. Identify one sentence in Didion's essay that relies on subordination as a method of combining three or more related

ideas. Be prepared to explain why subordination was the appropriate method for combining these ideas. (Refer to pages 163–164 and 180–181.)

Example

What it means is that tonight a Santa Ana will begin to blow, a hot wind from the northeast whining down through the Cajon and San Gorgonio Passes, blowing up sandstorms along Route 66, drying the hills and the nerves to the flash point.

2. Identify one sentence that relies on coordination for combining three or more related thoughts. Be prepared to explain why coordination was the appropriate method for combining these ideas. (Refer to pages 162–163 and 180–181.)

Example

My only neighbor would not come out of her house for days, and there were no lights at night, and her husband roamed the place with a machete.

3. Identify two short sentences that provide dramatic emphasis for an important point.

Example

That was the kind of wind it was.

4. Briefly characterize the *tone* that emanates from Didion's essay. Be as specific as possible. (Refer to pages 197–207.)

5. Give examples of the details that do the *showing:*

    • Details that help us see.

Example

The maid sulks.

    • Details that help us feel.

Example

Some unnatural stillness.

    • Details that help us hear.

Example

A hot wind from the northeast whining down.

    • Details that a camera would record.

Example

The sky had a yellow cast.

• Numerical details.

Example

On the first day, 25,000 acres of the San Gabriel mountains were burning.

RESPONDING TO YOUR READING

1. Explore your reactions to "Close to the Edge" by using the questions on page 91. Then respond with your own essay, analyzing the effects of a place, an event, or a relationship.

    You might trace the effects in your life from having a specific friend or belonging to a specific family or group. Or you might explain the effects on your family, school, or community of a tragic event (such as a suicide) or a fortunate one (say, a financial windfall). Or you might want to show how the socioeconomic atmosphere of your hometown or neighborhood or family has affected the person you have become. Or you might explain how the weather, landscape, or geography of your area affects people's values and behavior and lifestyle.

    Whatever the topic, be sure your discussion supports a definite viewpoint about the effects of something.

2. Explore your reactions to "Black Men and Public Space" by using the page 91 questions and those below.

    • For whom does Staples seem to be writing?

    • What assumptions does he make about his audience's knowledge and attitudes? Are these assumptions accurate? Why or why not?

    • What are the main issues here? How has this essay affected your thinking about these issues?

    • What point is Staples making about stereotypes?

    • What is this writer's attitude toward his subject? Toward his audience? How do we know? What are the signals?

    • How would you characterize the tone of this essay? Is it appropriate for this writer's audience and purpose?

Most of us want to be liked and accepted and respected. As you reread the essay, try to recall a situation in which you or a close person were the object of someone's hostility or rejection—say, because of resentment or fear or anger or scorn. (Or perhaps someone else was the object of yours!) Perhaps the reaction was based on a stereotype or misunderstanding or personal bias. Perhaps, after realizing rejection, you modified your behavior to fit in, you invented a self that seemed more acceptable. Identify your audience, and decide what you want these readers to be doing or thinking or feeling after reading your essay.

Describe the events and your reactions in enough detail for readers to visualize what happened and what resulted. Without preaching or moralizing, try to explain your view of this experience's *larger meaning*.

OPTIONS FOR ESSAY WRITING

1. Explain the effects of a major decision you or your family has made. How has the decision changed your life?

2. Analyze the effect computers have had on your generation.

3. Analyze the effect of a significant event in your life (death of a loved one, inheriting money, serious illness, divorce, moving a great distance, or the like).

4. Analyze how coming to college has affected a relationship in your life.

16

Explaining Similarities or Differences: Comparison and Contrast

Developing a Comparison • Developing a Contrast
• Developing a Combined Comparison and Contrast
• Guidelines for Comparison and Contrast
• A Special Kind of Comparison: Analogy
• Guidelines for Analogies • Applications

Comparison explains how things are similar; *contrast* explains how they are different. We use comparison and contrast (sometimes just called *comparison*) to evaluate things or to shed light on their relationship.

Whenever we set out to evaluate something by measuring it against something else, we confront this question:

Is *X* better than *Y*?

To reach a judgment about the relative merit or significance of X and Y, we examine them side by side. We might compare two (or more) cars, computers, business machines, political candidates, college courses, careers, or the like. In Chapter 1 (pages 18–19), Shirley Haley evaluates her parents' life-style by contrasting it with the life-style she envisions for herself. To evaluate recent economic progress by American women and minorities, we can compare numbers from two or three earlier decades with today's numbers: How much larger is the percentage of women who now have college degrees or high-income jobs? In each comparison, one item provides a basis for evaluating the other.

A second kind of comparison helps readers understand one thing in terms of another by answering this question:

What in *X* can shed light on *Y?*

To explain effects of the American high-fat diet on heart disease and cancer, we can compare disease rates in Japan (with its low-fat diet) with rates in our country. To reveal the danger posed by advocates of white supremacy, or of racial hatred in general, we can compare today's attitudes and behavior with those in Nazi Germany a half-century ago. When the two items are examined side by side, one helps illuminate the other.

In the following essay, a Mexican American explores the contrast between the original, Hispanic meaning of **macho** (as a term of respect) and its acquired meaning in American English (as a term of contempt). The way we use language reflects the way we think about ourselves as a culture. As you read, notice how this essay compels us to reconsider certain attitudes, values, and popular notions of desirable behavior.

Americanization Is Tough on "Macho"*

What is *macho?* That depends which side of the border you come from.

Although it's not unusual for words and expressions to lose their subtlety in translation, the negative connotations of *macho* in this country are troublesome to Hispanics.

Take the newspaper descriptions of alleged mass murderer Ramon Salcido. That an insensitive, insanely jealous, hard-drinking, violent Latin male is referred to as *macho* makes Hispanics cringe.

"Es muy macho," the women in my family nod approvingly, describing a man they respect. But in the United States, when women say, "He's so macho," it's with disdain.

The Hispanic *macho* is manly, responsible, hardworking, a man in charge, a patriarch. A man who expresses strength through silence. What the Yiddish language would call a *mensch.*

The American *macho* is a chauvinist, a brute, uncouth, selfish, loud, abrasive, capable of inflicting pain, and sexually promiscuous.

---

* Rose del Castillo Guilbault, "Americanization Is Tough on 'Macho'." Rose del Castillo Guilbault is a columnist for the San Francisco Chronicle. Reprinted by permission of the author.

Quintessential *macho* models in this country are Sylvester Stallone, Arnold Schwarzenegger and Charles Bronson. In their movies, they exude toughness, independence, masculinity. But a closer look reveals their machismo is really violence masquerading as courage, sullenness disguised as silence and irresponsibility camouflaged as independence.

If the Hispanic ideal of *macho* were translated to American screen roles, they might be Jimmy Stewart, Sean Connery and Laurence Olivier.

In Spanish, *macho* ennobles Latin males. In English it devalues them. This pattern seems consistent with the conflicts ethnic minority males experience in this country. Typically the cultural traits other societies value don't translate as desirable characteristics in America.

I watched my own father struggle with these cultural ambiguities. He worked on a farm for twenty years. He laid down miles of irrigation pipe, carefully plowed long, neat rows in fields, hacked away at recalcitrant weeds and drove tractors through whirlpools of dust. He stoically worked twenty-hour days during harvest season, accepting the long hours as part of agricultural work. When the boss complained or upbraided him for minor mistakes, he kept quiet, even when it was obvious the boss had erred.

He handled the most menial tasks with pride. At home he was a good provider, helped out my mother's family in Mexico without complaint, and was indulgent with me. Arguments between my mother and him generally had to do with money, or with his stubborn reluctance to share his troubles. He tried to work them out in his own silence. He didn't want to trouble my mother—a course that backfired, because the imagined is always worse than the reality.

Americans regarded my father as decidedly un-*macho*. His character was interpreted as nonassertive, his loyalty non-ambition, and his quietness, ignorance. I once overheard the boss's son blame him for plowing crooked rows in a field. My father merely smiled at the lie, knowing the boy had done it, but didn't refute it, confident his good work was well known. But the boss instead ridiculed him for being "stupid" and letting a kid get away with a lie. Seeing my embarrassment, my father dismissed the incident, saying "They're the dumb ones. Imagine, me fighting with a kid."

I tried not to look at him with American eyes because sometimes the reflection hurt.

Listening to my aunts' clucks of approval, my vision focused on the qualities America overlooked. "He's such a hard worker. So serious, so responsible." My aunts would secretly compliment my mother. The unspoken comparison was that he was not like some of their husbands, who drank and womanized. My uncles represented the darker side of *macho*.

In a patriarchal society, few challenge their roles. If men drink, it's because it's the manly thing to do. If they gamble, it's because it's how men relax. And if they fool around, well, it's because a man simply can't hold back so much man! My aunts didn't exactly meekly sit back, but they put up with these transgressions because Mexican society dictated this was their lot in life.

In the United States, I believe it was the feminist movement of the early '70s that changed *macho*'s meaning. Perhaps my generation of Latin women was in part responsible. I recall Chicanas complaining about the chauvinistic nature of Latin men and the notion they wanted their women barefoot, pregnant and in the kitchen. The generalization that Latin men embodied chauvinistic traits led to this interesting twist of semantics. Suddenly a word that represented something positive in one culture became a negative prototype in another.

The problem with the use of *macho* today is that it's become an accepted stereotype of the Latin male. And like all stereotypes, it distorts truth.

The impact of language in our society is undeniable. And the misuse of *macho* hints at a deeper cultural misunderstanding that extends beyond mere word definitions.

—Rose Del Castillo Guilbault

By *showing* instead of merely *telling*, Guilbault enables us to visualize the important distinctions that support her larger point about cultural differences.

We compare and contrast whenever similarities and differences can help us explore and explain something, as in the next essay. Here, the writer weighs the relative merits of two names to show readers that one name is better than the other.

"Campus Center" Versus "Student Union"

We refer to the building that houses the core of student activities at our school as the "Campus Center." Is this an accurate description of the space which provides the nucleus of university life?

Until about four years ago, the building was known as the "Student Union," a term appropriate to the place where students socialize, plan events, and debate issues. "A rose by any other name. . . ." you may be thinking. But to rechristen the building the "Student Union" would be in the best interest of our students.

"Campus Center" assigns no real meaning to the hub of so much student activity. The phrase calls to mind passive things: the large-screen television set and the couch potatoes who watch it all day, the video arcade, the billiard room—people just hanging around. "Campus Center" . . . repeat it a few times, and it sounds almost militaristic, controlled by forces reminiscent of some sort of police state—

perhaps the headquarters for Orwell's Thought Police. The architect of this university has already done what he could to make it resemble a missile-launching site, and so why throw around labels that further the effect?

"Student Union," on the other hand, carries active connotations, sounding as if people *do* things there. "Student Union" points to the meaningful student organizations housed in the building. When we think "Student Union," we think student action: the Student Senate, the Program Council, WUSM Radio, the Women's Center, the African-American Coalition, and so on. Whereas "Campus Center" is a value-neutral term that seems to connote the apathy that student organizers so often condemn, "Student Union" reminds us of our unity and alliance as a decisive force within the University. The "Student Union" belongs to us. The "Campus Center" belongs to someone else.

To revive the use of "Student Union" would be easy enough. We would merely be reversing a change made once before. Our newspapers and radio station have the tools to put "Student Union" back into our campus vocabulary. If we use the term in conversation, in announcements, on memos and posters, we might be surprised at how quickly our peers pick it up and pass it on. Instead of focusing on the building as a place for hanging around, the name would focus on the ideals embodied in the building and its organized student activities. "Student Union" reminds us that we as students have a say in what goes on.

—Lois Shea

Whenever readers need to know about similarities and differences, comparison and contrast are essential.

Developing a Comparison

A comparison is designed to answer this readers' question:

How are X and Y similar or alike?

The writer of this paragraph compares *drug habits* among people of all times and places to those among people of modern times:

Paragraph 1

Main point (1)   [1]All the natural narcotics, stimulants, relaxants, and hallucinants known to the modern botanist and pharmacologist were discovered by

Historical similarity
to modern habits
(2–3)

Religious similarity
to modern habits
(4–5)

Modern continuation
of habit (6–7)

Concluding point
based on
comparisons above
(8)

primitive [people] and have been in use from time immemorial. ²One of the first things that *Homo sapiens* did with his newly developed rationality and self-consciousness was to set them to work finding out ways to bypass analytical thinking and to transcend or, in extreme cases, temporarily obliterate the isolating awareness of the self. ³Trying all things that grew in the field or forest, they held fast to that which, in this context, seemed good—everything, that is to say, that would change the quality of consciousness, would make it different, no matter how, from everyday feeling, perceiving, and thinking. ⁴Among the Hindus, rhythmic breathing and mental concentration have, to some extent, taken the place of mind-transforming drugs used elsewhere. ⁵But even in the land of yoga, even among the religious and even for specifically religious purposes, *Cannabis indica* (marijuana) has been freely used to supplement the effects of spiritual exercises. ⁶The habit of taking vacations from the more-or-less purgatorial world, which we have created for ourselves, is universal. ⁷Moralists may denounce it; but, in the teeth of disapproving talk and repressive legislation, the habit persists, and mind-transforming drugs are everywhere available. ⁸The Marxian formula, "Religion is the opium of the people," is reversible, and one can say, with even more truth, that "Opium is the religion of the people."

—Aldous Huxley

Developing a Contrast

A contrast is designed to answer this readers' question:

How are *X* and *Y* different?

This paragraph contrasts the *beliefs* of Satanism with those of Christianity:

Paragraph 2

Main point (1)
First difference (2–3)

¹The Satanic belief system, not surprisingly, is the antithesis of Christianity. ²Their theory of the universe, their cosmology, is based upon the

notion that the desired end state is a return to a pagan awareness of their humanity. ³This is in sharp contrast to the transcendental goals of tradi-

Second difference (4) tional Christianity. ⁴The power associated with the pantheon of gods is also reversed: Satan's power is waxing (increasing); God's, if he still

Third difference (5–8) lives, waning. ⁵The myths of the Satanic church purport to tell the true story of the rise of Christianity and the fall of paganism, and there is a reversal here too. ⁶Christ is depicted as an early "con man" who tricked an anxious and powerless group of individuals into believing a lie. ⁷He is typified as "pallid incompetence hanging on a tree." ⁸Satanic novices are taught that early church fathers deliberately picked on those aspects of human desire that were most natural and made them sins, in order to use the inevitable transgressions as a means of controlling the popu-

Final—and major— lace, promising them salvation in return for obedi-
difference (9–10) ence. ⁹And finally, their substantive belief, the very delimitation of what is sacred and what is profane, is the antithesis of Christian belief. ¹⁰The Satanist is taught to "be natural; to revel in plea-sure and in self-gratification; to emphasize indul-gence and power in this life."

—Edward J. Moody

Developing a Combined Comparison and Contrast

A combined comparison and contrast is designed to answer this question from readers:

How are *X* and *Y* both similar and different?

This paragraph first contrasts *education* with *training* and, second, com-pares how each serves important needs of society:

Paragraph 3

Main point (1) ¹To understand the nature of the liberal arts college and its function in our society, it is impor-tant to understand the difference between *educa-*

Difference of purpose *tion* and *training*. ²Training is intended primarily
(2) for the service of society; education is primarily for

How "trained" people serve society (3–5)

Similarity of effects (6)

How "educated" people serve society (7–11)

Conclusion (12)

the individual. [3]Society needs doctors, lawyers, engineers, teachers to perform specific tasks necessary to its operation, just as it needs carpenters and plumbers and stenographers. [4]Training supplies the immediate and specific needs of society so that the work of the world may continue. [5]And these needs, our training centers—the professional and trade schools—fill. [6]But although education is for the improvement of the individual, it also serves society by providing a leavening of men and women of understanding, of perception and wisdom. [7]They are our intellectual leaders, the critics of our culture, the defenders of our free traditions, the instigators of our progress. [8]They serve society by examining its function, appraising its needs, and criticizing its direction. [9]They may be earning their livings by practicing one of the professions, or in pursuing a trade, or by engaging in business enterprise. [10]They may be rich or poor. [11]They may occupy positions of power and prestige, or they may be engaged in some humble employment. [12]Without them, however, society either disintegrates or else becomes an anthill.

—Harry Kemelman

Guidelines for Comparison and Contrast

Paragraphs 1, 2, and 3 are all developed according to these guidelines:

1. *Only items in the same general class can be compared or contrasted.* The items must be related in some way: dogs and cats, but not dogs and trees; men and women, but not women and bicycles; apples and oranges, but not apples and elephants. Items with nothing in common provide no logical basis for comparison or contrast.

2. *The comparison rests on a clear and definite basis: costs, uses, benefits, appearance, results, or the like.* Paragraph 1 compares people of all times for their drug habits; paragraph 2 compares Satanism and Christianity for their primary beliefs; Paragraph 3 compares education and training by their function in our society.

3. *A comparison or contrast shows likenesses or differences in order to make a point.* Depending on your purpose, your main point may be that X is better than Y, as useful as Y, or the like. The

paragraphs above, respectively, show (a) that drug habits throughout history have not changed, (b) that Satanism is the exact opposite of Christianity, and (c) that education and training are different in their purpose but both necessary to society.

4. *Both parts of the comparison or contrast receive equal treatment.* Points discussed for one item also are discussed (or implied) for the other, generally in the same order. Paragraphs 2 and 3 offer *observable* contrasts, giving roughly equal space to each item. In Paragraph 1, modern drug use habits (although briefly mentioned) is the other item in the comparison, an item suggested throughout the discussion, and one whose details readers easily can intuit from their own general knowledge. Paragraph 1, then, offers an *implied* comparison.

5. *The comparison or contrast is supported and clarified through examples.* Similarities and differences are shown through concrete, specific, and relevant examples.

6. *A comparison or contrast follows either a block pattern or a point-by-point pattern.* In the *block pattern,* first one item is discussed fully, then the next, as in Paragraph 3: "trained" people in the first block; "educated" people in the second. A block pattern is preferable when the overall picture is more important than the individual points.

   In the *point-by-point pattern,* one point about both items is discussed, then the next point, and so on, as in Paragraph 2: the first difference between Satanism and Christianity is in their respective cosmologies; the second is in their view of God's power; the third, in their myths about the rise of Christianity, and so on. A point-by-point pattern is preferable when specific points might be hard to remember unless placed side by side.

Block pattern	Point-by-point pattern

Item *A*
   first point
   second point
   third point, etc.
	first point of *A*/first point of *B*, etc.

Item *B*
   first point
   second point
   third point, etc.
	second point of *A*/second point of *B*, etc.

   The Shea essay (pages 314–315) follows a block pattern, while the Guilbault essay (pages 312–314) follows a point-by-point pattern.

A Special Kind of Comparison: Analogy

Ordinary comparison shows similarities between two things of the *same class* (two teachers, two styles of dress, two political philosophies). Analogy, on the other hand, shows similarities between two things of *different classes* (writing and skiing, freshman registration and a merry-go-round, a dorm room and a junkyard). By using one item to clarify another, analogy answers this readers' question:

> Can you explain X by comparing it to something I already know?

Analogies are good for emphasizing a point (**Some rain is now as acidic as vinegar**). But they are especially useful in translating something abstract, complex, or unfamiliar, as long as the easier subject is broadly familiar to readers. To translate how power dissipation in a resistor (as it restricts current flow) produces heat, you might use a kitchen toaster as an analogy. To understand that the toaster coil serves as a resistor, however (so that it can toast bread), readers would have to be familiar with toasters in general. Analogy therefore calls for particularly careful analyses of audience.

Besides naming things vividly, analogies help *explain* things. The following extended analogy from the *Congressional Research Report* helps us understand an unfamiliar technical concept (dangerous levels of a toxic chemical) by comparing it to something more familiar (a human hair).

Analogy
> A dioxin concentration of 500 parts per trillion is lethal to guinea pigs. One part per trillion is roughly equal to the thickness of a human hair compared to the distance across the United States.

Two common ways of using analogies are illustrated below (with each approach labeled for later reference).

ANALOGIES TO SOMETHING CONCRETE

As we discussed on pages 193–196, abstract ideas become clear through concrete support. A well-chosen analogy is an excellent way to provide a concrete comparison.

> [*abstract*]   [*concrete*]
> Maintaining a love relationship is like tending a garden.

> [*abstract*]   [*concrete*]
> Being illiterate is like being in prison.

Of course, these analogies would require a fully developed paragraph to make their meaning clear.

Here is a paragraph (part of the selection on pages 96–97) that explains an abstract concept (appreciation of the simple things all around us) through comparison with a concrete experience (finding a penny):

Paragraph 1

Main point (1–2)

Supporting points (3–4)

Analogy to a common event (with related examples) (5–7)

Concluding point drawn from the analogy (8–9)

¹I've been thinking about seeing. ²There are lots of things to see, unwrapped gifts and free surprises. ³The world is fairly studded and strewn with pennies cast broadside from a generous hand. ⁴But—and this is the point—who gets excited by a mere penny? ⁵If you follow one arrow, if you crouch motionless on a bank to watch a tremulous ripple thrill on the water and are rewarded by the sight of a muskrat paddling from its den, will you count that sight a chip of copper only, and go your rueful way? ⁶It is dire poverty indeed when a man is so malnourished and fatigued that he won't stoop to pick up a penny. ⁷But if you cultivate a healthy poverty and simplicity, so that finding a penny will literally make your day, then, since the world is in fact planted in pennies, you have with your poverty bought a lifetime of days. ⁸It is that simple. ⁹What you see is what you get.

—Annie Dillard

ANALOGIES TO SOMETHING FAMILIAR

Unfamiliar or complex things often can be understood through analogy to familiar things.

[*unfamiliar*]   [*familiar*]
Meditating is like diving into a clear, deep lake.

[*unfamiliar*]   [*familiar*]
The lungs of a heavy smoker look like charred meat.

[*complex*]   [*easier*]
A computer's memory is structured like post office mailboxes.

[*complex*]   [*easier*]
Punctuation marks work like road signs and traffic signals.

Here is a paragraph that helps us understand something unfamiliar (what an editor does to a manuscript) through a comparison to something familiar (what a mechanic does to a car):

Paragraph 2

Main point (about unfamiliar process) (1)

¹Having a manuscript under Ross's scrutiny was like putting your car in the hands of a skilled mechanic, not an automotive engineer with a bachelor of science degree, but a guy who knows what makes a motor go, and sputter, and wheeze, and sometimes come to a dead stop; a man with an ear for the faintest body squeak as well as the loudest engine rattle. ²When you first gazed, appalled, upon an uncorrected proof of one of your stories or articles, each margin had a thicket of queries and complaints—one writer got a hundred and forty-four on one profile. ³It was as though you beheld the works of your car spread all over the garage floor, and the job of getting the thing together again and making it work seemed impossible. ⁴Then you realized that Ross was trying to make your Model T or old Stutz Bearcat into a Cadillac or Rolls-Royce. ⁵He was at work with the tools of his unflagging perfectionism, and, after an exchange of growls or snarls, you set to work to join him in his enterprise.

Clarifying details of the unfamiliar process (2)

Details of the familiar process (3–5)

—James Thurber

Guidelines for Analogies

Paragraphs 1 and 2 both are developed according to these guidelines:

1. *The two subjects of the analogy are never of the same class or type.* If the paired subjects in the preceding paragraphs shared the same class (for example, if *editors* and *manuscripts* were paired, respectively, with *English teachers* and *student essays* instead of *mechanics* and *cars*), we would have ordinary comparison, not analogy.

2. *One of the subjects is used only to explain the other.* Analogy makes one item clear by using another. Unlike ordinary comparison, in which *both* subjects concern us equally, analogy has *one* subject of primary interest. In Paragraphs 1 and 2 we are interested in *finding pennies* or in *automobile repair* only to the extent that these subjects clarify the primary subjects.

3. *The easier subject must be one that is broadly familiar to readers.* If readers do not understand the secondary subject, then the analogy is worthless. An analogy between *computer memory* and

mailboxes in a post office would be lost on anyone who has never seen the inside of a typical post office. Likewise, an analogy between *punctuation marks* and *traffic signals* would be meaningless to persons newly arrived from an underdeveloped country that has no traffic signals. Analogy calls for careful analysis of the audience.

4. *An analogy is designed to support a specific main point.* The analogy itself has no value unless it supports and clarifies a main point.

5. *An analogy cannot serve as proof of anything.* Analogies provide new insights and perspectives only. They don't prove anything, because no two subjects are identical in all respects. The analogies in Paragraphs 1 and 2 merely show that the two subjects are alike in a way that clarifies each main point.

Application 16–1

PARAGRAPH WARM-UP: COMPARISON/CONTRAST

Using comparison or contrast (or both), write a paragraph discussing the likenesses or differences between two people, animals, attitudes, activities, places, or things. Identify clearly the situation, the audience, and your purpose.

Here are some possible subjects:

two places I know well

two memorable teaching styles (good or bad)

two friends' attitudes toward work

two similar consumer items

two pets I've had

the benefits of two kinds of exercise

two ways of spending a summer

Application 16–2

PARAGRAPH WARM-UP: ANALOGY

1. We often ignore or take for granted many beautiful or important things around us. Using Annie Dillard's paragraph (page 321) as a

model, develop an analogy to share with a stipulated audience an insight you've had about something special. (The paragraph you wrote for Application 7–9 might serve as a starting point here.)

2.   Using analogy, develop a paragraph explaining something abstract, complex, or unfamiliar by comparing it to something concrete, simpler, or familiar. ("Writing is like . . . "; "Love is like . . . "; "Meditating is like . . . "; "Osmosis works like . . . "). Identify a specific audience and purpose.

Application 16–3

ESSAY PRACTICE

After reading this essay, answer the study questions. Then select one of the essay assignments.

Meaningful Relationships

[1]I heard of a man and woman recently who had fallen in love. "Hopelessly in Love" was the woman's antique phrase for it. I hadn't realized people still did that sort of thing jointly. Nowadays the fashion is to fall in love with yourself, and falling in love with a second party seems to be generally regarded as bad form.

[2]It may be, of course, that many people are still doing it, but simply not admitting it publicly, perhaps on the assumption that it is a shameful act, as adultery used to be. Nowadays people discuss their adultery with strangers at parties and on airplanes, and not long ago I saw a married couple chatting about theirs on television, the way people used to discuss their car-repair problems. A possible explanation, I suppose, is that, in an age when the fashion is to be in love with yourself, confessing to being in love with somebody else is an admission of unfaithfulness to one's beloved. The truth is probably more complicated.

[3]Consider, for example, the situation of Ed and Jane, a hypothetical modern couple who see each other across a crowded room, feel inexplicable sensations not reducible to computer printouts and make human contact. After conventional preliminary events, they will naturally want to express what exists between them. Jane may announce that they "relate" beautifully. Ed may boast about how gratifyingly they "communicate." The beauty of their "relating" and the gratifications of their "communicating" may induce them to "establish a relationship." Why it is always a "relationship" they establish, and never a "communicationship," I don't know, but "relationship" is the universally approved term. On days when things go badly, they do not have a lovers' quarrel. Instead, Jane says that Ed is not "relating" and

Ed says that Jane is not "communicating." On days when things go well they boast about how "fulfilling" their "relationship" is. Ed and Jane do not dream of living happily ever after. They are more like the Bell telephone system. They aspire to heavy communicating in a fulfilling relationship.

⁴In fact, they are probably afraid of falling in love; and if, in spite of everything, they nevertheless do fall in love, they are too embarrassed to tell anybody. Why? One reason is that it is such an out-of-date thing to do. Falling in love is not scientific. It cannot be described in the brain-numbing jargon of sociology. It can only be described in the words of song writers. People in Cole Porter's antique old songs were always falling in love, and worse, talking about romance. Romance! Astaire and Rogers in a penthouse, and other such musty stuff. We have moved on to Mick Jagger, to John Lennon, who urged everybody to do it in the road instead of in the penthouse.

⁵Falling in love is archaic, like cookouts and tailfins on your Plymouth. Communicating, relating, experiencing fulfilling relationships—these are what up-to-date boys and girls engage in. When disaster strikes, it is not "the end of a love affair" to make them blue, but "the destruction of our relationship" to make them yearn for new "therapeutic experience."

⁶This grotesque terminology in which Americans now discuss what used to be called affairs of the heart is curious not only for its comic pseudoscientific sound, but also for the coolness with which it treats a passion formerly associated with heat. It takes a very cool pair of cats to talk about the grandest of passions as though it were only an exercise in sociology. Imagine Dante filling pages about the satisfactory nature of communicating with Beatrice, or Juliet raving on through five acts about her fulfilling relationship with Romeo.

⁷The way people talk, of course, reflects the way they think, and this avoidance of the language of love probably reflects a wish to avoid the consuming single-minded commitment to love to which the old words led, often no doubt to the dismay of people who uttered them. Why in our time we should tread so gingerly to avoid commitment to love to the second party is the subject for a monograph. Perhaps it comes from a fear of living too fully, perhaps from the current cultural fashion conditioning us to believe that whatever interferes with self-love will lead to psychic headache.

⁸Whatever the explanation, it is a bleak era for love, which makes it a time of dull joys, small-bore agonies and thin passions. "I could not love thee, dear, so much, lov'd I not honor more," the poet once could write. Today he could only say, "I could not have so fulfilling a relationship with thee, dear, had I not an even more highly intensified mental set as regards the absurd and widely discredited concept known as honor."

—Russell Baker

Questions About Content

1. Is the title appropriate? Explain.

2. How does this writer limit the broad subject "romantic love" to a manageable subject for an essay?

3. In your own words, restate the point of the comparison in a complete sentence.

4. List three reasons readers would find the content of this essay interesting.

5. Is this essay convincing? Explain.

Questions About Organization

1. Does this comparison follow the block pattern or the point-by-point pattern? Comment on the effectiveness of the pattern.

2. One subject of the comparison is discussed much more extensively than the other. Given that both parts of a comparison should receive equal treatment, is this imbalance justified? Explain.

3. In a brief outline, list the major topic of each body paragraph.

4. Which are the two most concrete paragraphs in the essay? Briefly explain their function. Why are they placed there in the essay?

5. Which topic sentence in the body serves two individual paragraphs? Is this an effective structure? Explain.

6. The body paragraphs vary greatly in length; is this variation justified? Explain.

7. Could there be other paragraph divisions for this essay? If so, give examples.

Questions About Style

1. Identify two analogies, and explain how they help make the point.

2. How do you interpret "small-bore agonies" in the final paragraph? How does this phrase reinforce the essay's primary meaning?

3. What is the outstanding stylistic feature of this essay? Give examples.

4. Characterize the tone. Give examples of word choice and sentence structure that contribute to the tone.

RESPONDING TO YOUR READING

1. Explore your reactions to *"Campus Center" Versus "Student Union"* by using the questions on page 91. Then respond with your own essay, comparing or contrasting two or more related items to help readers understand your preference.

   You might focus on a school-related topic, as in comparing your high school and college writing classes; or living in a dorm versus living in a fraternity or sorority; or living on campus versus commuting. Or you might compare the positions of two political candidates on local, state, or federal aid to education. Or you might compare two word processing systems.

   If you work part time, you might focus on a work-related topic, as in comparing two job procedures, two locations for a company branch, or two brands of machinery or equipment.

   Be sure your comparison supports a definite viewpoint and rests on a clear basis: costs, uses, benefits, appearance, or the like.

2. Explore your reactions to "Americanization Is Tough on 'Macho'" (pages 312–314) by using the page 91 questions and those below.

   - What are the main issues here? How has this essay affected your thinking about these issues?

   - What is the writer's attitude toward her subject? Toward her audience? How do we know? What are the signals?

   - What larger point is Guilbault making here about values and cultural differences? Summarize the main point in your own words.

   As you reread the essay, try to think of an example (perhaps from your own cultural background) in which "the cultural traits other societies value don't translate as desirable characteristics in America." Depending on your topic, your essay could present either a defense or a critique of American culture. Some possible topics for comparison: differing attitudes about owning guns, hunting, hard work and leisure, individualism, discipline, competition, old age, gender equality, status, marriage and divorce, career success, women in military combat, or crime and punishment.

   Instead of comparing values between different cultures, you might focus on differences between, say, your grandparent's generation and your own (for example, differing attitudes about gender or role models or heroes).

   Identify your audience, and decide what you want these readers to be doing or thinking or feeling after reading your essay.

Decide on either a point-by-point or block structure. Decide on a clear and definite basis for your comparison, and give enough examples to support your point. Try to explain your view of the larger meaning of this comparison.

3. After reading "Meaningful Relationships," compose an essay addressing this question: Besides the way people talk about it, in what way has America's perception of romantic love changed over the past couple of decades? By drawing your own comparison, explain why this change has been for better or for worse. For specific examples, you might wish to compare the portrayal of love in older versus recent movies, commercials, magazines, or songs. Or perhaps you could interview parents or grandparents. Be sure your comparison supports a definite point and rests on a clear basis: courtship rituals, premarital relationships, husband-and-wife roles, or the like.

OPTIONS FOR ESSAY WRITING

1. Football, baseball, and basketball all were invented in America, and each has been called "The American Sport." What features do all three sports have in common that reflect distinctively American values, interests, and character?

2. If you had your high school years to relive, what would you do differently?

3. During your years in school, you've had much experience with both good teaching and bad teaching. Based on your experiences, what special qualities are necessary for good teaching? Use a series of contrasts to make your point.

4. Some people use labels (*straight, freak, redneck, hick, nerd,* and the like) to categorize other people. The problem with such labels is that they are stereotypes. It's easy to say that John is a "typical jock" and thereby to ignore his complexity. Think of some label that someone might apply to you, and, through contrast, show how that label would be unfair and inaccurate.

5. Compose an essay on this assertion: "To some, money is a means; to others, an end."

17

Explaining the Exact Meaning: Definition

All successful writing shares one feature—*clarity*. Clear writing begins with clear thinking; clear thinking begins with an understanding of what all the terms mean. Therefore, clear writing begins with definitions that both reader and writer understand.

Words can signify two kinds of meaning: *denotative* and *connotative.* The denotations of words are the meanings in a dictionary. A word's denotation means the same thing to everyone. The denotation of *apple* is *the firm, rounded, edible fruit of the apple tree.* But words have connotations as well, overtones or suggestions beyond their dictionary meanings. A word can have different connotations for different people. Thus, *apple* might connote *Adam and Eve, apple pie, Johnny Appleseed, apple polisher, good health,* and so on. Denotative definition, then, answers these readers' questions.

What is it?

What is its dictionary meaning?

Connotative definition answers this question:

What does it mean or suggest to you?

For an illustration of the differences between denotative and connotative definitions, consider the word *survival,* defined in the dictionary as *the act of remaining alive.* In the next paragraph, the writer finds this denotative definition inadequate to make his point. He therefore provides his own connotative definition:

Main point (1)	[1]The question of the age, we like to think, is one of survival, and that is true, but not in the way
Denotative definition (2)	we ordinarily mean it. [2]The survival we ordinarily mean is a narrow and nervous one: simply the con-
	tinuation in their present forms, of the isolated
Cause-effect (3)	lives we lead. [3]But there is little doubt that most of us *will* survive as we are, for we are clearly pre-
	pared to accept whatever is necessary to do so: the deaths of millions of others, wars waged in our
Examples (4)	name, a police state at home. [4]Like the Germans who accepted the Fascists, or the French citizens who collaborated with the Germans, we, too, will be able to carry on "business as usual," just as we
Connotative definition (5)	do now. [5]Our actual crisis of survival lies else-where, in the moral realm we so carefully ignore, for it is there that our lives are at stake.

—Peter Marin

By showing what he *doesn't* mean by *survival,* the author helps us understand what he *does* mean in the final sentence. This technique is called *definition by negation.* We will encounter definition by negation again, along with other techniques, in the samples that follow.

Using Denotative Definitions

We use denotative definitions for two purposes: (1) to explain a term that is specialized or unfamiliar to our readers, and (2) to explain our exact definition of a word that has more than one meaning.

Most fields have their own specialized terms. Engineers, architects, and builders talk about *prestressed concrete, tolerances,* or *trusses;* psychologists and police officers refer to *sociopathic behavior* or *paranoia;* lawyers and real estate brokers discuss *liens, easements,* and *escrow accounts.* For readers outside the field, these terms must be defined.

Sometimes a term will be unfamiliar to some readers because it is new or no longer in use (*future shock, meltdown,* and *sexism*) or a slang word (*bad, heavy, freak, mad money*).

Once a term such as *paranoia* or *mad money* has been defined, its meaning is not likely to change in another context. And it is easy enough to figure out that technical terms should be defined for nonspecialist readers who have no idea what *prestressed concrete* or *escrow account* means. Some readers, though, are unaware that more familiar terms such as *guarantee, disability insurance, liability, lease,* or *mortgage* take on very specialized meanings in some contexts. What *guarantee* means in one situation is not necessarily what it means in another. Denotative definition then becomes crucial to full understanding by all parties.

CHOOSING THE LEVEL OF DETAIL

How much detail will a reader need to understand a term or a concept? Sometimes you can make your meaning clear with a synonym (a term with a similar meaning). Sometimes you will need a sentence. And often, you will need an entire paragraph—or an essay.

Using Synonyms to Define   Often, you can clarify the meaning of an unfamiliar word by using a more familiar synonym:

> To *waffle* means to be evasive and misleading.

> The *leaching field* (sievelike drainage area) needs 15 inches of crushed stone.

The definition of *leaching field* would be adequate in a report to a client whose house you are building. But in a town report titled "Ground-water Contamination from Leaching Fields" written for your local board of health, you would need an expanded definition.

Note: Be sure that the synonym clarifies your meaning instead of obscuring it. Don't say:

> A *tumor* is a neoplasm.

Do say:

> A *tumor* is a growth of bodily cells that occurs independently of surrounding tissue and serves no useful function.

Using Sentence Definitions   To be clear, a definition often requires more than a synonym. A sentence definition (which may be stated in more than one sentence) follows a fixed pattern: (1) the name of the item to be defined, (2) the class to which the item belongs, and (3) the features that make the item different from all others in its class. This is the pattern used in dictionaries.

Term	Class	Distinguishing features
carburetor	a mixing device	in gasoline engines that blends air and fuel into a vapor for combustion within the cylinders
transit	a surveying instrument	that measures horizontal and vertical angles
diabetes	a metabolic disease	caused by a disorder of the pituitary or pancreas and characterized by excessive urination, persistent thirst, and inability to metabolize sugar
brief	a legal document	containing all the facts and points of law pertinent to a case and filed by an attorney before arguing the case in court
stress	an applied force	that tends to strain or deform a body

In their presentation, these elements are combined into one or more complete sentences:

> Diabetes is a metabolic disease caused by a disorder of the pituitary or pancreas and characterized by excessive urination, persistent thirst, and inability to metabolize sugar.

Sentence definition is especially useful if you need to stipulate your precise definition for a term that has several possible meanings. In construction, banking, or real estate, *qualified buyer* can have different meanings for different readers, as can *remedial student* in education.

GUIDELINES FOR SENTENCE DEFINITIONS

1. *Classify the term precisely.* The narrower your class, the clearer your meaning. *Transit* is classified as a surveying instrument, not as a *thing* or as an *instrument*. *Stress* is classified as *an applied force;* to say that stress "is what . . . " or "takes place when . . . " is incorrect—these are not words of classification. Diabetes is classified as a *metabolic disease,* not as a *medical term.*

2. *Differentiate the term accurately.* Separate the expression from every other item in the same class. If the distinguishing features are too broad, they will apply to more than this one item. A definition of *brief* as *a legal document used in court* fails to differentiate *brief* from all other legal documents (wills, affidavits, and the like). Conversely, a definition of *carburetor* as *a mixing device used in automobile engines* is too narrow, because it ignores the carburetor's use in all other gasoline engines.

3. *Avoid circular definitions.* Do not repeat, as part of the distinguishing feature, the word you are defining. To say that *stress is an applied force that places stress on a body* is to give a circular definition.

EXPANDED DEFINITIONS

The sentence definition of *carburetor* on page 332 is adequate for a general reader who simply needs to know what a carburetor is. An instruction manual for mechanics, however, would define *carburetor* in much greater detail; these readers need to know how a carburetor works, how it is made, and what conditions cause it to operate correctly. Your choice of synonym definition, sentence definition, or expanded definition depends on the amount of information your readers need—and that, in turn, depends on why they need it.

As illustration of how the level of detail in a definition is keyed to the needs of the audience, consider this sentence definition:

> It [paranoia] refers to a psychosis based on a delusionary premise of self-referred persecution or grandeur (e.g., "The Knights of Columbus control the world and are out to get me" . . .), and supported by a complex, rigorously logical system that interprets all or nearly all sense impressions as evidence for that premise.

This definition is part of an article published in *Harper's*, a magazine with general readership. We can easily see that the audience will require a more detailed definition of this specialized term. Here is the expanded version:

Main point (1)

Sentence definition (2)

¹Paranoia is a word on everyone's lips, but only among mental-health professionals has it acquired a tolerably specific meaning. ²It refers to a psychosis based on a delusionary premise of self-referred persecution or grandeur (e.g., "The Knights of Columbus control the world and are out to get me" . . .), and supported by a complex, rigorously logical system that interprets all or nearly all sense

Effect-cause (3)

Process analysis (4)

Cause-effect (5–7)

Contrast (8)

impressions as evidence for that premise. [3]The traditional psychiatric view is that paranoia is an extreme measure for the defense of the integrity of the personality against annihilating guilt. [4]The paranoid (so goes the theory) thrusts his guilt outside himself by denying his hostile or erotic impulses and projecting them onto other people or onto the whole universe. [5]Disintegration is avoided, but at high cost; the paranoid view of reality can make everyday life terrifying and social intercourse problematical. [6]And paranoia is tiring. [7]It requires exhausting mental effort to construct trains of thought demonstrating that random events or details "prove" a wholly unconnected premise. [8]Some paranoids hallucinate, but hallucination is by no means obligatory; paranoia is an interpretive, not a perceptual, dysfunction.

—Hendrik Hertzberg and David C. K. McClelland

General readers are much more likely to understand this expanded definition than the sentence definition alone.

As we have seen in earlier sections, synonyms and sentence definitions are part of most writing. But, in turn, expanded definition relies on the various strategies for development discussed in those earlier sections. The specific strategies you choose for expanding a definition will depend on your subject, purpose, and audience needs.

Strategies for development are not rigid, prescribed forms into which you must bend and squeeze your writing; rather, they are the channels of logical thought and clear expression. Thus, the writers of the selection above, defining *paranoia*, combine those development patterns most likely to answer the questions they can anticipate from readers:

What causes paranoia? [*effect-cause*]

How does it happen? [*process analysis*]

What are the effects of paranoia? [*cause-effect*]

How is paranoia different from other mental illnesses? [*contrast*]

Notice how the following definition uses various development strategies to clarify the meaning of a slang term that is no longer in common use:

Main point (1)

[1]During my teen years I never left the house on my Saturday night dates without my mother slipping me a few extra dollars—mad money, it

Contrast and division (2)

was called. ²I'll explain what it was for the benefit of the new generation in which people just sleep with each other: the fellow was supposed to bring me home, lead me safely through the asphalt jungle, protect me from slithering snakes, rapists, and

Division (3)

the like. ³But my mother and I knew young men were apt to drink too much, to slosh down so many rye-and-gingers that some hero might well lead me in front of an oncoming bus, smash his daddy's car into Tiffany's window or, less gal-

Cause-effect (sentence definition) (4)

Cause-effect as analogy (5)

lantly, throw up on my dress. ⁴Mad money was for getting home on your own, no matter what form of insanity your date happened to evidence. ⁵Mad money was also a wallflower's rope ladder; if a guy you came with suddenly fancied someone else, well, you didn't have to stay there and suffer; you could go home.

—Anne Roiphe

Here again the writer combines development strategies that answer readers' questions about her main point:

Why does this generation not worry about *mad money?* [*contrast*]

What behavior did a young woman expect (or dread) from a date? [*division*]

What was mad money for? [*cause-effect*]

This expanded definition, from an auto insurance policy, defines *damages for bodily injury to others*, a phrase that could have many possible meanings:

Main point (1)

Sentence definition (2)

Cause-effect (3–6)

¹Under this coverage, we will pay damages to people injured or killed by your auto in Massachusetts accidents. ²Damages are the amount an injured person is legally entitled to collect through a court judgment or settlement. ³We will pay only if you or someone else using your auto with your consent is legally responsible for the accident. ⁴The most we will pay for injuries to any one person as a result of any one accident is $5,000. ⁵The most we will pay for injuries to two or more people as a result of any one accident is a total of $10,000. ⁶This is the most we will pay as the result of a single accident no matter how many autos or premiums are shown on the Coverage

Negation (7)   Selections page. [7]We will *not* pay: for injuries to
                              guest occupants of your auto; for accidents outside
                              of Massachusetts or in places in Massachusetts
                              where the public has no right of access; for injuries
                              to any employees of the legally responsible person
                              if they are entitled to Massachusetts workers'
                              compensation benefits.

This definition is designed to answer two basic questions:

Under what conditions will the insurer pay damages?

Under what conditions will the insurer not pay?

Thus the development patterns of *cause-effect* and *negation* (showing what something *isn't*) most logically serve the purpose of this definition.

Using Connotative Definitions

A denotative definition can take us only so far. It cannot communicate the special meaning a writer may intend. In such cases, connotative definitions explain *exactly* what we mean. Connotative definitions explain terms that hold personal meanings for the writer beyond their mere dictionary definitions. Because they introduce readers to the writer's complex, private associations, connotative definitions almost always call for expanded treatment.

In the next paragraph, the denotative definition of *house (a structure serving as a dwelling)* is replaced by a more personal, artistic, and spiritual definition:

Main point (1)*   [1]What is a house? [2]A house is a human cir-
Analogies (2–4)   cumstance in Nature, like a tree or the rocks of the
                                 hills; a good house is a technical performance where
                                 form and function are made one; a house is integral
                                 to its site, a grace, not a disgrace, to its environ-
                                 ment, suited to elevate the life of its individual
                                 inhabitants; a house is therefore integral with the
                                 nature of the methods and materials used to build
                                 it. [3]A house to be a good home has throughout what
                                 is most needed in American life today—integrity.
                                 [4]Integrity, once there, enables those who live in that
                                 house to take spiritual root and grow.
                                                              —Frank Lloyd Wright

---

* A question is a good beginning for an expanded definition.

For other people, *house* might connote a place to live, something to buy and sell, or peace and security. But to this great architect, *house* takes on a special meaning, one that he explains through a series of analogies.

Denotative definition often presents a persuasive challenge for writers, especially when we try to persuade people to accept a particular definition of a term that carries multiple, conflicting meanings (*freedom, love, patriotism,* or the like), and especially when the meaning we advocate is unconventional or controversial. In the following essay, an African American develops her own connotative definition of a term that, for her, carries personal meanings beyond its dictionary definition. As you read, think about how this writer supports her assertion that meaning is determined by the social context in which a word is used.

The Meanings of a Word*

Language is the subject. It is the written form with which I've managed to keep the wolf away from the door and, in diaries, to keep my sanity. In spite of this, I consider the written word inferior to the spoken, and much of the frustration experienced by novelists is the awareness that whatever we manage to capture in even the most transcendent passages falls far short of the richness of life. Dialogue achieves its power in the dynamics of a fleeting moment of sight, sound, smell, and touch.

I'm not going to enter the debate here about whether it is language that shapes reality or vice versa. That battle is doomed to be waged whenever we seek intermittent reprieve from the chicken and egg dispute. I will simply take the position that the spoken word, like the written word, amounts to a nonsensical arrangement of sounds or letters without a consensus that assigns "meaning." And building from the meanings of what we hear, we order reality. Words themselves are innocuous; it is the consensus that gives them true power.

I remember the first time I heard the word *nigger.* In my third-grade class, our math tests were being passed down the rows, and as I handed the papers to a little boy in back of me, I remarked that once again he had received a much lower mark than I did. He snatched his test from me and spit out that word. Had he called me a nymphomaniac or a necrophiliac, I couldn't have been more puzzled. I didn't know what a nigger was, but I knew that whatever it meant, it was something he shouldn't have called me. This was verified when I raised my hand, and in a loud voice repeated what he had said and watched the teacher scold him for using a "bad" word. I was later to

---

* Gloria Naylor, "The Meanings of a Word," "Hers" column, *The New York Times,* February 20, 1986. Reprinted by permission of Sterling Lord Literistic, Inc. Copyright © 1986 by Gloria Naylor.

go home and ask the inevitable question that every black parent must face—"Mommy, what does *nigger* mean?"

And what exactly did it mean? Thinking back, I realize that this could not have been the first time the word was used in my presence. I was part of a large extended family that had migrated from the rural South after World War II and formed a close-knit network that gravitated around my maternal grandparents. Their ground-floor apartment in one of the buildings they owned in Harlem was a weekend mecca for my immediate family, along with countless aunts, uncles, and cousins who brought along assorted friends. It was a bustling and open house with assorted neighbors and tenants popping in and out to exchange bits of gossip, pick up an old quarrel, or referee the ongoing checkers game in which my grandmother cheated shamelessly. They were all there to let down their hair and put up their feet after a week of labor in the factories, laundries, and shipyards of New York.

Amid the clamor, which could reach deafening proportions—two or three conversations going on simultaneously, punctuated by the sound of a baby's crying somewhere in the back rooms or out on the street—there was still a rigid set of rules about what was said and how. Older children were sent out of the living room when it was time to get into the juicy details about "you-know-who" up on the third floor who had gone and gotten herself "p-r-e-g-n-a-n-t!" But my parents, knowing that I could spell well beyond my years, always demanded that I follow the others out to play. Beyond sexual misconduct and death, everything else was considered harmless for our young ears. And so among the anecdotes of the triumphs and disappointments in the various workings of their lives, the word *nigger* was used in my presence, but it was set within contexts and inflections that caused it to register in my mind as something else.

In the singular, the word was always applied to a man who had distinguished himself in some situation that brought their approval for his strength, intelligence, or drive:

"Did Johnny *really* do that?"

"I'm telling you, that nigger pulled in $6,000 of overtime last year. Said he got enough for a down payment on a house."

When used with a possessive adjective by a woman—"my nigger"—it became a term of endearment for her husband or boyfriend. But it could be more than just a term applied to a man. In their mouths it became the pure essence of manhood—a disembodied force that channeled their past history of struggle and present survival against the odds into a victorious statement of being: "Yeah, that old foreman found out quick enough—you don't mess with a nigger."

In the plural, it became a description of some group within the community that had overstepped the bounds of decency as my family defined it. Parents who neglected their children, a drunken couple who fought in public, people who simply refused to look for work, those with excessively dirty mouths or unkempt households were all "trifling niggers." This particular circle could forgive hard times, unemployment, the occasional bout of depression—they had gone through all of that themselves—but the unforgivable sin was a lack of self-respect.

A woman could never be a "nigger" in the singular, with its connotation of confirming worth. The noun *girl* was its closest equivalent in that sense, but only when used in direct address and regardless of the gender doing the addressing. *Girl* was a token of respect for a woman. The one-syllable word was drawn out to sound like three in recognition of the extra ounce of wit, nerve, or daring that the woman had shown in the situation under discussion.

"G-i-r-l, stop. You mean you said that to his face?"

But if the word was used in a third-person reference or shortened so that it almost snapped out of the mouth, it always involved some element of communal disapproval. And age became an important factor in these exchanges. It was only between individuals of the same generation, or from any older person to a younger (but never the other way around), that *girl* would be considered a compliment.

I don't agree with the argument that use of the word *nigger* at this social stratum of the black community was an internalization of racism. The dynamics were the exact opposite: the people in my grandmother's living room took a word that whites used to signify worthlessness or degradation and rendered it impotent. Gathering there together, they transformed *nigger* to signify the varied and complex human beings they knew themselves to be. If the word was to disappear totally from the mouths of even the most liberal of white society, no one in that room was naive enough to believe it would disappear from white minds. Meeting the word head-on, they proved it had absolutely nothing to do with the way they were determined to live their lives.

So there must have been dozens of times that *nigger* was spoken in front of me before I reached the third grade. But I didn't "hear" it until it was said by a small pair of lips that had already learned it could be a way to humiliate me. That was the word I went home and asked my mother about. And since she knew that I had to grow up in America, she took me in her lap and explained.

—Gloria Naylor

Naylor offers various instances in which a single term is used *ironically* (that is, to signify meanings clearly opposite or different from the term's ordinary meanings).

Unless you are certain that readers know the exact or special meaning you intend, always define a term the first time you use it.

Application 17–1

Adequate formal sentence definitions require precise classification and detailed differentiation. Tell whether you think each of these definitions is adequate for a general reader. Rewrite those that seem inadequate. If necessary, consult dictionaries and specialized encyclopedias. Discuss your revision in class.

1. A bicycle is a vehicle with two wheels.

2. A transistor is a device used in transistorized electronic equipment.

3. Surfing is when one rides a wave to shore while standing on a board specifically designed for buoyancy and balance.

4. Bubonic plague is caused by an organism known as *Pasteurella pestis.*

5. Mace is a chemical aerosol spray used by the police.

6. A Geiger counter measures radioactivity.

7. A cactus is a succulent.

8. In law, an indictment is a criminal charge against a defendant.

9. A prune is a kind of plum.

10. Friction is a force between two bodies.

11. Luffing is what happens when one sails into the wind.

12. A frame is an important part of a bicycle.

13. *Hypoglycemia* is a medical term.

14. An hourglass is a device used for measuring intervals of time.

15. A computer is a machine that handles information with amazing speed.

16. A Ferrari is the best car in the world.

17. To meditate is to exercise mental faculties in thought.

Application 17–2

PARAGRAPH WARM-UP: DENOTATIVE DEFINITION

Using denotative definition, write a paragraph explaining the meaning of a term that is specialized, new, or otherwise unfamiliar to your reader. List in the margin the strategies for expansion you've used. Begin your paragraph with a formal sentence definition (term-class-differentiation). Select a term from one of the lists below, from your major (defined for a nonmajor), or from your daily conversation with peers (defined for an elderly person).

Identify clearly the situation, the audience, and your purpose.

Specialized terms	Slang terms
summons	jock
generator	Yuppie
dewpoint	nerd
capitalism	turkey
salt marsh	groupie
economic recession	fox
microprocessor	to break
water table	boss
T-square	getting it together
editorial	awesome
fashion	macho

Application 17–3

PARAGRAPH WARM-UP: CONNOTATIVE DEFINITION

Using connotative definition, write a paragraph explaining the special meaning or associations that a term holds for you. Select a term from the list below, or provide one of your own. List in the margin the expansion strategies you've used. Identify clearly the situation, the audience, and your purpose.

patriotism	education	freedom
trust	marriage	courage
friendship	God	peace
progress	guilt	morality
beauty	the perfect date	happiness
adult	sex appeal	fear

Application 17–4

ESSAY ANALYSIS AND PRACTICE

After reading this essay, answer the study questions. Then select one of the essay assignments.

The Belated Father

[1]There is a small clipping, no more than 2 square inches, that has been in my file marked "Fathers" since last fall. It's a simple story about a judge in western Massachusetts who, when confronted with a 15-year-old kid in trouble, made an unusual judgment. He sentenced the father to 30 days of dinner at home.

[2]There are some other things in the folder. One is a letter to an advice column from a woman whose husband has never kissed their baby son because he said, "I felt funny kissing a guy." Behind that letter is a statistic: "Ten percent of the children in this country live in fatherless homes."

[3]There is also a quote from a novel about the children of the sixties, written by Stephen Koch. It says, "Who among those fiery sons, with their vague and blasted eyes, really connected with his father; who even knew, let alone admired, what the father did in that invisible city of his? Fatherhood meant delivering, or not delivering, checks. It meant not being around, or being unwelcome when around. It meant either shouting or that soul-crushing silence most deeply installed in the soul of any red-blooded American boy: Dad mute behind his newspaper."

[4]I wish there were something else in the file folder, some story, some role model you could applaud.

[5]There are so many young fathers who don't want to be like their own dads. They feel awkward when they find themselves alone with their fathers today. They flip through their own mental files on the subject. There is Father Knows Best and Father Knows Nothing, Father as Pal, and Father as Trans-parent. There is even an occasional full-time father—who trips in all the pitfalls of full-time mothers.

[6]None of these will do. They don't fit. They don't feel right. So these sons are trying to devise their own role models, to be their own first generation. They are becoming—what shall we call them?—working fathers.

[7]Margaret Mead has written that "human fatherhood is a social invention." Maybe so. But they are re-inventing it. They want to be involved in the full range of their children's lives, to know which days the kids have to wear sneakers for gym and which kid would starve before he'd eat cauliflower.

[8]They are learning to deal with kids when they are crying or

dirty or hungry. As one father said, "When I was a kid, my father would play ball with me, but the minute I hurt my knee, we'd both call for my mother. I don't want to divide my kids like that."

9He wants the kind of relationship that is only woven in the intimacy of daily, time-consuming routines during which you "learn" what they call intuition—the second sense that tells you one kid is worried and another is sad, and the difference between a cry that is tired and one that is hungry or hurt. These fathers don't want to be Sunday events.

10On the other hand, they have new guilts. They feel guilty if they miss the school play and guilty if they are tired or out of town. They can't push it down justifying their absence with the need to Make It, or with the notion that children are women's work.

11They wonder: "Can I be a successful worker and a successful father?" Their bosses are usually men of their father's generation whose offices are geared to full-time mothers and absent fathers. If they refuse overtime will they get ahead? What if they can't travel their way to a better job?

12At the office they suddenly find themselves wondering, Did the babysitter show? I wonder if the bully in the playground is bothering Bobby again? Finally they wonder whether they have enough energy left over from working and fathering for their own lives and plans and marriages.

13And when they describe all this, all this that is so new to them, they notice their wives quietly smiling. These fathers you see, are becoming—well, how should we put it? Like us.

—Ellen Goodman

Questions About Content

1. Does the title adequately forecast what is to follow? Explain.

2. Does this essay have a thesis statement? If so, where is it?

3. Why will readers find the content of this essay interesting?

4. Is this expanded definition primarily denotative or connotative? Explain.

5. What is the primary expansion strategy in this definition? Explain.

6. Which paragraph is developed through negation?

7. What is the major development strategy in paragraphs 7–12?

Questions About Organization

1. How many paragraphs make up the introduction? What is the major development strategy in the introduction? Is this strategy effective? Explain.

2. Is the one-sentence paragraph (4) effective? What role does it serve?

3. What role does paragraph 6 serve?

4. Trace the line of thought in this essay. Is this the most effective order? Explain.

5. Does the conclusion relate back to the introduction and the thesis? Explain.

6. Are most paragraphs too short? Explain.

Questions About Style

1. What are the two most notable stylistic features in this essay?

2. Identify the major devices that increase coherence.

3. The writer sometimes uses sentence fragments. Where are they? Are they effective? Explain.

4. What is the author's attitude toward her subject? Identify four terms conveying that attitude.

5. Identify four concrete and specific images that make the essay vivid.

RESPONDING TO YOUR READING

1. Along with changing times come changes in our way of seeing. Some terms that held meanings for us two or three years ago may have acquired radically different meanings by now. If we once defined *success* narrowly as social status and income bracket, we might now define it in broader words: leading the kind of life that puts us in close touch with ourselves and the world around us, or some such. In similar ways, the meanings of many other terms (*education, friendship, freedom, maturity, self-fulfillment, pain, love, home, family, career, patriotism*) may have changed for us. Although some terms take on more positive meanings, others acquire more negative ones. The meaning of *marriage* will depend on whether the person defining it has witnessed (or experienced) marriages that have been happy and constructive or bitter and destructive. And quite often an entire society's definition of something changes, *marriage* being a good example.

    Your assignment is to identify something that has changed in meaning, either for you individually or for our society as a whole. Discuss both the traditional and the new meanings (choosing a serious, ironic, or humorous point of view) in such a way that your definition makes a specific point or commentary, either stated or implied, about society's values or your own. Use Goodman's essay as a model.

2. Explore your reactions to "The Meanings of A Word" (pages 337–339 by using the page 91 questions. Respond with your own essay that supports or challenges the assertion that meaning is determined by the social context in which a word is used. Perhaps you belong to an in-group (family, friends, club, ethnic group) that uses certain words in ironic or special ways to signify meanings that could be appreciated only by the members of that particular group. Perhaps you could discuss a slang term or a term of alienation used as a term of affection or respect. Your essay should make a clear and definite point about the larger meaning behind the examples you provide.

Identify your audience and decide what you want these readers to be doing or thinking or feeling after reading your essay.

OPTIONS FOR ESSAY WRITING

1. Write an expanded definition of "The American Dream"—what this expression means to you or how its meaning has changed for you.

2. Write an expanded definition of *man* or *woman* based on images created by a magazine *(Playboy, Esquire, Cosmopolitan, Ms.)* or by television commercials.

18

Developing a Persuasive Argument

Anticipating Audience Resistance • Having a Debatable Point
• Supporting Your Claim • Appealing to Reason
• Recognizing Illogical Reasoning • Appealing to Emotion
• Applications

Many earlier essays in this book can be called "persuasive"—to the extent that they move readers to agree with particular viewpoints such as these:

- that media reports on African-Americans often are biased (page 255)

- that the "wifely" stereotype persists in today's generation (92)

- that the weather can influence human behavior (304)

- that many of today's young fathers seek real involvement as parents (342)

Although these essays employ various development strategies (illustration, cause-effect, and so on), their underlying goal is to persuade readers to see things the writer's way. Once they have sufficiently enlightened their readers, these writers can expect little disagreement.

But sometimes we write for the *primary* goal of persuasion; we decide to take a stand on an issue about which people always disagree—no matter how enlightened they become. All kinds of issues routinely provoke argument: about whether something is true or false or good or bad, about what caused something, about what should be done. Examples: *Has television produced a generation of couch potatoes? Do the risks of nuclear power outweigh its advantages? Should your school require athletes to maintain good grades? Should your dorm be coed? Does your close friend really have an alcohol problem?* In their answers to questions such as these, people disagree. And so we write in hopes of winning readers over to our side.

In a free society, controversy is expressed everywhere. Whatever your stand on any controversy, you can expect some readers to disagree— no matter how long and how brilliantly you argue. But even though you won't change *everyone's* mind, a persuasive argument is likely to influence *some people*. No matter how controversial the issue, your argument still can make a difference.

Anticipating Audience Resistance

Argument focuses on its audience. It may ask them to accept an opinion or to support a position or to take action or to change their behavior. But because it addresses issues in which people are directly involved, an argument provokes *resistance* from its readers.

Persuading an audience to accept a conflicting point of view might well be the ultimate measure of a writer's skill. People rarely change their minds—without good reason. When you challenge someone's stand on an issue, or try to change people's behavior, expect a defensive reaction and questions such as these:

Why should I even read this?

Why should I change my mind?

How can I be sure you are right?

Can you prove it?

How do you know?

Why should I do it?

Says who?

Your problem is getting readers to admit you might be *right*, which means, of course, they will also have to admit they might be *wrong*. And the size of your problem depends ultimately on who your readers are, what you want them to do, and how strongly they identify with their position. (People who are undecided are easier to persuade than those whose "minds are made up.") The bigger the readers' stake in the issue, the more personal their involvement, the more resistance you can expect. To overcome this resistance, you have to put yourself in your audience's position—you have to see things *their* way before you argue for *your* way. Before you can make readers budge even an inch, before you can create contact, you have to make them realize that your position is worth considering.

Making a good argument requires that you bring together all the strategies and resources you've acquired so far, along with features specific to argumentative writing:

1. a main point or claim that the audience finds debatable

2. convincing support for the claim

3. appeals to the audience's reason

4. appeals to the audience's emotions (as appropriate)

5. a clear and unmistakable line of thought

The final test of any argument is whether its *audience* finds it convincing.

Having a Debatable Point

The main point in an argument must be debatable (something open to dispute, something that can be viewed from more than one angle). Mere statements of fact are not debatable:

Facts

Several nearly disastrous accidents have occurred recently in nuclear power plants.

Women outlive men.

Economic policies of the Clinton administration have led to increases in student loan programs.

More than 50 percent of traffic deaths are alcohol related.

Because these statements can be verified (shown to be true—at least with enough certainty so that most people would agree), they cannot be debated. Nor can matters of taste or personal opinion be debated:

Statements of personal taste or opinion

I love oatmeal.

Salmon is my favorite fish.

Catholics are holier than Baptists.

Bill Clinton's speaking style puts me to sleep.

I hate the taste of garlic.

Likes or dislikes are not issues to be argued; the fact of your preference in such matters already is established. Questions of taste or personal opinion never can be resolved, because they rest on no objective reasons.

Even many assertions that call for expository development are not debatable (for most audiences). Consider these topic or thesis statements:

Viewpoints that can be verified

During the last decade, the Moral Majority has gained political influence.

Many of today's music videos demean women or advocate sexual violence.

Competition for good jobs in the 1990s is stiffer than ever.

Police roadblocks help deter drunk driving.

Too many young people are dying because of alcohol abuse.

The truth or validity of these assertions can be proved. And once the facts are established, the audience has no choice but to say, "Yes, it's true."

What, then, is a debatable point? It is one that cannot be proved true, but only more or less probable. For example, few readers would debate the notion that electronic games have altered the play habits of millions of American children. But some readers would debate the notion that electronic games are dominating children's lives. Some other debatable points:

Debatable points

The political activities of the Moral Majority violate the constitutional separation of church and state.

Music videos that demean women or advocate sexual violence should be censored.

Schools should place more emphasis on competition.

Police roadblocks are a justifiable deterrent against drunk driving.

Our state should raise the drinking age to 21.

No amount of reasoning by any expert and no supporting statistics can *prove* the rightness or wrongness of these claims. But even though controversial issues never can be resolved, writers can argue (more or less persuasively) for one side or the other. And—unlike an assertion of personal opinion or taste—the validity of an arguable assertion can be measured by the quality of support the writer presents. How does the assertion hold up against *opposing* assertions? In argument, we try to decide on the more reasonable approach. The winning argument is the one that presents the best case.

Always state your arguable point directly and clearly as a thesis. Although other development strategies (especially description and narration) sometimes allow the thesis merely to be implied, argumentative writing almost never does. Let readers know exactly where you stand.

The following essay presents the debatable assertion that electronic games are bad for children. As you read this essay, think about the ways our writer supports his claim. Is the support persuasive? Why, or why not?

No, You Can't Have Nintendo

My wife and I are the kind of mean parents whom kids grumble about on the playground. We're among that ever-shrinking group of parents known as Nintendo holdouts. We refuse to buy a Nintendo set. (Nintendo, for those of you who have been living in a cave for the past few years, is something that you hook up to your TV set that enables you to play various games on your home screen.) Around Christmastime, my son made a wish list, and I noticed that Nintendo was No. 1. I said, "You know you're not going to get Nintendo." He said, "I know I'm not going to get it from *you*. But I might get it from *him*." Alas, Santa, too, let him down.

I've heard parents' rationalizations about the games: "They're good for hand-eye coordination." (So is playing ball.) "It's something kids can do without an adult watching." (So is—dare I say that word?—reading.) "While he's playing at the screen, I can relax for a few minutes." (Who among us hasn't used the electronic babysitter from time to time? But "a few minutes"? Who are we kidding?)

I don't think that playing a video game now and then is really harmful to children. But the children I know are so obsessed with these games that they have prompted at least one second-grade teacher (my son's) to ban the word Nintendo from the classroom. When I asked my 7-year-old if the teacher wouldn't let the kids talk about the games because that's all they were *talking* about, he said, "No. That's all we were *thinking* about."

Our society is already so computerized and dehumanized that kids don't need one more reason to avoid playing outside or going for a walk or talking with a friend. I'd still feel this way even if there were nothing intrinsically wrong with games whose objectives are to kill and destroy.

I know, I know. There are games other than those like Rampage, Robocop, Motor Cross Maniacs, Bionic Commando, Dr. Doom's Revenge, Guerrilla War and Super Street Fighter. But aren't the violent games the ones the kids love to play for hours? And hours. And hours. My son told me he likes the "killing games" the best, hasn't had much experience with "sports games," and likes "learning games" the least because they are "too easy." (Manufacturers take note.) My 5-year-old daughter told me she enjoyed playing Duck Hunt at a friend's house. The beauty of this game is that even very young players can have the fun of vicariously shooting animals. And then there's the game with my favorite title—an obvious attempt to combine a graceful sport with exciting action: Skate or Die.

Some might try to convince us that these violent electronic games are good for a child's self-esteem and development. For years psychologists have been telling us how important fairy tales are to help children work out their fears and fantasies about good and evil, life and death. Maybe electronic games are just a modern way of doing this. Maybe, but. . . .

Maybe, but I don't remember kids reading and rereading "Hansel and Gretel" instead of playing outdoors when I was a kid. I don't remember hearing about children stealing money so they could buy copies of "Little Red Riding Hood." I don't remember many of my childhood friends skipping school so they could stay home and read "The Tortoise and the Hare." But this is what's going on with video and computer games.

The January [1990] issue of the *Journal of the American Academy of Child and Adolescent Psychiatry* (foreboding enough title for you?) featured an article entitled "Pathological Preoccupation with Video Games." The author believes that some game manufacturers try to develop programs that "deliberately promote habituation," and the goal of some of the people who make up these games is "to induce an altered level of concentration and focus of attention in the gamester."

If you have children, or know any, doesn't this "altered level of concentration and focus" sound familiar? If not, try talking to a child while he is staring at that screen, pushing buttons. He won't hear you unless the words you happen to be saying are, "I just bought a new game for you."

In case you couldn't tell, I'm worried that electronic games are dominating children's lives. There are games that simulate sports like baseball and basketball, and that's all some kids know about the sports. Someday soon, a young couple will take their children to their first baseball game and hear the kids exclaim. "This is great. It's almost like the *real baseball* we play on our home screen." When I took my son to a recent Lakers basketball game, the thing that seemed to excite him most (in addition to the self-flushing urinal) was a video game in the lobby. You see, if a kid didn't want to be bored watching some of the greatest athletes in the world play, he could just put a quarter in the machine and watch lifeless electronic images instead.

My son's teacher was right. Kids do play and talk about these games too much. They even have books and magazines that kids can study and classes so they can get better at the games. And that's what's got me worried. I'm just concerned that this activity is so absorbing, kids are going to grow up thinking that the first people to fly that airplane at Kitty Hawk were the Super Mario Brothers.

I don't like to discourage children from doing something they're good at; in this case, I must. And believe me, my desire to see them play the games less does not diminish how impressed I am by their skill—they seem to be getting better and better at these games at a younger and younger age. If you believe in evolution, you have to assume that right now DNA is coming together in new ways to create a "Nintendo gene" in our children which they'll pass along to their children. So, our grandchildren will be *born* with the ability to play electronic games. And, about the "Nintendo gene": I've got a feeling it's going to be dominant.

—Lloyd Garver

To support his claim, Garver offers powerful examples of various types of "video domination." Can you identify all his examples? (Try underlining them.) Why do you suppose Garver delays his thesis until paragraph 10? Is this an effective strategy here? Explain.

Supporting Your Claim

Chapter 6 shows how any credible assertion rests on opinions derived from facts. But facts out of context can be interpreted in various ways. Legitimate argument offers objective reasons, reliable sources, solid evidence, careful interpretation, and valid conclusions.

OFFERING CONVINCING REASONS

Any argument is only as convincing as the *reasons* that support it. No matter how "right" you think you are, you have to make your readers agree. And before readers will change their minds, they need to know *why*. They expect you to complete a version of this statement.

My position is _____ because _____.

Your reasons follow the "because."

To admit you are *right*, opponents also have to admit they are *wrong*—something few of us are likely to do without powerful reasons.

Arguing effectively, however, doesn't simply mean unloading on your reader every reason you can think of. Use only those reasons likely to move your specific audience. Assume, for instance, that all students living on your campus have a meal plan with a 15-meal requirement (for weekdays), costing $1800 yearly. You belong to a group trying to reduce the required meals to 10 weekly. Before seeking students' support and lobbying the administration, your group constructs a list of reasons supporting its position. A quick brainstorming session produces this list:

> The number of required weekday meals should be reduced to ten per week because:
>
> 1. Many students dislike the food.
> 2. Some students with only afternoon classes like to sleep late and should not have to rush to beat the 9:00 a.m. breakfast deadline.
> 3. The cafeteria atmosphere is too noisy, impersonal, and dreary.
> 4. The food selection is too limited.
> 5. The price of a yearly meal ticket has risen unfairly and is now more than 5 percent higher than last year's price.

Reviewing this list, you quickly spot a flaw: all these reasons rest almost entirely on *subjective* grounds, on matters of personal taste or opinion. For every reader who dislikes the food or sleeps late, there probably is one who likes the food or rises early—and so on. None of your intended audience (students, administrators) is likely to judge these reasons as very significant.

If you want your reasons to be judged significant, base them on *objective* evidence and on goals and values you and your readers *share*.

Offer Objective Evidence   Evidence is any information that supports your claim. Evidence is objective when it can be verified (shown to be factual) by everyone involved. Common types of objective evidence include statistics, examples, and expert testimony.

Numbers can be highly convincing. Before considering other details of your argument, many readers are interested in the "bottom line" (costs, savings, profits, and so on).

> Roughly 30 percent of the 500 students we surveyed in the cafeteria eat only two meals per day.

Any statistics you present have to be accurate, trustworthy, and easy for readers to understand and verify. (See pages 372–374 for advice on avoiding statistical fallacies.) Always cite your sources.

By showing specific instances of your point, examples help audiences *visualize* the idea or concept. For instance, the best way to explain what you mean by "wasteful" is to show "waste" occurring:

> From 20 to 25 percent of the food prepared never is eaten.
>
> Each dorm suite has its own kitchen, but these hardly are being used.

Good examples have persuasive force; they give readers something solid, a way of understanding even the most surprising or unlikely claim. Always use examples that your audience can identify with and that fit the point they are designed to illustrate.

Expert testimony lends authority and credibility to any claim. Readers like to know what the experts have to say:

> Food service directors from three local colleges point out that their schools' optional meal plans have been highly successful.

To be credible, however, an expert has to be unbiased and considered reliable by the audience.

Appeal to Shared Goals and Values   Although objective evidence can be persuasive, evidence alone isn't always enough to change a reader's mind. Audiences expect a writer to share their goals and values. If you hope to connect, you have to identify at least one goal you and your audience have in common: "What do we both want most?" In the meal plan issue, for example, we can assume that everyone is primarily concerned with eliminating wasteful practices. Any persuasive argument therefore will have to take this goal into account:

> These changes in the meal plan would eliminate waste of food, labor, and money.

Audiences in various situations have various goals (job security, being appreciated, a sense of belonging, safety, prosperity, excitement, or whatever). Be sure your argument focuses on a common, central goal.

Our goals are shaped by certain values: friendship, loyalty, honesty, equality, fairness, and so on (Rokeach 57–58). Make sure your argument appeals to the values you and your audience share. In the meal plan case, *fairness* seems as if it would be an important value:

No one should have to pay for meals she or he doesn't eat.

If you hope to be persuasive, provide arguments *that have real meaning for your readers.*

Here is how your group's final list of reasons might read:

The number of required weekday meals should be reduced to ten per week because:

1. No one should have to pay for meals she or he doesn't eat.

2. Roughly 30 percent of the 500 students we surveyed in the cafeteria eat only two meals per day.

3. From 20 to 25 percent of the food prepared never is eaten—a waste of food, labor, and money.

4. Each dorm suite has its own kitchen, but these hardly are being used.

5. Between kitchen suites and local restaurants, students on only the Monday-through-Friday plan do survive on weekends. Why couldn't they survive just as well during the week?

6. Food service directors from three local colleges point out that their schools' optional meal plans have been highly successful.

Any reasonable audience should find this argument compelling: each reason is based on a verifiable fact or (as in item 1) good sense. Although these reasons might not move all audience members to support your cause, readers will have to admit your argument is sound; they will understand *why* you've taken your stand.

Always place yourself in the audience's position. Think about reasons *they* will find important—reasons that might very well differ from those *you* find important.

Finding objective evidence to support a claim often requires that we go beyond our own experience by doing some type of research. But to arrive at the *best* conclusion (not merely the easiest or most convenient), we need to be able to trust our sources, our findings, and our interpretations.

CHOOSING RELIABLE SOURCES

Whether your evidence comes from reading, observing, or listening, make sure that each source is sufficiently current to provide the latest information on your topic. Also, each source should be reputable, relatively unbiased, authoritative, and borne out by similar sources. Say you are researching the alleged benefits of low-impact aerobics for reducing stress among employees at a fireworks factory. You could expect claims in a professional journal such as the *New England Journal of Medicine* to have bases in scientific fact. Also, a reputable magazine, such as *Scientific American,* would be a reliable source of evidence or of informed opinion. On the other hand, you might wisely suspect the claims in supermarket scandal sheets or movie magazines. Even claims in monthly "digests," which offer simplified and mostly undocumented "wisdom" to mass audiences, should be verified.

You would need to interview a representative sample of people who have practiced aerobics for a long time: people of both sexes, different ages, different lifestyles before they began aerobics, and so on. Even reports from ten successful practitioners would be a small sample unless those reports were supported by laboratory data. On the other hand, with a hundred reports from people ranging from students to judges and doctors, you might not have "proved" anything, but the persuasiveness of your evidence would increase.

Your own experience often is an inadequate base for generalizing. You cannot tell whether your experience is representative, regardless of how long you might have practiced aerobics. Interpret your experience only within the broader context of sources.

Some issues (the need for defense spending or causes of inflation) always are controversial and never will be resolved. Although we can get verifiable data and can reason persuasively on some subjects, no close reasoning by any expert and no supporting statistical analysis will "prove" anything about a controversial subject. For instance, one could only *argue* (more or less effectively) that federal funds will or will not alleviate poverty or unemployment. Some problems simply are more resistant to solution than others, no matter how reliable and valid the sources.

SEEKING OBJECTIVE EVIDENCE

Objective evidence consists of facts, examples, statistics, expert testimony, or informed opinion. It can stand up under testing because it can be verified (shown to be true). Subjective evidence consists of uninformed opinion or data that was obtained unscientifically. It may collapse under testing unless the opinion is expert and unbiased.

Base your conclusions on objective evidence. Early in your research, you might read an article that makes positive claims about low-impact aerobics, without providing data on measurements of pulse, blood pressure, or metabolic rates. Although your own experience and opinion might agree with the author's, you should not hastily conclude that this form of exercise benefits everyone. So far, you have only two opinions—yours and the author's—without scientific support (e.g., tests of a cross-section under controlled conditions). Conclusions now would rest on subjective evidence. Only after a full survey of reliable sources can you decide which conclusions are supported by the bulk of your evidence.

INTERPRETING YOUR EVIDENCE CAREFULLY

Interpreting the evidence means trying to reach the truth of the matter: an overall judgment about what the data mean and what conclusion or action they suggest. Unfortunately, even the best research does not always yield answers that are clear or conclusive or about which we can be certain.

As possible outcomes of research, we need to be able to recognize three distinct and very different levels of certainty:

1. The ultimate truth: the *conclusive answer:*

   Truth is *what is so* about something, the reality of the matter, as distinguished from what people wish were so, believe to be so, or assert to be so. From another perspective, in the words of Harvard philosopher Israel Scheffler, truth is the view "which is fated to be ultimately agreed to by all who investigate."* The word *ultimately* is important. Investigation may produce a wrong answer for years, even for centuries. . . . Does the truth ever change? No. . . . One easy way to spare yourself any further confusion about truth is to reserve the word *truth* for the final answer to an issue. Get in the habit of using the words, *belief, theory,* and *present understanding* more often. (Ruggiero 21–22)

   People often are mistaken in their certainty about the *truth.* For example, in the second century A.D., Ptolemy's view of the universe concluded that the earth was its center—and though untrue, this judgment was based on the best information available at that time. And Ptolemy's view survived for thirteen centuries, even after new information had discredited this belief. When Galileo proposed a more truthful view in the fifteenth century, he was labeled a heretic.

   Conclusive answers, of course, are the research outcome we seek, but we often have to settle for something less certain.

---

* From *Reason and Teaching,* New York: Bobbs-Merrill, 1973.

2. The *probable answer:* the answer that stands the best chance of being true or accurate—given the most we can know at this particular time. Probable answers are subject to revision in the light of new information.

3. The *inconclusive answer:* the realization that the truth of the matter is far more elusive or ambiguous or complex than we expected.

Before arguing any issue, we must decide what level of certainty our findings warrant. Otherwise, we might invent an unwarranted conclusion for inconclusive material.

When the issue is controversial, our own bias might cause us to overestimate the certainty of our findings.

> Expect yourself to be biased, and expect your bias to affect your efforts to construct arguments. Unless you are perfectly neutral about the issue, an unlikely circumstance, at the very outset . . . you will believe one side of the issue to be right, and that belief will incline you to . . . present more and better arguments for the side of the issue you prefer. (Ruggiero 134)

Because personal bias is hard to transcend, *rationalizing* often becomes a substitute for *reasoning:*

> You are reasoning if your belief follows the evidence—that is, if you examine the evidence first and then make up your mind. You are rationalizing if the evidence follows your belief—if you first decide what you'll believe and then select and interpret evidence to justify it. (Ruggiero 44)

Personal bias is inescapable but manageable—as long as we recognize it.

Finding the truth, especially in a complex issue or problem, is often a process of elimination, of ruling out or avoiding errors (fallacies) in reasoning. Common errors that distort our interpretations are discussed on pages 367–374.

AVOIDING SPECIOUS CONCLUSIONS

Specious conclusions are deceptive because they seem correct at first glance but prove invalid when scrutinized. Conclusions based on subjective evidence or faulty reasoning are specious.

Assume you are an education consultant evaluating the accuracy of IQ testing as a measure of intelligence and as a predictor of academic performance. Reviewing the evidence, you find a correlation between low IQ scores and low achievers. You then verify your statistics by examining a cross-section of reliable sources. Should you feel justified in concluding that IQ tests do measure intelligence and predict performance accurately? This conclusion might be specious unless you could show that

1. Neither parents nor teachers nor the children tested had seen individual test scores and had thus been able to develop biased expectations.

2. Regardless of their IQ scores, all children had been exposed to an identical curriculum at an identical pace, instead of being "tracked" on the basis of individual scores.

Your data could be interpreted only within the context of these two variables. Even objective evidence can support specious conclusions, unless it is interpreted within a context that accounts for all major variables.

The critical-thinking strategies we have just considered are part of the process that distinguishes legitimate research from mere information gathering.

Later in this chapter we will discuss the specific kinds of logical fallacies that can make conclusions specious.

Appealing to Reason

Keep in mind that argument is not separate and different from other types of writing discussed earlier in the book. In argument we always rely on some combination of description, narration, and exposition. Many persuasive arguments, however, are built around one or both of these reasoning patterns: *induction* (reasoning from specific evidence to a general conclusion) and *deduction* (applying a proven generalization to a specific case). But before looking at inductive and deductive strategies separately, let's consider how they work together to create sound logic.

Just about any daily decision (including the ones you're asked to make in this book) is the product of inductive or deductive reasoning, or both. Suppose that on registration day you learn you've been assigned to Math 101 with Professor Digit. You immediately decide to request a transfer to some other section. Let's trace the reasoning that led to your decision.

First, you reasoned inductively, from this specific evidence to a generalization:

*   *Fact:* Your older brother, a good mathematician and a serious student, received a *D* from Professor Digit two years ago, even

though you saw your brother slaving over his math assignments night after night.

- *Fact:* 60 percent of Professor Digit's students receive a *D* or *F*.

- *Fact:* Professor Digit often remarks, in class, that he despises teaching "dull-witted, first-year students."

- *Fact:* Two friends, both good students, failed Professor Digit's course. Each repeated the course with a different instructor: one received a *B+*, one a *B*.

- *Fact:* About one-third of Professor Digit's students drop his course after receiving their first grade

Based on this evidence, you reached this generalization:

Professor Digit seems to grade his students unfairly.

By reviewing and compiling the evidence, you were able to arrive at an *informed* opinion (a probability, not a fact). You reached this opinion via *inductive reasoning*. Armed with this generalization, in turn, you were able to use *deductive reasoning* to reach a conclusion:

Generalization	Professor Digit seems to grade his students unfairly.
Specific instance	I am one of Professor Digit's students.
Conclusion	I am likely to be graded unfairly.

Based on this conclusion, you decided to request a transfer to some other section.

We use induction and deduction repeatedly, often unconsciously. Specific facts, statistics, observations, and experiences lead us inductively to generalizations such as these:

Pre-med majors must compete for the highest grades.

Politicians can't always be trusted.

Big cities can be dangerous.

A college degree alone does not ensure success.

This college has a fine reputation.

On the other hand, deductive reasoning leads us from generalizations to specific instances to conclusions.

Generalization	Big cities can be dangerous.
Specific instance	New York is a big city.
Conclusion	New York can be dangerous.
Generalization	Pre-med majors must compete for the highest grades.
Specific instance	Brigitte will be pre-med major next year.
Conclusion	Brigitte will have to compete for the highest grades.

When we write to convince others that our reasoning is sound, we need to use these processes deliberately and consciously—and to be careful about how sweepingly we state our generalizations.

USING INDUCTION

We use induction in two situations: to move from various items of specific evidence to some related generalization, and to establish the cause or causes of something. Assume you've been dating someone for a while, but in the last week you've made these observations:

> Eloise hasn't returned my phone calls in a week.
>
> She always wants to go home early.
>
> She yawns a lot when we're together.
>
> She talks to everyone but me at parties.
>
> She does anything to avoid being alone with me.

Based on this evidence, you reason inductively to the generalization:

> Eloise is losing interest in me.

The same kind of reasoning establishes the possible or probable causes of Eloise's aloofness. As you reflect on the relationship, you recall a number of inconsiderate things you've done recently:

> I've been awfully short-tempered lately.
>
> I forgot all about her birthday last week.
>
> I'm usually late for our dates.

A few times, I've made wisecracks about her creepy friends.

In planning a date, I never ask for her opinion.

Thus, you conclude that your own inconsiderate behavior probably has caused your relationship with Eloise to suffer.

Induction is a good way to establish probability, arrive at generalization. Although generalizations aren't *proof* of anything, the better your evidence, the more likely your generalizations are accurate. Avoid generalizing from too little evidence. That Eloise yawns a lot would not be sufficient basis to conclude that she is losing interest in you. (Maybe she's ill or chronically tired!) Be sure readers can follow your reasoning and can see how your evidence adds up to your generalization. If Eloise had yawned during only one evening, that fact alone would not support the hasty generalization that your relationship is on the rocks. Provide enough facts, examples, statistics, and informed opinions to make your assertions believable.

As illustration of inductive reasoning, consider this passage from a 1963 letter by Martin Luther King, Jr., to white clergy after he was jailed for organizing a demonstration in Birmingham, Alabama.

A key statistic (1)
An informed opinion (2)

Acknowledgment of opposing views (3)
Examples (4)

[1]We have waited for more than 340 years for our constitutional and God-given rights. [2]The nations of Asia and Africa are moving with jetlike speed toward gaining political independence, but we still creep at horse-and-buggy pace toward gaining a cup of coffee at a lunch counter. [3]Perhaps it is easy for those who have never felt the stinging darts of segregation to say, "Wait." [4]But when you have seen vicious mobs lynch your mothers and fathers at will and drown your sisters and brothers at whim; when you have seen hate-filled policemen curse, kick, and even kill your black brothers and sisters; when you have seen the vast majority of your twenty million Negro brothers smothering in an airtight cage of poverty in the midst of an affluent society; when you suddenly find your tongue twisted and your speech stammering as you seek to explain to your six-year-old daughter why she can't go to the public amusement park that has just been advertised on television, and see tears welling up in her eyes when she is told that Funtown is closed to colored children, and see ominous clouds of inferiority beginning to form in her little mental sky, and see her beginning to distort her personality by developing an unconscious bit-

terness toward white people; when you have to con-
coct an answer for a five-year-old son who is asking,
"Daddy, why do white people treat colored people
so mean?"; when you take a cross-country drive and
find it necessary to sleep night after night in the
uncomfortable corners of your automobile because
no motel will accept you; when you are humiliated
day in and day out by nagging signs reading "white"
and "colored"; when your first name becomes "nigger," your middle name becomes "boy" (however
old you are) and your last name becomes "john,"
and your wife and mother are never given the
respected title "Mrs."; when you are harried by day
and haunted by night by the fact that you are a
Negro, living constantly at tiptoe stance, never
quite knowing what to expect next, and are plagued
with inner fears and outer resentments; when you
are forever fighting a degenerating sense of "nobodi-
ness"—then you will understand why we find it dif-

A generalization
from specifics (5)
Main point as a
direct appeal (6)

ficult to wait. 5There comes a time when the cup of
endurance runs over, and [people] are no longer willing to be plunged into the abyss of despair. 6I hope,
sirs, you can understand our legitimate and
unavoidable impatience.

—Martin Luther King, Jr.

This argument is intended to make Dr. King's readers see things from his
point of view. Notice how the inductive argument is organized: sentence
4 carries the burden of support for Dr. King's stand. And the support itself
is organized for greatest effect on the audience, with examples that
progress from the injustice he has witnessed to the injustice he and his
family have suffered to the humiliation he feels. Not only does he provide ample evidence to support his closing generalization (African
Americans have reason to be impatient), but his evidence also adds up
logically—and leads dramatically—to his conclusion.

An argument is only as strong as the objective evidence that supports it. It takes more than determination alone to change people's
minds; it takes solid evidence and sound reasoning as well.

USING DEDUCTION

You reason deductively when you use generalizations to arrive at specific conclusions. Once the generalization "African Americans have legitimate cause for impatience" is established *inductively* (and accepted), one
can argue deductively:

Generalization	African Americans have legitimate cause for impatience.
Specific instance	Ms. Smith is African American.
Conclusion	Ms. Smith has legitimate cause for impatience.

The conclusion is valid because the generalization is accepted and the specific instance is a fact. Both these conditions *must* exist in order for the conclusion to be sound.

Deductive reasoning applies to specific situations generalizations that are accepted as valid:

Generalization	Students who are required to pay for meals they don't eat are treated unfairly.
Specific instance	Many students at our college are required to pay for meals they don't eat.
Conclusion	Many students at our college are treated unfairly.

Here is how you might use deductive reasoning daily:

> If you know that Professor Jones gives no make-up exams, and you sleep through her final, then you can expect to flunk her course.

> If you know that Batmobiles need frequent repairs, and you buy a Batmobile, then you can expect to spend many hours repairing your car.

The soundness of deductive reasoning can be measured by sketching an argument in the form of a *syllogism*, the basic pattern of deductive arguments. Any syllogism has three parts: a major premise, a minor premise, and a conclusion—as shown here:

Major premise	All humans are mortal.
Minor premise	John is human.
Conclusion	John is mortal.

If readers accept both premises, they have no choice but to accept your conclusion. For the conclusion to be valid, the major premise must state an accepted generalization and the minor premise must state a factual instance of that generalization. And the conclusion must express the same degree of certainty as the premises (that is, if a "usually" appears in a premise, it must appear in the conclusion as well). Also, the syllogism must be stated correctly, the minor premise linking its subject with the subject of the major premise; otherwise, the syllogism is faulty, like this:

A faulty syllogism   All human beings are mortal.

John is mortal. [*Minor premise is incorrectly stated; many creatures are mortal, but not human.*]

John is a human being.

Each premise in a syllogism is usually derived from inductive reasoning. Because every human being we've known so far has been mortal, we can reasonably conclude that *all* human beings are mortal. And once we have examined and studied John thoroughly and decided that he is a human being, we can connect the two premises to arrive at the conclusion that John is mortal.

Illogical deductive arguments usually result from a faulty major premise (or generalization). You usually can verify a minor premise easily (merely by observing John, to determine if he is a human being). But the major premise is a generalization; unless you have enough inductive evidence, your generalization can be faulty. How much evidence is *enough*? Let your good judgment tell you. Base your premise on *reasonable* evidence, so that your generalization reflects reality as most people would know it. Avoid unreasonable premises such as these:

Faulty generalizations   All men are male chauvinists.

Cats are sneaky and mean.

School is boring.

Men with long hair are drug addicts.

People can't be trusted.

Frailty, thy name is woman.

Notice the problem when one such generalization serves as the major premise in an argument:

Major premise   People can't be trusted.

Minor premise   My mother is a person.

Conclusion   My mother can't be trusted.

In many deductive arguments, the generalizations are not stated directly; instead they are implied, or understood:

> Joe is harming his health with cigarettes. [*Implied generalization: Cigarette smoking harms health.*]
>
> Sally's low verbal scores on her college entrance exam suggest that she will need remedial help in composition. [*Implied generalization: Students with low verbal scores need extra help in composition.*]

Here's what happens to the conclusion when the unstated generalization is faulty:

> Dr. Jones is a college professor, and so she must be absent-minded. [*Implied generalization: All college professors are absent-minded.*]
>
> Martha is a feminist, and so she must hate men. [*All feminists hate men.*]
>
> He's our president, and so what he says must be true. [*Presidents are never mistaken or dishonest.*]

In addition to incorrect or unsupported generalizations, another danger in deductive arguments is the *overstated generalization;* that is, making a limited generalization apply to all cases. Be sure to modify your assertions with qualifying words such as *usually, often, sometimes,* and *some,* instead of absolute words such as *always, all, never,* and *nobody.* Notice how these generalizations are overstated:

> All Dobermans are vicious.
>
> Politicians never keep their promises.

Rephrase these to make them reasonable and realistic:

> Some Dobermans are vicious.
>
> Politicians seldom keep their promises.

And when you apply these generalizations, remember that the conclusion that follows must also be qualified.

This paragraph illustrates a deductive argument.

> These ought to be the best of times for the human mind, but it is not so. All sorts of things seem to be turning out wrong, and the century seems to be slipping through our fingers here at the end, with almost all promises unfulfilled. I cannot begin to guess at all the

causes of our cultural sadness, not even the most important ones, but I can think of one thing that is wrong with us and eats away at us: we do not know enough about ourselves. We are ignorant about how we work, about where we fit in, and most of all about the enormous, imponderable system of life in which we are embedded as working parts. We do not really understand nature, at all. We have come a long way indeed, but just enough to become conscious of our ignorance. It is not so bad a thing to be totally ignorant; the hard thing is to be partway along toward real knowledge, far enough to be aware of being ignorant. It is embarrassing and depressing, and it is one of our troubles today.

—Lewis Thomas

The deductive argument runs like this:

Implied generalization	People who don't know enough about themselves are in a sad state of mind.
Specific instance	We don't know enough about ourselves.
Conclusion	Therefore, we are in a sad state of mind.

The argument is valid because it meets these criteria:

- The major premise is acceptable.

- The minor premise is verifiable.

- The argument is not overstated. Notice the limiting words:

  all sorts of things [*not* all things]

  almost all promises [*not* all promises]

  one thing that is wrong [*not* everything]

  one of our troubles [*not* all of our troubles]

- The author limits his argument to *one* instance or problem ("we do not know enough about ourselves").

Recognizing Illogical Reasoning

Whether you argue inductively or deductively, beware of the kinds of illogical reasoning called *fallacies* (assertions and statements derived from faulty logic). Because they reveal flaws in your thinking, fallacies weaken your case. By recognizing the most common fallacies, you should be able to avoid them.

MAKING FAULTY GENERALIZATIONS

As we have seen, induction *leads* to a generalization, but deduction *proceeds from* a generalization. And because we all love to generalize, we have to be particularly wary of making two kinds of major errors. Generalizations can be faulty for two reasons:

1. Because they are hasty (based on insufficient or irrelevant evidence), as we have seen in the section on inductive reasoning.

2. Because they are far too broad and sweeping. Something true in one case need not be true in all cases.

How true are these generalizations?

> Blondes have more fun.
>
> Television is worthless.
>
> Humanities majors do not get good jobs.
>
> Money buys happiness.

A common version of faulty generalization is *stereotyping,* the simplistic and trite assignment of characteristics to groups.

> All politicians are crooks.
>
> Southern cops are brutal.
>
> The French are hot tempered.
>
> The Irish are big drinkers.
>
> Elderly people are senile.
>
> Women cry easily.

BEGGING THE QUESTION

You beg the question when you assume that a debatable premise (or premises) underlying your assertion already has been supported convincingly. In other words, you are "begging" readers to accept your premise before you have shown it to be reasonable, as in these examples:

> Useless subjects like composition should not be required.
>
> Voters should reject Candidate *X*'s unfair accusation.
>
> Books like *X* and *Y,* which destroy the morals of our children, should be banned from our libraries.

Such arguments assume in one of their premises what the arguer is supposed to be proving. If a subject is useless, obviously it should not be required. But that it *is* useless is precisely what has to be established. Likewise, Candidate *X*'s accusations have to be proved unfair, and books such as *X* and *Y* have to be proved corrupting. In each of these cases, the arguer is "begging the question" by asking for the desired conclusion without the effort of supporting it by reasoning. Any sound argument is based on valid premises.

AVOIDING THE QUESTION

As we will see in the next section, some appeals to emotions, of course, are legitimate (pity, fear, and the like). But you avoid the question when you distract readers from the real issue with material that is irrelevant or that obscures the issue by making an irrational appeal to emotions.

An appeal to pity

He should not be punished for his assault conviction because as a child he was beaten severely by his parents. [*Has no legal bearing on the real issue: his crime.*]

An appeal to fear

If we outlaw guns, only outlaws will have guns. [*Ignores the question of the deaths and injuries caused by guns.*]

An appeal to normalcy

She is the best person for the teaching job because she is happily married and has two lovely children. [*Has nothing to do with the real issue: her qualifications as a teacher.*]

An appeal to flattery

A person with your sophistication surely will agree that marriage is outmoded. [*Has nothing to do with the conclusion that remains to be verified.*]

An appeal to authority or patriotism

Uncle Sam stands behind savings bonds. [*Ignores the question of whether savings bonds are a good investment: Although they are safe, they often pay lower interest than some other investments.*]

Snob appeal (persuading readers to accept your assertion because they want to be identified with respected, heroic, or notable people)

A real man knows that *Musk* cologne is the best. [*Has nothing to do with the issue of individual preference or quality.*]

As any intelligent person knows, Candidate A will make a good president. [*Has nothing to do with the candidate's qualifications.*]

Michael Jackson drinks Pepsi Cola, so it must be the best. [*Has nothing to do with the quality of the item.*]

USING THE BANDWAGON APPROACH

The bandwagon approach gets readers to agree by claiming that everyone else agrees. It urges readers to follow the crowd and thereby avoids the real issue.

No one in our sorority would date men from that fraternity.

Everyone has tried marijuana at least once.

More Cadillac owners are switching to Continentals than ever before. [*Of course, if the numbers provided real evidence, the assertion would be legitimate.*]

ATTACKING YOUR OPPONENT

Another way to ignore the real question is by attacking your opponent through name-calling or derogatory statements about his or her character (*ad hominem argument*):

The effete intellectual snobs in academia have no right to criticize our increase in military spending. [*Calling people names does not discredit their argument.*]

He was once convicted for perjury, so why should we believe what he says? [*How do we know that he hasn't since been honest?*]

College students are too immature to know what they want, so why should they have a say in the college curriculum? [*College students often are young but not necessarily immature.*]

USING FAULTY CAUSAL REASONING

Causal reasoning tries to explain *why* something happened or *what* will happen—often truly complex questions. As illustrated on pages 289–292, a cause can have more than one effect, and vice versa. A faulty causal argument oversimplifies the cause-and-effect relationship through errors like these:

> Running improves health. [*Ignores the fact that many runners develop injuries and that some even drop dead while running.*]

> Albert receives good grades because he is brilliant. [*Ignores the possibility that, although Albert may be bright, perhaps he also studies hard or takes easy courses.*]

A common instance of faulty causal argument is assigning the wrong cause or ignoring other causes:

> Investment builds wealth. [*Ignores the role of knowledge, timing, and luck in successful investing.*]

Another mistake is to suggest an unwarranted causal relationship merely because one event follows another (*post hoc fallacy*):

> Right after buying a rabbit's foot, Felix won the state lottery.

Yet another version of faulty causal arguing is *rationalization,* a way of denying the real causes of our failures:

> I flunked math because the teacher was awful and the book was boring. [*Not because I hardly studied!*]

> Because I became a father at 19, I was never able to go to college. [*Not because I was too lazy to spend my evenings doing anything but watching television!*]

IMPOSING THE EITHER-OR FALLACY

The either-or fallacy occurs when a writer reduces a complex issue to only two extreme positions or sides—black or white—even though other choices exist.

> Deadlines force students to hand in something not carefully done, just to make sure it's on time. [*Ignores the possibility of doing it on time and doing it well.*]

> We have the choice between polluting our atmosphere or living without energy. [*Leaves out the possibility of generating clean energy.*]

> Marry me, or I'll kill myself.

Like all other appeals to emotion instead of reason, this kind of argument may influence some readers for a while but certainly will crumble when scrutinized.

USING FAULTY STATISTICAL REASONING

The purpose of statistical analysis is to determine the meaning of a collected set of numbers. In research, surveys and questionnaires often lead to some kind of numerical interpretation ("What percentage of respondents prefer X?" "How often does Y happen?" and so on).

Numbers have special appeal because they seem more precise, more objective, and less ambiguous than words. They are easier to summarize, measure, compare, and analyze. But, through error or abuse, numbers can be totally misleading.

> One journalist explains how radio or television "phone-in" surveys produce grossly distorted "data": Although ninety percent of callers, say, express support (or opposition) toward this or that viewpoint, the people who call tend to be those with the greatest anger or the strongest feelings about the issue—usually a mere two or three percent of the total audience (Fineman 24).

Before relying on any set of numbers, we need to know exactly where they come from, how they were collected, and how they were analyzed (Lavin 275–76).

Faulty statistical reasoning produces conclusions that are unwarranted, inaccurate, or downright deceptive. Here are some typical fallacies:

- *The meaningless statistic:* when exact numbers are used to quantify something so inexact or vaguely defined that it should only be approximated (Huff 247; Lavin 278): "Only 38.2 percent of college graduates end up working in their specialty." "Boston has 3,247,561 rats." An exact number looks impressive, but it can hide the fact that certain subjects (child abuse, cheating in college, virginity, drug and alcohol abuse on the job, eating habits) cannot be counted exactly because respondents don't always tell the truth (because of denial or embarrassment or merely guessing).

- *The undefined average:* when the mean, median, and mode are confused in determining an average (Huff 244; Lavin 279). The *mean* is the result of adding up the value of each item, then dividing by the number of items. The *median* is the result of ranking all the values from high to low, then choosing the middle value. The *mode* is the value that occurs most often.

Each of these three measurements represents some kind of average. But unless we know which "average" is being presented, we cannot possibly interpret the figures accurately.

Assume, for instance, that we are calculating the average salary among female vice presidents at XYZ Corporation (ranked from high to low):

Vice President	Salary
A	$90,000
B	90,000
C	80,000
D	65,000
E	60,000
F	55,000
G	50,000

In the above example, the mean salary (total salaries divided by people) equals $70,000; the median salary (middle value) equals $65,000; the mode (most frequent value) equals $90,000. Each is legitimately an "average," and each could be used to support or refute a particular assertion (for example, "Women receive too little" or "Women receive too much").

Research expert Michael Lavin sums up the potential for bias in reporting averages:

> Depending on the circumstances, any one of these measurements may describe a group of numbers better than the other two. . . . [But] people typically choose the value which best presents their case, whether or not it is the most appropriate to use. (279)

Unethical use of statistics misleads and manipulates the audience.

- *The distorted percentage figure:* when percentages are reported without explanation of the original numbers used in the calculation (Adams and Schvaneveldt 359; Lavin 280): "75 percent of respondents prefer our brand over the competing brand"— without mention that only four people were surveyed. Or "66 percent of employees we hired this year are women and minorities, compared to the national average of 40 percent"— without mention that only three people have been hired this year, by a company that employs 300 (mostly white males). Even the most impressive looking numbers can be misleading.

  Another fallacy in reporting percentages is in failing to account for the margin of error. For example, a claim that the majority of people surveyed prefer Brand X might be based on the fact that 51 percent of respondents expressed this preference; but if the survey carried a 2 percent margin of error, the claim could be invalid.

- *The bogus ranking:* when items are compared on the basis of ill-defined criteria (Adams and Schvaneveldt 212; Lavin 284): "Last year, the Batmobile was the number-one selling car in America" —without mention that some competing car makers actually sold *more* cars to private individuals, and that the Batmobile figures were inflated by hefty sales to rental-car companies and corporate fleets. Unless we know how the ranked items were chosen and how they were compared (the criteria), a ranking can produce a scientific-seeming number based on a completely unscientific method.

These are only a few examples of statistics that seem highly persuasive but that in fact cannot be trusted. As producers *and* consumers of information, we have an ethical responsibility to seek out the truthful answers, not merely those that are most comforting or convenient.

Even when the statistics are valid and reliable, we need to interpret them realistically. Consider, for example, the legitimate finding that rates for certain cancers double among people who are exposed for prolonged periods to electromagnetic radiation (from power lines and appliances). What this statistic may mean is that the incidence of cancer actually increases from 1 in 10,000 to 2 in 10,000.

Appealing to Emotion

Emotion is no substitute for reason, but some audiences are not persuaded by reason alone. In fact, the audience's attitude toward the writer is often the biggest factor in persuasion—no matter how solid the argument. Audiences are more receptive to people they like, trust, and respect. And so an emotional appeal can help connect reader and writer.

Emotional appeals should address readers' virtues—*not* their weaknesses. Appeals to honesty, fairness, humor, and common sense are legitimate ways of strengthening an already good argument. On the other hand, appeals to closed-mindedness, prejudice, paranoia, and ignorance (as in the logical fallacies covered earlier) merely hide the fact that an argument offers no authentic support. Emotional appeals cannot rescue unsupportable arguments.

Complex emotional transactions between writer and reader defy simple formulas, but we find limited guidance through the following strategies:

- Try to identify with the reader's feelings.
- Show respect for the reader's views.
- Try to sound reasonable.
- Know when and how to be forceful.
- Know when to be humorous.

Each of these strategies for effective emotional appeals is discussed below.

SHOWING EMPATHY

To show empathy is to identify with the reader's feelings and to express genuine concern for the reader's welfare. Consider the lack of empathy in this paragraph:

> Dear Buck,
>
> After a good deal of thought I've decided to write to you about your weight problem. Let's face it: you're much too fat. Last week's shopping trip convinced me of that. Remember the bathing suit you liked, the one that came only in smaller sizes? If you lost weight, you might be able to fit into those kinds of suits. In addition to helping you look attractive, the loss of 30 or 40 pounds of ugly fat would improve your health. All you have to do is exercise more and eat less. I know it will work. Give me a call if you need any more help or suggestions.

Although this writer makes the problem vivid to the reader and supports the assertions, this argument is almost certain to fail. The writer's superior attitude can't help but alienate the reader. Here is a revised version, now with a distinct expression of empathy.

> Dear Buck,
>
> Remember that great bathing suit we saw in Stuart's the other day, the one you thought would be perfect for the beach party but that didn't come in your size? Because the party is still 3 weeks away, why not begin dieting and exercising so you can buy the suit? I know that losing weight is awfully hard, because I've had to struggle with that problem myself. Buck, you're one of my best friends, and you can count on me for support. A little effort on your part could make a big difference in your life.

The tone of this version communicates the writer's genuine interest in Buck's welfare—and feelings. Without taking a superior position, the writer manages to appeal to Buck's desire for self-improvement. Empathy is especially important in an argument encouraging some specific action on the reader's part.

ACKNOWLEDGING OPPOSING VIEWS

Because an argument addresses readers on the opposing side, you must do everything possible to get them over to your side. *Before* arguing your case, show respect for your readers by acknowledging the merit in their position, as in this passage:

Orienting statement (1–3)

Acknowledgment of opposing view (4–5)

Writer's argument (6–9)

¹Well, the moon was there. ²The moment there was a chance to get on it, someone was bound to try. ³The process was accelerated by national rivalries, but it would have happened even if the U.S. or the Soviet Union alone had had a monopoly on rocketry. ⁴For any great country has a supply of brave and spirited [people] who would have been ready for any adventure technology might give them. ⁵That is grand: it makes one proud of belonging to the same species. ⁶But there is something else that is perhaps not so grand, that is unarguable and also sinister. ⁷That is—there is no known example in which technology has been stopped being pushed to the limit. ⁸Technology has its own inner dynamic. ⁹When it was possible that technology could bring off a moon landing, then it was certain that sooner or later, the landing would be brought off—however much it cost in human lives, dollars, rubles, social effort.

—C. P. Snow

This writer takes a controversial position on an event that is almost sacred in American history. But by showing respect for the popular view, he decreases readers' resistance to his own position. Your acknowledgment of opposing views shows that you understand that no arguable position can be *proved* correct. Readers respect fairness.

MAINTAINING A MODERATE TONE

Another way to connect with readers is through a moderate and balanced tone. People are more likely to listen to you if they like you! Resist the temptation to overstate your case to make your point. Stay away from emotionally loaded words that boil up in the heat of argument. This writer is unlikely to win converts:

> Scientists are the culprits responsible for the rape of our environment. Although we never see these beady-eyed, amoral eggheads actually destroying our world, they are busy in their laboratories dreaming up new ways for industrialists and developers to ravage the landscape, pollute the air, and turn all our rivers, lakes, and oceans into stinking sewers. How anybody with a conscience or a sense of decency would become a scientist is beyond me.

Granted, this piece is forceful and sincere and does suggest the legitimate point that scientists share responsibility—but the writer doesn't seem very likable. The paragraph is more an attack than an argument. Besides generalizing recklessly and providing no evidence for the assertions, the writer uses emotionally loaded words (*eggheads, stinking sewers*) that overstate the position. A good argument appeals to *reason*, not just *emotion*. The tone of overstatement here surely will make readers skeptical. Always avoid extreme positions.

Here is another version of the paragraph above. Because the main point is controversial, this writer understates it, thus making the argument more convincing:

> [1]It might seem unfair to lay the blame for impending environmental disaster at the doorstep of the scientists. [2]Granted, the rape of the environment has been carried out, not by scientists, but by profiteering industrialists and myopic developers, with the eager support of a burgeoning population greedy to consume more than nature can provide and to waste more than nature can clear away. [3]But to absolve the scientific community from complicity in the matter is quite simply to ignore that science has been the only natural philosophy the western world has known since the age of Newton. [4]It is to ignore the key question: who provided us with the image of nature that invited the rape, and with the sensibility that licensed it? [5]It is not, after all, the normal thing for people to ruin their environment. [6]It is extraordinary and requires extraordinary incitement.
>
> —Theodore Roszak

Notice how the argument begins by acknowledging the opposing view (sentences 1–2). The tone is firm yet reasonable. When the writer points the blame at scientists, in sentences 3–4, he offers evidence.

The writer softens his tone while making his point by using a rhetorical question in sentence 4. *Rhetorical questions* are really statements in the form of questions; because the answer is obvious, readers can be expected to provide it for themselves. Used sensibly, a rhetorical question can be a good way of impelling readers to confront the issue (as the question in sentence 2 of the letter to Buck, page 371) without offending them.

When you use rhetorical questions, do so with caution. They can easily alienate readers, especially if the issue is personal:

> Your constant tardiness is an inconvenience to everyone. It's impossible to rely on a person who is never on time. Do you know how many times I've waited in crummy weather for you to pick me up? What about all the appointments I've been late for? Or how about all the other social functions we haven't "quite" made it to on time? It's annoying to everyone when you're always late.

Notice how the aggressive tone of this piece is heightened because of the rhetorical questions. The writer seems to be throwing his friend's bad habit into his face. Such a tone only makes readers defensive.

How big is the problem, and how forceful should you be? Some strong issues may *deserve* the emotional emphasis created by rhetorical questions. This is another kind of decision you need to make continually about your audience and purpose. Notice how this paragraph combines the force of rhetorical questions with a touch of humor.

> I was pleased to have a glimpse of you last night as you honked your horn and whizzed by me (am I right?) at about 100 miles per hour. Perhaps I'm straining the bonds of our friendship, but here goes. Why do you drive so fast? Don't you have any regard for others? Isn't the world moving fast enough already? I know: You're suicidal—right? Often the ones hurt because of people like you are innocent bystanders: children, senior citizens, little dogs, kitty cats. Is there anything on this list that you do slow down for? And how about yourself? Suppose you wrecked your car and yourself as well. Have you ever thought about being hospitalized for the rest of your life? How about death? That's pretty final. Come on: slow down and live; enjoy the world around you; get a less powerful car; take the bus; ride a bike; walk; call me—I'll give you a ride. Next time you drive by me, I hope to see something more than a flash of light.

Rhetorical questions seem appropriate here because the drastic situation called for drastic persuasive measures. Notice also the short sentences for emphasis.

USING SATIRE IN APPROPRIATE CIRCUMSTANCES

Just how forceful can we be with our tone? For example, how can we express anger or frustration or outrage without seeming to preach? Is it possible to confront readers without alienating them? No one enjoys being "told off" or ridiculed, but in certain situations a jolt of lucid observation might help readers overcome denial in order to face an issue realistically. Satire is one vehicle for exposing folly, stupidity, ignorance, or corruption—for "telling it like it is."

Satire usually relies on irony and sarcasm to make its point. *Irony* is a form of expression that states one thing while clearly meaning another. For instance, Gloria Naylor (pages 337–339) describes how the ordinarily alienating and degrading term "nigger" sometimes is used ironically by some African Americans as a term of affection or respect. *Sarcasm* employs a more blatant form of irony to mock or to ridicule. For instance, in the essay that follows, a professor of English takes a hard look at certain contemporary attitudes about education and offers this sarcastic observation:

> I, too, used to think that knowledge was important and that we should encourage hard work and perseverance. Now I realize that the concept of rewards for merit is elitist and, therefore, wrong in a society that aims for equality in all things. We are a democracy. What could be more democratic than to give exactly the same grade to every student?

As you read the whole essay, think about how the satirical perspective compels us to examine our own attitudes.

A Liberating Curriculum

A blessed change has come over me. Events of recent months have revealed to me that I have been laboring as a university professor for more than 20 years under a misguided theory of teaching. I humbly regret that during all those years I have caused distress and inconvenience to thousands of students while providing some amusement to my more practical colleagues. Enlightenment came to me in a sublime moment of clarity while I was being verbally attacked by a student whose paper I had just proved to have been plagiarized from *The Norton Anthology of English Literature.* Suddenly, I understood the true purpose of my profession, and I devised a plan to embody that revelation. Every moment since then has been filled with delight about the advantages to students, professors and universities from my Plan to Increase Student Happiness.

The plan is simplicity itself: at the end of the second week of the semester, all students enrolled in each course will receive a final grade of A. Then their minds will be relieved of anxiety, and they will be free to do whatever they want for the rest of the term.

The benefits are immediately evident. Students will be assured of high grade-point averages and an absence of obstacles in their march toward graduation. Professors will be relieved of useless burdens and will have time to pursue their real interests. Universities will have achieved the long-desired goal of molding individual professors into interchangeable parts of a smoothly operating machine. Even the environment will be improved because education will no longer consume vast quantities of paper for books, compositions and examinations.

Although this scheme will instantly solve countless problems that have plagued education, a few people may raise trivial objections and even urge universities not to adopt it. Some of my colleagues may protest that we have an obligation to uphold the integrity of our profession. Poor fools, I understand their delusion, for I formerly shared it. To them, I say: "Hey, lighten up! Why make life difficult?"

Those who believe that we have a duty to increase the knowledge of our students may also object. I, too, used to think that knowledge was important and that we should encourage hard work and perseverance. Now I realize that the concept of rewards for merit is elitist and, therefore, wrong in a society that aims for equality in all things. We are a democracy. What could be more democratic than to give exactly the same grade to every single student?

One or two forlorn colleagues may even protest that we have a responsibility to significant works of the past because the writings of such authors as Chaucer, Shakespeare, Milton and Swift are intrinsically valuable. I can empathize with these misguided souls, for I once labored under the illusion that I was giving my students a precious gift by introducing them to works by great poets, playwrights and satirists. Now I recognize the error of my ways. The writings of such authors may have seemed meaningful to our ancestors, who had nothing better to do, but we are living in a time of wonderful improvements. The writers of bygone eras have been made irrelevant, replaced by MTV and People magazine. After all, their bodies are dead. Why shouldn't their ideas be dead, too?

If any colleagues persist in protesting that we should try to convey knowledge to students and preserve our cultural heritage, I offer this suggestion: honestly consider what students really want. As one young man graciously explained to me, he had no desire to take my course but had enrolled in it merely to fulfill a requirement that he resented. His job schedule made it impossible for him to attend at least 30 percent of my class sessions, and he wouldn't have time to do much of the reading. Nevertheless, he wanted a good grade. Another student consulted me after the first exam, upset because she had not studied and had earned only 14 points out of a possible 100. I told her that, if she studied hard and attended class more regularly, she could do well enough on the remaining tests to pass the course. This encouragement did not satisfy her. What she wanted was an assurance that she would receive at least a B. Under my plan both students would be guaranteed an A. Why not? They have good looks and self-esteem. What more could anyone ever need in life?

I do not ask for thanks from the many people who will benefit.

I'm grateful to my colleagues who for decades have tried to help me realize that seriousness about teaching is not the path to professorial prestige, rapid promotion and frequent sabbaticals. Alas, I was stubborn. Not until I heard the illuminating explanation of the student who had plagiarized from the anthology's introduction to Jonathan Swift did I fully grasp the wisdom that others had been generously offering to me for years—learning is just too hard. Now, with a light heart, I await the plan's adoption. In my mind's eye, I can see the happy faces of university administrators and professors, released at last from the irksome chore of dealing with students. I can imagine the joyous smiles of thousands of students, all with straight-A averages and plenty of free time.

My only regret is that I wasted so much time. For nearly 30 years, I threw away numerous hours annually on trivia: writing, grading and explaining examinations; grading hundreds of papers a semester; holding private conferences with students; reading countless books; buying extra materials to give students a feeling for the music, art and clothing of past centuries; endlessly worrying about how to improve my teaching. At last I see the folly of grubbing away in meaningless efforts. I wish that I had faced facts earlier and had not lost years because of old-fashioned notions. But such are the penalties for those who do not understand the true purpose of education.

—Roberta F. Borkat

Some readers might feel offended or defensive about such a harsh assessment; however, satire deliberately seeks confrontation—not diplomacy. Unlike those rhetorical strategies that *close* the distance between writer and reader, satire often serves to *widen* this distance! Be sure, therefore, that you understand its purpose and potential effect on your audience before deciding on a satirical perspective in your own writing.

ADDING HUMOR WHERE APPROPRIATE

In some situations, your raising an issue—no matter how legitimate—is likely to make your reader defensive. Sometimes a bit of humor can rescue an argument that might cause hard feelings because it seems overly sarcastic. In the next paragraph, the writer wanted to call attention to his roommate's sloppiness. With such a delicate issue, the writer decided to add some humor and exaggeration to his argument.

Jack,

If you never see me alive again, my body will be at the bottom of your dirty clothes pile that rises like a great mountain in the center of our room. How did I end up there? Well, while doing my math I ran out of paper and set out for my desk to get a few pieces—despite the risk I knew I was taking. I was met by a 6-foot wall of dirty laundry. You know how small our room is; I could not circumnavigate the pile. I thought I'd better write this note before going to the janitor's room for a shovel to dig my way through to my desk. The going will be tough and I doubt I'll survive. If the hard work doesn't kill me, the toxic fumes will. Three years from now, when you finally decide to do your wash, just hang my body up as a reminder to stash your dirty clothes in your closet where they will be out of sight and out of smell.

Your dead roommate

Of course, humor sometimes works and occasionally doesn't. Always anticipate how your audience will react; otherwise, humor can backfire.

What determines whether your argument creates contact with readers is *how* you say what you have to say. Different purposes and audiences invariably call for different tones—a major decision in persuasive writing.

Make your tone moderate but not voiceless. Readers need to sense a real person behind the words. In the following essay, Laurie Simoneau asks dorm students and parents to support a request for thermostats in each dorm room. As you read the essay, think about how the support, the appeals, and the tone combine for a persuasive argument.

The Sweatbox and the Icebox: Dorm Students Need Thermostats

It's 9 A.M. I peel my sweat-soaked body off the soggy sheet and turn off my alarm. I wipe my moist forehead and chin with a tissue and lick my parched lips. Even though my window is wide open, the heat repels the cold November air. After showering I study my cracked lips and dry, blotchy skin. Infuriated, I dress and head for class.

Upstairs, my friend Lisa crawls out of bed at the sound of her own alarm. She shivers—despite the flannel pajamas, sweatshirt, and wool socks she put on last night in a vain attempt to retain body heat. Her window is shut tight, and so is her heating vent. Lisa complains often to the Housing Office, but her room still freezes.

Within days, the Student Health Office is overrun by sniffling, hacking, sneezing, retching students who must each day either leave the dorms in a sweat, only to face harsh November winds, or who freeze all night long, take hot morning showers, then freeze again until they reach the warmth of the classroom. And these aren't isolated cases: I've surveyed all students in my dorm, and 80 percent complained about room temperatures.

The extreme temperatures of many dorm rooms are hurting students' health and performance. They are getting sick. They are unable to study in the discomfort of their own rooms. They sleep poorly, and they are furious.

The problem has an obvious cause: among the eight rooms in each suite are only two thermostats. And so the occupants of these two rooms adjust the heat to a temperature they find comfortable. As a result, rooms at other points on the heating pipe receive too little or too much heat. The logical solution: install thermostats in the remaining six rooms of every suite.

The cost of dorm housing more than doubles the cost of tuition (for state residents). Students choose dorms over off-campus housing because of the "positive living-learning environment" promised in the college brochures. But many of us, I think, would now scoff at the mention of such a promise. What these sweating shivering, sniffling, hacking, sneezing, retching students request is a comfortable room temperature *throughout* the dorms. What they need are thermostats.

I ask all students and parents involved to please phone or write the Housing Office (555-1515) to voice your complaint and your request. With your support we can create the "positive living-learning environment" all residential students desire and deserve.

—Laurie Simoneau

In addition to presenting objective evidence (examples, etc.), Laurie writes in a forceful tone. Is such a tone appropriate here? Why, or why not?

Application 18–1

Which of these statements are debatable? Be prepared to give the reasons for your choices. (Review pages 348–349.)

1. Grades are an aid to education.

2. 40 percent of incoming first-year students at our school never graduate.

3. Physically and psychically, women are superior to men.

4. Pets should not be allowed on our campus.

5. Computer courses are boring.

6. Every student should be required to become computer literate.

7. The computer revolution is transforming American business.

8. Computer prices are dropping by as much as 25 percent yearly.

9. French wines are better than domestic wines.

10. French wines generally are more subtle and complex than domestic wines.

11. French wines are overpriced.

·12. College is not for everyone.

Application 18–2

Using your own subjects or those below, develop five arguable assertions. (Review pages 348–349.)

> *Examples*
>
> [*sex*] The sexual revolution has created more problems than it has solved.
>
> [*a personal gripe*] The heavy remedial emphasis at our school causes many introductory courses to be substandard.

taxes	law	a classroom incident
sex	music	jobs
drugs	war	a personal gripe
pollution	dorm life	a suggestion for improving something

Application 18–3

The statements below are followed by false or improbable conclusions. What specific supporting evidence would be needed to justify each conclusion so that it is not a specious generalization? (First, you need to infer the missing generalization or premise; then you have to decide what evidence would be needed for the premise to be acceptable.) (Review pages 358–359.)

> *Example*
>
> Only 60 percent of incoming first-year students eventually graduate from this college. Therefore, the college is not doing its job.

To consider this conclusion valid, we would have to be shown that:

1. All first-year students want to attend college in the first place.
2. They are all capable of college-level work.
3. They did all assigned work promptly and responsibly.

1. Eighty percent of African-American voters in Alabama voted for George Blank as governor. Therefore, he is not a racist.

2. Fifty percent of last year's college graduates did not find the jobs they wanted. Therefore, college is a waste of time and money.

3. She never sees a doctor. Therefore, she must be healthy.

4. This house is expensive. Therefore, it must be well built.

5. Felix is flunking first-year composition. Therefore, he must be stupid.

6. My parents never argue. Therefore, they must be happily married.

7. Abner has never had an accident in two years of driving. Therefore, he must be a good driver.

Application 18–4

Select one of these general claims, and list five specific items that would inductively support each. (Review pages 359–363.)

Example

General claim
We have little cause to be optimistic about our global future.

Inductive support
1. Our environment is becoming more and more polluted.

2. Nuclear arms capability is proliferating.

3. Energy shortages threaten the economic survival of industrialized countries.

4. The earth's population will double in 35 years.

5. Changing weather patterns threaten the world's agricultural production.

1. We have good cause to be optimistic about our global future.

2. College is not for everyone.

3. Grades are (an aid, a detriment) to education.

4. Our school (should, should not) drop student evaluation of teachers.

5. Television has made a (positive, negative) contribution to the education of the young in this country.

Application 18–5

PARAGRAPH WARM-UP: INDUCTIVE REASONING

Using Dr. King's paragraph (page 362) as a model, write a paragraph in which you use inductive reasoning to support a general conclusion about one of these subjects (after you have narrowed it) or about one of your own choice.

highway safety	minorities
a college core requirement	the legal drinking age
the changing role of women	credit cards

Identify your audience and purpose. Provide enough evidence so that readers can follow your chain of reasoning to your conclusion.

Application 18–6

Assume that someone recently has made a decision that you disagree with (say, the dean has imposed a curfew because of several assaults on campus, or a friend has decided to drop out of school). Write a letter to the specific person or group involved, arguing that the decision was unwise, unfair, or in some way harmful. Persuade the audience to change its mind. Provide enough evidence for your assertion, and use a tone that is diplomatic and reasonable. Reserve your main point for the end of your argument.

Application 18–7

One of these conclusions is valid. The others rely on implied generalizations that are faulty or overstated. Identify the errors and revise. (Review pages 365–368.)

1. Because Martha claims to be a feminist, she should support the Equal Rights Amendment.

2. Harold smokes marijuana, so he is likely to develop lung cancer.

3. Hubert, a typical male, seems threatened by feminists.

4. Because Mary is now a suburbanite, she will probably become an alcoholic.

5. Because I'm a poor writer, my English instructor must think I'm stupid.

Application 18–8

PARAGRAPH WARM-UP: DEDUCTIVE REASONING

Select an accepted generalization from this list or use one of your own as the topic statement in a paragraph using deductive reasoning. (Review pages 359–367.)

- "Beauty is in the eye of the beholder."

- "That person is richest whose pleasures are the cheapest."

- Some teachers can have a great influence on a student's attitude toward a subject.

- A college degree doesn't guarantee career success.

Application 18–9

Assume that you have a younger sibling or friend who is thinking about attending your college. Based on what you know about your reader's needs, write a letter that argues for or against attending.

Application 18–10

Identify the fallacy in each of these sentences and revise the assertion to eliminate the error. (Review pages 367–374.)

Example

Faulty   Television is worthless. [*sweeping generalization*]

Revised   Commercial television offers too few programs of educational value.

1. Mary dropped out of school because Professor Quantum gave her an F in math.

2. Because our product is the best, it is worth the high price.

3. America—love it or leave it.

4. Three of my friends praise their Jettas, proving that Volkswagen makes the best car.

5. My grades last semester were poor because my exams were unfair.

6. Anyone who was expelled from Harvard for cheating could not be trusted as a president.

7. Until college students contribute to our society, they have no right to criticize our government.

8. Because he is a devout Christian, he will make a good doctor.

9. Anyone with common sense will vote for this candidate.

10. You should take up tennis; everyone else around here plays.

11. Poverty causes disease.

12. Convex running shoes caused Karl Crane to win the Boston Marathon.

Application 18–11

Revise this paragraph so that its tone is more moderate and reasonable, more like an intelligent argument than an attack. Feel free to add personal insights that might help the argument.

> People who argue that marijuana should remain outlawed are crazy. Beyond that, many of them are mere hypocrites—the boozers of our world who squander their salary in bars and come home to beat the wife and kids. Any intelligent person knows that alcohol burns out the brain, ruins the body, and destroys the personality. Marijuana is definitely safer; it leaves no hangover; it causes no physical damage or violent mood changes, as alcohol does; and it is not psychologically or physically addictive. Maybe if those redneck jerks who oppose marijuana would put down the beer cans and light a joint, the world would be a more peaceful place.

Application 18–12

After reading this paragraph, answer the questions that follow.

> [1]Responsible agronomists report that before the end of the year millions of people, if unaided, might starve to death. [2]Half a billion

deaths by starvation is not an uncommon estimate. ³Even though the United States has done more than any other nation to feed the hungry, our relative affluence makes us morally vulnerable in the eyes of other nations and in our own eyes. ⁴Garret Hardin, who has argued for a "lifeboat" ethic of survival (if you take all the passengers aboard, everybody drowns), admits that the decision not to feed all the hungry requires of us "a very hard psychological adjustment." ⁵Indeed it would. ⁶It has been estimated that the 3.5 million tons of fertilizer spread on American golf courses and lawns could provide up to 30 million tons of food in overseas agricultural production. ⁷The nightmarish thought intrudes itself. ⁸If we as a nation allow people to starve while we could, through some sacrifice, make more food available to them, what hope can any person have for the future of international relations? ⁹If we cannot agree on this most basic of values— feed the hungry—what hopes for the future can we entertain? ¹⁰Technology is imitable and nuclear weaponry certain to proliferate. ¹¹What appeals to trust and respect can be made if the most rudimentary of moral impulses—feed the hungry—is not strenuously incorporated into national policy?

—James R. Kelly

1. Is this argument inductive or deductive? Explain.

2. Does the author appeal to our emotions? If so, where and how?

3. In which sentences does he support his position with hard evidence?

4. Restate the main point as a declarative sentence. Is the point arguable? Explain.

5. Identify one short sentence that provides emphasis. Explain how it reinforces the author's position.

6. Are the rhetorical questions effective here? Explain.

Application 18–13

RESPONDING TO YOUR READING

1. Explore your reactions to "No, You Can't Have Nintendo" (pages 350–352) by using the page 91 questions. Then respond with an essay of your own. You might challenge Garver's view by pointing out the benefits of electronic games. Or you might support his view by pointing out other electronic forms of "contemporary

domination" (say, televised sports, political advertising, product advertising, sitcom views of the world, violence toward women in television shows, and so on). Or you might take some middle position on the issue. Whatever your stance, be sure to support your view with clear, logical reasoning and solid evidence.

2. Explore your reactions to "A Liberating Curriculum" by using the page 91 questions and those below.

- For whom does Borkat seem to be writing?

- What do you suppose Borkat wants her audience to be thinking or feeling after reading this essay? Does she achieve her purpose? Explain.

- What assumptions does she make about her audience's knowledge and attitudes? Are these assumptions accurate? Why or why not?

- What is this writer's attitude toward her subject? Toward her audience? How do we know? What are the signals?

- What are the main issues for her? How has this essay affected your thinking about these issues?

- What point is Borkat making about educational expectations? Restate her point in your own words.

- Is this essay's tone appropriate for the writer's audience and purpose? Explain.

- Are the rhetorical questions effective? Explain.

Respond to Borkat with an essay of your own. You might wish to challenge her view by arguing your own ideas about "what students really want" or the "true purpose of education." (See, for example, essay option number 15, page 27.) You might support her view by citing evidence from your own experience. Or you might develop your own satirical treatment of some topic you think warrants a certain measure of mockery or ridicule. If you do settle on a satirical perspective, try to anticipate its effect on your audience. Remember that the purpose of satire is to wake people up—but not to alienate them to the extent that they end up rejecting what you have to say. Whatever we write for readers has consequences!

Decide carefully on your audience and on what you want these readers to be doing or thinking or feeling after reading your essay. Be sure your essay supports a clear and definite point.

WORKS CITED

Adams, Gerald R., and Jay D. Schvaneveldt. *Understanding Research Methods.* New York: Longman, 1985.

Fineman, Howard. "The Power of Talk." *Newsweek* 8 Feb. 1993: 24–28.

Huff, Darrell. *How to Lie with Statistics.* New York: Norton, 1954.

Lavin, Michael R. *Business Information: How to Find It, How to Use It.* 2nd ed. Phoenix: Oryx, 1992.

Rokeach, Milton. *The Nature of Human Values.* New York: Free Press, 1973.

Ross, Raymond S. *Understanding Persuasion.* 3rd ed. Englewood Cliffs: Prentice, 1990.

Ruggiero, Vincent R. *The Art of Thinking.* 3rd ed. New York: Harper, 1991.

19

Composing Various Arguments

Shaping to Reveal Your Line of Thought
• **Observing Audience Guidelines**
• **Observing Ethics Guidelines**
• **Specific Goals of Argument** • **Applications**

Persuasion, at best, is risky business, because no single approach is guaranteed to work. Your own approach will depend on the people involved, the relationships, and the topic. And if the audience is truly resistant, even the best arguments might fail. Although you have no way of predicting whether your efforts will succeed, the chances improve immensely when your argument is emphatic, engaging, and fair.

Shaping to Reveal Your Line of Thought

As you plan, draft, and revise your argument, give it a shape that emphasizes key material, a shape readers can recognize. Readers want to be able to follow your reasoning; they expect to *see* how you've arrived at your conclusions.

Like other writing for other aims, persuasive writing has an introduction, body, and conclusion. But within this familiar shape, your argument should do some special things as well.

Standard shape for an argument

Introduction (Attracts and Invites Your Readers and Provides a Forecast)

- Identify the issue clearly and immediately. Show the audience that your essay deserves their attention.

- Acknowledge the opposing viewpoint *accurately* and concede its merit.

- Offer at least one point of your own that your audience can agree with.

- As you build to your thesis, offer *significant* background material so that your readers are fully prepared to understand your position.

- State a clear, concrete, and *definite* thesis. Never delay your thesis without good reason. (For now, you might list supporting points in your thesis statement.) Of course, if your thesis is highly controversial, you might want to delay it until you've had a chance to offer some convincing evidence.

- Do all these things in no more than a few paragraphs.

Body (Offers the Support and Refutation)

- Use reasons that rest on *impersonal* grounds of support.

- In one or more paragraphs *each,* organize your supporting points for best emphasis (from least to most important or dramatic or compelling, or vice versa). If you think your audience has little interest, begin with the more powerful material. Sometimes you can sandwich weaker points between stronger points. But if all your points are equally strong, begin with the most familiar and acceptable to your audience—to elicit some early agreement. In general, try to save the strongest points for last.

- Develop each supporting point with concrete, specific *details* (facts, examples, narratives, quotations, or other evidence that can be verified empirically or logically). Never be vague.

- Using transitions and other connectors, string your supporting points and their supporting evidence together to show a definite line of reasoning.

- In at least one separate paragraph, refute opposing arguments (including any anticipated readers' objections to your points) —unless you've done your refuting earlier or throughout.

Conclusion (Sums Up Your Case and Makes a Direct Appeal)

- Summarize your main points and your refutation, emphasizing your strongest material. (Keep things short and sweet.) Offer a view of the Big Picture.

- End by appealing directly to readers for a definite action (where appropriate).

- Let readers know what they should be doing or thinking or feeling after reading your argument.

The sample arguments in Applications 19–1 through 19–4 are each shaped around some version of this model. Virtually no argument, however, rigidly follows the order or specifications outlined here. Select whatever shape you find useful in your situation—as long as it reveals your line of thought.

By shaping your argument deliberately, you stand the best chance of moving your audience to accept or appreciate—or at least understand clearly—your way of seeing something controversial.

Observing Audience Guidelines

Whenever you set out to persuade, remember this principle:

No matter how brilliant, any argument rejected by its audience is a failed argument.

If readers find reason to dislike you or conclude that your argument has no meaning for them personally, they usually reject *anything* you say.

Connecting with an audience means being able to see things from their perspective. The following guidelines can help you make that connection.

1. *Be clear about what you want.* Diplomacy is important, but people won't like having to guess about your purpose.

2. *Never make a claim or ask for something you know readers will reject outright.* Be sure readers can live with whatever you're requesting or proposing. Offer a genuine choice.

3. *Anticipate your audience's reaction.* Will they be defensive, surprised, annoyed, angry, or what? Try to address their biggest objections beforehand.

4. *Avoid extreme personas.* **Persona** is the image or impression of the writer's personality suggested by the tone of a document. Resist

the urge to "sound off," no matter how strongly you feel. Audiences tune out aggressive people—no matter how sensible the argument. Try to be likable and reasonable. Admit the imperfections in your case. A little humility never hurts.

5. *Find points of agreement with your audience.* Focusing early on a shared value or goal or concern can reduce conflict and help win agreement on later points.

6. *Never distort the opponent's position.* A sure way to alienate people is to cast the opponent as more of a villain or simpleton than the facts warrant.

7. *Try to concede SOMETHING to the opponent.* Surely the opposition's position is based on at least one good reason. Acknowledge the merits of that case before arguing for your own. Instead of seeming like a know-it-all, show some empathy and willingness to compromise.

8. *Use only your best material.* Not all your reasons or appeals will have equal strength or significance. Decide which material—from your *audience's* view—best advances your case.

9. *Make no claim or assertion unless you can support it with good reasons.* "Just because" does not constitute adequate support!

10. *Use your skills responsibly.* The obvious power of persuasive skills creates tremendous potential for abuse. People who feel they have been bullied or manipulated or deceived become enemies.

The following persuasive letter observes the previous guidelines. Our writer, Christopher Biddle, has applied earlier to a state university for mid-year acceptance as a full-time transfer student. But, facing severe budget cuts, the university decided not to review any applications for mid-year transfer. And so Biddle appeals directly to the University president.

As you read Biddle's letter, think about the ways it makes a human connection and how it appeals to reason.

Dear President Mason:

As fall semester ends, I face bleak prospects: After three semesters of excellent work as a special student, I had planned to begin the new year fully enrolled at State U. Enter the budget cuts.

Having reached the credit limit for special students, I'm now looking at the end of my academic career for at least a semester, if not forever.

I realize that the budget cuts mandated drastic measures on your part. However, the decision not to review mid-year transfer applications may already have served its purpose. If so, might there be time to review those applications and admit the very best applicants on a space-available basis?

Of all the tough decisions you've had to make in this financial crisis, the decision not to review mid-year applications must have been one of the toughest. On one hand, you have a responsibility not to "water down" the education of those students already admitted. On the other hand, you have a responsibility toward students who have been working hard at junior colleges or as special students, all in hopes of being admitted this winter. It's not fair for the presently enrolled students to have their classes overcrowded by mid-year transfers, but then again, it's not fair for the transfer students to be denied a chance.

The legislature understandably needs to receive a loud and clear message that State U is struggling. And I see the danger of legislators interpreting transfer admissions as a sign of "business as usual"—a sign that State U has weathered these cuts and thus might be able to handle further cuts.

I don't envy your role in the decision process, and I'm in no position to fault your handling of the issue. Maybe this is just the kind of "blood" our legislature had to see.

Through state house demonstrations (of which I was a part), countless protest letters and phone calls, and political SOS's from higher education officials, we have implored the legislators to ease up. And they have been forced to listen. Almost as soon as they had announced the latest round of cuts, the legislature felt compelled to soften the blow by almost one-third. Maybe the university's political hardball helped.

But the point now has been made. State U has profited from its decision not to review mid-year applications, and there still may be time to counteract the losses.

Besides benefiting the students themselves, mid-year transfers would benefit the university. A transfer student occupying an otherwise empty seat costs State U no money; tuition dollars, in fact, bring money in. And assuming that only the best students are admitted, they enhance the entire student body.

Of course, some majors already are overcrowded, and so transfers would have to be admitted on a space-available basis. The Registrar assures me that he has worked with the admissions office in earlier years to fill last-minute spaces with transfers as late as mid-January. And the Admissions Director claims that her office's role in this process is "the easy part."

I realize that even the "easy part" might not be so easy at this late stage, but I would love to see the university give it a try.

Picture State U after the budget cuts, and what do you see? The football, basketball, and hockey teams are still playing. The radio station is still broadcasting.

What's missing from this picture? Students. A couple of dozen highly motivated transfer students. So what's the big deal? The university can get by without these students.

The big deal is that the university exists to educate. Without a football team you can still have a university. Without a track team, without a swimming pool, even without a radio station or newspaper you can still have a university. As long as teachers are teaching students, there is still a university. But take away the students, and what's the point? Students should come first, and they should go last.

Respectfully,

Christopher B. Biddle

Christopher B. Biddle

Befitting the relationship with his reader, the tone is forceful but respectful and *reasonable.* Biddle is careful to ask for nothing the reader would consider extreme or outrageous. Instead of special consideration for himself only ("Make an exception for me") he asks that *all* transfer applications be reviewed ("Give us all a fair chance"). And by citing the views of other university officials, Biddle shows he has done his homework on this issue.

Observing Ethics Guidelines

We argue to change readers' thinking, but not "to win" at any cost. An effective argument is not necessarily an *ethical* argument. For instance, advertisers effectively advance an implied argument that goes something like this: "Our product is just what you need!" Some of their more specific claims: "Our artificial sweetener is made of proteins that occur naturally in the human body [amino acids]" or "Our potato chips contain no cholesterol." Such claims are technically accurate, but misleading: amino acids in artificial sweeteners can alter body chemistry to cause headaches, seizures, and possibly brain tumors; potato chips are loaded with saturated fat—from which the liver produces cholesterol. While the advertiser's claims may be factual, these facts are incomplete, and they imply misleading conclusions. Can you think of other examples from advertising or politics?

Whether such miscommunication occurs deliberately or through neglect, a message is unethical when it prevents readers from making their best decision. To be ethical, writing must meet standards of honesty, fairness, and concern for everyone involved.*

To help ensure that whatever you write is ethical, ask yourself these questions:

- Do I avoid exaggeration, understatement, sugarcoating, or any distortion that leaves readers at a disadvantage?

- Do I really know what I'm talking about—instead of "faking" certainty?

- Have I explored all sides of the issue?

- Are my information sources valid, reliable, and unbiased?

- Am I being honest and fair with everyone involved?

- Am I reasonably sure that what I'm saying harms no innocent persons or damages their reputation?

- Do I give readers all the understanding and information they need for making an informed decision?

- Do I state the case clearly, instead of hiding behind fallacies or generalities?

- Do I inform readers of the consequences or risks of what I am advocating?

- Do I give credit to all contributors and all sources of ideas and information?

When we argue, we often are tempted to emphasize anything that advances our case and to ignore anything that impedes it. But readers always expect fair treatment. Don't let them down by merely doing "whatever it takes" to be persuasive.

---

* This list largely was adapted from Stephen H. Unger, *Controlling Technology: Ethics and the Responsible Engineer.* New York: Holt, 1982: 39–46; Richard L. Johannesen, *Ethics in Human Communication,* 2nd Edition. Prospect Heights, Illinois: Waveland, 1983: 21–22; George Yoos, "A Revision of the Concept of Ethical Appeal." *Philosophy and Rhetoric 12* (Winter 1979): 41–58; Judi Brownell and Michael Fitzgerald, "Teaching Ethics in Business Communication." *The Bulletin of the Association for Business Communication 55.3* (1992): 15–18; John Bryan, "Down the Slippery Slope: Ethics and the Technical Writer as Marketer." *Technical Communication Quarterly 1.1* (1992): 73–88.

Specific Goals of Argument

We argue so that readers will see things our way. In this sense, all arguments share a goal. But arguments can differ considerably in their intended effect on readers—in what they ask readers to do. The goal of an argument might be to influence readers' opinions, seek readers' support, propose some action, or change readers' behavior. Let's look more closely at different arguments that seek different levels of involvement from readers.

ARGUING TO INFLUENCE READERS' OPINIONS

An argument intended to change an opinion is aimed for minimal involvement from its readers. Maybe you want readers to agree that specific books and films should be censored, that women should be subject to military draft, that grades are a detriment to education, that yuppies are ruining city neighborhoods. Or maybe you seek agreement on the reverse of any of these positions. The specific goal behind any such argument is merely to get readers to change their thinking, to say "I agree."

ARGUING TO ENLIST READERS' SUPPORT

In seeking readers' support for our argument, we ask readers not only to agree with a position but to take a stand as well. Maybe you want readers to vote for a candidate, reject a plan for fluoridating the public water supply, lobby for additional computer equipment at your school, or help enforce dorm or library "quiet" rules. The goal in this kind of argument is to get readers actively involved, to get them to ask "How can I help?"

MAKING A PROPOSAL

The world is full of problems to solve. And *proposals* are designed precisely to solve problems. The type of proposal we examine here typically asks readers to take some form of direct action (to improve dorm security, fund a new campus organization, or improve working conditions). But before readers can be persuaded to *act*, they have to agree that the problem is worth their attention. And once they've agreed, readers need a definite plan for solving the problem. A proposal writer's job, specifically, is to satisfy these four criteria:

1. spell out the problem (and its causes) in enough detail to convince readers of its importance

2. point out the benefits of solving the problem

3. offer a realistic solution

4. urge the reader to act on the proposed solution

Proposal writers have to think very carefully about *exactly* what they want their readers to do. This kind of argument seeks to get readers to say "Let's do it."

ARGUING TO CHANGE READERS' BEHAVIOR

Persuading readers to change their behavior is perhaps the biggest challenge in argument. Maybe you want your boss to treat employees more fairly, or a friend to be less competitive, or a teacher to be more supportive in the classroom. Whatever your goal, readers are bound to take your argument personally. And the more personal the issue—the more readers are asked to do—the greater resistance you can expect. This kind of argument is especially difficult because it is more personal than a proposal. With it we try to get readers to say, "I was wrong. From now on, I'll do it differently."

SAMPLE ARGUMENTS

The four essays shown in Applications 19–1 through 19–4, respectively, are addressed to readers who have an increasing stake or involvement in the issue. By reading and comparing these essays, you will get a good sense of how writers in various argumentative situations can reveal persuasively *their* way of seeing.

Application 19–1

ESSAY PRACTICE: ARGUING TO INFLUENCE READERS' OPINION

The writer of this essay argues that traditional city neighborhoods are losing their character as they are transformed into suburb-like havens for affluent young professionals. Read the essay, and answer the questions that follow. Then (as your instructor requests) select one of the essay assignments.

The Evils of Gentrification

[1]As a child, I always dreamed of living in a big city. It didn't matter which, so long as it had more people than I could possibly know and more places than I could ever visit. In the small Midwestern suburb where I grew up, I knew every face, building, and street sign by heart. A single city neighborhood seemed to possess

more diversity, excitement, and character than all the shopping malls, manicured lawns, and clean suburban streets I had ever seen. I was eager to leave those clean streets behind.

²But now I find that the very presence of people like myself—men and women between the ages of 18 and 34 who are choosing to stay single and childless—is changing the face of American cities, making them oddly like the suburbs where we grew up. We have altered the landscape to suit our needs. Our socioeconomic status has given us the power to spend, and thus, the power to transform neighborhoods once defined by racial and ethnic characteristics. The blacks and the Jews and the Irish have dispersed; we, the baby boom kids, have taken their place.

³This process has been given the rather awkward title of "gentrification," but I would prefer to leave that term in the hands of the sociologists who coined it. No single word can describe a phenomenon that forces the neighborhood dry cleaner to close his doors and brings in a $1-a-scoop ice cream store to take his place. That is what happened on Columbus Avenue in New York City, the "New Town" lakefront neighborhood in Chicago, the Montrose section of Houston, the Capitol Hill neighborhood in Washington, D.C., and the other areas where the young, affluent baby boom spenders gather to live and consume.

⁴Nor can a sociological term match the experience of a walk down the Main Streets of these new neighborhoods, all born within the last decade. On New York's Columbus Avenue, young people pack the sidewalks each night, eating $5 hamburgers at high-tech restaurants and buying $15 glitter socks at new-wave boutiques. For groceries they must walk 10 minutes to the nearest A&P; for a pair of Keds sneakers or a haircut, they must go even farther. The barber shop is gone, the shoe store is gone, the grocery is gone.

⁵The attraction of these new neighborhoods is simple: as young people delay marriage and children, they more desperately need, and thus seek, the company of others like themselves. The marketplace understands that need and exploits it, which is why young people on Capitol Hill are spending more than $500 a month for studio apartments that only a few years ago cost half as much. In Chicago, you could live in the Northwest Side's ethnic neighborhoods and pay next to nothing for rent—but where would you go to buy a half-pound of chocolate-chip cookies at midnight?

⁶And so we move into these tiny, overpriced apartments, driving out the poor, the middle class, and even the children, turning the neighborhood into the exclusive domain of the singles and the childless. As of 1980, Manhattan had a population-per-household of 1.96; that's the second lowest in the nation, right behind the Kalawao leper colony in Hawaii.

⁷It isn't merely those who decide to delay marriage and children

who have prompted the change, but also the growing homosexual population that will remain permanently childless and affluent. Even in macho Houston, the gay population has come into the open as an economic force. Although the rest of Houston may look down its nose at the Montrose section's newfound gay chic, it can't help but appreciate the potent power of money to create a viable neighborhood.

[8]I say viable because many people defend this process of neighborhood transformation. They argue that the new stores and restaurants provide a city-to-city anchor for a nomadic society; one can move from Chicago to Boston and find a virtually identical neighborhood to live in. There's hardly a city left in America that doesn't have some sort of "gentrified" quarter—from San Francisco, where one might argue that the whole city has been transformed, to Washington, where changes are just beginning.

[9]I can't really argue with that defense. It is comforting to find good restaurants close by, nice stores, perhaps a theater showing a movie I want to see. But it also feels suspiciously like something I grew up with in that small Midwestern suburb: the shopping mall. A day spent in Chicago's New Town is not all that different from a day at the giant Woodfield Mall in the Chicago suburb of Schaumburg.

[10]So now, thanks to the sheer economic force of my generation, I don't have to move back to the suburbs. The suburbs have moved to me. I can walk out my door and find all the stores I want; I don't even have to drive. I can buy a baseball cap with horns on each side, a take-out container of homemade linguini with clam sauce, a greeting card that will make me seem quite clever. Everything I want is right in front of me—everything except the city of my childhood dreams.

—David Blum

Questions About Content

1. Does the writer acknowledge the opposing viewpoint? If so, where?

2. Does the writer concede anything to his opponents (give them credit for anything)? Explain.

3. Does the thesis grow out of sufficient background details? Explain.

4. Does the writer offer convincing reasons for his case? Explain.

5. Does the writer make too much of an emotional appeal? Explain

Questions About Organization

1. Which strategy of expository development is used most here?

2. Trace the line of thought by summarizing the topic of each paragraph. Is the material arranged in the best order?

3. Why did the writer use a two-paragraph introduction? Explain.

Questions About Style

1. What is the notable style feature of this essay? Explain and illustrate.

2. How would you characterize the tone? Is it appropriate for the audience and purpose? Does the writer avoid any extreme personas? Explain.

RESPONDING TO YOUR READING

Explore your reactions to "The Evils of Gentrification" by using the questions on page 91. Then respond with your own essay arguing for or against a physical change (that has occurred or will occur) in some part of your environment.

The change might involve your community, your neighborhood, your school, some favorite hideaway, a place where you work, or the like. Perhaps your old high school is facing a proposed change from traditional classroom space to an "open concept" (various classes clustered around an open area, each class in a cubicle). Or perhaps your favorite lakeside retreat is now giving way to condominium development.

Be sure your essay has a discoverable thesis, and addresses a specific audience affected by the change in some way. Although this essay will make an emotional appeal, your argument should not rest solely on subjective grounds (how you *feel* about it), but also on factual details.

To organize this essay, use a comparison-contrast structure (page 319).

OPTIONS FOR ESSAY WRITING

1. Several years ago, students at a leading university (call it Ivy University) voted in support of this position: that the school infirmary stockpile cyanide capsules to be made available to all personnel in the event of a global nuclear war. Argue for or against the position expressed by the students at Ivy University.

2. Argue for or against this assertion: Parents have the right to make major decisions in the lives of their teenagers.

3. Are grades an aid to education?

4. Sally and Sam have two children, ages 2 and 5. Sally, an attorney, is currently not working but has been offered an attractive full-time job. Sam believes Sally should not work until both children are in school. Should Sally take the job? Why, or why not?

5. In 1977, voters in Dade County, Florida, repealed an ordinance protecting homosexuals from discrimination in housing and

employment. More recently, voters in Colorado took a similar position. Defend or attack these public decisions.

6. Should college scholarships be awarded for academic achievement or promise rather than for financial need?

7. Should books and films and music be censored?

8. Defend the "American Way of Life" to a person from another country (say, a foreign exchange student) who has criticized it as too commercial, hectic, and superficial.

9. Should women be drafted?

10. Imagine that you have just read this passage in a newspaper column:

> Ten years ago, only about two-thirds as many Americans were graduating from college as now, and plenty of jobs were available requiring college degrees. Nowadays, by contrast, there are no longer enough upper-level jobs to absorb the flood of college graduates. We are producing an "overqualified" generation, some of whom must wind up in jobs not requiring higher education, or even in no jobs at all. The resulting personal frustration and social unrest are the fault of an overexpanded higher education system.
>
> I am not arguing, however, that more young people should be denied the *chance* to go to college. Instead of reducing admissions, we should cut back on the awarding of degrees. In other words, we don't flunk enough students out; in fact, with grade inflation, we now flunk almost *nobody* out. If the lower third of each class were dropped after two years, the excess of degrees would vanish, with beneficial effects for the nation.

Respond to the passage. If you agree, offer further support, if you disagree, suggest an alternative, giving support for your idea.

11. We live in an imperfect world. Everywhere are problems to be solved. During your more than 12 years in school, you've undoubtedly developed legitimate gripes about the *quality* of American education. Based on your experiences *and* perceptions *and* research, think about one specific problem in American education, and argue for its solution. Remember, you are writing an argument, not an attack; your goal is not to offend but to persuade readers—to get them over to your way of seeing.

After making sure that you have enough inductive evidence to support your main generalization, write an editorial essay for your campus newspaper: identify the problem; analyze its cause(s); and propose a solution. Possible topics:

- too little (or too much) attention given to remedial students
- too little (or too much) emphasis on *practical* education (career training)
- too little (or too much) emphasis on competition
- teachers' attitudes
- parents' attitudes
- students' attitudes

12. Should people be allowed to choose the sex of their child?

13. Should police force the homeless into shelters in cold weather?

14. Should minors who commit violent crimes be tried as adults and, in certain cases, be subject to the death penalty?

15. Should beauty pageants be outlawed?

Application 19–2

ESSAY PRACTICE: ARGUING TO ENLIST READERS' SUPPORT

This essayist argues that school athletes should meet minimal academic standards as a condition for participating in team sports. Read the essay, and answer the questions that follow. Then (as your instructor requests) select one of the essay assignments.

Standards You Meet and Don't Duck

[1]I'm telling you about my son Mark, not because I want to embarrass him, but because I find it useful in discussing public-policy questions to ask what I would advocate if the people affected by my policy proposals were members of my own family.

[2]Mark, who is not quite 12, is a good kid: friendly, bright, a good athlete and (potentially) a very good student. But he has a tendency to be lazy about his studies.

[3]So at the beginning of the year, I issued an edict: He would perform acceptably well in school or he wouldn't be allowed to play organized sports outside school.

[4]He talked me into a modification: Rather than penalize him for last year's grades, earned before the new rule was announced, let him sign up for the Boys Club league now, and take him off the team if his mid-terms weren't up to par.

[5]Well, the mid-terms came out, and the basketball team is struggling along without the assistance of my son the shooting guard.

⁶All of which is a roundabout and perhaps too personal a way of saying my sentiments are with the Prince George's County (Md.) school officials. My suburban Washington neighbors, confronted with angry parents, disappointed students and decimated athletic teams, are under pressure to modify their new at-least-C-average-or-no-extracurriculars policy.

⁷I hope they will resist it. The new policy may not be perfect, but it reflects a proper sense of priorities, which is one of the things our children ought to be learning. It may turn out to be a very good thing for all concerned—including the 39 percent of the county's students who are temporarily ineligible for such outside activities as athletics, cheerleading, dramatics and band.

⁸I've heard the arguments on the other side, and while I don't dismiss them out of hand, they fall short of persuading me that the new standards are too tough or their application too rigid. I know that for some students, the extracurriculars are the only thing that keep school from being a complete downer. I know that some youngsters will be tempted to pass up Algebra II, chemistry and other tough courses in order to keep their extracurricular eligibility (weighted grade points could solve that problem). And I know that for students whose strengths are other than academic, success in music or drama or sports can be an important source of self-esteem.

⁹Still I support the C-average rule—partly because of my assumption that it isn't all that tough a standard. We're not talking here about bell-shaped curves that automatically place some students above the median and some below it. I suspect that we're talking less about acceptable academic achievement than about acceptable levels of exertion. I find it hard to believe that Prince George's teachers will flunk kids who really do try: who pay attention in class, turn in all their work, seek special assistance when they need it and also bring athletic glory to their schools. (If it turns out that some youngsters are being penalized for inadequate gifts rather than insufficient effort, I'd support some modification of the rule.)

¹⁰The principal value of the new standard is that it helps the students, including those in the lower grades, to get their own priorities right: to understand that while outside activities can be an ego-boosting adjunct to classroom work, they cannot be a substitute for it. Even the truly gifted, whose nonacademic talents might earn them college scholarships or even professional careers, need as solid an academic footing as they can get.

¹¹Pity, which is what we often feel for other people's children, says give the poor kids a break. Love, which is what we feel for our own, says let's help them get ready for real life—not by lowering the standards but by providing the resources to help them meet the standards. One principal who saw 38 percent of his students fall below the eligibility cutoff agrees. Said Thomas Kirby: "I don't see any point in

having a kid who can bounce a basketball graduate from high school and not be able to read."

—William Raspberry

Questions About Content

1. Does the writer acknowledge the opposing viewpoint, and does he address his opponents' biggest objection to his position?

2. Where is the thesis? Is it easily found?

3. Does the writer offer sound reasons for his case? Explain.

4. Does the writer offer impersonal (as well as personal) support? Explain.

Questions About Organization

1. Is the introduction effective? Explain.

2. Does the writer place his strongest material near the beginning or the end of the essay? Is this placement effective?

3. How does the writer achieve coherence and smooth transitions between paragraphs?

Questions About Style

1. Comment on the sentence variety in this essay.

2. Does the writer avoid an extreme persona here (say, sounding like a righteous parent)? Explain.

3. Characterize the tone of the essay. Is it appropriate?

RESPONDING TO YOUR READING

Explore your reactions to "Standards You Meet and Don't Duck" by using the questions on page 91. Then respond with your own essay supporting or opposing the author's view. Your goal is to get readers involved.

Perhaps you will want to argue from the viewpoint of athletes who are affected by such grade standards. Or you might argue for some other school requirement, as in urging your old high school (or your college) to require an exit essay of its graduating seniors to ensure an acceptable level of literacy. Or maybe you feel that some other standard has been neglected or that some school requirements are unfair.

Whatever your position, be sure that your essay has a discoverable thesis and that you address a specific audience whose support you seek. In order to be persuasive, base your support not only on personal grounds (how you feel about it), but on impersonal grounds (verifiable evidence), as well.

OPTIONS FOR ESSAY WRITING

1. Write a response to the assertion that the liberal arts have become an unaffordable luxury. Be sure to consider the arguments for and against specialized vocational education versus a broadly humanistic—but less "practical"—education. What do you think?

2. Your college is thinking of abolishing core requirements. Write an essay to the dean in which you argue for or against this change.

3. Should first-year composition be required at your school? Support your position with a convincing argument addressed to the faculty senate.

4. Should your school (or institute) drop students' evaluations of teachers? What are the pros and cons of students' evaluations? Write to the student and faculty senates.

5. Perhaps you belong to a fraternity, a sorority, or some other organized group. Identify an important decision your group has to make. Write an essay supporting your position on the issue to the group.

6. Your community is about to vote on whether to fluoridate its public water supply. Do some research, and write an editorial supporting your position on fluoridation. As an alternate assign-ment, take a stand on some other decision facing your community or family, and write an essay defending your position to a stipulated audience.

7. The Cultural Affairs Committee at your school has decided to sponsor a concert next fall, featuring some popular singer or musical group. Although the committee (mostly faculty) is aware that today's music reflects great diversity in personal taste and musical style, the committee members are uncertain about which performer or group would be a good choice for the event. In fact, most committee members admit to being ignorant of the characteristics that distinguish one performance or recording from another. To help in the decision, the committee has invited the student body to submit essays (not letters) arguing for a performer or group. Free tickets will be awarded to the writer of the best essay. Compose your response.

8. Should your school have an attendance policy? Or a plagiarism policy?

9. Should your school have a foreign language requirement?

10. Challenge an attitude or viewpoint that is widely held by your audience. Maybe you want to persuade your classmates that the

time required to earn a bachelor's degree should be extended to five years. Or maybe you want to claim that the campus police should (or should not) wear guns. Or maybe you want to ask students to support a 10-percent tuition increase in order to make more computers and software available.

What kind of resistance can you anticipate? How will you connect with readers? How can you avoid outright rejection of your claim? What reasons will have meaning for your audience? What tone would be appropriate? Present your case in a persuasive argument.

Application 19–3

ESSAY PRACTICE: MAKING A PROPOSAL

This proposal addresses a fairly common problem: a large television set in the campus center is causing congestion and wasting students' time. One student decides to confront the problem by writing a proposal to the director of the campus center.

Read the proposal carefully, and answer the questions that follow. If your instructor so requests, select one of the essay assignments.

A Proposal for Better Use of the Television Set
in the Campus Center

¹Leaving the campus center yesterday for class, I found myself stuck in the daily pedestrian jam on the second-floor landing. People by the dozens had gathered on the stairway for their daily dose of "General Hospital." Fighting my way through the mesmerized bodies, I wondered about the appropriateness of the television set's location, and of the value of the shows aired on this set.

²Along with the recent upsurge of improvements at our school (in curriculum and standards), we should be considering ways to better use the campus center television. The tube plays relentlessly, offering soap operas and games shows to the addicts who block the stairway and main landing. Granted, television for students to enjoy between classes is a fine idea, but no student needs to attend college to watch soap operas. By moving the set and improving the programs, we could eliminate the congestion and enrich the learning experience.

³The television needs a better location: out of the way of people who don't care to watch it, and into a larger, more comfortable setting for those who do. Background noise in the present location makes the set barely audible; and the raised seating in front of the set places the viewers on exhibit to all who walk by. A far better location would be the back wall of the North Lounge, outside the Sunset Room—a large,

quiet, and comfortable space. Various meetings sometimes held in this room could be moved instead to the browsing area of the library.

⁴More important than the set's location is the quality of its programs. Videotaped movies might be a good alternative to the shows now aired. Our audiovisual department has a rich collection of excellent movies and educational programs on tape. People could request the shows they would like to see, and a student committee could be responsible for printing showtime information.

⁵The set might also serve as a primary learning tool by allowing communications students to create their own shows. Our school has the videotaping and sound equipment and would need only a faculty adviser to supervise the project. Students from scriptwriting, drama, political science, and journalism classes (to name a few) could combine their talents, providing shows of interest to their peers. We now have a student news program that is aired evenings on a local channel, but many who live some distance off campus cannot receive this channel on their sets at home. Why not make the program accessible to students during the day, here on campus?

⁶With resources already in our possession, we can make a few changes that will benefit almost everyone. Beyond providing more efficient use of campus center space, these changes could really stimulate people's minds. I urge you to allow students and faculty to vote on the questions of moving the television set and improving its programs.

—Patricia Haith

Questions About Content

1. Where is the thesis? Is it easily found?

2. Does the proposal satisfy the four criteria outlined on page 399? Explain.

3. For her primary audience, does the writer offer the best reasons for her case? Explain.

4. For a different audience (say, students who avidly follow the soap operas), would the writer have to change her material at all? Explain.

5. Is this argument primarily inductive or deductive?

6. Does the writer establish agreement with the reader? If so, where?

Questions About Organization

1. Which expository strategy is used most in this essay?

2. Is the narrative introduction effective? Explain.

3. Is the conclusion effective? Explain.

Questions About Style

1.   What are two outstanding features of style in this essay? Explain.

2.   Is the tone of this essay appropriate for its audience and purpose? Explain.

3.   Is the writer's voice likable? Explain.

OPTIONS FOR ESSAY WRITING

Identify a problem in your school, community, family, or job. Develop a proposal for solving the problem. Stipulate a definite audience for your proposal. Here are some possible subjects:

- improving living conditions in your dorm
- improving security in your dorm
- creating a day-care center on campus
- saving labor, materials, or money on the job
- improving working conditions
- eliminating a traffic hazard in your neighborhood
- increasing tourist trade in your town
- improving the services of your college library
- finding ways for an organization to raise money
- improving the food service on campus
- establishing more equitable use of computer terminals on campus
- improving faculty advisement of students

Be sure to spell out the problem, explain the benefits of change, offer a realistic plan, and urge your readers to definite action. Think very carefully about *exactly* what you want your readers to do.

Application 19–4

ESSAY PRACTICE: CHANGING THE READER'S BEHAVIOR

This essay is in the form of a complaint letter written by an employee to her boss. It illustrates the challenge of trying to influence another person's behavior. Read it carefully, and answer the questions that follow. Then select one of the essay assignments.

Letter to the Boss

¹For several months I have been hesitant to approach you about a problem that has caused me great uneasiness at work. More recently, however, I've found that several other employees are equally upset, and I feel, as one of your close friends, that I should explain what's wrong. With you as our boss, we all have an exceptional employer-employee relationship, and I'd hate to see one small problem upset it.

²John, when you have criticism about any one of us at work, you never seem to deal directly with that specific person. When the chefs were coming in late, you didn't confront them directly to express your displeasure; instead, you discussed it with the other employees. When you suspected Alan's honesty and integrity as a bartender, you came to me rather than to Alan. I learned yesterday from the coat-checker that you are unhappy with the [waitpersons] for laughing and joking too much. And these are just a few of many such incidents.

³I understand how difficult it is to approach a person with constructive criticism—in fact, it's taken me several months to mention this problem to you! Having been on the receiving end of grapevine gossip, though, I would accept the complaint much more gracefully if it came directly from you. Many of the employees are needlessly upset, and our increasing dissatisfaction harms the quality of our work.

⁴Because I've never been a supervisor, I can only imagine your difficulty. I'm sure your task is magnified because when you bought this restaurant last spring, we employees all knew one another, but you knew none of us. You've told me many times how important it is for you to be a friend to all of us, but sometimes friendship can stand in the way of communication.

⁵Our old boss used to deal with the problem of making constructive suggestions in this way: Every other Saturday evening we would have a meeting at which he would voice his suggestions and we would voice ours. This arrangement worked out well, because none of us felt singled out for criticism, and we all had the chance to discuss any problems openly.

⁶I value your friendship, and I hope you will accept this letter in the sincere spirit in which it's offered. I'm sure that with a couple of good conversations we can work things out.

—Marcia White

Questions About Content

1. Bracket all facts in this letter, and underline all statements of opinion (see Chapter 6). Are all opinions supported by facts? Explain.

2.   Does the writer acknowledge the opposing viewpoint? Explain.

3.   Is this letter likely to be convincing? Explain.

4.   Does the writer admit the imperfections in her case? Explain.

Questions About Organization

1.   Explain the function of the introductory paragraph. Is the writer guilty of "beating around the bush"? Explain.

2.   Which body paragraphs are deductive? Which inductive?

3.   Is the arrangement of the body paragraphs effective? Explain.

4.   Is the final body paragraph too indirect? Explain.

5.   Which is the most concrete paragraph? Explain its function.

6.   Are the second and third body paragraphs necessary? Explain.

7.   Is the conclusion effective? Explain.

Questions About Style

1.   In the second and third body paragraphs, identify one example of coordination, and explain how this structure reinforces the writer's meaning.

2.   Identify and give examples of one outstanding stylistic feature in this essay.

3.   How would you characterize the tone? Is it appropriate for the situation, audience, and purpose? Identify three sentences that contribute to this tone.

4.   Identify three sentences in which the writer expresses empathy with her reader.

5.   Is the writer's voice likable? Explain.

OPTIONS FOR ESSAY WRITING

1.   Everyone has habits that annoy others or are harmful in some way. Identify a bad habit of a friend, relative, co-worker, or someone you spend a lot of time with, and write an essay (as a letter) trying to persuade the person to break the habit. As additional encouragement, suggest specific actions that your reader might take to overcome the habit. (Stay away from the classic, cigarette smoking.)

You're writing to someone close to you, so, besides being concrete and direct, be diplomatic. Your primary goal here is not to "tell someone off" (much as you might like to!) but to help your friend change for the better. To make sure your reader confronts the problem, you need to be candid and outspoken. To be sure you don't lose a friend, you need to be patient, diplomatic, and supportive.

Make careful decisions about *what* you say and *how* you say it.   Say something nice once in a while, but be sincere (anybody can spot a phony). First, identify the problem clearly; then, point out the causes and the reasons for change; and finally, offer suggestions for change. Pay close attention to your tone. You want to sound like an honest friend, not a judge. Because you anticipate defensiveness on the part of your reader, decide on ways of getting your message across to overcome that defensiveness.

2.   Think of a situation in which you recently encountered problems—in a job, in school, or as a consumer. Choose something about which you have a major complaint. Write an essay (as a letter) to the person in charge or otherwise responsible, laying out the issues and suggesting appropriate changes.

3.   Someone close to you is trying to make an important decision and has asked your advice. Respond in a persuasive essay.

SECTION FOUR

RESEARCH
AND
CORRESPONDENCE

20
Developing a Research Report

The Research Report Process • Discovering a Research Topic
• Using the Library • Finding Adequate Information Sources
• Taking Notes • Assessing Your Inquiry
• Developing a Working Thesis and Outline
• Writing a First Draft • Documenting Your Sources
• Revising Your Research Report • A Sample Research Project
• Applications

We do research to obtain facts or expert opinions or to increase our understanding of issues. For example, we might want to inquire about the price range of building lots on Boca Grande Island or the latest findings in AIDS research. Or we might want to inquire about what experts are saying about the long-term effects of global warming. Or we might want to inquire about the causes of the Israeli-Palestinian conflict or the role of the banking industry in rain-forest destruction.

Research is not only a college skill, but also a life skill. For example, if you learn that your well water is contaminated with benzene, should you merely ask for your neighbor's opinion about the dangers, or should you track down the real answers for yourself?

In the workplace, *information* has become the ultimate commodity. And workplace professionals are expected to locate all kinds of information daily (How do we market this product? How do we avoid accidents like this one? How can we keep costs down? How can we

417

attract dependable employees? Are we headed for a recession?). We all need to know where and how to look for answers, and how to communicate our findings *on paper.*

Any kind of significant research is for some purpose: to answer a question, to make an evaluation, to establish a principle. We set out to discover whether diesel engines are efficient and dependable for a purpose: we're thinking about buying a car equipped with one; we're trying to decide whether to begin producing them; or the like. Research is the way to find your own answers, to submit your opinions to the test of fact, to reach the conclusion that has the greatest chance of being accurate. A research report records and discusses your findings. It provides the information that leads to an informed conclusion.

The Research Report Process*

A research report that *makes a difference* involves a lot more than cooking up any old thesis, collecting the first bunch of stuff you come across, and then blending in some juicy quotations and paraphrases that supposedly "prove" you've done the assigned work. Research is a highly deliberate form of inquiry, a process of *problem solving.* And, as in any problem solving, we cannot begin to solve the problem until we have clearly defined it.

Granted, there are certain procedures in the research process that follow a recognizable sequence:

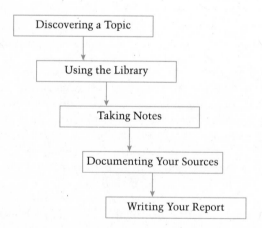

Later sections in this chapter and the next treat these more "procedural" stages of the research process.

---

* My thanks to SMU librarian Shaleen Barnes for inspiring this whole section.

But research writing never is merely a "by-the-numbers" set of procedures ("First, do this; then, do that"). Intertwined with each of the procedural stages are the inquiry stages of the process, the many careful decisions that accompany any legitimate inquiry:

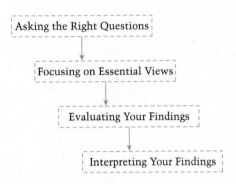

Let's consider how each inquiry stage of the research process enables us to develop the kind of inquiry that makes a real difference.

ASKING THE RIGHT QUESTIONS

The answers you uncover will depend on the questions you ask. Suppose, for instance, you've decided to research the 1989 spill of 11 million gallons of oil into Alaska's Prince William Sound: The immediate problem was the tanker Exxon *Valdez* hitting a shoal. But what *specific* parts of the problem interest you? (The events that led up to the disaster? Ways the spill could have been avoided or better contained? Environmental effects? Economic effects? Or what?) Before you settle on a definite question, you need to navigate a long list of possible questions, some of which are shown in the Figure 20.1 tree chart.

Any *one* of the questions (or clusters of questions) from our tree chart could serve as the topic of a worthwhile research report on such a complex topic. By asking the right questions, you discover a focus and a topic that you can research in real depth—instead of settling for a superficial and simplistic approach to a complex issue. (Perhaps you can think of other questions we might add to our chart.)

FOCUSING ON ESSENTIAL VIEWS

Let's assume you've settled on this question for research: "Has the cleanup from the Exxon *Valdez* disaster been adequate?" To answer this

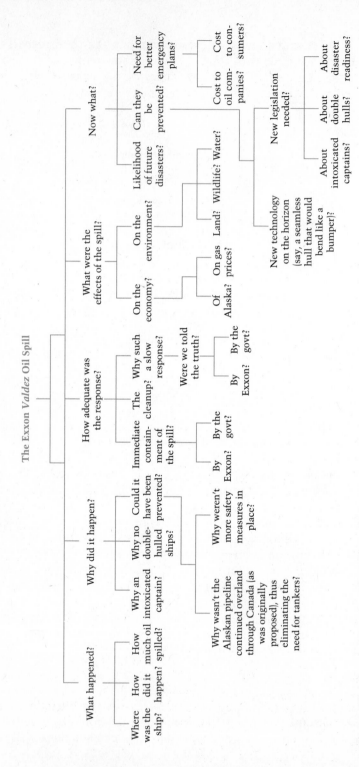

Figure 20.1 Some Questions for Researching a Topic

question fairly and accurately, you would have to consider all sides of the story:

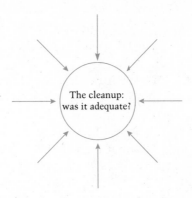

Here are some essential points of view on the cleanup:

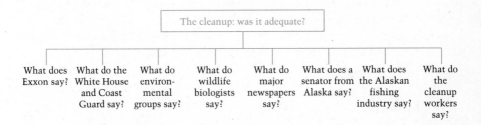

We do research to discover the right answer—or the answer that stands the best chance of being right. Rather than settling for the first or most comforting or convenient answer, we have an ethical obligation to consider all perspectives. Even "expert" testimony may not be the final word, because experts often disagree or they can be mistaken. To reach a balanced and objective conclusion, you need to survey the entire spectrum of viewpoints.

EVALUATING YOUR FINDINGS

Once you have collected all the essential evidence about your topic, you need to decide how much of it is legitimate. Consider, for example, the fact that Exxon filed a $2 billion suit against the federal government, claiming the Coast Guard interfered with the cleanup by prohibiting early use of chemical dispersants. How would you evaluate Exxon's claim?

Questions for evaluating a particular finding

- Is this information accurate, reliable, and relatively unbiased?
- Can the claim be verified by the facts?
- How much of it (if any) is useful?
- Is this the whole story?
- Does something seem to be missing?
- Do I need more information?

Not all the material will have equal value. Some might be distorted or incomplete or misleading. Information might be tainted by the bias of the source. (For instance, a particular source might understate or overstate certain facts, depending on whose interests that source represents—say, the Exxon Corporation or the government or an environmental group.) Ethical researchers rely on evidence that represents a fair balance of views. They don't merely emphasize findings that support their own biases or assumptions.

Remember that the purpose of research is not to prove the "rightness" of some initial assumption you might have had; instead, you do research to find the *right* answers. And only when your inquiry nears completion can you settle on a *definite* thesis—based on what the facts suggest.

INTERPRETING YOUR FINDINGS

Once you've decided which of your findings seem legitimate, you need to decide what they all mean:

Questions for interpreting your findings

- What do all these facts or observations mean?
- Do any findings conflict?
- Are other interpretations possible?
- Should I reconsider the evidence?
- What are my conclusions?
- What, if anything, should be done?

The interpretation should fit your evidence and should lead to an accurate conclusion—an overall judgment about what the findings mean. (For example, "The cleanup has been woefully inadequate" or "The cleanup seems to have been thorough," etc.)

Even the best research can produce contradictory or indefinite conclusions. For example, some people argue that the crude oil remaining on Alaskan shores will be "scrubbed" clean within a decade by the fierce winter tides—making any further cleanup unnecessary. Others charge that this view is an oil-company "cop-out." An accurate conclusion would have to come from your analyzing all views and deciding that one outweighs the others—or that only time will tell.

Never force a simplistic conclusion on a complex issue. Sometimes the best conclusion you can come up with is an indefinite conclusion: "Although controversy continues over the adequacy of the cleanup, the upcoming winter seasons will tell whether Mother Nature has been able to finish the job." A wrong conclusion is far worse than no definite conclusion at all.

Discovering a Research Topic

Perhaps the crucial step in developing a research report is to decide on a worthwhile topic. Begin with a subject that has real meaning for you, and then decide on the specific question you want to ask about it. This chapter's opening pages showed how the subject of the Exxon *Valdez* oil spill might be approached. Now let's try another subject.

What would you like to know about? Let's say you're disturbed about all the chemicals used to preserve or enhance flavor and color in foods. Maybe this can be your subject: *food additives and preservatives.*

What specific part of this subject would you like to focus on? This will be your *topic*, and it will be phrased as a question. Suppose you are majoring in elementary education and are especially interested in children's behavior. To identify the possible questions you might ask, you develop a tree chart (as on page 420), and finally you decide to focus your inquiry on this question: *What effects, if any, do food additives and preservatives have on children's behavior?*

Here is advice to help you avoid choosing the wrong kind of topic:

1.   Avoid topics that are too broad. The topic "Do food additives and preservatives affect children?" would have to include children's growth and development, their intelligence, their susceptibility to diseases, and so on. A six- to twelve-page research report simply offers too little space to cover that broad a topic.

2.   Avoid topics that limit you to a fixed viewpoint *before* you've done your research: "Which behavior disorders in children are caused by food additives and preservatives?" Presumably, you haven't yet established that such chemicals have *any* harmful effects (except perhaps from hearsay or from something you've

read somewhere). Therefore, save any definite conclusions (along with your definite thesis) until you've had a chance to evaluate your information. Your initial research is meant to find the facts, not to prove some point. *Allow your thesis to grow from your collected facts, instead of manipulating the facts to fit your thesis.*

3. Avoid topics that have been exhausted (abortion, capital punishment, life on Mars, the Bermuda Triangle)—unless, of course, you can approach such a topic in a fresh way, like this: "Could recent technological developments to help a fetus survive outside the womb cause the Supreme Court to reverse its 1972 ruling on abortion?" In other words, if the topic is a familiar one, try to answer a question that would offer a new perspective.

4. Avoid topics that can be summed up in an encyclopedia entry or in any one source: "The Life of Thoreau," "How to Cross-Country Ski," or "The History of Microwave Technology." From a different angle, of course, any of these areas might produce good topics: "Was Thoreau ever in love?"; "How do injury rates compare between cross-country and downhill skiing?"; "How safe are microwave ovens?" Research on the latter topics would yield material from which you could draw your *own* conclusions.

5. Avoid religious, moral, or emotional topics that offer no objective basis for informed conclusions: "Is euthanasia moral?"; "Will Jesus save the world?"; "Should prayer be allowed in public schools?" Any conclusions about these kinds of topics rest on personal opinion, not fact. Questions debated throughout the ages by philosophers, judges, and social thinkers are unlikely to be answered definitively in your research paper—or anywhere else, for that matter.

6. Avoid any topic chosen from desperation. Sometimes you won't be able to decide exactly what it is you want to know until you visit the library a few times. If you can't find a definite topic this early, begin with a subject of general interest, and browse through library sources for ideas.

Far more important than the subject you choose is the *question* you decide to ask about it. Don't be surprised or discouraged if you spend many hours in search of the right question. The quality of your whole research project will depend on the quality of your decisions at this stage.

As soon as you decide on a definite topic, you will want to make sure enough information is available from a sufficient variety of perspectives to provide an accurate and balanced view. To check for sources, you will need to know how to use the library.

Using the Library

Inexperienced researchers sometimes are confused about where to begin a library search. Here are various options:

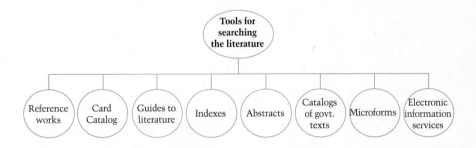

Where you begin your own search will depend on whether you seek background and basic facts or the very latest information. If you are an expert in the field, you might simply do a computerized search or browse through the specialized journals. But if you have only limited knowledge or if you need to focus your topic, you probably will want to begin with general reference sources.*

REFERENCE WORKS

Reference works include encyclopedias, almanacs, handbooks, dictionaries, histories, and biographies. These can be a good starting point because they provide background and bibliographies that can lead to more specific information. One drawback to reference books is that some may be outdated. Always check the last copyright date.

Reference works are in a special section marked "Reference"—usually on the main floor of the building. All reference works will be indexed in the "Subject" card catalog, with a "Ref." designation above the call number.

Bibliographies   Bibliographies are lists of publications about a subject, within specified dates. Although they provide a comprehensive view of

---

* University of Massachusetts Dartmouth librarian Ross LaBaugh advises students to begin with the popular, general literature, and then to work toward journals and other specialized sources: "The more accessible the source, the less valuable it is likely to be."

major sources, bibliographies quickly become dated. Ask a librarian about recent bibliographies on your subject. (Some bibliographies are issued yearly, or even weekly.)

Annotated bibliographies (which include an abstract for each entry) are most helpful because they can help you identify the most useful sources. A sample listing of bibliographies (shown with annotations):

MLA International Bibliography of Books and Articles on the Modern Languages and Literatures. A comprehensive listing, published annually by the Modern Language Association.

Bibliographic Index. Updated three times yearly, a listing (by subject) of bibliographies that contain at least 50 citations; to see which bibliographies are published in your field, begin here.

A Guide to U.S. Government Scientific and Technical Resources. A list of everything published in these broad fields by the government.

Bibliographic Guide to Business and Economics. A list of all major business and economic publications.

Health Hazards of Video Display Terminals: An Annotated Bibliography. One of many bibliographies focused on a highly specific subject.

Shorter, more specific bibliographies appear as parts of books and journal articles. To locate bibliographies that are whole volumes in themselves, look in the card catalog under "Bibliography" as a subject or title heading. For recent sources on food additives, for example, you might begin with the *Bibliographic Index.*

Encyclopedias Use encyclopedias to find basic information (which might be outdated). Sample listings:

Encyclopedia Britannica

Cassell's Encyclopedia of World Literature

Encyclopedia of Social Sciences

Encyclopedia of Food Technology

Journals, newsletters, and other publications from professional organizations (such as the American Medical Association or the Institute of Electrical and Electronics Engineers) are a valuable source of specialized information. The *Encyclopedia of Associations* offers a yearly listing of over 80,000 societies and non-profit organizations worldwide that range from agricultural to scientific and technical, from labor unions to religious groups. For information on food additives and behavior you might want to contact the American Psychological Association.

Dictionaries   Besides carrying general definitions, dictionaries can focus on specific disciplines or they can give biographical information. Sample listings:

Webster's Third New International Dictionary of the English Language. Considered the best general dictionary.

Dictionary of Engineering and Technology

Dictionary of Telecommunications

Dictionary of American Biography

Handbooks   Handbooks amass key facts (including formulas, tables, advice, and examples) about a field in condensed form. Often aimed at users experienced in the field, some handbooks may not be useful to newcomers. Sample listings:

Business Writer's Handbook

Fire Protection Handbook

The McGraw-Hill Computer Handbook

Almanacs   Ranging from general to specific, almanacs have factual and statistical data. Sample listings:

World Almanac and Book of Facts

Almanac for Computers

Almanac of Business and Industrial Financial Ratios

Directories   Directories offer information about organizations, companies, people, products, services, statistics, or careers, often including addresses and phone numbers. This material usually is updated annually. Sample listings:

The Career Guide: Dun's Employment Opportunities Directory

Directory of Computer Software

Standard & Poor's Register of Corporations, Directors, and Executives

Directory of Grants in the Humanities

Directory of American Firms Operating in Foreign Countries

Directory of Financial Aids for Women

The Radical Right: A World Directory

A growing number of directories and other reference works are accessible by computer.

Reference works are published for every discipline. If you were researching the effects of food additives, you would want to start with titles such as the *McGraw-Hill Encyclopedia of Food, Agriculture, and Nutrition* or the *RC Handbook of Food Additives.* Look for your subject in the card catalog, and then check for any subheadings such as "Handbooks, Manuals, etc." or "Dictionaries." These will be the books that get you started.

THE CARD CATALOG

Printed Catalog Entries   All books, reference works, indexes, periodicals, and other materials held by a library usually are listed in its card catalog under three headings: *author, title,* and *subject.* Thus you have at least three access points for retrieving an item, as shown in Figures 20.2, 20.3, and 20.4.

Your library may place author, title, and subject cards in one alphabetical file or may provide individual catalogs labeled "Author," "Title," and "Subject." First decide whether you seek a specific title, an author, or material about a subject. Then look in the card catalog under one of those three access points (title, author, or subject).

Locating the Card   Say you are looking for a book on food additives by James Erlichman. Locate the "E" cards in the "Author" section of the catalog. Figure 20.2 shows a typical author catalog card.

Library of Congress Guide to Subject Headings   If you know neither authors nor titles of works on your subject, use the *subject* listing. To identify related subject headings under which you might find material on your topic, consult the *Library of Congress Subject Headings* (large books in the card catalog area). For material on food additives, for instance, you might scan the listings under *Food preservatives;* among other entries, you would see these:

Food preservatives

Allergic reactions

Canning and preserving, food

Chemical food additives

Food adulteration

Food contamination

Food processing

Processed foods

You now have an array of subjects under which to search for useful material in the card catalog.

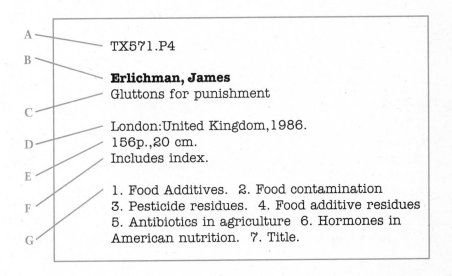

A.   TX571.P4

B.   **Erlichman, James**
     Gluttons for punishment

C.   London:United Kingdom,1986.

D.   156p.,20 cm.
     Includes index.

E.   1. Food Additives. 2. Food contamination
F.   3. Pesticide residues. 4. Food additive residues
     5. Antibiotics in agriculture 6. Hormones in
G.   American nutrition. 7. Title.

A.   The call number. Each book has a different call number under the coding system by which books are classified. Books are arranged on the shelves in the order of their respective call numbers. This number is your key for locating the book.

B.   The author's name, listed last name first. (On some cards the author's name is followed by his or her date of birth—and death, if he or she was deceased at the time of the book's last printing.)

C.   The title of one book written by this author.

D.   City of publication, publisher, and publication date.

E.   Technical information: This book has 156 pages, a vertical length of 20 centimeters.

F.   Special information about the book: This book includes an index.

G.   Other headings under which this book is listed in the card catalog: In the subject section, the book is listed under six different headings; it is also listed alphabetically by title.

Figure 20.2 A Catalog Card Classified by Author

```
TX 571. P4

Gluttons for punishment
Erlichman, James
```

Figure 20.3 Partial Catalog Card Classified by Title

```
TX 571. P4

Food additives
Erlichman, James
Gluttons for punishment
```

Figure 20.4 Partial Catalog Card Classified by Subject

Electronic Catalog Entries In place of printed entries, libraries increasingly are automating their card catalogs. Fast and easy to use, electronic card catalogs offer additional access points (beyond *author*, *title*, and *subject*) including:

- *Descriptor:* for retrieving works on the basis of a key word or phrase in the subject heading ("food additives" or "diet and behavior").

- *Document type:* for retrieving works in a specific format (videotape, audiotape, compact disk, motion picture).

- *Organizations and Conferences:* for retrieving works produced under the name of an institution or professional association (Brookings Institution, American Heart Association).

- *Publisher:* for retrieving works produced by a particular publisher (Little, Brown and Co.).

- *Combination:* for retrieving works by combining any available access points (a book about a particular subject by a particular author or institution).

The next page displays the first three screens you might encounter in an automated search using the descriptor FOOD ADDITIVES. If the computer responds to your descriptors with a "no record" screen, consult the *Library of Congress Subject Headings* (page 428) for other possible key terms.

A Sample Search of an Electronic Card Catalog   You begin by pressing any key, and the computer responds with a screen that lists options for getting help or for searching the catalog from various access points:

Type of searches:				Press Help key for HELP		
1	AU	=	Author	8 PU	=	Publisher
2	OC	=	Organization or conference	9 SH	=	Subject heading
3	TI	=	Title	10 DT	=	Document type
4	UT	=	Uniform or collective title	11		Combination
5	DE	=	Descriptor	12		ISBN
6	CN	=	Call number	13		ISBN
7	SE	=	Series	14		Numeric

Enter the NUMBER of your search request and press RETURN:

After selecting the DE search mode, you type in your key words (FOOD ADDITIVES), then press RETURN. This next screen appears (the first of several with all 42 entries). Notice that published conference proceedings (#1) and relevant journals (#2) are listed along with books, their authors, and publication dates:

Key Word: FOOD ADDITIVES (42 records)

1 Conf. on food add. . . National Dietetics Assoc. 1990
2 Journal of food tech. . . Inst. for Nutrition Res. 1982-
3 Food additives. . . Nishern, Diana. 1982
4 Food add. and cancer risk. . . Kassler, Wm. J. 1978
5 Food add. and fed. policy. . . Hunter, Beatrice T. 1975
6 Food add. and hyperact. child. . . Conners, C. K. 1980
7 Food add. approval process. . . United States. 1987
8 Food additives book. . . Feydberg, Nicholas. 1982
9 Food add. handbook. . . Lewis, Richard J. 1989
10 Food add. series. . . World Health Org. 1972

Entry #6 seems promising, so you select it and then press RETURN. The computer responds with detailed bibliographic information on your selected item, a screen showing the electronic equivalent of the entry you would find in the printed card catalog:

```
Selection:
RJ 506.H9. C65

AUTHOR       Conners, C. Keith
TITLE        Food additives and hyperactive children

PUBLISHER    New York: Plenum Press
DATE         c 1980
PHYS.FEAT.   xv,: 167 p. ; ill.; 24 cm.

SUBJECTS     1. Hyperactive ch.  2. Food additives--
             toxicology.  3. Food additives--adverse
             effects.  4. Hyperkinesis  in infancy
             and childhood.
```

After recording the data that you need to retrieve entry #6 from the library shelves, you decide to look more closely at entry #9, and so on, scrolling through the several screens that list all 42 entries.

Through a computer network such as *Internet,* an electronic catalog can be searched from home or office or anywhere in the world. (The search illustrated on page 431 was done from this author's university office via campus network.)

Caution: Any misspelling or typographical error in entering key terms can result in a false indication of "no record."

GUIDES TO LITERATURE

If you simply don't know which books, journals, indexes, and reference works are available for your topic, consult a guide to literature. For a general listing of books in various disciplines, see Walford's *Guide to Reference Material* or Sheehy's *Guide to Reference Books.*

For sources in specific disciplines, consult specialized guides such as *The Encyclopedia of Business Information Sources* or *Sources of Information in the Social Sciences.* Ask your reference librarian about literature guides for your topic.

INDEXES

Indexes are lists of books, newspaper articles, journal articles, or other works on particular subjects. They are excellent sources for current information. Because different indexes list sources in different ways, always read the introductory pages for instructions. Or ask a librarian for help.

Book Indexes   All books currently being published (up to a set date) are listed in book indexes by author, title, or subject. Sample indexes (shown with annotations):

Books in Print. An annual listing of all books published in the United States.

Cumulative Book Index. A monthly worldwide listing of books in English.

Forthcoming Books. A listing every two months of U.S. books to be published.

Scientific and Technical Books and Serials in Print. An annual listing of literature in science and technology.

New Technical Books: A Selective List with Descriptive Annotations. Issued 10 times yearly.

Technical Book Review Index. A monthly listing (with excerpts) of book reviews.

Medical Books and Serials in Print. An annual listing of works from medicine and psychology.

In research on food additives, you might check the current issue of *Medical Books and Serials in Print* or *Scientific and Technical Books and Serials in Print.* But no book is likely to offer the very latest information because of the time required to publish a book manuscript (from several months to one year).

Newspaper Indexes   Most newspaper indexes list articles by subject. These indexes are especially useful for current topics. The *New York Times Index* is best known, but other major newspapers have their own indexes. Sample titles:

Boston Globe Index

Christian Science Monitor Index

Wall Street Journal Index

For your research, you might check recent editions of the *Boston Globe Index.* To locate publications that offer radical viewpoints, you might consult the *Alternative Press Index.*

Periodical Indexes   For recent information in magazines and journals, consult periodical indexes. To find useful indexes, first decide whether you seek general or specialized information.

One most general index is the *Magazine Index,* a subject index (on microfilm) of 400 general periodicals. A popular index is the *Readers' Guide to Periodical Literature,* listing articles from 150 general magazines and journals. Because the *Readers' Guide* is updated every few weeks, you can locate current material. Figure 20.5 shows a section from one of its pages.

As in many indexes, subjects and their subheads in the *Readers' Guide* are listed alphabetically. Each article is listed in this order: article title, author (if known), periodical title, volume and page numbers, and date. Codes for abbreviated journal titles are at the front of each volume.

Assume you are researching the physiological effects of food additives and preservatives. As you turn to a recent issue (Figure 20.5) of the *Readers' Guide,* you find many entries under the general heading "Food." Scanning the entries under "Food Additives," you spot an item that looks useful: A primer on "food additives"—item *A.* From that entry you gain this information: because no author's name is given, the article probably was written by a staff writer; the periodical's name is *FDA Consumer;* the volume number is 22; the article is found on pages 12–17 of the October 1988 issue. Item B refers to other headings under which you might find relevant articles. Under "Food Allergy" are other possibly useful articles, shown checked (especially since certain reactions to food can trigger abnormal behavior).

Consult the periodicals holdings list to determine which periodicals are held by your library. Copies are available in the area where indexes are shelved. If you find an index reference to an article not held by your library, ask your librarian to see if the article is available in nearby libraries or through interlibrary loan.

If the article is in a very recent issue, look on the current periodical shelves, usually arranged alphabetically by title, to find your issue. In some libraries, older issues are bound together in hardcover bindings instead of being microfilmed. Ask your librarian to explain the use of microfilm files and readers.

General indexes such as the *Readers' Guide* list only nonspecialized sources of information. For specialized information, consult indexes that list journal articles in specific disciplines, such as *Ulrich's International Periodicals Directory.* Another comprehensive source of specialized information, the *Applied Science and Technology Index* carries a monthly listing, by subject, of articles in more than 200 scientific and technical journals.

For business articles, consult the *Business Periodicals Index,* with its monthly subject listing of articles and book reviews from 270 business periodicals.

Other broad indexes that cover specialized fields in general include the *Business Index, General Science Index,* and *Humanities Index.* The *Statistical Reference Index* lists statistical works not published by the government.

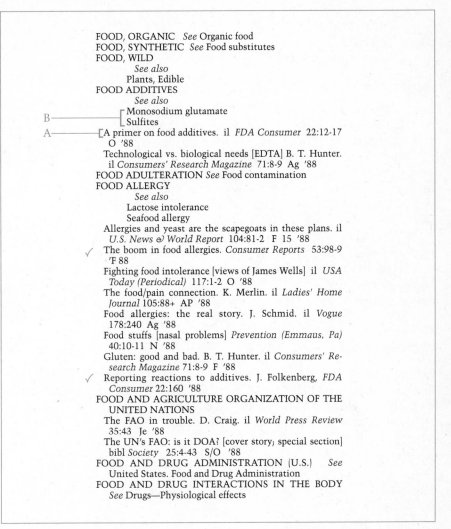

FOOD, ORGANIC   *See* Organic food
FOOD, SYNTHETIC   *See* Food substitutes
FOOD, WILD
   See also
   Plants, Edible
FOOD ADDITIVES
   See also
B   Monosodium glutamate
        Sulfites
A   A primer on food additives. il *FDA Consumer* 22:12-17
   O '88
   Technological vs. biological needs [EDTA] B. T. Hunter.
   il *Consumers' Research Magazine* 71:8-9 Ag '88
FOOD ADULTERATION *See* Food contamination
FOOD ALLERGY
   See also
   Lactose intolerance
   Seafood allergy
   Allergies and yeast are the scapegoats in these plans. il
   U.S. News & World Report 104:81-2 F 15 '88
  ✓ The boom in food allergies. *Consumer Reports* 53:98-9
   'F 88
   Fighting food intolerance [views of James Wells] il *USA
   Today (Periodical)* 117:1-2 O '88
   The food/pain connection. K. Merlin. il *Ladies' Home
   Journal* 105:88+ AP '88
   Food allergies: the real story. J. Schmid. il *Vogue*
   178:240 Ag '88
   Food stuffs [nasal problems] *Prevention (Emmaus, Pa)*
   40:10-11 N '88
   Gluten: good and bad. B. T. Hunter. il *Consumers' Re-
   search Magazine* 71:8-9 F '88
  ✓ Reporting reactions to additives. J. Folkenberg, *FDA
   Consumer* 22:160 '88
FOOD AND AGRICULTURE ORGANIZATION OF THE
   UNITED NATIONS
   The FAO in trouble. D. Craig. il *World Press Review*
   35:43 Je '88
   The UN's FAO: is it DOA? [cover story; special section]
   bibl *Society* 25:4-43 S/O '88
FOOD AND DRUG ADMINISTRATION (U.S.)   *See*
   United States. Food and Drug Administration
FOOD AND DRUG INTERACTIONS IN THE BODY
   See Drugs—Physiological effects

Figure 20.5 Section of a Page from the *Readers' Guide to Periodical Literature*

  Along with these broad indexes, some disciplines have their own specific indexes. Sample listings:

Agricultural Index

Education Index

Energy Index

F & S Index of Corporations and Industries

Environment Index

Index to Legal Periodicals

International Nursing Index.

Chapters in books or current essays about an artist, author, issue, region, figure, or other topic in humanities and social sciences may be part of larger collections. To locate such material, consult the *Essay and General Literature Index.* Each year, the *Index* lists thousands of essays and articles (by subject and author) that have been published in nearly 300 volumes of collected essays and miscellaneous works.

Your library may have other indexes. Ask the reference librarian to help you identify appropriate indexes for your subject.

Having looked in the reference books that provide an overview of the psychological effects of food additives, you might now turn to *Psychological Abstracts* or *Index Medicus* for journal literature.

ABSTRACTS

Beyond indexing various works, abstracts briefly describe each article. The abstract can save you from going all the way to the journal in order to decide whether to read the article or to skip it.

Abstracts usually are titled by discipline. A sample list:

Biological Abstracts

Computer Abstracts

Engineering Index

Environment Abstracts

Excerpta Medica

Forestry Abstracts

International Aerospace Abstracts

Metals Abstracts

In researching food additives and behavior, you would see this entry in the April 1993 volume of *Psychological Abstracts*, under the subject heading "Behavior Disorders":

13862. **Baden, Anne D. & Howe, George W.** (Vanderbilt U, Peabody Coll, Nashville, TN) **Mothers' attributions and expectancies regarding their conduct-disordered children.** *Journal of Abnormal Child Psychology,* 1992(Oct), Vol 20(5), 467--485. —Mothers of 40 conduct-disordered children (aged 11-18 yrs) and 40 matched control children completed questionnaires measuring their attributions regarding the causes of their children's misbehavior and their expectancies of parental effectiveness. Results indicate that parents of conduct-disordered children were more likely to regard their children's misbehavior as intentional and to attribute it to stable, global causes beyond the parents' control. They also were less likely to see their own parenting as effective. These parents hold cognitive stances of blame and helplessness that contribute to aversive parent behavior and withdrawal in the face of escalating child aggressiveness. The parent's blameful stance becomes part of a cognitive-affective set that increases the likelihood of reciprocated aggression with the child, thus playing an important role in family coercion cycles.

Abstracts increasingly are searchable by computer. Check with your librarian.

For some current research, you might consult abstracts of doctoral dissertations in *Dissertation Abstracts International.*

THE REFERENCE LIBRARIAN

A reference librarian specializes—as the title implies—in *referring* people to sources of information. Therefore, don't be afraid to ask for assistance. Even professional researchers sometimes need help. The reference librarian can save you hours of time by showing you how to use indexes or microfilm and microfiche readers, and how to locate reference books or bibliographies. Moreover, he or she can order items from other libraries (but this takes time; plan ahead).

INDEXES TO FEDERAL GOVERNMENT PUBLICATIONS

The federal government publishes maps, periodicals, books, pamphlets, manuals, monographs, annual reports, research reports, and a remarkable array of other information. Kinds of information available to the public include presidential proclamations, congressional bills and reports, judiciary rulings, some reports from the Central Intelligence Agency, and publications from all other government agencies (Departments of Agriculture, Commerce, Transportation, and so on). Here is a brief sampling of the countless titles available in this gold mine of information:

Decisions of the Federal Trade Commission

Economic Report of the President

Effects of New York's Fiscal Crisis on Small Business

Journal of Research of the National Bureau of Standards

Major Oil and Gas Fields of the Free World

Siting Small Wind Turbines

Much of this information can be searched by computer as well as in printed volumes.

Your best bet for tapping this valuable but complex resource is to ask the librarian in charge of government documents for help. If your library does not own the publication you seek, it can be obtained through an interlibrary loan.

Here are the basic access tools for documents issued or published at government expense as well as for many privately sponsored documents:

1. *The Monthly Catalog of the United States Government* is the major access to government publications and reports; it is indexed by author, subject, and title. The indexes provide the catalog entry number that leads you, in turn, to a complete citation for a work.

2. *Government Reports Announcements & Index* is a listing published every two weeks by the National Technical Information Service (NTIS), a branch of the U.S. Department of Commerce that serves as a clearinghouse for scientific and technical information—all stored in a computer database. The collection stores summaries of more than 1 million federally sponsored research reports published and patents issued since 1964. About 70,000 new summaries are added annually in 22 subject categories ranging from aeronautics to medicine and biology. Full copies of any of these summarized reports are available from NTIS.

3. *The American Statistics Index* is a yearly guide to statistical publications of the U.S. government. It is divided into two sections: *Index* and *Abstracts* (an index with summaries). The *Index* volume lists material by subject and provides geographic (federal, state, and so on), economic (income, occupation, and so on), and demographic (sex, marital status, race, and so on) breakdowns. The *Index* volume refers you to a number and entry in the *Abstracts* volume.

In addition to these three basic access tools, the government issues *Selected Government Publications*, a monthly list of roughly 150 titles (with descriptive abstracts). These titles range from highly general (*Questions About the Oceans*) to highly technical (*An Emission-Line Survey of the Milky Way*). Although this list may be of interest, it is by no means a refined research tool.

The government also publishes bibliographies on hundreds of sub-jects, ranging from "Accidents and Accident Prevention" to "Home Gardening of Fruits and Vegetables." Ask your librarian for information about such subject bibliographies.

MICROFORMS

Microform technology enables vast quantities of printed information to be reproduced and stored on rolls of microfilm or packets of microfiche. (This material is read on machines that magnify the reduced image. Ask your librarian for assistance.) Among the growing array of microform products are government documents, technical reports, newspapers, busi-ness directories, and translated documents from worldwide (Lavin 12).

A valuable business resource, for example, is *Business NewsBank*, a microfiche index to articles on business and economic development from over 450 U.S. cities. Also on microfilm are specialized indexes such as the *Business Index*, and more general indexes such as the *Magazine Index*. Typical of the many valuable works stored on microfilm are *The War in Vietnam: Classified Histories by the National Security Council* and *Herstory Collection*, documenting the roots of the women's movement.

USING ELECTRONIC INFORMATION SERVICES

Libraries increasingly offer computerized services. In addition to elec-tronic card catalogs, access to libraries worldwide is facilitated by the *Internet** or some similar network. Some libraries expect to store elec-tronic versions of all their material within 25 years (Watkins 19).

Compact Disks and Diskettes   One compact disk (CD) stores an entire encyclopedia and provides instant access to any part. CD technology offers reference resources like these: *Science Citation Index, Population Statistics, Ulrich's International Guide to Periodicals,* and products ranging from corporate directories to government reports. Even weekly job listings from the nation's largest Sunday newspapers are becoming available on CDs ("On Line" 19).

One popular index on compact disk is *InfoTrac*™, a monthly listing of articles from some 900 business, technical, and general magazines and journals. As in printed indexes, entries are arranged by subject headings and subheadings. If you type in "food additives," the system responds with a list of entries you can print out.

---

* A global computer network for academic information, the *Internet* is used by millions of researchers, students, and businesspeople.

Other databases on CD include *Government Publications Index*™, a monthly listing of U.S. government literature, and *LegalTrac*™, a monthly listing of entries from 750 legal publications. *Lotus One Source*™ provides corporate profiles and financial summaries for over 15,000 U.S. companies, research reports on stocks, and article summaries from major business sources. Ask at your library about disk-based indexing services.

For smaller bodies of specialized information (census and stock-market data, economic profiles of U.S. cities, and so on), files on diskettes can be purchased (Lavin 19).

Mainframe Databases   Most college libraries subscribe to retrieval services that can access thousands of individual databases stored on centralized computers. From a library terminal (or in some cases, a microcomputer), you can access indexes, journals, books, monographs, dissertations, and reports. Compared with CDs, mainframe databases tend to be more specialized and more current, sometimes updated daily.

Mainframe retrieval services offer three types of databases, or some combination: *bibliographic, full-text,* and *factual* (Lavin 14). Bibliographic databases list publications in a field; entries can be searched according to author, title, subject, document type (report, article, dissertation) or other access point. Some bibliographic databases include abstracts of each entry.

Full-text databases display the entire article or document (usually excluding graphics) directly on the computer screen, and then will print the article on command.

Factual databases provide specialized facts of all kinds: global and up-to-the minute stock quotations, weather data, lists of new patents filed, and credit ratings of major companies, to name a few.

Until recently, searching mainframe databases has required the skills of a librarian or other trained professional. But new, "end-user systems" now offer simplified menus for each step of the search process (Lavin 16).

Three popular database services are discussed in the following sections. OCLC helps you locate titles you have already identified as useful. Dialog and BRS help you identify useful titles.

The Online Computer Library Center (OCLC)   You can easily compile a comprehensive list of works on your subject at any library that belongs to the Online Computer Library Center. The OCLC database, in Columbus, Ohio, stores more than 19 million records with the same information found in a printed card catalog. Using the library's computer terminal, you type in author or title. Within seconds, you get a free listing of the publication you seek and information about where to find it. If your library doesn't have the publication, your librarian can activate the Interlibrary Loan System (ILS). The system forwards requests to libraries holding the material. Once a lender indicates (via its terminal) that it will supply the material, the system stops forwarding the request, and notifies your librarian that the request has been filled. Your order will arrive at the library by mail in a week or two.

Dialog   Many libraries subscribe to Dialog, a comprehensive technical database. You retrieve information by typing in key terms that enable the computer to scan bibliography lists for titles containing those terms. Say you need information on possible *health hazards* from *household electrical equipment*. You instruct the computer to search Medline, a medical database (one of 150 Dialog databases in science, technology, medicine, business, and so on), for titles including the words italicized above (or synonymous words, such as *risk, danger, appliances*). The system would provide full bibliographies and abstracts of the most recent medical articles on your topic.

Besides bibliographic information on published works, dissertations, and conference papers, Dialog also provides financial and product information about companies, names and addresses of company officers, statistical data, and patent information. Here are just a few of Dialog's databases:

AIDS Weekly

American Journal of Diseases of Children

Career Placement Registry

Conference Papers Index

Electronic Yellow Pages (for Retailers, Services, Manufacturers)

Enviroline

Oceanic Abstracts

Philosopher's Index

U.S. Exports

Water Resources Abstracts

Despite its expense ($150 hourly or more for many of its databases), a sizable number of college libraries subscribe to Dialog. Companies who have full-time database researchers also subscribe.

BRS   Bibliographic Retrieval Services (BRS) is another popular database providing bibliographies and abstracts from life sciences, physical sciences, business, or social sciences. These are a few from the more than fifty BRS databases:

American Chemical Society Journals

Dissertation Abstracts International

Government Reports Announcements & Index

Harvard Business Review

International Pharmaceutical Abstracts

Military and Federal Specifications and Standards

Pollution Abstracts

Robotics Information Database

Many college libraries now subscribe to the BRS system.

A Sample Automated Search   Assume you are continuing your research into the effects of food additives on children. You have done a brief search through the "manual" indexes and, for a comprehensive view, you decide on an automated search, using your library's BRS service. You ask a librarian for help, and the two of you sit at the terminal and begin.

After logging into the BRS system, you instruct the computer to search all the databases under the group headings "Life Sciences" and "Social Sciences," using the key words *food, additive, children,* and *behavior.* The computer responds with a listing of each database under "Life Sciences" and "Social Sciences" and the number of articles (containing the key words in each). For instance, the *Drug Information/ Alcohol Use-Abuse* database has no articles; *Medline* has nine; *International Pharmaceutical Abstracts* has one article; and so on. You notice that the *Psycinfo* Database (PSYC) lists 16 articles (since 1967). Because you are most interested in the psychological effects of additives (versus, say, the physiological effects), you instruct the computer to list the titles of all these articles. Here is the list (partial):

1

TI THE FEINGOLD DIET: A CURRENT REAPPRAISAL

2

TI FOOD ADDITIVES: THE CONTROVERSY CONTINUES

[The list continues to number 16.]

15

TI THE FUNCTIONAL RELATIONSHIP BETWEEN ARTIFICIAL FOOD COLORS AND HYPERACTIVITY

16
TI HYPERKINESIS AND LEARNING DISABILITIES LINKED TO THE INGESTION OF
ARTIFICIAL FOOD COLORS AND FLAVORS

*END OF DOCUMENTS IN LIST

In this list are several titles of interest, but number 15 seems most relevant to your topic. You now instruct the computer to print the full bibliographic information (including the abstract) about this article. The computer responds:

Accession number	AN 03410 64-2.
Author	AU ROSE-TERRY
Institution	IN NORTHERN ILLINOIS U.
Title	TI THE FUNCTIONAL RELATIONSHIP BETWEEN ARTIFICIAL FOOD COLORS AND HYPERACTIVITY
Source	SO JOURNAL OF APPLIED BEHAVIOR ANALYSIS 1978 WIN VOL 11(4) 439-446
Abstract	AB THE PRESENCE OF A FUNCTIONAL RELATIONSHIP BETWEEN THE INGESTION OF ARTIFICIAL FOOD COLORS AND AN INCREASE IN THE FREQUENCY AND/OR DURATION OF SELECTED BEHAVIORS THAT ARE REPRESENTATIVE OF THE HYPERACTIVE BEHAVIOR SYNDROME WAS EXPERIMENTALLY INVESTIGATED. TWO 8-YR-OLD FEMALES, WHO HAD BEEN ON B. F. FEINGOLD'S (1975–1976) K-P DIET FOR A MINIMUM OF 11 MONTHS, WERE THE SUBJECTS STUDIED. [The abstract continues.]

*END OF DOCUMENT

After reviewing the abstract, you decide to obtain the complete article, and so you make a note to check your library's holdings or to order a copy through interlibrary loan. (Some reprints can be ordered directly through the computer terminal.) You turn again to the list of titles to see if others seem promising.

Once you've searched the PSYC database to your satisfaction, you may decide to look at Medline or some other database on the list that was shown to have articles with your key words in the title.

Benefits and Limitations of Automated Searches   Online searches have several advantages over manual searches (that is, flipping pages by hand).

- They are rapid: you can review ten or fifteen years of an index in minutes.

- They are detailed: beyond listing titles and sources, an automated search often provides abstracts.

- They are current: the index usually comes online about six weeks before the printed copies.

- They are thorough: the system can search not only for titles but for key words (or word combinations) found in the title *or* the abstract.

- They are efficient: you can extract from the database only the information you need, without tracking material that turns out useless.

But automated searches have limitations as well. Most computerized bibliographies include no entries before the mid-1960s; earlier information requires a manual search. Also, a manual search provides the whole "database" (the bound index or abstracts). As you browse, you often *randomly* discover something useful. This randomness, of course, is impossible with an automated search, which can give you the illusion of having surveyed all that is known on your topic.* Finally, automated searches can be expensive, depending on how many databases you search and how long you spend online. (The average cost of a BRS search is about $30.) Some schools offer students one free search, but if your school does not, you pay the cost.

For any automated search, keep in mind that a manual (random) search almost always is needed as well. And a thorough search calls for a preliminary conference with a trained librarian.

Finding Adequate Information Sources

As soon as you are familiar with your library, make sure enough information for your topic is available. Do a quick search of the card catalog, reference books, and indexes. Compile a working bibliography of at least a dozen works. Maybe you won't use all this material, or maybe you will need more—but you now have a place to begin. Your bibliography will

---

*University of Massachusetts Dartmouth librarian Charles McNeil cautions against assuming that computer access yields the best material: "The material in the computer is what is cheapest to put there." Librarian Ross LaBaugh alerts users to a built-in bias in databases: "The company that assembles the bibliographic or full-text database often includes a disproportionate number of its own publications." Like any collection of information, a database can reflect the biases of its assemblers.

grow as you read. And many books you examine will have their own bibliographies, which lead to additional sources.

For some topics, you will want to list *primary* as well as *secondary* information sources. Primary research is a first-hand study of the topic; its sources are observation, questionnaires, interviews, inquiry letters, works of literature, or personal documents (letters, diaries, journals). If your topic is the love life of Thoreau, a good primary source will be his journals, poems, and letters. Secondary research is based on information and conclusions that other researchers—by their primary research—have compiled in books and articles. Whenever your topic permits, try to combine these approaches. Have a look for yourself.

Recording Findings

Findings should be recorded in ways that enable you to easily locate, organize, shuffle, and control the material as you work with it.

TAKING NOTES

Notecards are convenient because they are easy to organize and reorganize. Follow these suggestions for using notecards:

1. Begin by making separate bibliography cards for each work you plan to consult (Figure 20.6). Record the complete entry, using the identical citation format that will appear in your report. (See pages 457–463 for sample entries.) Take time to record the information

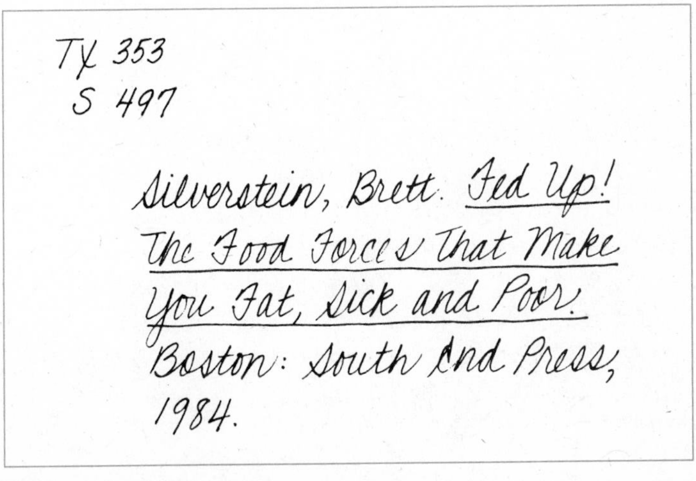
TX 353
S 497

Silverstein, Brett. Fed Up! The Food Forces That Make You Fat, Sick and Poor. Boston: South End Press, 1984.

Figure 20.6 A Bibliography Card

for your bibliography accurately. Doing so will save you from having to relocate a source at the last minute or having to eliminate one because you can't properly document it.

2. Skim the entire work to locate relevant material.

3. Go back and decide what to record. (Use a separate card for each item.)

4. Decide how to record the item: as a quotation or a paraphrase. When quoting others directly, be sure to record words and punctuation accurately. When restating or adapting material in your own words, be sure to preserve the original meaning and emphasis.

QUOTING THE WORK OF OTHERS

When you borrow exact wording, whether the words were written or spoken (as in an interview or presentation), you must place quotation marks around all borrowed material. Even a single borrowed sentence or phrase, or a single word used in a special way, needs quotation marks, with the exact source properly cited.

If your notes fail to identify quoted material accurately, you might forget to credit the source in your report. Even when this omission is unintentional, writers face the charge of *plagiarism* (misrepresenting as one's own the words or ideas of someone else).

In recording a direct quotation, copy the selection word for word (Figure 20.7) and include the page number(s). If your quotation omits parts of a sentence, use an *ellipsis* (three periods equally spaced: . . .) to

> Silverstein, Brett.   *Fed Up!* p. 39.
>
> "Sometimes the chemicals are added to food
> in a real attempt to improve it.
> More often, additives are used so that food
> can be processed by machine, canned or
> frozen, dehydrated or drowned in liquid,
> shipped across the country, and stored for
> months, while retaining some small resemblance
> to what some of us remember as fresh food."

Figure 20.7 Notecard for a Quotation

indicate each part that you have omitted from the original. If your quotation omits the end of a sentence, the beginning of the subsequent sentence, or whole sentences or paragraphs, show the ellipsis with four
periods (. . . .).

> If your quotation omits parts . . . use an ellipsis. . . . If your quota-
> tion omits the end. . . .

Be sure that your elliptical expression is grammatical and that the omitted material in no way distorts the original meaning.

If you insert your own comments within the quotation, place them
inside brackets to distinguish your words from those of your source:

> "This profession [aircraft ground controller] requires exhaustive
> attention."

(For more on brackets, see page 574.)

Introducing quotations with your own expressions requires attention to audience needs and proper grammar. Generally, integrated quotations are introduced by phrases such as "Jones argues that," "Smith
suggests that," so that readers will know who said what. But, more
importantly, readers must see the relationship between the quoted idea
and the sentence that precedes it. You therefore want to use a transitional phrase that emphasizes this relationship by looking back as well
as ahead:

> After you decide to develop a program, "the first step in the pro-
> gramming process. . . ."

Besides showing how each quotation helps advance the main
idea you are developing, your integrated sentences should be grammatical:

> "The agricultural crisis," Marx acknowledges, "resulted primari-
> ly from unchecked land speculation."
>
> "She has rejuvenated the industrial economy of our region,"
> Smith writes of Berry's term as regional planner.

(For quoting long passages and for punctuating at the end of a quotation,
see pages 571–572.)

Use a direct quotation only when precision or clarity or emphasis requires the exact words from the original. Avoid excessively long
quoted passages. Research writing is more a process of independent
thinking, in which you work with the ideas of others in order to reach
your own conclusions; you should therefore paraphrase, instead of quoting, much of your borrowed material.

PARAPHRASING THE WORK OF OTHERS

We paraphrase not only to preserve the original idea, but also to express it in a clearer or simpler or more direct or emphatic way—without distorting the idea. Paraphrasing means more than changing or shuffling a few words; it means restating the original idea in your own words and giving full credit to the source.

To borrow or adapt someone else's ideas or reasoning without properly documenting the source is plagiarism. To offer as a paraphrase an original passage only slightly altered—even when you document the source—also is plagiarism. Equally unethical is to offer a paraphrase, although documented, that distorts the original meaning.

An effective paraphrase generally displays all or most of the following elements (Weinstein 3):

- reference to the author early in the paraphrase, to indicate the beginning of the borrowed passage

- key words retained from the original, to preserve the meaning

- original sentences restructured and combined, for emphasis and fluency

- needless words from the original deleted, for conciseness

- your own words and phrases that help explain the author's ideas, for clarity

- a citation (in parentheses) of the exact source, to mark the end of the borrowed passage and to give full credit

- preservation of the author's original intent

Figure 20.8 shows an entry paraphrased from the passage in Figure 20.7. Notice that the writer signals the beginning of the paraphrase by citing the author, and the end by citing the source.

Paraphrased material is not enclosed within quotation marks, but it has to be documented to acknowledge your debt to the source. Failing to acknowledge ideas, findings, judgments, lines of reasoning, opinions, facts, or insights not considered *common knowledge* (page 454) is plagiarism—even when these are expressed in your own words.

Assessing Your Inquiry

The inquiry phases of the research process present a minefield of potential errors in where we search, how we interpret, and how we reason: we might ask wrong questions; we might rely on wrong sources; we might misinterpret findings; we might reason illogically.

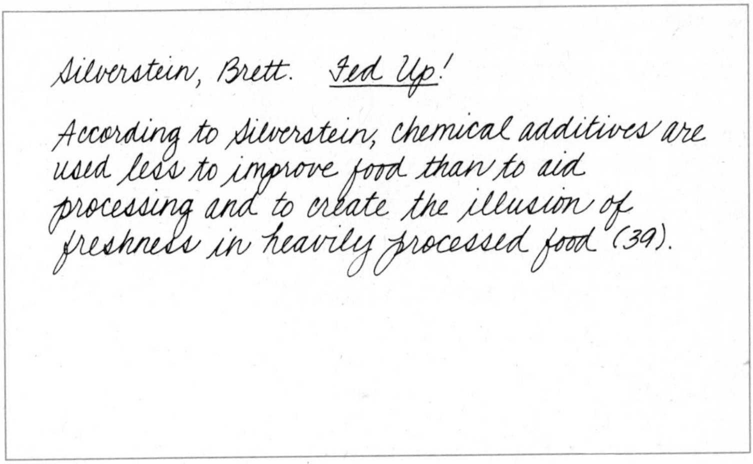

Silverstein, Brett. Fed Up!

According to Silverstein, chemical additives are used less to improve food than to aid processing and to create the illusion of freshness in heavily processed food (39).

Figure 20.8 Notecard for a Paraphrase

Before preparing the actual report, we therefore need to examine critically our methods, our interpretations, and our reasoning. The following checklist helps guide our assessment.

Inquiry Checklist

(Numbers in parentheses refer to the first page of discussion.)

Methods

☐ Did I ask the right questions? (419)

☐ Are the sources current enough to convey the latest that is known? (356)

☐ Is each source reliable, relatively unbiased, and borne out by other, similar sources? (356)

☐ Is the evidence verifiable? (356)

☐ Is a balance of viewpoints represented? (420)

☐ Do I need more information? (422)

Interpretations

☐ What do the findings mean? (357)

☐ Do the facts conflict? (423)

☐ Are other interpretations possible? (422)

☐ What conclusions are warranted by my findings? (423)

Reasoning

☐ Am I reasoning instead of rationalizing? (358)

☐ Am I confident that my causal reasoning is correct? (370)

☐ Can all the numbers and statistics be trusted? (372)

☐ Have I resolved (or at least acknowledged) any conflicts among my findings? (423)

☐ Do I avoid conclusions that are specious or forced? (358)

☐ Have I decided whether my final answer is definitive, or only probable, or even inconclusive? (357)

☐ Is this the most reasonable conclusion (or merely the most convenient)? (423)

☐ Do I allow for other possible interpretations or conclusions? (422)

☐ Have I accounted for all sources of bias, including my own? (358)

☐ Should I reconsider the evidence? (422)

This kind of careful assessment is what separates legitimate inquiry from mere information gathering.

Developing a Working Thesis and Outline

Don't expect to identify your thesis until you have evaluated and interpreted your findings (as discussed on pages 421–423). *How* you finally arrive at a thesis and outline is immaterial; *that* you arrive sooner or later is essential. To get there, use the following strategies—in whichever order works best for you.

Begin with a general view. Encyclopedias are a good place to find general information. Or you can read a book or pamphlet that offers a comprehensive view before you move to specialized articles in periodicals. Specialized dictionaries and newspaper or magazine articles also provide background. Ask your reference librarian to help you find sources.

Learn to skim. Open a book and look over the table of contents and the index. Check the introduction for an overview or thesis. In long articles, look for headings that may help you locate specific information. Short articles and pamphlets usually should be read fully.

To skim effectively, you have to concentrate. If you feel yourself drifting, take a break.

Be selective about note taking. Resist the temptation to copy or paraphrase every word. As you read, try to develop your own interpretation. Your finished report should be a combined product of your insights and collected facts you've woven together.

Remember that you are not merely collecting views, but screening and evaluating facts to answer a definite question—the question you formulated for your research topic in the first place. Your summary answer to that question will be your thesis, and it will be based on the most accurate and reliable information you have been able to find. On page 423 you phrased your topic as this question:

Research topic   *What effects, if any, do food additives and preservatives have on children's behavior?*

As you near completion of your research, you should be in a position to give at least a tentative answer to that question:

Tentative thesis   Some common food additives and preservatives play a definite role in childhood behavior disorders.

As your research proceeds, you might revise this tentative thesis any number of times. But at least for now, you have a working sense of direction.*

Now that you have identified a definite direction, you need a road map—a working outline. Perhaps your topic-as-question suggested its own rough outline earlier. However, you've probably had to do some reading first in order to assemble some sort of rough, working outline:

I. The role of diet in behavior disorders
    A. Children's sensitivity to small doses of chemicals
    B. Abnormal behavior as an allergic response to some foods

II. Effects of specific additives and preservatives
    A. On physical aggression
    B. On classroom behavior
    C. On scholastic performance
    D. On peer socialization

III. Diet control in management of behavior disorders
    A. Exclusion of flavoring and coloring substances
    B. Exclusion of specific food preservatives and salicylates

---

* In some cases, of course, your research will produce contradictory findings or indefinite conclusions, and so you might have to settle for an inconclusive thesis such as this one: *Although food additives are a suspected cause of childhood behavior disorders, the link has not yet been demonstrated.* Be sure your interpretations and conclusions fit the best evidence you've collected. Never settle on a thesis that cannot be justified by the evidence.

Each of these parts, of course, can be divided into its own subparts as your research continues. By the time you compose your final outline (see the sample on pages 476–477), the shape of your report may have changed radically.

Writing a First Draft

When you have collected and reviewed your material, organized your notecards, and settled on a workable thesis, you are ready to write the first draft of your report.

Begin by revising your working outline. At this stage, try to develop a detailed formal outline, using at each level either topic phrases or full sentences. (A topic outline is shown on page 451, and a sentence outline on pages 45–46.) Be consistent: use all phrases or all sentences.

A formal outline depends on logical notation and consistent format. *Notation* is the system of numbers and letters marking the logical divisions of your outline. *Format* is the arrangement of your material on the page (indention, spacing, and so on). Proper notation and format show the subordination of some parts of your topic to others. Be sure all sections and subsections are ordered, capitalized, lettered, numbered, punctuated, and indented to show how each part relates to other parts and to the whole. The general pattern of outline notation goes like this:

    I.
        A.
            1.
            2.*
        B.
            1.
            2.
                a.
                b. (1)†
                      (2)
        C.
    II.   etc.

(For a discussion of a sample formal outline, see page 474.)

---

* Any division must yield at least two subparts. You could not logically divide "Types of Strip Mining" into "1. Contour Mining" without other subparts. If you cannot divide your major topic into at least two subtopics, change your original heading.

† Further subdivisions can be carried as far as needed, as long as the notation for each level of division is individualized and consistent.

When your outline is complete, check your tentative thesis to make sure no changes are needed there. The thesis should promise *exactly* what your report will deliver.

Now you can begin to write. To maintain control over the material, concentrate on only one section at a time. Students often find this the most intimidating part of research: pulling together a large body of information in a report. Don't frantically throw everything on the page simply to get done. Remember that your final report will be the only concrete evidence of your labor.

Begin by classifying your notecards in groups according to the section of your outline to which each card is keyed. Next, find a flat surface. Take the notecards for your introduction and arrange them in order. Now, lay them out in rows, as you would lay out playing cards. Thus armed with your outline, your statement of purpose, your ordered notecards, and your expertise, you are ready to write your first section.

As you move from subsection to subsection, provide commentary and transitions, and document each source. When you complete your introductory section, proceed to the others, weaving ideas together by following the outline (and modifying as needed).

Documenting Your Sources

Documenting research means acknowledging one's debt to each information source. Proper documentation satisfies professional requirements for ethics, efficiency, and authority.

WHY YOU SHOULD DOCUMENT

Documentation is a matter of *ethics* in that the originator of borrowed material deserves full credit and recognition. Moreover, all published material is protected by copyright law. Failure to credit a source could make you liable to legal action, even if your omission was unintentional.

Documentation is also a matter of *efficiency*. It provides a network for organizing and locating the world's printed knowledge. If you cite a particular source correctly, your reference will enable interested readers to locate that source themselves.

Finally, documentation is a matter of *authority*. In making any claim (say, "A Mercedes-Benz is more reliable than a Ford Taurus") you invite challenge: "Says who?" Data on road tests, frequency of repairs, resale value, construction quality, and owner comments can help validate your claim by showing its basis in *fact*. A claim's credibility increases in relation to the expert references supporting it. For a controversial topic, you may need to cite several authorities who hold various views, as in this next example, instead of forcing a simplistic conclusion on your material:

> Opinion is mixed as to whether a marketable quantity of oil rests under Georges Bank. Cape Cod Geologist John Blocke feels that extensive reserves are improbable ("Geologist Dampens Hopes" 3). Oil geologist Donald Marshall is uncertain about the existence of any oil in quantity under Georges Bank ("Offshore Oil Drilling" 2). But the U.S. Interior Department reports that the Atlantic continental shelf may contain 5.5 billion barrels of oil (Kemprecos 8).

Readers of your research report expect the *complete* picture.

WHAT YOU SHOULD DOCUMENT

Document any insight, assertion, fact, finding, interpretation, judgment or other "appropriated material that readers might otherwise mistake for your own" (Gibaldi and Achtert 155). Specifically, you must document

- any source from which you use exact wording
- any source from which you adapt material in your own words
- any visual illustration: charts, graphs, drawing, or the like.

You don't need to document anything considered *common knowledge:* material that appears repeatedly in general sources. In medicine, for instance, it is common knowledge that foods high in fat cause some types of cancer. Thus, in a research report on fatty diets and cancer, you probably would not need to document that well-known fact. But you would document information about how the fat/cancer connection was discovered, subsequent studies (say, of the role of saturated versus unsaturated fats), and any information for which some other person could claim specific credit. If the borrowed material can be found in only one specific source, and not in multiple sources, document it. When in doubt, document the source.

HOW YOU SHOULD DOCUMENT

Borrowed material has to be cited twice: at the exact place you use that material, and at the end of your document. Documentation practices vary widely, but all systems work almost identically: a brief reference in the text names the source and refers readers to the complete citation, which enables the source to be retrieved.

Many disciplines, institutions, and organizations publish their own documentation manuals. Here are a few:

Style Guide for Chemists

Geographical Research and Writing

Style Manual for Engineering Authors and Editors

IBM Style Manual

NASA Publications Manual

When no specific format is stipulated, consult one of the two general manuals discussed in the next section or the *Chicago Manual of Style*, 14th ed., by the University of Chicago Press, which covers documentation in the humanities, related fields, and natural sciences. The formats in any of these three manuals can be adapted to most research writing.

The next section illustrates citations and entries for MLA documentation style, and then presents alternatives with APA (American Psychological Association) style.

MLA DOCUMENTATION STYLE

Traditional documentation used superscripted numbers (like this: [1]) in the text, followed by full references at page bottom (footnotes) or at document's end (endnotes) and, finally, by a bibliography. But a more current form of documentation appears in the *MLA Handbook for Writers of Research Papers*, 4th ed., New York: Modern Language Association, 1995. MLA style replaces footnote and endnote numbers with parenthetical references, which briefly identify the source (in parentheses). Full documentation then appears in a "Works Cited" section at report's end.*

A parenthetical reference usually includes the author's surname and the exact page number of the borrowed material:

Cancer risk increases when magnetic fields measure consistently higher than 2.5 milligauss (Abelson 241).

Readers seeking the complete citation for Abelson can move easily to "Works Cited," listed alphabetically by author:

Abelson, Philip H. "Effects of Electric and Magnetic Fields."

Science 21 July 1989: 240–46.

This complete citation includes page numbers for the entire article.

---

* In the MLA system, footnotes (and endnotes) now are used only to comment or expand on material in the text, or to comment on sources or suggest additional sources. Place these notes at page bottom or in a "Notes" section at document's end.

Guidelines for Parenthetical References   For clear and informative parenthetical references, observe these guidelines:

- If your discussion names the author, do not repeat the name in your parenthetical reference; simply give the page number:

  Abelson describes recent evidence indicating that cancer risk increases when magnetic fields measure consistently higher than 2.5 milligauss (241).

- If you cite two or more works in a single parenthetical reference, separate the citations with semicolons:

  (Jones 32; Leduc 41; Gomez 293–94)

- If you cite two or more authors with the same surname, include the first initial in your parenthetical reference to each author:

  (R. Jones 32) (S. Jones 14–15)

- If you cite two or more works by the same author, include the first significant word from each work's title, or a shortened version:

  (Lamont, Biophysics 100–01) (Lamont, Diagnostic Tests 81)

- If the work is by an institutional or corporate author or is unsigned (that is, author unknown), use only the first few words of the institutional name or the work's title in your parenthetical reference:

  (American Medical Assn. 2) ("Distribution Systems" 18)

To avoid distracting your readers, keep each parenthetical reference as brief as possible. (One method is to name the source in your discussion, and to place only the page number in parentheses.)

For a paraphrase, place the parenthetical reference *before* the closing punctuation mark. For a quotation that runs into the text, place the reference *between* the final quotation mark and the closing punctuation mark. For a quotation set off (indented) from the text, place the reference two spaces *after* the closing punctuation mark.

Works Cited Entries for Books   Any citation for a book should contain the following information (found on the book's title and copyright pages): author, title, editor or translator, edition, volume number, and facts about publication (city, publisher, date).

Type the first line of each entry flush with the left margin. Indent the second and subsequent lines five spaces. Double-space within and between each entry. Skip one horizontal space after any closing period in an entry,* and one space after any comma or colon.

Following are examples of complete citations as they would appear in the "Works Cited" section of your document. Shown italicized after each citation is its corresponding parenthetical reference as it would appear in the text.

SINGLE AUTHOR

Kerzin-Fontana, Jane B. Technology Management: A Handbook.

3rd ed. Delmar.: American Management Assn., 1992.

Parenthetical reference: (Kerzin-Fontana 3–4)

List only the first city, if several are listed on the title page. For Canada include the province abbreviation after the city. For all other countries include an abbreviation of the country name.

TWO OR THREE AUTHORS

Aronson, Linda, Roger Katz, and Candide Moustafa. Toxic Waste

Disposal Methods. Englewood Cliffs: Prentice, 1991.

Parenthetical reference: (Aronson, Katz, and Moustafa 9)

Shorten publishers' names (as in "Simon" for Simon & Schuster; "GPO" for Government Printing Office; or "Yale UP" for Yale University Press).

MORE THAN THREE AUTHORS

Santos, Ruth J., et al. Environmental Crises in Developing

Countries. New York: Harper, 1990.

"Et al." is the abbreviated form of the Latin "et alia," meaning "and others."

Parenthetical reference: (Santos et al. 111–23)

---

* Only those periods that separate different items in the entry (say, author's name from the work's title) are followed by two spaces. Those periods that end an abbreviation within one particular item (say, "29 Dec." or "Mary H. Gordon") are followed by only one space.

AUTHOR NOT NAMED

Structured Programming. Boston: Meredith, 1989.

Parenthetical reference: (Structured 67)

TWO BOOKS BY THE SAME AUTHOR

Chang, John W. Biophysics. Boston: Little, 1989.

---. Diagnostic Techniques. New York: Radon, 1990.

Parenthetical references: (Chang, Biophysics 123–26); (Chang, Diagnostic 87)

When citing more than one work by the same author, do not repeat the author's name; simply type three hyphens followed by a period. List the works alphabetically by title.

ONE OR TWO EDITORS

Morris, A. J., and Louise B. Pardin-Walker, eds. Handbook of New

Information Technology. New York: Harper, 1993.

Parenthetical reference: (Morris and Pardin-Walker 34)

For more than three editors, name only the first, followed by "et al."

QUOTATION OF A QUOTATION

Kline, Thomas. Automated Office Systems. New York: Random,

1989.

Sturtevant, John. White-Collar Productivity.

Boston: Houghton, 1991.
Parenthetical reference: (qtd. in Sturtevant 116)

When your source (as in Sturtevant, above) has quoted another source, list each source in its appropriate alphabetical place in your "Works Cited" page. Use the name of the original source (here, Kline) in your text and precede your parenthetical reference with "qtd. in."

SELECTION IN AN ANTHOLOGY (COLLECTED WORKS BY VARIOUS AUTHORS)

> Anderson, Paul V. "What Survey Research Tells Us about Writing
>
> at Work." Writing in Nonacademic Settings. Ed. Lee Odell and
>
> Dixie Goswami. New York: Guilford, 1985. 3–83.
>
> *Parenthetical reference: (Anderson 31)*

The page numbers in the complete citation are for the selection cited from the anthology.

Works Cited Entries for Periodicals   A citation for an article should give this information (as available): author, article title, periodical title, volume or number (or both), date (day, month, year), and page numbers for the entire article—not just the pages cited. List the information in the order given here, as in the following examples.

MAGAZINE ARTICLE

> Main, Jeremy. "The Executive Yearning to Learn." Fortune 3 May
>
> 1982: 234–48.
>
> *Parenthetical reference: (Main 235–36)*

No punctuation separates the magazine title and date. Nor is the abbreviation "p." or "pp." used to designate page numbers.

If no author is given, list all other information:

> "Distribution Systems for the New Decade." Power Technology
>
> Magazine 18 Oct. 1990: 18+.
>
> *Parenthetical reference: ("Distribution Systems" 18)*

This article began on page 18 and then continued on page 21. When an article does not appear on consecutive pages, give only the number of the first page, followed immediately by a plus sign. A three-letter abbreviation denotes any month spelled with five or more letters.

ARTICLE IN A JOURNAL WITH NEW PAGINATION IN EACH ISSUE

Thackman-White, Joan R. "Computer-Assisted Research."

American Librarian 51.1 (1992): 3–9.

Parenthetical reference: (Thackman-White 4–5)

Because each issue for that year will have page numbers beginning with "1," readers need the number of this issue. The "51" denotes the volume number; the "1" denotes the issue number. Omit "The" or "A" or any other introductory article from a journal or magazine title.

ARTICLE IN A JOURNAL WITH CONTINUOUS PAGINATION

Barnstead, Marion H. "The Writing Crisis." Writing Theory 12

(1989): 415–33.

Parenthetical reference: (Barnstead 418)

When page numbers continue from issue to issue for the full year, readers won't need the issue number, because no other issue in that year repeats these same page numbers. (You may, however, include the issue number if you think it will help readers retrieve the article more easily.) The "12" denotes the volume number.

NEWSPAPER ARTICLE

Baranski, Vida H. "Errors in Technology Assessment." Boston

Times 15 Jan. 1993, evening ed.: sec. 2:3.

Parenthetical reference: (Baranski 3)

When a daily newspaper has more than one edition, cite the specific edition after the date. Omit any introductory article in the newspaper's name (not The Boston Times). If no author is given, list all other information. If the newspaper's name does not contain the city of publication, insert it, using brackets: "Sippican Sentinel [Marion, MA]."

Works Cited Entries for Other Kinds of Materials Miscellaneous sources range from unsigned encyclopedia entries to nonprint sources to software packages. A full citation should give this information (as available): author, title, city, publisher, date, and page numbers.

ENCYCLOPEDIA, DICTIONARY, OR OTHER ALPHABETIC REFERENCE

"Communication." The Business Reference Book. 1987 ed.

Parenthetical reference: ("Communication")

If the entry is signed, begin with the author's name. For any work arranged alphabetically, omit page numbers in both the complete citation and the parenthetical reference. For a well-known reference book only an edition (if stated) and a date are needed. For other reference books give the full publication information.

PERSONALLY CONDUCTED INTERVIEW

Nasser, Gamel. Chief Engineer for Northern Electric. Personal

Interview. Rangeley, ME. 2 Apr. 1992.

Parenthetical reference: (Nasser)

PUBLISHED INTERVIEW

Lescault, James. "The Future of Graphics." Executive Views of

Automation. Ed. Karen Prell. Boston: Haber, 1992. 216–31.

Parenthetical reference: (Lescault 218)

The interviewee's name is placed in the entry's author slot.

UNPUBLISHED LETTER

Rogers, Leonard. Letter to the author. 15 May 1993.

Parenthetical reference: (Rogers)

QUESTIONNAIRE

Taylor, Lynne. Questionnaire sent to 612 Massachusetts business

executives. 14 Feb. 1992.

Parenthetical reference: (Taylor)

PAMPHLET OR BROCHURE

Waters, Joan L. Investment Strategies for the 90's. San Francisco:

Blount Economics Assn., 1990.

Parenthetical reference: (Waters)

If the work is unsigned, begin with its title.

LECTURE

Dumont, R. A. "Managing Natural Gas." UMass

Dartmouth, 15 Jan. 1993.

Parenthetical reference: (Dumont)

If the title is not known write Address, Lecture, or Reading but do not use quotation marks. Include the sponsor and the location if they are available.

DATABASE SOURCE

Wilford, John Noble. "Corn in the New World: A Relative

Latecomer." New York Times 7 Mar. 1995, late ed.:

C1 + . New York Times Online. Online. America Online.

8 Mar. 1995.

Parenthetical reference: (Wilford)

SOFTWARE

Levy, Michael C., et al. Statmaster: Exploring and Computing

Statistics. Diskette. Boston: Little. 1988.

Parenthetical reference: (Levy)

Name the appropriate computer, the kilobytes, the software format ("disk"), and include any other useful information.

CORPORATE AUTHOR OR GOVERNMENT PUBLICATION

Presidential Task Force on Acid Rain. The Role of Acid Rain in

Deforestation. Washington: GPO, 1992.

Parenthetical reference: (Presidential Task Force 108–12)

The shortened version in the previous parenthetical reference avoids interrupting the flow of the text.

OTHER ITEMS (UNPUBLISHED REPORTS, DISSERTATIONS, AND SO ON)

> Author (if known), title (in quotes), sponsoring organization or
>
> publisher, date, page number.

For any work that has group authorship (corporation, committee, task force), cite the name of the group or agency in place of the author's name.

The "Works Cited" List   In your "works cited" section, arrange entries alphabetically by author's surname. When the author is unknown, list the title alphabetically according to its first word (excluding introductory articles). For a title that begins with a digit ("5," "6," etc.), alphabetize the entry as if the digit were spelled out.

On pages 500–504 you will find a list of works cited by Shirley Haley in her research report.

APA DOCUMENTATION STYLE

One popular alternative to MLA style appears in the *Publication Manual of the American Psychological Association,* 3rd ed. Washington: American Psychological Association, 1993. APA style is useful when writers wish to emphasize the publication dates of their references. A parenthetical reference in the text briefly identifies the source, date, and page number:

> Beyond motivation and communication skills, interpersonal skills
>
> are the ultimate requirement for success in marketing (Splaver,
>
> 1987, p. 14).

The full citation then appears in the alphabetic listing of "References," at report's end:

> Splaver, S. (1987). Your personality and your career. New York:
>
> Simon & Schuster.

Because it emphasizes the date, APA style (or some similar author-date style) is preferred in the sciences and social sciences, where information quickly becomes dated.

Guidelines for Parenthetical References   APA's parenthetical references resemble MLA's (pages 455–463), but a comma separates each item in the reference, and "p." or "pp." precedes the page number. When a subsequent reference to a given work follows closely after the initial reference, the date need not be included. For additional guidelines governing parenthetical references, consult the *APA Manual.*

The List of References   APA's "References" section is an alphabetic listing equivalent to MLA's "Works Cited" section. Like "Works Cited," the reference list includes only those works actually cited. (A bibliography usually would include background works or works consulted as well.) APA entries, however, differ somewhat from MLA entries. For comprehensive examples of entries in the reference list, consult the *APA Manual* (usually available at the reserve desk).

Revising Your Research Report

After completing and documenting a first draft, use the Revision Checklist in Chapter 4, along with the following checklist, to revise the report.

Research Report Checklist

Numbers in parentheses refer to the first page of discussion.

Content

- ☐ Does the report grow from a clear thesis? (450)
- ☐ Is the title accurate and unbiased? (62)
- ☐ Does the evidence support the conclusion? (422)
- ☐ Is the report based on reliable sources and evidence? (352–359)
- ☐ Is the information complete? (113)
- ☐ Does the report avoid reliance on a single source? (420)
- ☐ Is your evidence free of weak spots? (353)
- ☐ Are all data clearly and fully interpreted? (422)
- ☐ Can anything be cut? (43)
- ☐ Is anything missing? (113)
- ☐ Are all sources other than common knowledge documented? (454)
- ☐ Are direct quotations used sparingly and appropriately? (446)
- ☐ Are all quotations accurate and grammatical? (447)

☐   Is the report free of excessively long quotations? (447)

☐   Are all paraphrases accurate and clear? (448)

☐   Is all quoted material clearly identified in the report? (446)

☐   Is the documentation complete and correct? (453)

Organization

☐   Does the introduction state clearly the purpose and thesis? (44)

☐   Does the report itself follow the outline? (452)

☐   Is each paragraph focused on one main thought? (123)

☐   Do conclusions rest fully on the data discussed and inter-preted? (423)

☐   Is the line of reasoning clear and easy to follow? (44)

Application 20–1

Prepare a research report by completing these steps. (Your instructor might establish a timetable for completing the phases outlined here.)

PHASE ONE: PRELIMINARY STEPS

1. Choose a topic of *immediate practical importance,* something that affects you or your community directly. (The list of topics on pages 466–468 should give some ideas.) Develop a tree chart that will enable you to ask the right questions.

2. Identify a specific audience and its intended use of your information.

3. Narrow your topic, and check with your instructor for approval and advice.

4. Identify the various viewpoints that will enable you to achieve your own balanced viewpoint.

5. Make a working bibliography to ensure that your library holds sufficient resources. Don't delay this step!

6. List the information you already have about your topic.

7. Write a clear statement of purpose and submit it to your instructor.

8. Make a working outline.

PHASE TWO: COLLECTING, EVALUATING, AND INTERPRETING DATA

1. In your research, move from the general to the specific; begin with general reference works for an overview.

2. Skim the sources, looking for high points.

3. Evaluate each finding for accuracy, reliability, fairness, and completeness.

4. Take notes selectively. Don't record everything! Use notecards.

5. Interpret your findings and decide what they all mean.

6. Settle on your thesis.

7. Use the page 449 checklist to assess your methods, interpretations, and reasoning.

PHASE THREE: ORGANIZING YOUR DATA AND WRITING YOUR REPORT

1. Revise and adjust your working outline, as needed.

2. Follow the introduction-body-conclusion format.

3. Concentrate on only *one* section of your report at a time.

4. Fully document all sources of information.

5. Write your final draft according to the page 464 checklist.

6. Proofread carefully.

DUE DATES

- List of possible topics due:
- Final topic due:
- Working bibliography and working outline due:
- Notecards due:
- Revised outline due:
- First draft of report due:
- Final draft of report with full documentation due:

Here are some possible research projects for Phase One.

1. Does alcohol consumption have any effect on academic performance? What do the latest studies indicate? Find out and prepare a report.

2. Does jogging really promote good health?

3. Find out which geographic sections of the United States are experiencing greatest prosperity and population growth (or the greatest hardship and population decrease). What are the major reasons? Trace the recent history of this change.

4. Some observers claim that productivity in American industry is on the decline. Find out whether this claim is valid. If it is, identify the reasons.

5. Assume that you and a business partner have developed a desktop duplicating machine (or some other product) that can be manufactured at low cost. What are the intricacies involved in applying for and getting a patent for your product?

6. How safe are artificial sweeteners?

7. What is the present status of women and minorities in your specialty? Assess their hiring and promotional opportunities, relative salaries, and percentages in executive positions. Do comparative data over the past decade suggest a trend toward equal opportunity?

8. Is the present famine in Africa likely to worsen? What needs to be done?

9. Why have SAT scores declined? What needs to be done?

10. How will the computer revolution affect our lives by the year 2010?

11. The federal government is planning at least two national sites for disposal of spent nuclear fuel rods and other high-level radioactive waste. State governments plan many more sites for disposal of low-level nuclear waste and other toxic waste. Find out the proposed locations for these sites and determine whether the site planned closest to your area poses any health or economic threat.

12. Home buyers (especially of older homes) face a frightening array of possible hazards, including chlordane sprayed for termites; wood preservatives; urea formaldehyde foam insulation; radon gas (radioactive) or chemical contamination in well water; lead paint; and asbestos. Research the effects of these hazards for someone you know who is buying a home.

13. Can peanut butter, black pepper, potatoes, and buttered toast cause cancer? Which of the commonest "pure" foods can be most carcinogenic? Find out and write a report for your cafeteria dietitian.

14. Assume you are the health officer in a town less than one mile from a massive radar installation. Citizens are worried about the effects of microwave radiation. Do they need to worry? Find the facts and write your report.

15. Assume you are the health officer in a town where a power company easment allows high-voltage lines to run immediately adjacent to the elementary school playground. Are the children endangered by electromagnetic disturbances? Parents and the school committee want to know. Find out and write your report.

16. The "coffee generation" wants to know about the properties of caffeine and the chemicals used on coffee beans. What are the effects of these substances on the human body? Write your report, making specific recommendations about precautions coffee drinkers can take.

17. Are there any recent inventions that could help decrease our reliance on fossil fuels in ways that are economical and practical? Find out and prepare a report for your U.S. senator.

18. What is the latest that scientists are saying about the implications of global warming caused by rain forest destruction and ozone depletion? Find out and prepare a report to be published in your campus newspaper.

19. Are video display terminals (computer screens) a health hazard? Find out and write a report for people who work in front of a computer.

20. Does acupuncture have measurable medical benefits? Your classmates want to know.

21. Assume that you and some classmates have been offered a great deal on the purchase of waterfront land in south Florida. Is the land likely to be under water within a couple of decades? Find out and write a report for your classmates.

Application 20–2

Consult the *Library of Congress Subject Headings* for alternative headings under which you might find information in the card catalog for your semester report topic. List at least five headings.

Application 20–3

List five major reference works in your major or on your topic by consulting Sheehy, Walford, or a more specific guide to literature.

Application 20–4

Using the card or electronic catalog, locate and list the full bibliographic citation (author's name, title of work, place and publisher, date) for five books in your major or on your semester report topic, all published within the past two years.

Application 20–5

Using one of the latest book indexes, identify one book in your major or on your semester topic published within the past three years. Give the full bibliographic citation.

Application 20–6

Identify a major periodical index in your major or on your topic. Locate a recent article on a specific topic (say, the use of artificial intelligence in medical diagnosis). Photocopy the article and submit it to your instructor along with the full bibliographic citation.

Application 20–7

Consult the appropriate librarian and identify two databases you would search for information on your semester topic.

Application 20–8

If your library offers students a free search of mainframe databases, ask your librarian for help in preparing an electronic search for your research report.

Application 20–9

Using the *Monthly Catalog or Government Reports Announcements and Index*, locate and photocopy a recent government publication in your major or on your topic.

Application 20–10

Determine whether your library offers OCLC and/or InfoTrac™ services. Use whichever service is available to locate the titles of two current books or articles in your major or on your topic. Give full bibliographic citations.

Application 20–11

List the titles of each of these specialized reference works on your topic: a bibliography, an encyclopedia, a dictionary, a handbook, an almanac (if available), and a directory.

Application 20–12

Identify a major abstract collection on your topic. Using the abstracts, locate a recent and relevant article. Photocopy the abstract and the article.

WORKS CITED

Gibaldi, Joseph, and Walter S. Achtert. *MLA Handbook for Writers of Research Papers.* 3rd ed. New York: Modern Language Assn., 1988.

Lavin, Michael R. *Business Information: How to Find It. How to Use It.* 2nd ed. Phoenix: Oryx, 1992.

"On Line." *Chronicle of Higher Education* 14 Oct. 1992, sec A: 19.

Watkins, Beverly T. "Many Campuses Start Building Tomorrow's Electronic Library." *Chronicle of Higher Education* 2 Sep. 1992, sec A: 1+.

Weinstein, Edith K. Unpublished review.

21
A Sample
Research Project

Discovering a Worthwhile Topic
• **Focusing the Inquiry** • **Searching the Literature**
• **Recording and Reviewing Findings** • **Settling on a Thesis**
• **Writing and Documenting the Research Report**

Writers who take short cuts or who try making something from nothing never get far—especially in the case of research writing. A useful research report evolves through deliberate problem-solving stages (focusing, searching, recording, reviewing, reasoning) that precede the actual "writing" stages (planning, drafting, revising).

In this chapter we will follow one student writer's problem-solving, from the day her report was assigned until the day she submitted her final draft.

Discovering a Worthwhile Topic

As soon as Shirley Haley learned that a research report was due in six weeks, she began to search for a worthwhile topic. Although Haley had many college friends who had adjusted to the hectic pace of the first-year student, she knew others who were not doing so well: some had developed insomnia; others had gained or lost a good deal of weight; one friend was sleeping more than 12 hours a day. Other disorders ranged from compulsive eating and indigestion to chronic headaches and skin problems— all seemingly since the beginning of the semester. Haley wondered why, beyond the obvious pressures of college life, so many of her friends had become so unhealthy. She decided to search for answers.

A psychology major, Haley had recently read about *stress* in an introductory textbook. She wondered if there could be a connection between stress and the problems she was witnessing among her friends.

Focusing the Inquiry

Haley was fortunate in being able to settle quickly on a topic that had real meaning for her and that was pretty well focused to begin with. But to come up with the right answers, she would have to ask all the right questions. Here is her tree chart:

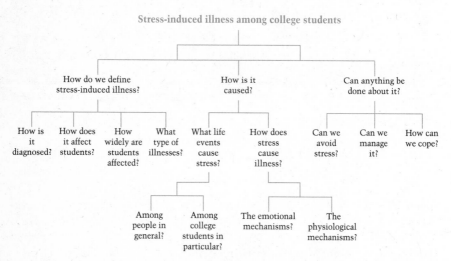

These questions gave Haley the kind of detailed perspective that would lend real direction to her research.

Once she knew the specific kinds of information she was looking for, Haley focused on the various viewpoints that would give her a balanced picture:

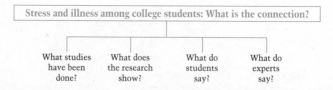

Now that she knew what questions to ask and from whom to get the answers, Haley was ready to do her research.

Searching the Literature

On her first trip to the library, Haley went straight to the *Readers' Guide to Periodical Literature*; because she had already read a description of stress in her psychology textbook, she felt no need to begin with such general reference works as encyclopedias and specialized dictionaries. In the most recent volume of the *Readers' Guide* was a sizable collection of articles under the heading "Stress." Haley also checked under the heading "College students"; there, under the subheading "Psychology," she found additional relevant titles. Then she checked through further volumes of the *Readers' Guide*, going back several years. Whenever she came across a promising title, she recorded the full citation on a bibliography card.

Next Haley searched through recent volumes of *Psychological Abstracts* (arranged like the *Readers' Guide*, but more specialized) for any studies that might have been done on stress and college students. Besides finding yet more titles in this index, she was able to look up and read abstracts of articles whose titles seemed promising. Under "Stress," she found an overwhelming number of titles—too many to follow up. But under "College Students," she found listings for some key articles that seemed to address her friends' health problems.

Now Haley checked her library's periodicals holdings list (see page 434) to determine which of these key articles were available in this library. Some, she found, were collected in bound volumes; others were on microfilm. With the help of a librarian, she learned how to locate and read articles on a microfilm reader. The librarian also assisted by ordering through interlibrary loan two articles not held in that library.

Then Haley proceeded to the card catalog, where she jotted down a few book titles and call numbers. Once in the stacks, she was able to browse through the books on the shelves. She also checked book and article titles in the "Selected Bibliography" section of her psychology textbook. Every time she discovered another promising source, she recorded the citation on a bibliography card.

Recording and Reviewing Findings

Now that she had a good stock of sources, Haley began to skim the most promising works for key information. She was careful to evaluate each finding for accuracy, reliability, fairness, and completeness. Whenever she came across useful material, she recorded it on a notecard, being careful to indicate the source and page numbers and to record quotations word for word. In her reading, she found a good body of information on stress management, and so she decided to structure her report in this way:

Problem → Causes and Effects → Solutions

Settling on a Thesis

After a long time reading and thinking about her findings, Haley settled on her overall interpretation—her judgment about the *meaning* of all this material. In this case, the evidence clearly pointed toward a definite conclusion: Stress was indeed a real factor in students' poor health. Now she could formulate a tentative thesis:

> *Stress is a definite cause of illness among college students.*

Although Haley would later refine and expand her thesis, she had, for now, a good focal point for developing her report.

Writing and Documenting the Report

Haley continued to read, record information, outline, and organize her notecards. Finally, she decided she knew enough to write her first draft. Using the revision checklists, she reworked a first and then a second draft and completed the final draft that appears on the following pages. Read this final draft carefully, paying close attention to the writer's decisions that are discussed on the facing pages. (The numbers in the margins of the report refer to the points discussed on the facing pages.)

Discussion of the Sample Research Report

1. *Title page:* Most instructors expect students to prepare a title page for a research report. Many reports for government, business, and industry are prefaced by a title page with these standard items: report title, author's name, course or department, intended reader's name, and date of submission. Haley centers and spaces these items for visual appeal. The title page is not numbered.

2. *Outline* (on next two pages): You might be asked to submit your final outline with your report—either as a topic or a sentence outline. Haley prefaces her sentence outline with her thesis, so that readers can understand her plan at a glance. She divides her report into three major sections (The Problem, Specific Causes, and Possible Solutions) to reveal a clear and sensible line of thought. This shape is a version of effect-to-cause development (see pages 297–298).

    After each roman numeral is a sentence summarizing that major section. After each capital letter or number is a topic or orienting sentence coinciding with a paragraph or group of paragraphs in the report. Notice that each level of division in the outline yields at least *two* parts. Outline pages are not numbered, but the first page carries the heading "Outline."

1

Students Under Stress: College Can

Make You Sick

By

Shirley Haley

English 101, Section 1432

Professor Lannon

December 8, 1993

Outline

Thesis: Because of disruptive changes and pressures in
          their personal, social, and academic lives, college
          students are highly vulnerable to the physical
          effects of stress.

I. The Problem: Stress increasingly is recognized as a
   definite cause of physical disorders.

   A. The mechanisms have been studied for years, but
       stress is still making us sick.

   B. Stress has a technical and a personal definition, and
       both are accurate.

   C. More and more of us suffer the physical effects of
       stress.

   D. College students are among the groups most affected.

II. Specific Causes: Stress-induced illness is caused by a
    series of emotional responses that have physical
    consequences.

   A. Stress originates when the body works too hard to
       maintain equilibrium.

       1. If the alarm reaction persists, the body is forever
           ready for action.

       2. Psychosomatic illness is not imaginary.

2

B. A 1967 study showed a connection between the stress of common life events and illness.

C. Even a series of ordinary events in the lives of college students can cause dangerous levels of stress.

D. Various studies of college students confirm the stress-illness link.

III. Possible Solutions: Now that the problem is recognized, solutions are being found.

A. The effect stress has on us depends on how well we cope.

    1. We need both coping strategies and help from others.

    2. Without coping mechanisms, we are almost certain to be overwhelmed.

B. Students need to develop more realistic expectations of college life.

    1. College orientation should be more realistic.

    2. Stress-management courses should be offered by more colleges.

C. Some type of stress-management training should be available to every college student.

3

The Problem: Stress-Induced Illness

Stress can cause physical illness. The mechanisms have been studied for years, but stress is still making us sick.

4

Over 60 years ago, the search began for a link between stress and illness. Walter Cannon identified the "fight or flight" response in 1929. Showing that emotional arousal causes physical reactions such as increased respiration and pulse rate and elevated blood pressure, Cannon laid the groundwork for stress research. In the 1930s Dr. Adolf Mayer, who began using charts of patients' life events to aid

5

his medical diagnoses, recorded "the changes of habit, of school entrances, graduations or changes, or failures; the various jobs . . . and other important events" (Dohrenwend and Dohrenwend 3). And Hans Selye in 1936 described the body's reaction to stress as "the syndrome of just being

6

sick" ("Stress Concept" 72).

Stress has a technical and a personal definition. Technically, stress is a response to life events that disrupt the physical being. In personal terms, stress is part of what happens when a person falls in or out of love, receives good or bad news, drives a car, receives a traffic ticket, takes final

7

exams, or graduates. All life experiences, good and bad, entail stress. In fact, some degree of anxiety is a good motivator--we work better under stress. According to Dr. Kenneth Greenspan, director of the stress lab at New York Presbyterian Hospital, "as with a violin string, there is an optimal note: not all slack

3. *Headings and page numbering:* Haley uses section headings as signals to aid readability and help keep readers on track. This first page of the text is not numbered, but, as we will see, the second page is numbered "2."

4. *Background information:* Haley designs her first paragraph to grab our attention by showing immediately that stress makes us sick. She summarizes a half-century of stress research to emphasize that the whole stress issue is much more than a fad. Brief quotations from authorities lend credibility to Haley's opening sentence.

5. *Using quoted material:* Haley introduces brief quotes by naming the author and by combining the quotations with her own words to make complete sentences. No comma or other punctuation precedes these quotations, because they are phrased as part of Haley's sentences.

6. *Citing sources:* Haley cites each source in parentheses, inside the period, but outside any quotation marks. Because one of the authors cited in the first paragraph has more than one work listed in Haley's "Works Cited" section, Haley is careful to list a shortened version of this work's title when she refers to that author.

7. *Defining the problem:* Observing a principle of all communication, Haley *defines* her subject before going on to discuss it. And she clarifies her definition with concrete examples of stressful situations. Haley is careful to point out that *some* stress can be beneficial, but that too much is destructive. She summarizes this distinction between levels of stress by quoting an authority.

2

--not all taut" (Adler and Gosnell 107). But when stress becomes excessive, it endangers our physical health.

More and more of us suffer physical effects of stress: ulcers and colitis, fatigue and exhaustion, high blood pressure and headache. Stress probably makes us susceptible to infectious disease and cancer by inhibiting our "natural killer (NK) cells." These killer cells help the body fight colds, flu, pneumonia, and other infections, and they destroy malignant cells. In a recent study, young adults who reported highly stressful lives showed decreased NK cell activity and a high rate of infectious illness (Bower 141).

Stress has warning signs, cues to seek help before our bodies actually break down. Among the commonest signs are an overpowering urge to cry or run away, persistent anxiety for no reason, insomnia, and a feeling of being "keyed up." (See Appendix A for other signs.) Overeating and alcohol or drug use are often the result of stress beyond endurance, an attempt to run away (Selye, Stress of Life 175).

Among the groups most exposed to life changes, and thus most affected by stress, are college students. In 1984 counselor Fred B. Newton at Kansas State University tried to develop a general character profile of students, to assess counseling needs. He found major problems to be worry, stress, and anxiety; 76 percent of students surveyed described the college environment as negative or, at best neutral, "a hassle," "a runaround"; and the most important need was for warm, accepting relationships

8.   *Relating the material to the audience:* Readers always want to know what something means to *them personally;* Haley therefore includes a paragraph on the common effects and signs of stress. By helping her audience relate to the material early in the report, Haley stimulates our interest enough to make us want to keep reading.

9.   *Referring to appendices:* Haley refers us to an appendix at report's end for details that we might find useful but that would interrupt the flow of the report itself.

10.   *Thesis paragraphs:* Now that Haley has given us background information on stress in general and sparked our personal interest, she can focus specifically on stress in the lives of college students. Haley designs this paragraph and the next to lead into her thesis (top of page "4").

3

11 (542–43). A 1992 study found that students' main sources of stress were "fear of falling behind, finding the motivation to study, time pressures, financial worries, and concern about academic ability" (Tyrell 185–88). Research also indicates that anxiety about exams, especially in math and physical sciences, is a major stress producer (Everson et al. 5–6).

Students' battles with stress can begin early. Even before graduating high school they worry about being admitted to the college of their choice. Or they feel they have to measure up to parents' achievements and expectations, or keep up with successful brothers or sisters. "Second-rate doesn't rate at all in a majority of the households from which these [students] come--and they know it" (Brooks 613). Transition to college creates more stress as students leave a friendly and familiar environment for one that seems impersonal and demanding, academically and socially (Compas 243). Moreover, today's students struggle with tuition increases, reductions in financial aid, and feelings of hopelessness about finding decent jobs after graduation (Cage 26).

Such disruptive changes and pressures in their personal, social, and academic lives make students vulnerable to the physical effects of stress.

12

Specific Causes of Stress-Induced Illness

Stress originates when the body works too hard to maintain the equilibrium necessary for a healthy life. Any

11. *Citing sources:* Because Haley has mentioned the author's name
     in her paragraph, she merely lists the page numbers in her
     parenthetical citation.

12. *Tracing the causes:* Before Haley covers the disruptive situations
     that cause stress, she spends three paragraphs explaining how the
     body reacts to such situations. This background is essential to our
     understanding of the connection Haley later makes between life
     events and illness.

4

disruption or demand, good or bad, sets off an adjustment that allows the body to regain its equilibrium. When a stimulus sets off this adjustment, when an "alarm reaction" puts the body "on alert," adrenaline prepares the body for action: blood pressure rises to increase blood flow to muscles; digestion temporarily shuts down; blood sugar rises to increase energy; perspiration increases; and other physical changes occur, to prepare the body for "fight or flight" (Selye, "Stress Concept" 76).

If the alarm reaction persists, the body is forever ready for action. That is when stress becomes destructive. We can run away from a speeding car as we cross the street, and when the danger passes, so does the stress. But we can't run away from some inner threat, such as the pressure for good grades. And as the stress endures, our bodies become less able to maintain the equilibrium needed for health.

Psychosomatic illness is not imaginary; it is real disease that can be diagnosed and treated. But the cause of psychosomatic illness is unmanaged stress. Until the stress is controlled, the disease can't be cured. Because of previous illness or heredity, one organ or system (heart, digestive system, skin) in a person's body tends to be most vulnerable. This part of the body is like the weak link in a chain; no matter what pulls the chain, good or bad, the chain breaks (Selye, "Stress Concept" 77).

13. *Interpreting research findings:* This paragraph shows us that
     Haley is *interpreting* her material, not merely giving us a
     collection of findings to sort out for ourselves.

5

14   A connection between the stress of common life events and illness was demonstrated in a 1967 study. First, researchers assigned point values to 43 specific life events (divorce, illness, marriage, job loss). After collecting health histories, the researchers asked their subjects to total the points for recent events in their lives. (The scale ranged from 100 points for the death of a spouse to 11 for a traffic violation--see Appendix B for a full listing.) Comparing the health histories to point totals, the researchers discovered that any group of life events totaling 150 or more points in one year was connected to a major illness (requiring physician's care) for 93 percent of the subjects. And the harmful effects of a high point total lasted as long as two years (Holmes and Masuda 50–56).

15   Even a collection of ordinary events in students' lives can place them in a danger category, as shown in Table 1:

Table 1: A Life-Events Scale for College Students

Event	Point Value
Beginning or ending of school	26
Change in living conditions	25
Revision of personal habits	24
Change in work hours or conditions	20
Change in residence	20
Change in church activities	19
Change in social activities	18
Loan of less than $10,000	17
Change in sleeping habits	16
Change in eating habits	15

Source: Adapted from Holmes and Rahe, Table 3: 216.

The life events in Table 1 alone total 200 points--

14. *Establishing the link:* In this paragraph, Haley describes the major study that demonstrated the stress-illness connection. Here again, she refers us to an appendix for details.

15. *Focusing on college students:* Haley now interprets her general findings in specific relation to college students. This paragraph leads into a detailed discussion of studies done on college students.

16. *Using visuals:* To illustrate her numerical data, Haley decides to use a table. She is careful to number the table, to introduce it, to cite her source, and to interpret the data for her readers. If the table were longer than one text page, she would place it in an appendix (see pages 498–499). Besides tables, other visuals (charts, graphs, diagrams, maps, photos) can provide concrete and vivid illustrations.

6

disregarding any other points students collect from out-of-school experiences.

17   Studies of college students confirm the stress-illness link. John Jemmott analyzed saliva of first-year dental students for an antibody that fights tooth decay and respiratory infections. Students who placed a higher value on close friendship than on success consistently secreted more of this antibody than did students with a drive for power and success—especially during exams (Stark 77). Highly motivated students thus would seem more vulnerable to physical disorders, especially under stress (Taulbee 7).

18   Using a health questionnaire and a life-events scale tailored for college students, other researchers have established a definite connection between "high levels of life change and reported illness" (Kutash and Schlesinger 194). More than half the medical students in one study "experienced major health changes" within two years after entering school. A college life-events scale was given to 54 incoming first-year medical students; those with the highest scores reported most illness before the end of the second year (Holmes and Masuda 64). The stress of starting school can strongly affect one's health.

In a related study, Holmes found a connection between life changes and the number of injuries sustained by 100 college football players. High scores on the life-change survey equaled more injuries on the field. Of the ten players

17. *One topic sentence serving multiple paragraphs:* Haley discusses too many studies here to include in one paragraph. Instead, she breaks up her material into three paragraphs and lets her one topic sentence serve all three.

18. *Citing supplementary sources:* Rather than giving a laundry list of all studies that confirm the stress-illness link, Haley merely states that such information is available, giving us a parenthetical citation so that we can locate the sources if we wish. Instead of listing every item she discovered in her research, Haley is *selective*, giving us only what we need.

7

who had multiple injuries, seven were from the group with highest scores in the life-events survey (Holmes and Masuda 66).

Stress-induced illness can be self-perpetuating. A recent study suggests that stressful events can initiate symptoms that then help create further stressful events: "For example, divorce of one's parents may lead to symptoms of depression [anxiety, insomnia, loss of appetite, hopelessness, etc.], which in turn may lead to disruption of interpersonal relationships and poor performance in school" (Compas 242). Merely treating the symptoms--without confronting the causes--traps many students in this cycle of stress and illness.

Possible Solutions

Because stress is unlikely to disappear, our only solution is to learn to cope. "It is our ability to cope with the demands made by the events in our lives, not the quality or intensity of the events, that counts. What matters is not so much what happens to us, but the way we take it" (Selye, "Stress Concept" 83). And "the way we take it" has a lot to do with heredity, with the coping strategies we've learned, and with the helping resources available to us now.

Stress management requires coping strategies and help from others--what Aaron Antonovsky terms "resistance resources": for instance, the ability to see all alternatives

19. *Transition:* Haley uses a transitional sentence to sum up the causes and to lead into her discussion of solutions, the final major section of her report.

20. *Arriving at solutions:* Notice Haley's line of reasoning throughout this section: from the importance of coping, to specific coping strategies, to students' coping needs, to programs designed to help students cope. The report is clear because Haley's line of thought is clear. She has taken the time to *shape* her material.

8

to a problem, to see ourselves in more than a single role (so
that failure in one role isn't devastating), to recover our
balance quickly and to move on, and our ties to others
(252). "On the simplest level," says Antonovsky, "a person
who has someone who cares for him [or her] is likely to
more adequately resolve tension than one who does not"
(252). The importance of ties to others is confirmed by
Newton's findings that students have a great need for friendship and belonging (543).

Without coping mechanisms, we are likely to be overwhelmed. Richard Lazarus of the University of California at
Berkeley suggests: "coping is the core problem [of stress],"
and George Vaillant of Harvard speculates that "stress does
not kill us so much as ingenious adaptation to stress . . .
facilitates our survival" (Adler and Gosnell 108).

For students, coping depends on realistic expectations
of college life. Newton's study at Kansas State found that
students tend to be unrealistic about their chances of succeeding in college. They suffer from what Levine calls the
Titanic Ethic: "They see doom in the world around them but
still feel they [personally] will somehow survive" (qtd. in
Newton 541). Students are so certain of survival, they make
few plans for coping with anticipated problems; instead they
rely on the hope that problems will take care of themselves
(Newton 540–542).

To help students avoid shattered expectations, college

21.   *Punctuating quotations:* On page 1 of this report, we saw that Haley inserted no punctuation before the quotations she had integrated with her own sentences. When she inserts her own comment, however (as in "says Antonovsky"), within the quotation, she sets the comment off with commas.

   When using an independent clause to introduce a quotation, she precedes the quotation with a colon.

   Following a quotation, commas and periods belong inside the quotation marks. Any other punctuation following a quotation belongs outside the quotation marks—unless it belongs to the quoted material itself (*What did he mean when he said "I'm through"?* or *His response was "I'm through!"*).

22.   *Using brackets in quotations:* To clarify some quotations, Haley inserts a word or phrase in brackets. The brackets are a signal that the writer has altered the original quotation; the bracketed comments are Haley's, not the author's.

23.   *Using ellipses in quotations:* Haley uses ellipses (. . .), here and in the second paragraph of her report, to shorten otherwise long quotations. In fact, no quotation in the report is more than a few lines long. A research report does not merely catalog other people's ideas and words. Instead, writers filter this material, giving it their own concise shape—without, of course, distorting the original information.

   If Haley had used a quotation of more than four typewritten lines, she would have set it off by indenting it ten spaces and typing it double-spaced, without quotation marks.

24.   *Quoting an indirect source:* In her research, Haley came across a key phrase—"the Titanic Ethic"—to characterize college students. But she found this phrase quoted from the original in another source, and this second source gave no page number from the original. Unable to trace the original source, Haley includes the abbreviation "qtd."—for "quoted in"—in the parenthetical citation of her indirect source. As we will see, she includes in "Works Cited" all the bibliographic information available on the original source (that is, Levine).

9

25 orientation should be more realistic. Newton suggests that, besides playing games, registering, testing, and waving good-bye until fall, orientation should include stress-management counseling and a no-nonsense look at all sides of college life (541).

Realistic approaches to college life also must include the effective use of leisure time. A recent study indicates that students who know how to relax through recreational activities (hobbies, sports, exercise groups) report reduced feelings of stress (Mounir and McKinney 7–9).

At least one school has begun offering, for credit, a course in stress management. University of Minnesota counselor John Romano offers "Psychology and the Management of Stress." The course's goal is to "teach students how to implement personal change strategies before emotional and physical crises develop." Focus is on three areas: diet, exercise, and life-style (Romano 533–534). In all three areas, students learn to accept responsibility for changing their lives.

26 College can be especially stressful, a time of massive and profound change. The stress from such change can cause serious illness. Although stress is unavoidable, it can be managed. Stress-management training should be offered to all students, to make them aware of the realities of college life and of their responsibility for their own well-being. Students who do learn to manage stress will be less likely to find that college makes them sick.

25. *Paraphrased and summarized material:* To save space and
improve coherence, Haley paraphrases throughout her report.
Here Haley derived her paraphrase and summary from this
original passage:

> Selective blindness may be a more difficult illness to prevent when the fan-
> tasy vision may seem more pleasant than reality. As a recommendation, to
> shock students into an awareness of reality now may be more beneficial
> than the rude awakening of tomorrow. So far, the best suggestion is to con-
> duct "future shock" and "future cope" workshops that confront students
> with situations and problems that will need to be resolved. Perhaps, orien-
> tation programs should strive to show more of the realities of college life
> rather than the present-day programs of welcoming, testing, registering,
> and saying "I'll see you in the fall."

26. *Conclusion:* Haley's closing suggestions are keyed specifically to
her thesis, thus summarizing and rounding out the discussion and
reemphasizing the major points. Having followed Haley's line of
thought throughout the report, we can readily accept her
conclusions.

10

Appendix A: Warning Signals of Stress

Stress has definite warning signals, emotional and physical.

Here are the commonest:

Emotional Signs of Stress

- being emotionally very "up" or very "down"
- impulsive behavior and emotional instability
- uncontrollable urge to cry or run away
- inability to concentrate
- feelings of unreality
- loss of "joy of life"
- feeling "keyed up"
- being easily startled
- nightmares; insomnia
- a general sense of anxiety or dread

Physical Signs of Stress

- pounding heart (may indicate high blood pressure)
- constantly dry throat and mouth
- weakness; dizziness
- feelings of tiredness
- trembling; nervous tics
- high-pitched, nervous laughter
- grinding of teeth
- constant aimless motion
- excessive perspiring
- diarrhea; indigestion; queasy stomach
- headaches
- pain in neck or lower back (because of muscle tension)
- excessive or lost appetite
- proneness to accidents

Source: Adapted from Selye, The Stress of Life: 175.

27.   *Appendices* (including the one on the next two pages): To expand
items in the report without cluttering the text, Haley includes
two appendices at the end of her text—but before her "Works
Cited" section.

An appendix is a catchall for material that is important but
difficult to integrate into the body of a report. Typical material in
an appendix includes:

- details of an experiment
- specific measurements
- maps
- quotations longer than one page of text
- photographs
- long lists or visuals using more than one full page
- texts of laws, regulations, literary passages, and so on

Haley is careful to use her appendices correctly by including
no needless information or by leaving no vital material out of the
report itself. Readers should not have to turn to appendices to
understand the text of the report. Haley distills the essential facts
from her appendices and includes this distillation in the text of
her report.

Each appendix is labeled clearly, and a separate one is used
for each major item. At appropriate places in her report, Haley
refers us to her appendices for supplementary information: "(See
Appendix A. . .)".

11

Appendix B: Stress Values of Common Life Events

In their 1967 study, Holmes and Rahe ranked life events in

descending order according to their stress value. This table

shows the rating scale.

Social Readjustment Rating Scale

Rank	Life Event	Mean Value
1	Death of spouse	100
2	Divorce	73
3	Marital separation from mate	65
4	Detention in jail or other institution	63
5	Death of a close family member	63
6	Major personal injury or illness	53
7	Marriage	50
8	Being fired at work	47
9	Marital reconciliation with mate	45
10	Retirement from work	45
11	Major change in the health or behavior of a family member	44
12	Pregnancy	40
13	Sexual difficulties	39
14	Getting a new family member (e.g., through birth, adoption, oldster moving in, etc.)	39
15	Major business readjustment (e.g., merger, reorganization, bankruptcy, etc.)	39
16	Major change in financial state (e.g., a lot worse off or a lot better off than usual)	38
17	Death of a close friend	37
18	Changing to a different line of work	36
19	Major change in the number of arguments with spouse (e.g., either a lot more or a lot less than usual regarding child rearing, personal habits, etc.)	35
20	Taking out a mortgage or loan for a major purchase (e.g., for a home, business, etc.)	31
21	Foreclosure on a mortgage or loan	30
22	Major change in responsibilities at work (e.g., promotion, demotion, lateral transfer)	29
23	Son or daughter leaving home (e.g., marriage, attending college, etc.)	29
24	Trouble with in-laws	29

12

Appendix B (Continued)

Rank	Life Event	Mean Value
25	Outstanding personal achievement	28
26	Wife beginning or ceasing work outside the home	26
27	Beginning or ceasing formal schooling	26
28	Major change in living conditions (e.g., building a new home, remodeling, deterioration of home or neighborhood)	25
29	Revision of personal habits (dress, manners, associations, etc.)	24
30	Trouble with the boss	23
31	Major change in working hours or conditions	20
32	Change in residence	20
33	Changing to a new school	20
34	Major change in usual type and/or amount of recreation	19
35	Major change in church activities (e.g., a lot more or a lot less than usual)	19
36	Major change in social activities (e.g., clubs, dancing, movies, visiting, etc.)	18
37	Taking out a mortgage or loan for a lesser purchase (e.g., for a car, TV, freezer, etc.)	17
38	Major change in sleeping habits (a lot more or a lot less sleep, or change in part of day when asleep)	16
39	Major change in number of family get-togethers (e.g., a lot more or a lot less than usual)	15
40	Major change in eating habits (a lot more or a lot less food intake, or very different meal hours or surroundings)	15
41	Vacation	13
42	Christmas	12
43	Minor violations of the law (e.g., traffic tickets, jaywalking, disturbing the peace, etc.)	11

Source: "The Social Readjustment Scale": 216.

13

Works Cited

Adler, Jerry, and Mariana Gosnell. "Stress: How It Can Hurt." Newsweek 21 Apr. 1980: 106–08.

Antonovsky, Aaron. "Conceptual and Methodological Problems in the Study of Resistance Resources and Stressful Life Events." Dohrenwend and Dohrenwend. 245–58.

Bower, Bruce. "Setting the Stage for Infection." Science News 26 Aug. 1989: 141.

Brooks, Andre A. "Educating the Children of Fast-Track Parents." Phi Delta Kappan Apr. 1990: 612-15.

Cage, Mary C. "Students Face Pressures as Never Before, But Counseling Help Has Withered." Chronicle of Higher Education 18 Nov. 1992: A2+.

Compas, Bruce E., et al. "A Prospective Study of Life Events, Social Support, and Psychological Symptomatology During the Transition from High School to College." American Journal of Community Psychology 14 (1986): 241–56.

Dohrenwend, Barbara Snell, and Bruce P. Dohrenwend. "A Brief Historical Introduction to Research on Stressful Life Events." Dohrenwend and Dohrenwend. 1–5.

---, eds. Stressful Life Events. Their Nature and Effects. New York: Wiley, 1974.

Everson, Howard T., et al. "Test Anxiety and the Curriculum: The Subject Matters." Anxiety, Stress, and Coping: An International Journal 6.1 (1993): 1–8.

28. *Works Cited* (including the continuation on the next page): One inch from the top of the page is the centered heading "Works Cited." Two spaces below the heading is the first entry. Each entry is double spaced, with second and subsequent lines indented five spaces from the left margin. Entries are in alphabetical order, with double spacing between them. Each page of the "Works Cited" section follows the numbering of the text pages.

29. An entry for a signed article in a weekly magazine. Article titles appear in quotation marks; book or periodical titles are underlined or italicized. All key words in the title are capitalized. Articles, prepositions, or conjunctions are capitalized only if they come first or last.

30. To cite three works from the same collection, Haley uses the cross-reference "Dohrenwend and Dohrenwend" and the page numbers. Whenever two or more works from the same collection are cited, the only information you need is the editor's name and the page numbers—as long as the main entry itself (with complete information) is somewhere in the "Works Cited" list.

31. A newspaper article. The introductory article ("The") in the newspaper's name is omitted.

32. Multiple works by the same author are listed alphabetically according to their titles. Three hyphens followed by a period denote a second work by the same author.

33. The work compiled by the editors above, and the main entry for the cross-references mentioned in item 30.

34. An entry for a work with three or more authors or editors cites only the first person's name, followed by "et al."

14

Holmes, Thomas H., and Minoru Masuda. "Life Change and
    Illness Susceptibility." Dohrenwend and Dohrenwend.
    45–72.

Holmes, Thomas H., and R. H. Rahe. "The Social
    Readjustment Scale." Journal of Psychosomatic Research
    11 (1967): 213–18.

Kutash, Irwin L., and Louis B. Schlesinger, eds. Handbook on
    Stress and Anxiety. San Francisco: Jossey, 1980.

Levine, A. When Dreams and Heroes Died: A Portrait of
    Today's College Student. San Francisco: Jossey, 1980.

Mounir, Raghet, and Jennifer McKinney. "Campus Recreation
    and Perceived Academic Stress." Journal of College
    Student Development 34.1 (1993): 5–10.

Newton, Fred B., et al. "The Assessment of College Student
    Needs: First Step in a Prevention Response." Personnel
    and Guidance Journal 62 (1984): 537–43.

Romano, John L. "Stress Management and Wellness:
    Reaching Beyond the Counselor's Office." Personnel and
    Guidance Journal 62 (1984): 533–36.

Selye, Hans. "The Stress Concept: Past, Present, and
    Future." Stress Research: Issues for the 80's. Ed. Cary
    L. Cooper. Chichester, England: Wiley, 1983: 69–87.

---. The Stress of Life. Rev. ed. New York: McGraw, 1976.

Stark, Elizabeth. "Stressing Yourself Sick." Psychology Today
    Sep. 1983: 77.

35.   An entry for a scholarly journal.

36.   An entry for a work compiled by editors.

37.   An entry for a book with one author.

38.   A period followed by two spaces separates any citation's three major items: author, title, publication data. Only one space follows a comma or colon.

39.   An entry for an article in a collection of works compiled by an editor.

40.   An entry for a book that is a revised edition. If no edition number or name is given on the title page, the book is cited as a first edition. Otherwise, the edition is identified by number, name, or year, as given on the title page. Publishers' names are shortened (as in "McGraw" for "McGraw-Hill" or "Harper" for "HarperCollins").

41.   Three-letter abbreviations denote months with five or more letters. Volume numbers for magazines are not cited. No punctuation separates magazine title and date.

15

42 "Study Pinpoints Stress-Illness Link." <u>Science News</u> 15 Dec.

1979: 40.

Taulbee, P. "Study Shows Stress Decreases Immunity."

<u>Science News</u> 2 July 1983: 7.

43 Tyrell, Jeanne. "Sources of Stress among Psychology

Undergraduates." <u>Irish Journal of Psychology</u> 13.2

(1992): 184–92.

42.   An entry for an unsigned article in a weekly newsletter.

43.   For page numbers having more than two digits, only the final two
      digits appear in the second number.

22

Composing Business Letters and Memos

In business writing, you share information with readers who will use it for a practical purpose. Readers might use your information to perform a task, answer a question, solve a problem, or make a decision. A business document is designed to give readers the exact information they need for taking specific action.

Uses of Business Writing Skills

In the work world, your value to any organization will depend on how well you communicate what you know. In any field, almost anyone in a responsible position writes daily. Managers write progress reports, personnel evaluations, requisitions, and instructions—among other documents. Computer specialists write documentation explaining to customers how to use software and hardware. Contractors write proposals, bids, and specifications for banks and customers. Engineers and architects plan, on paper, the structure of a project before contracts are awarded and construction begins. In this era of rapidly changing technology, good communication is more than ever crucial.

When you enter the work world, employers first judge your writing by your application letter and résumé. If you join a large organization, your retention and promotion may be decided by executives you have never met. Thus, your letters, memos, and reports will be seen as a measure of the overall quality of your work. As you advance, your ability to communicate may become even more important than your technical background. The higher your goals, the more skill in writing you will need.

Specific Features of Business Writing

Besides having the general features of worthwhile content, sensible organization, and readable style, business writing has several specific features: (1) constant focus on the reader's need for information, (2) efficiency, (3) accuracy, (4) a "you" perspective, and (5) a professional format.

A FOCUS ON THE READERS' INFORMATION NEEDS

Business writing is for readers who will use your information for some purpose. You might write to *define* something—as to insurance customers who want to know what "variable annuity" means. You might write to *describe* something—as to an architectural client who wants to know what a new addition to her home will look like. You might write to *explain* something—as to a stereo technician who wants to know how to eliminate bass flutter in your company's new line of speakers. You might write to *persuade* someone—as to your vice president in charge of marketing who wants to know if it's a good idea to launch an expensive advertising campaign for a new oil additive. Whatever your specific purpose, as a business writer you do not write for yourself, but to inform and persuade others.

Business writing does more than merely record information. Instead of telling readers everything you know, be selective; tailor your message to the specific needs of your readers.

When you write for a specific reader or a small group of readers, you can focus sharply on your audience by asking these questions:

1. Who wants the letter or report? Who else will read it?

2. Why do they want it? How will they use it? What purpose do I want to achieve?

3. What is the technical background of the audience?

4. How much does the audience already know about the subject? What material will have informative value?

5. What exactly does the audience need to know, and in what format (letter, memo)? How much is enough?

6. When is the document due?

The more you can learn about your audience's exact expectations and needs, the more useful you can make your document. In your audience's view, which material will be most important? Be sure to answer this question before you decide what to say.

EFFICIENCY

Professors read to *test* our knowledge; colleagues, customers, and supervisors read to *use* our knowledge. Workplace readers hate waste and expect efficiency. Every sentence and word should carry its own weight, advancing the writer's meaning.

In any system, efficiency is the ratio of useful output to input. For the product that comes out, how much energy goes in?

In an efficient system, the output nearly equals the input.

Similarly, a document's efficiency can be measured by how hard readers work to understand the message. Is the product worth the reader's effort?

No reader should have to spend ten minutes deciphering a message worth only five minutes. Consider, for example, this wordy message:

> We are in receipt of your recent correspondence indicating your interest in the position listed below. Your correspondence has been duly forwarded to the office with candidate selection responsibility for consideration. You may expect to hear from the aforementioned office relative to your application as the selection process progresses.

Inefficient messages drain the readers' energy; they are too easily misinterpreted; they waste time and money. Notice how hard we had to work with the message above to extract information that could be expressed this efficiently:

> We have received your application for the position listed below and have forwarded it to the office that will select candidates. At each stage in selection, we will inform you of the status of your application.

Never make readers work needlessly.

Here are some of the most frequent errors that cause a document to be inefficient:

- more (or less) information than readers need
- irrelevant or uninterpreted information
- confusing organization
- more words than readers need
- fancier or less precise words than are needed
- uninviting appearance or confusing layout

Inefficient documents are produced by writers who lack a clear sense of purpose, audience, meaning, organization, or style. In style matters, we *think* in plain English, but we sometimes forget to *write* that way. We might say to ourselves:

> I want a better job.

but instead we might write:

> I desire to upgrade my employment status.

Whatever their cause, inefficient documents make readers work too hard.

ACCURACY

Because readers use business writing to make decisions and take action, accuracy is vital. Names, dates, places, costs, and measurements have to be spelled out and exact.

A business letter can be considered a contract; therefore, if you write to a customer with an offer of a service or product at a specified cost, you are making a legal commitment. Be sure to tell customers exactly what they will and will not get for their money. Notice how, in Figure 22.1, the writer provides exact specifications and figures—and spells out exceptions to the repairs outlined in the estimate.

Business writing should convey only *one* meaning and should allow only *one* interpretation insofar as possible.

A "YOU" PERSPECTIVE

In speaking face to face, you automatically adjust your delivery as you observe the listener's reactions: a smile, a frown, a raised eyebrow, a nod. Even in a phone conversation, a listener can signal approval, anger, and so on. In writing, however, you can easily forget that a flesh-and-blood person will be reacting to what you are saying—or seem to be saying.

The "you" perspective is an element of effective tone; by careful word choice, you show your readers respect—you create genuine contact. Put yourself in their place; consider how readers will react to what you've written.

Business writing should create a relationship that encourages readers to be on your side. Try to be sensitive to the reader's position. Show some empathy by letting readers know you understand their way of seeing. Assume, for instance, that your tuition is due but your college loan is late. You write to ask the registrar for an extension. Which of these two closing paragraphs is more likely to get the reader on your side?

> (a) It is imperative that I receive this extension of my tuition due date. I appreciate your cooperation.

> (b) May I have this brief extension of my tuition due date, without causing too much inconvenience? Your patience in this difficult time would be a great help.

The second version displays a "you" perspective; it focuses on the reader instead of the writer.

Even one carelessly chosen word can offend readers. In a letter complaining about the monitor on your new computer, you have the choice of saying, "Although the amber screen causes very little eyestrain, the character resolution is not sharp enough for lengthy word-processing use" or "The monitor is lousy for word processing." Clearly, "lousy" is a poor choice here because of the implied insult to the manufacturer or dealer and fails to describe the problem (i.e., poor resolution).

Put yourself in the reader's place as you consider these examples. Imagine you are an employer screening applicants for a position with

LEVERETT LAND & TIMBER COMPANY, INC.   creative land use
                                        quality building materials
                                        architectural construction

January 17, 19XX

Mr. Thomas E. Muffin
Clearwater Drive
Amherst, Massachusetts 01002

Dear Mr. Muffin:

I have examined the damage to your home caused by the ruptured
water pipe and consider the following repairs to be necessary and of
immediate concern:

> Exterior:
> Remove plywood soffit panels beneath overhangs
> Replace damaged insulation and plumbing
> Remove all built-up ice within floor framing
> Replace plywood panels and finish as required
>
> Northeast Bedroom--Lower Level:
> Remove and replace all sheetrock, including closet
> Remove and replace all door casings and baseboards
> Remove and repair windowsill extensions and moldings
> Remove and reinstall electric heaters
> Respray ceilings and repaint all surfaces

This appraisal of damage repair does not include repairs and/or
replacements of carpets, tile work, or vinyl flooring. Also, this
appraisal assumes that the plywood subflooring on the main level has
not been severely damaged.

Leverett Land & Timber Company, Inc. proposes to furnish the
necessary materials and labor to perform the described damage
repairs for the amount of four thousand one hundred and eighty
dollars ($4,180).

Sincerely,

J.A. Jackson

Gerald A. Jackson
President

GAJ/cb

Figure 22.1 A Letter-as-Contract

your company. Which of these opening would you find appealing? Which applicants seem most *likable?*

> (a) I recently read of your opening for a field geologist. One of my professors, Dr. R. D. Loner, worked for you and claims that your company was beneficial to her career. My taking the position would be a great opportunity to advance my career in geology. *(The tone here is self-serving; an employment letter should emphasize what the applicant can offer—not vice versa.)*

> (b) I am applying for a position as a computer clerk. Most of my programming experience has been with PASCAL. I have experience programming in a variety of languages. I was referred to you by Chris Mather, who works as a computer clerk in your firm. His interest and enthusiasm encouraged me to write. *(The Dick-and-Jane sentence structure and diction, along with a nonexistent "you" perspective, add up to a dreary tone here.)*

> (c) While attending Eastern University, I have followed closely your company's financial statements and have become highly interested in your sales growth. Therefore, when Roberta Lowny, Vice President of Sales for Bando Sportswear, told me of an opening in your fabric sales division, I decided to write immediately. *(This writer shows genuine interest in—and knowledge about—the company, focusing on the reader, not on himself.)*

> (d) Does your company have a summer position for a student determined to become a technical writer? If so, I think you will find me qualified. *(Here again, the focus is on the company, with a confident but diplomatic tone that seems forceful but likable.)*

Here are some closings from employment letters. Which ones seem written by a person you would want to meet?

> (a) I would like to arrange an interview to discuss this position. Please phone me at your convenience. *(This sounds like a military order—a faceless writer telling a faceless reader what to do.)*

> (b) I would like an interview as soon as possible. *(Being bossy with a prospective boss is no way to create a likable tone.)*

> (c) I hope you agree that I am the type of engineer DGH is seeking. Please allow me to further discuss career opportunities with you. *(This closing is confident yet diplomatic, focusing on the company's needs and moving the reader to action.)*

> (d) Hardworking, efficient, and eager to learn, I am anxious to apply my skills. Please consider me for a summer position. *(The "you"*

perspective clearly is implied by the writer's summation of what she can offer the reader.)

Readers are much more likely to side with you if they *like* you—if they feel as if they *matter*.

One way to destroy a "you" perspective and alienate readers is by inflating words (see pages 199–201) and using a category of trite expressions called *letterese:* overblown phrases some writers think they need to appear important. Here are a few of the clichés that invade letters, memos, and reports, creating artifical distance between writer and reader.

Letterese	Translation into plain English
As per your request	As you requested
I am cognizant of the fact.	I know.
I beg to differ.	I disagree.
This writer	I
At the present time	Now
In the immediate future	Soon
Due to the fact that	Because
I wish to express my gratitude.	Thank you.
At this point in time	Now

Letterese denies contact. Write as you would *speak* in a classroom.

A PROFESSIONAL FORMAT

Readers first react to the *appearance* of a document; they expect a professional format. Simply stated, format is the arrangement of words on the page: indention; margins; line spacing; typeface; and standard letter, memo, or report form. What your document looks like and how it is arranged may be just as important as what it says. A professional format helps you look good and invites the reader's attention.

Use high-quality (20-lb. bond, $8\frac{1}{2} \times 11$-inch) white paper with a minimum fiber content of 25 percent. Type neatly, avoid erasures, and make sure you have clean typewriter keys and a fresh ribbon. If you write on a word processor, avoid using a dot-matrix printer for your final draft; instead, use a letter-quality printer or retype on a good typewriter.

In addition to these general requirements, letters and memoranda have specific format requirements, discussed later.

Business Letters

The general purpose of any business letter is to create goodwill toward the writer and the company. Here is a sampling of the kinds of letters you can expect to write routinely:

- sales letters designed to create interest in a product or service

- letters of instruction outlining a procedure to be carried out by the reader

- letters of recommendation for friends, fellow workers, or past employees.

- letters of transmittal to accompany mailed reports and other documents

- letters to inquire about a product, procedure, or person

- letters to complain about service or products and to request adjustment

- letters to apply for jobs

You may also write responses to letters received by your company.

A full discussion of letters would more than fill a textbook. In this chapter, therefore, we cover only three common types of letters: the inquiry letter, the complaint letter, and the letter of application, along with its accompanying résumé.

Unless readers request otherwise, your letter should conform to specific format requirements. Use uniform margins, spacing, and indention: frame your letter with a $2^1/_2$-inch top margin and side and bottom margins of 1 to $1^1/_4$ inches; single space within paragraphs and double space between; avoid hyphenating at the end of a line.

If your letter takes up more than one page, begin each additional page seven spaces from the top, with a line identifying the addressee, the date, and the page number:

Marcia James, June 25, 1994, p. 2

Begin your text two spaces below this line. Place at least two lines of your paragraph at the bottom of page 1 and at least two lines of your final text on page 2.

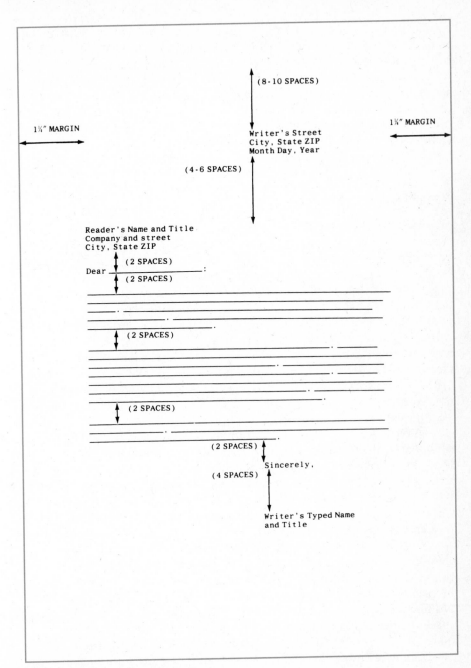

Figure 22.2 A Semiblock Letter Form

Your $9^1/_2$-by-$4^1/_8$-inch envelope should be of the same quality as the stationery. Center your reader's address, single-spaced. Use only accepted abbreviations. Place your own single-spaced address in the upper left corner.

Also, use an accepted letter form. Although several letter forms are acceptable, and your company may have its own, we discuss one common form: semiblock, with no indentions, as shown in Figure 22.2. The line spacing from page top to writer's address, and then to reader's address, is variable. Depending on length, adjust this upper spacing so the letter appears centered on the page. All *other* spacing is fixed.

INQUIRY LETTERS

Inquiry letters may be solicited or unsolicited. You often write the first type as a consumer requesting information about an advertised product. Such letters are welcomed because the reader stands to benefit. You can be brief: "Please send me your brochure on . . . ," for example.

Other inquiries will be unsolicited; that is, not in response to an ad, but requesting information for a report or project. Here, you are asking your reader to spend time reading your letter, considering your request, collecting the information, and writing a response. Always apologize for any imposition, express appreciation, and state a reasonable request clearly and briefly (long, involved inquiries are likely to go unanswered).

In order to ask specific questions, do your homework. Don't expect the respondent to read your mind. A general question ("Please send me all your data on . . . ") is likely to be ignored.

A typical inquiry situation: You are preparing a research report on the feasibility of harnessing solar energy for home heating in northern climates. You learn that a nonprofit research group has been experimenting in energy systems. After deciding to write for details, you plan and compose your inquiry.

In your introduction, tell the reader who you are and why you want information. Maintain the "you" perspective with an opening statement that sparks interest and goodwill.

In the body of your letter, write specific and clearly worded questions that are easy to understand and answer. If you have several questions, arrange them in a list. (Lists help readers organize their answers, increasing your chances of getting all the information you want.) Number each question, and separate it from the others, perhaps leaving space for responses right on the page. If you have more than five or six questions, consider placing them in an attached questionnaire.

Conclude by explaining how you plan to use the information and, if possible, how your reader might benefit. If you have not done so earlier, specify a date by which you need a response. Offer to send a copy of your finished report. Close with a statement of appreciation. Include a stamped, self-addressed envelope.

Your letter might look like the one below.

234 Western Road
Arlington, VT 05620
March 10, 19xx

Director of Energy Systems
The Earth Research Institute
Petersham, ME 04619

Dear Director:

As a student at Evergreen College, I am preparing a report (April 15 deadline) on the feasibility of solar energy as a viable source of home heating in northern climates.

While gathering data on home solar heating, I encountered references (in *Scientific American* and elsewhere) to your group's pioneering work. Would you please allow me to benefit from your experience? I specifically would appreciate answers to these four questions:

1. At this stage of development, have you found active or passive solar heating more practical?

2. Do you hope to surpass the 60 percent limit of heating needs supplied by the active system? If so, what level of efficiency do you expect to achieve, and how soon?

3. What is the estimated cost of building materials for your active system, per cubic foot of living space?

4. What metal do you use in collectors to obtain the highest thermal conductivity at the lowest maintenance costs?

Your answers, along with any recent findings you can share, will enrich a learning experience I will put into practice next summer by building my own solar home. I would be glad to send you a copy of my report, along with the house plans I have designed. Thank you.

Sincerely yours,

Leslie Greene

Leslie Greene

COMPLAINT LETTERS

A complaint letter requests an adjustment for defective goods or poor services, or it complains about unfair treatment, or the like. You would be mistaken to begin a complaint letter with the intention of telling someone off. Everyone likes to sound off now and then, but your real purpose is to achieve a desired result: a refund, a replacement, improved service, better business relations, or even an apology. Most businesses will grant all reasonable claims; they do so to retain customers' goodwill.

Imagine that you are in this situation: Recently you bought an expensive stereo, with top-of-the-line speakers, from a franchised dealer in New Jersey. Three weeks after your purchase you moved to Wisconsin, and five weeks later you noticed distortion of heavy bass sounds in your speakers. The problem is that your guarantee requires that you return the equipment to the store where it was purchased. You decide to write to the store, requesting they arrange for a local franchised dealer to repair or replace your speakers.

First, identify your reason for writing. Maintain the "you" perspective by stating your claim *objectively*. Include enough information for a fair evaluation.

In the body section, explain and support your claim. (If you were writing to a jeweler, you would explain that your new wristwatch gains an hour a day, instead of merely saying it's defective.) Identify the faulty item clearly, giving serial and model numbers. Describe the deficiency, and explain how it has caused you inconvenience, expense, loss of time, and so on. Propose what you consider a fair adjustment, phrasing your statement so that the reader will feel inclined to honor your request. Be absolutely clear about whether you desire a replacement, a refund, or something else.

Conclude by requesting a specific action. Indicate your goodwill and confidence in the reader's integrity. Thanking the reader in advance would be inappropriate, but once your claim has been resolved, you might write a thank-you note.

Here is how your letter to the stereo dealer might read:

> 534 Hartford Way
> Madison, WI 20967
> March 20, 19xx

Stereo Components, Inc.
143 Main Street
Newark, NJ 10311

ATTENTION: Service Department

SUBJECT: Bass Distortion in Toneway Speakers

Given your excellent reputation, I'm sure you will do everything possible to help me with a perplexing service problem.

On December 10, 19xx, I bought a component system (sales receipt #114621) from your outlet. Three weeks later, I moved to Wisconsin, and after eight weeks of using the system, I noticed distortion in heavy bass sounds in my speakers.

As a classical music fan, I bought your best speakers (Toneway 305's, #3624 and 3625) because of their extra-wide bass range. Their distortion of lower ranges of percussion and keyboard sounds, however, is increasing to the point of actual vibration, making my expensive system useless.

My speaker guarantee states that items for repair or replacement must be returned to the *original* retailer. But because we are now hundreds of miles apart, that arrangement would cost me considerable time and money—and further delay my use of the stereo. Under these circumstances, could you please arrange for a franchised dealer in the Madison area to honor my guarantee directly?

Yours truly,

Raymond Fields

Instead of the standard salutation ("Dear _____:"), the previous letter has an attention line and a subject line. Use an attention line when writing to an organization and when you want a specific person (whose name you don't know), title, or department to receive your letter. The subject line forecasts what your letter is about and is a good device for getting a busy reader's attention.

Sometimes we have to complain about *issues* rather than products or services. The following letter (with addresses and signature not shown) complains about a political decision.

Dear Governor King:

I protest your support of the sale of oil leases on the Georges Bank fishing grounds. As a registered voter of the Commonwealth and a resident of a coastal town, I am convinced that such oil leases would violate the interests of Massachusetts and New England citizens.

In 1988, New Bedford *[a nearby city]* was second in the nation in dollar value of seafood landed. Much of this catch was made up of such prized species as scallops, cod, haddock, flounder, and lobster. This revenue supported much of the local population in fishing and related jobs, such as fish processing and ship repair. Similar situations exist in many of our coastal communities, including Gloucester, Boston, and Provincetown. An industry with this much impact on the state cannot be ignored.

Offshore oil rigs certainly will affect the area's ecology. Sediment, garbage, and oil produced by normal operations on an oil platform will pollute the area surrounding the rigs—an area very close to the scallop and flounder grounds of Georges Bank.

Given the circular water current on the bank, a major blowout or oil spill would not be carried out to sea, but would concentrate on the fishing grounds, thus destroying one of the world's great seafood resources.

The possibility of such a disaster greatly outweighs the benefits from any oil found on the fishing grounds. I therefore ask, in the best interest of the Commonwealth, that you withdraw your support for offshore drilling and join the citizens who are fighting to prevent it.

Notice how this writer spells out the complaint, forcefully but diplomatically encouraging the reader to change his position.

RÉSUMÉS AND JOB APPLICATIONS

In the job market, many applicants compete for few openings. Whether you are applying for an attractive summer job, an internship, or your first professional job, or are changing careers in midlife, you have to wage an effective campaign to market yourself. Your résumé and application letter *must* stand out among those of other applicants.

The Résumé   The résumé summarizes your experience and qualifications. Written before your application letter, it provides background information to support your letter. In turn, the letter will emphasize specific parts of your résumé and will discuss how your background is suited to that job. The résumé gets you the interview, not the job.

Employers generally spend less than 60 seconds scanning a résumé. They look for an obvious and persuasive answer to this question: *What can you do for us?* An employer expects a résumé

1. to look good (conservative and tasteful, on high-quality paper)

2. to read easily (headings, typeface, spacing, and punctuation that provide clear orientation)

3. to provide information the employer needs for making an interviewing decision

Employers generally discard résumés that are mechanically flawed, cluttered, sketchy, or hard to follow. Don't leave readers guessing or annoyed; make your résumé perfect.

Organize your information within these categories:

- name, address, and phone number
- career objectives
- educational background
- work experience
- personal data
- interests, activities, awards, and skills
- references

Select and organize material to emphasize what you can offer. Don't just list *everything*; be selective. (We're talking about *communicating* instead of merely delivering information.) Don't abbreviate, because some readers may not know the referent. Use punctuation to clarify and emphasize, not to be "artsy" or "unique." Try to limit your résumé to a single page, as most employers prefer.*

Begin preparing your résumé at least one month before your job search. You will need that much time to do a first-class job. Your final version can be duplicated for various targets (but each application letter has to be freshly typed or printed).

NAME, ADDRESS, AND PHONE NUMBER

At page top list your full name, mailing address, and phone number (many interview invitations and job offers are made by phone). If your school and summer address differ, include both, indicating dates on which you can be reached at each.

CAREER OBJECTIVES

Have a clear idea of the *specific* jobs for which you *realistically* qualify. Resist the impulse to be all things to all people. The key to a successful résumé is the image of *you* it projects—disciplined and purposeful, yet flexible. State your specific job and career goals:†

> Intensive care nursing in a teaching hospital, with the eventual goal of supervising and instructing.

Do not borrow a trite or long-winded statement from some placement brochure.

---

* Of course, if you are changing jobs or careers, or if your résumé looks cramped, you might need a second page.

† To save space, you can omit your statement of career objectives from the résumé and include it in your letter instead.

EDUCATIONAL BACKGROUND

If your education is more impressive than your work experience, place it first. Begin with your most recent school and work backward, listing degrees, diplomas, and schools *beyond* high school (unless prestige, program, or your achievement warrants its inclusion). List the courses that have directly prepared you for the job you seek. Include any schools attended or courses completed while you were in military service. If you finance part or all of your education by working, say so, indicating the percentage of your contribution.

WORK EXPERIENCE

If you have solid work experience, place it before your education. Beginning with your most recent job and working backward, list and clearly identify each job, giving dates and names of employers. Tell whether the job was full-time, part-time (hours weekly), or seasonal. Tell exactly what you did in each job, indicating promotions. If the job was major (and related to this one), describe it in detail; otherwise, describe it briefly. Include any military experience. If you have no real work experience, show you have potential by emphasizing your preparation and by writing an enthusiastic letter.

Do not use complete sentences in your job descriptions; they take up room best left for other items. But do use action verbs throughout (**supervised, developed, built, taught, opened, managed, trained, solved, planned, directed,** and so on). Such verbs emphasize your vitality and help you stand out.

PERSONAL DATA

An employer cannot legally discriminate on the basis of sex, age, race, color, religion, national origin, physical features, or marital status. Therefore, you aren't required to provide this information or a photograph. But if you believe that any of this information could advance your prospects, by all means include it.

INTERESTS, ACTIVITIES, AWARDS, AND SKILLS

List hobbies, sports, and other pastimes; memberships in teams and organizations; offices held; and any recognition for outstanding performance. Include dates and types of volunteer work. Employers know that persons who seek well-rounded lives are likely to take an active interest in their jobs. Be selective in this section. List only items that show the qualities employers seek.

REFERENCES

Your list of references names four or five persons *who have agreed* to write strong, positive assessments. Often a reference letter is the key to getting an employer to want to meet you; choose your references carefully.

Select references who can speak with authority about your ability and character. Avoid members of your family and close friends not in your field. Choose instead among professors, previous employers, and community figures who know you well enough to write concretely on your behalf.

Ask each reference for only one letter, with no salutation, to be sent to the placement office for your placement dossier. Your dossier is a folder containing your credentials: college transcript, letters of recommendation, and any other items (such as a notice of a scholarship award or letter of commendation) that document your achievements. In your letter and résumé, you talk about yourself; in your dossier, others talk about you. An employer impressed by what you say about yourself will want to read what others think and will request a copy of your dossier. By collecting recommendations in one folder, you spare your references from writing the same letter over and over.

Visit your placement office to inquire about setting up a dossier (or placement folder).

Opinion is divided about whether names and addresses of references belong in a résumé. If saving space is important, simply state "References available on request," keeping your résumé only one page long. But if your résumé already takes up more than one page, you probably should include names and addresses of references. (An employer might recognize a name, and thus notice *your* name among the crowd of applicants.) If you are changing careers, a full listing of references is especially important.

Composing the Résumé   With data collected and references lined up, you are ready to compose your actual résumé. Imagine you are a 23-year-old student at a community college, working on an A.A. degree in Hotel and Restaurant Management. Before college, you worked at related jobs for more than three years. You now seek a summer position with a resort. You have spent two weeks compiling information for your résumé and obtaining commitments from four references. Figure 22.3 shows your résumé. Notice that this résumé mentions nothing about salary. Wait until this matter comes up in your interview, or later.

When fully satisfied with your résumé, consider having your model typeset or laser printed. This one prototype, in turn, will yield as many copies as you need. For neat copies, use a photocopying machine, laser printing, or offset printing; *never* send out carbon, Thermofax, or mimeographed copies.

James David Purdy

203 Elmwood Avenue
San Jose, California 90462
Tel.: (214) 316-2419

Professional Objective Customer relations for a hospitality chain, eventually leading to market management responsibilities.

Education 1990-1993 San Jose City College, San Jose, California
Associate of Arts degree in Hotel/Restaurant Management, expected June 1993. Grade point average: 3.25 of a possible 4.00. All college expenses financed by scholarship and part-time job (20 hours weekly).

Employment

1990-1993 Peek-a-Boo Lodge, San Jose, California
Began as a desk clerk and am now desk manager (part-time) of this 200-unit resort. Responsible for scheduling custodial and room service staff, convention planning, and customer relations.

1988-1990 Teo's Restaurant, Pensacola, Florida
Began as waiter, advanced to cashier, and finally to assistant manager. Responsible for weekly payroll, banquet arrangements, and supervising dining-room and lounge staff.

1987-1988 Encyclopaedia Britannica, Inc., San Jose, California
Sales representative (part-time). Received top bonus twice.

1986-1987 White's Family Inn, San Luis Obispo, California
Worked as busboy, then waiter (part-time).

Personal Awards
Captain of basketball team; Lion's Club Scholarship.

Special Skills
Speak French fluently; expert skier.

Activities
High school basketball and track teams (3 years); college student senate (2 years); Innkeepers' Club—prepared and served monthly dinners at the college (2 years).

Interests
Skiing, cooking, sailing, oil painting, and backpacking.

References Placement Office, San Jose City College, San Jose, CA 94062

Figure 22.3 A Résumé for a Summer Job

Now, with your résumé prepared, you are ready to plan and compose the application letter.

The Application Letter   Although it elaborates on your résumé, your application letter must emphasize your personal qualities and qualifications convincingly. Your résumé presents raw facts; your application letter relates these facts to the company to which you are applying. The tone and insight you bring to your discussion suggest a good deal about who you are. The letter is your chance to explain how you see yourself fitting into the organization. Your purpose is to interpret your résumé and show an employer how valuable you will be. Your letter's immediate purpose is to secure an interview.

Never send a photocopied letter. You can base different letters to different employers on one model—with appropriate changes—but prepare each letter fresh.

Sometimes you will apply for jobs advertised in print or by word of mouth (solicited applications). At other times you will write "prospecting" letters to organizations that have not advertised but might need someone like you (unsolicited applications). Either letter should be tailored to the situation.

THE SOLICITED LETTER

Imagine you are James Purdy (whose résumé appears on page 525). In *Innkeeper's Monthly*, you read this advertisement and decide to apply:

Resort Management Openings

Liberty International, Inc., is accepting applications for summer management positions at our new Lake Geneva Resort. Applicants must have three years' practical experience, along with formal training in hotel/restaurant management. Please apply by June 1, 1993, to:

Elizabeth Borden
Personnel Director
Liberty International, Inc.
Lansdowne, Pennsylvania 24135

Now plan and compose your letter.

Introduction. Create a confident tone by directly stating your reason for writing. Name the exact job, and remember you are talking *to* someone; use the pronoun "you" instead of awkward or impersonal constructions such as "One can see from the enclosed résumé." If you can, establish a connection by mentioning a mutual acquaintance—but only with that person's permission. Finally, after referring to your enclosed résumé, discuss your qualifications.

Body. Concentrate on the experience, skills, and aptitudes you can bring to *this job*. Don't come across as a jack-of-all-trades. Avoid flattery ("I am greatly impressed by your remarkable company"). Be specific. Replace "much experience," "many courses," or "increased sales" with "three years of experience," "five courses," or "a 35 percent increase in sales between June and October 1991." Support your claims with *evidence* and show how your qualifications will benefit this employer.

Instead of writing "I have leadership skills," write "I was student senate president during my senior year and captain of the lacrosse team." Create a dynamic tone by using *active* voice and action verbs:

Weak	Increased responsibilities were steadily given me.
Stronger	I steadily assumed increasing responsibilities.

Trim the fat from your sentences:

Flabby	I have always been a person who enjoys a challenge.
Lean	I enjoy a challenge.

Express self-confidence:

Unsure	It is my opinion that I will be a successful manager because . . . .
Confident	I will be a successful manager because . . . .

Never be vague:

Vague	I am familiar with the 1022 interactive database management system and RUNOFF, the text-processing system.
Definite	As a lab grader for one semester, I kept grading records on the 1022 database management system and composed lab procedures on the RUNOFF text-processing system.

Also, avoid "letterese." Write in plain English, and remember that an enthusiastic tone can go a long way. Your attitude can be as important as your background, in some instances.

Conclusion. Restate your interest and emphasize your willingness to retrain or relocate (if necessary). If your reader is nearby, request an interview; otherwise, request a phone call, stating times you can be reached. Leave your reader with the impression you are worth knowing.

Revision. Never settle for a first draft—or a second or third! This letter is your model for letters serving in varied circumstances. Make it perfect.

After several revisions, James Purdy finally signed the letter shown in Figure 22.4.

Purdy wisely emphasized practical experience because his background is varied and impressive. An applicant with less experience would emphasize education instead, discussing courses and activities.

THE UNSOLICITED LETTER

Ambitious job seekers do not limit their search to advertised openings. The unsolicited, or "prospecting," letter is a good way to uncover possibilities beyond the Help Wanted section.

Because your unsolicited letter is unexpected, attract attention immediately. Don't begin: "I am writing to inquire about the possibility of obtaining a position with your company." By now, your reader is asleep. If you can't establish a connection through a mutual acquaintance, use a forceful opening:

> Does your resort have a place for a summer manager with college work in hospitality management, proven commitment to quality service, and customer-relations experience that extends far beyond mere textbook learning? If so, please consider my application.

Employers will regard the quality of your application as an indication of the quality of work you will do. Businesses spend much money and time projecting favorable images. The image you project, in turn, must meet their standards.

Business Memorandum Reports

In the workplace, decision makers rely on short reports, usually in the form of memoranda, as a basis for *informed* decisions on matters as diverse as the most comfortable office chairs to buy or the best recruit to hire for management training.

People on the job must communicate rapidly and precisely. Here are some of the kinds of memorandum reports you might write on any workday:

- a request for assistance on a project
- a requisition for parts and equipment

203 Elmwood Avenue
San Jose, California 90462
April 22, 1993

Ms. Elizabeth Borden
Personnel Director
Liberty International, Inc.
Lansdowne, Pennsylvania 24135

Dear Ms. Borden:

Please consider my application for a summer management position
at your Lake Geneva resort. I will graduate from San Jose City
College in June with an Associate of Arts degree in Hotel/
Restaurant Management. Dr H. V. Garlid, my nutrition professor,
has described her experience as a consultant for Liberty
International and encouraged me to apply.

For two years I worked as a part-time desk clerk and I am now the
desk manager at a 200-unit resort. This experience, along with
customer relations work described in my resume, has given me a
clear and practical understanding of customers' needs and expectations. As an amateur chef, I know of the effort, attention, and
patience required to prepare fine food. Also, my skiing and sailing
background might be useful in your recreation program.

I have confidence in my hospitality management skills. My
experience and education have prepared me to work well with
others and to respond creatively to changes, crises, and added
responsibilities.

If my background meets your needs, please phone me any weekday
after 4 p.m. at (214) 316-2419.

Yours truly,

James David Purdy

James David Purdy

Figure 22.4 An Application Letter

- a proposal for a new project
- a set of instructions
- a cost estimate for materials and labor on a new project
- a report of your progress on a specific assignment
- an hourly or daily account of your work activities
- a report of your inspection of a site, item, or process
- a record of a meeting

The major form of written communication in organizations, memos leave a "paper trail" of directives, inquiries, instructions, requests, recommendations, and so on. Whereas letters go outside the organization, memos remain inside.

The standard memo has a heading that names the organization and identifies the sender, recipient, subject (often in caps or underlined for emphasis), and date. (Placement of these items may differ among firms.) Other memo elements are shown in Figure 22.5.

Memo reports cover every conceivable topic. The two broad types are informational reports and recommendation reports.

INFORMATIONAL REPORTS

Informational reports supply knowledge about products, services, operations, or anything about which readers need to be informed.

In your own field, you may be asked to report, say, research findings comparing the cost or quality of similar products. These findings may lead to contracts with certain suppliers. The informational report in Figure 22.6 shows how data in memo form can serve as a basis for decision making. Notice that the writer *interprets* her information for the reader. Unless your reader requests otherwise, provide an interpretation of your findings.

RECOMMENDATION REPORTS

Recommendation reports interpret data, draw conclusions, and make recommendations, often in response to a specific reader request. When the report is *solicited* (requested by the reader), make your recommendation at the very beginning; then justify it.

Here is a typical situation in which a solicited report serves as a basis for action: Mary Noll, a biology major, works part-time as a lab technician for an environmental testing company. Customers have recently complained about waiting too long for results of tests they've ordered. During a staff meeting, Mary comments that one of the com-

NAME OF ORGANIZATION

MEMORANDUM
Date: (also serves as a chronological record for future reference)
To: Name and title (the title also serves as a record for reference)
From: Your name and title (your initials for verification)
Subject: GUIDELINES FOR FORMATTING MEMOS

Subject Line
Announce the memo's purpose and contents on the subject line, to orient
readers to the subject and help them gauge its importance.

Introductory Paragraph
Unless you have a reason for being indirect, state your main point
immediately.

Topic Headings
When discussing multiple subtopics, include headings (as we do here).
Headings help you organize and they help readers locate information
quickly.

Paragraph Spacing
Do not indent the first line of paragraphs. Single space within
paragraphs and double space between them.

Second-page Notation
When the memo exceeds one page, begin the second and subsequent
pages with the recipient's name, date, and page number. For example:
Ms. Baxter, June 12, 19XX, page 2. Place this information three lines
from the page top and begin your text three lines below.

Memo Verification
Do not sign your memos. Initial the "From" line, after your name.

Copy Notation
When sending copies to people not listed on the "To" line, include a copy
notation two spaces below the last line, and list, by rank, the names and
titles of those receiving copies. For example,

Copies: J. Spring, V.P., Production
           H. Baxter, General Manager, Production

Figure 22.5 Standard Memo Format

CALVIN COLLEGE

MEMORANDUM

DATE: February, 15, 19XX

TO: Professor Smith
            Writing Instructor

FROM: Susan Grimes, Student

SUBJECT: CONSUMER SURVEY OF COMPARATIVE RETAIL PRICES
            FOR DILANTIN TABLETS

I surveyed comparative prices for a Dilantin prescription by calling six local pharmacies.

SIX LOCAL PHARMACIES CLASSIFIED IN DESCENDING
ORDER OF THEIR RETAIL PRICE FOR DILANTIN

Pharmacy	Price/100 tablets
Hargrove Pharmacy, Harwich	$4.14
Cascade Village Pharmacy, Hyannis	4.14
Murphy's Rexall, Sandwich	4.10
Apothecary, Dennis Village	3.89
Consumer's Pharmacy, Harwich	2.79
Dunn's Pharmacy, Hyannis	2.19

These data are important to me because I must take Dilantin every day. The 100 tablets last only about one month and the expense of this medicine quickly adds up. The data indicate that my best choice for future Dilantin purchases is Dunn's Pharmacy in Hyannis.

Figure 22.6 An Informational Report in Memo Form

TO: Don Spring, Personnel Director   April 18, 19XX

FROM: Mary Noll, Biology Division

ABOUT: The Need to Hire Additional Personnel

Introduction and Recommendation

With 26 active employees, GBI has been unable to keep up with scheduled contracts. As a result, we have a contract backlog of roughly $500,000. This backlog is caused by understaffing in the biology and chemistry divisions.

To increase production and ease the workload, I recommend that GBI hire three general laboratory assistants.

The lab assistants would clean glassware and general equipment; feed and monitor the fish stock; prepare yeast, algae, and shrimp cultures; prepare stock solutions; and assist scientists in tests and procedures.

Cost and Benefits

While costing $28,080 yearly (at $4.50/hour), three full-time lab assistants would have a positive effect on overall productivity.

1.   Uncleaned glassware no longer would pile up, and the fish-holding tanks could be cleaned daily (as they should be) instead of weekly.

2.   Because other employees no longer would need to work more than 40 hours weekly, morale would improve.

3.   Research scientists would be freed from general maintainance work (cleaning glassware, feeding and monitoring the fish stock, etc.). With more time to perform client tests, the researchers could eliminate our backlog.

4.   Clients no longer would have cause for impatience.

Conclusion

Increased production at GBI is essential to maintaining good client relations. These additional personnel would allow us to continue a reputation of prompt and efficient service.

Figure 22.7 A Solicited Recommendation Report

pany's problems is that employees have too heavy a workload. The personnel director asks Mary for a report outlining the problem and recommending a solution. Mary's report appears in Figure 22.7.

When the report is *unsolicited* (initiated by the writer), begin by spelling out the problem in enough detail to alert the reader; justify your solution *before* giving it. When they have sufficient background, readers are more inclined to act favorably on a recommendation they haven't solicited. In Figure 22.8, the writer structures his unsolicited report so the reader will understand the basis for the recommendation. Whenever you expect your reader to react negatively or to need persuading, give the explanation *before* the main point.

For recommendation reports and other persuasive writing tasks covered in this chapter, review the advice in Chapters 18 and 19.

Application 22–1

These sentences need overhauling before being included in a letter. Identify the problems, and revise as needed.

1. Pursuant to your ad, I am writing to apply for the scholarship.

2. I need all the information you have about methane-powered engines.

3. You idiots have sent me a faulty disk drive!

4. It is imperative that you let me know of your decision by January 15.

5. You are bound to be impressed by my credentials.

6. I could do wonders for your company.

7. I humbly request your kind consideration of my application.

8. If you are looking for a winner, your search is over!

9. I have become cognizant of your experiments and wish to ask your advice about the following procedure.

10. You will find these instructions easy enough for an ape to follow.

11. I would love to work for your wonderful company.

12. As per your request, I am sending the county map.

13. I am in hopes that you will call soon.

14. We beg to differ with your interpretation of this leasing clause.

15. I am impressed by the high salaries paid for this kind of work.

EASTERN UNIVERSITY

April 18, 19XX

TO: Mr. Frank Jones, Physical Plant Director

FROM: Joseph J. Gutt, Student Representative

SUBJECT: Improved Lighting Around the Library

Recently, several near-accidents--all within a few feet of the library's main entrance--suggest a critical need for better lighting around the library.

Increased lighting is not a luxury, subject to budget cuts; it is a necessity in preventing accidents and crime. The rising number of thefts and assaults on campus bears out the need for better lighting, not only outside the library, but in all areas of the campus. Though the lighting problem is campuswide, the library (the facility used most at Eastern, especially evenings) seems a logical place to begin.

Everyone is aware of rising electrical costs, but I'm sure you will agree that the University would find a lawsuit more expensive than a few light bulbs. If a student or visitor were to be injured, the University could face a damage suit, not to mention incurring a good deal of bad publicity.

Please install additional exterior lights around the library before a serious misfortune occurs. I make this recommendation on behalf of the many students and faculty who have expressed to me their fear and concern.

Figure 22.8 An Unsolicited Recommendation Report

Application 22–2

Collaborative Project: Bring to class a copy of a business letter addressed to you or a friend. Compare letters. Choose the most and the least effective. Working in small groups, revise the least effective letter, and then compare your revision with those from other groups.

Application 22–3

Write and mail an unsolicited letter of inquiry about the topic you have investigated, or will investigate, for a research assignment. In your letter you might request brochures, pamphlets, or other informational literature, or you might ask specific questions. Submit to your instructor a copy of your letter and the response.

Application 22–4

Write and mail an inquiry letter about an item or service you have seen advertised. Ask no fewer than six questions, and provide any explanations you think necessary to help the reader answer your questions fully. Write as a prospective customer, not as a student. Turn in the advertisement with your letter. Your instructor might also ask for a copy of the reply.

Application 22–5

1. As a student attending a state college, you learn that your governor and legislature have cut next year's operating budget for all state colleges by 20 percent. This cut will cause the firing of many young and popular faculty members, drastic reduction in student admissions, reduction in financial aid, cancellation of new programs, and erosion of college morale and quality of instruction. Write a complaint letter to your governor or your legislative representative, expressing your strong disapproval and justifying a major change in the proposed budget.

2. Write a complaint letter to a politician about some issue affecting your school or community.

3. Write a complaint letter to an appropriate school official about a campus problem.

Application 22–6

Write a letter of complaint about some problem you have had with goods or services. State your case clearly and objectively and request a specific adjustment.

Application 22–7

Write a letter applying for a part-time or summer job in response to a specific ad. Choose an organization related to your career goal. Identify the exact hours and calendar period during which you are free to work. Include a résumé. Submit a copy of the ad along with your documents.

Application 22–8

Assume a friend has asked you for help with this application letter. Read it carefully, evaluate its effectiveness, and rewrite as needed.

> Dear Ms. Brown:
>
> Please consider my application for the position of assistant in the Engineering Department. I am a second-year student majoring in Electrical Engineering Technology. I am presently an apprentice with your company and would like to continue my employment in the Engineering Department.
>
> I have six years' experience in electronics, including two years of engineering studies. I am confident my background will enable me to assist the engineers, and I would appreciate the chance to improve my skills through their knowledge and experience.
>
> I would appreciate the opportunity to discuss the possibilities and benefits of a position in the engineering department at Concord Electric. Please phone me any weekday after 3:00 P.M. at (467) 568-9867. I hope to hear from you soon.
>
> Sincerely,

Application 22–9

Research the writing skills you will need in your career. (Begin by looking at the *Dictionary of Occupational Titles* in your library's reference section. You might also interview a successful person in your profession.) Why and for whom will you write on the job? Explain in a memo to your instructor.

Application 22–10

Assume you are a training manager for XYZ Corporation. After completing this section of the text and the course, what advice about the writing process would you have for a beginning writer who will need to write frequent reports on the job? In a one-page (single-spaced) memo to new employees, explain the writing process briefly, and give a list of guidelines these beginning writers can follow.

Application 22–11

We all would like to see changes in our school's policies or procedures, whether they are changes in our major, school regulations, social activities, grading policies, registration procedures, or the like. Find some area of your school that needs obvious changes, and write a recommendation report to the person who might initiate the change. Explain why the change is necessary, and describe the benefits. Follow the format on page 534.

Application 22–12

You would like to see some changes in this course to better reflect your career plans. Perhaps you feel too much emphasis is placed on writing and too little on reading. Or maybe there's too much lecturing and not enough discussion. Write a recommendation report to your instructor, justifying the reasons for the changes you propose. Illustrate specific benefits resulting from your plan for you and your classmates. Do *not* try to justify spending less time doing course work.

Application 22–13

Think of an idea you would like to see implemented in your job. Write a recommendation report persuading your audience that your idea is worthwhile.

Application 22–14

Identify a dangerous or inconvenient area or situation on campus or in your community (endless cafeteria lines, a poorly lit intersection, slippery stairs, a poorly adjusted traffic light). Observe the problem for several hours during a peak-use period. Write a memo to a *specifically identified* decision maker describing the problem, listing your observations, making recommendations, and encouraging reader support or action.

Appendix A: Review of Grammar, Punctuation, and Mechanics

Sentence Parts • Sentence Types • Common Sentence Errors
• Effective Punctuation • Effective Mechanics

No matter how vital and informative a message may be, its credibility can be damaged by basic errors. Any of these errors—an illogical, fragmented, or run-on sentence; faulty punctuation; or a poorly chosen word—stands out and mars otherwise good writing. Not only do such errors confuse and annoy the reader, but they also speak badly for the writer's attention to detail. Your career will make the same demands for good writing that your English classes do. The difference is that evaluation (grades) in professional situations usually shows in promotions, reputation, and salary.

Table A-1 displays the standard correction symbols along with their interpretation and page references. When your instructor marks a symbol on your paper, turn to the appropriate section for explanations and examples that will help you make corrections quickly and easily.

Sentence Parts

Aside from a few exceptions we discuss later, a sentence is a statement that contains a subject and a verb and expresses a complete idea. More important than this textbook definition of *sentence*, however, is our

Table A.1 Correction Symbols

Symbol	Meaning	Page*	Symbol	Meaning	Page
ab	abbreviation	575	, /	comma	562
agr p	pronoun/referent agreement	554	-- /	dash	574
agr sv	subject/verb agreement	552	... /	ellipses	572
appr	inappropriate diction	198	! /	exclamation point	560
bias	biased tone	203	– /	hyphen	576
ca	pronoun case	554	ital	italics	573
cap	capitalization	578	( ) /	parenthesis	573
chop	choppiness	179	. /	period	559
cl	clutter word	176	? /	question mark	560
coh	paragraph coherence	131	" / "	quotation mark	571
cont	contraction	570	; /	semicolon	560
coord	coordination	162	qual	needless qualifier	177
cs	comma splice	549	red	redundancy	171
dgl	dangling modifier	156	rep	needless repetition	171
¶ dev	paragraph development	113	ref	faulty reference	158
euph	euphemism	189	ro	run-on sentence	551
exact	inexact word	190	shift	sentence shift	556
frag	sentence fragment	545	sp	spelling	580
gen	generalization	188	str	paragraph structure	122
len	paragraph length	124	sub	subordination	163
mod	misplaced modifier	156	trans	transition	142
noun ad	noun addiction	174	trite	triteness	187
over	overstatement	188	un	paragraph unity	129
par	parallelism	160	v	voice	164
pct	punctuation	558	var	sentence variety	182
ap/	apostrophe	569	w	wordiness	170
[ ] /	brackets	574	ww	wrong word	190
: /	colon	561	#	numbers	579
			¶	begin new paragraph	123
			no ¶	no paragraph	123

*Numbers refer to the first page of major discussion in the text.

innate understanding of how groups of words function as sentences. As an illustration, consider this nonsense statement:

In the cronk, the crat midingly pleted the mook smurg.

Although the only words we recognize in the example are **in** and **the**, we can say that this is a sentence. Why? Because in some place, something did something to something else. Specifically, the statement has a subject, **crat**, which did the doing; it has a verb, **pleted**, which is in the past tense; it has an adverb, **midingly**, which modifies the verb, telling us how the crat pleted; it has an adjective, **mook**, which modifies **smurg**; it has three nouns, **cronk**, **crat**, and **smurg; cronk** is the object of the preposition **in,** and **smurg** is the object of the verb **pleted**. And so, without understanding the words, we can see we already know something about language—how words work to make up a sentence. We don't know what this particular idea is, but we do know that it is complete.

Let's look at these sentence parts, and others, in more detail.

SUBJECT

The subject is the actor of the sentence—the noun or pronoun that usually precedes the predicate (the verb and other words that explain it) and about which we say something or ask a question.

The **cat** eats too much.

Why does the **cat** eat too much?

The **big, fat, lazy cat sitting on the table** eats too much.

In this last sentence, the simple subject is **cat,** and the complete subject (with all the words that explain the simple subject) is **The big, fat, lazy cat sitting on the table**.

PREDICATE

The predicate is made up of the verb and any words that modify and explain it. The predicate usually is what is said about the subject's action or being.

The cat **eats**.

Who **is** a fat cat?

The cat **eats until he can no longer stand up**.

In this last sentence, the simple verb is **eats**, and the complete predicate (with all the words that explain the simple predicate) is **eats until he can no longer stand up**.

OBJECT

An object is something that is acted on either directly or indirectly by a verb, or that is governed by a preposition.

Direct Object   A direct object is a noun or noun substitute that receives or is otherwise affected by the predicate's action.

> The cat drank the **bowl of milk**.
>
> Why did the cat eat **the mouse**?
>
> I don't know **where the cat is**.
>
> **What** did the cat eat?

Indirect Object   An indirect object is a noun or noun substitute that states to whom or for whom (or to what or for what) the predicate acts.

> I gave **the cat** a bowl of milk.
>
> He built **his friend** a house.

Usually the indirect object could be replaced by a prepositional phrase beginning with **to** or **for**.

> I gave a bowl of milk **to the cat**.
>
> He built a house **for his friend**.

Object of the Preposition   The object of the preposition is a noun or noun substitute that is joined to another part of the sentence by a preposition (**across**, **after**, **between**, **by**, **for**, **in**, **near**, **up**, **with**, and other "relationship" words). The words **cat** and **friend** in the two sentences above are objects of the preposition, as is **floor** in the next:

> The fat cat collapsed on the **floor**.

OBJECTIVE COMPLEMENT

An objective complement is a word or group of words that further explains the subject's action on the direct object.

> The cats elected Jack **president**.
>
> I consider him **a villain**.

SUBJECTIVE COMPLEMENT

A subjective complement is a word or group of words that further explains the subject. Subjective complements always follow linking verbs (**be**, **seem**, **feel**, **taste**, or any other verb that indicates a condition of being and that has no object).

> Jack is **angry**.
>
> All cats appear **alert and vigilant**.

PHRASE

A phrase is a group of related words that lacks either a subject or a predicate, or both. These are the kinds of phrases:

Infinitive phrase	Jack likes **to be fat**. [*functions as direct object*]
Prepositional phrase	Jack is content to sit **on the table**. [*functions as adverb*]
Verbal phrase	Jack **will be eating** until his dying day. [*functions as verb*]
Gerund phrase	**Eating constantly** can be damaging. [*functions as noun*]
Participial phrase	**Hoping for more food**, Jack meowed loudly. [*functions as adjective*]

CLAUSE

A clause is a group of related words that contains a subject and a predicate. It may be independent (main) or dependent (subordinate). An independent clause can stand alone as a sentence.

> The cat eats too much.

A dependent clause cannot stand alone as a sentence; it can serve as a noun, an adjective, or an adverb. A dependent clause always needs an independent clause to complete its meaning.

Noun clause	Jack hopes **he can eat forever**. [*as direct object*] **Anyone Jack meets** is a potential meal ticket. [*as subject*]
Adjective clause	Jack, **who eats constantly**, is the fattest cat in town. [*modifies "Jack"*]
Adverb clause	Jack is fat **because he eats too much**. [*modifies the subjective complement "fat"*]

Now let's look at the types of sentences that can be made by combining these sentence parts.

Sentence Types

SIMPLE SENTENCES

A simple sentence contains one independent clause and expresses one complete thought.

> **Jack eats**.
>
> **Jack eats** too much.
>
> On any given day, **Jack eats** too much.
>
> On any given day, **Jack**, the fat, lazy cat, **eats** too much dry and canned food for any small animal.

Each of these sentences is a simple sentence. Although the subject and verb are gradually expanded, and objects, adjectives, adverbs, and prepositional phrases are added, the kernel sentence still is **Jack eats**.

COMPOUND SENTENCES

A compound sentence contains two or more independent clauses, each with a subject and a predicate. The clauses usually are joined by coordinating conjunctions (**and, but, or, nor, for**) or by a semicolon or colon.

> Jack eats constantly **and** he gets fatter.
>
> Jack eats constantly; he gets fatter.

Ideas in a compound sentence are roughly equal in importance; therefore, they are expressed in equal (parallel) grammatical form.

Jack **eats** all morning, and he **sleeps** all afternoon, and he **prowls** all night.

COMPLEX SENTENCES

A complex sentence has two or more clauses that are *not* equal in importance. Instead, it has a dependent clause and an independent clause; the former depends on the latter to complete its meaning.

Because Jack eats too much, **he is fat.** [*second clause is independent*]

Have you seen the cat who eats too much? [*first clause is independent*]

Because one clause depends on the other, they should not be separated by anything stronger than a comma. Words such as **which, although, after, when,** and **because** (subordinating conjunctions) placed at the beginning of an independent clause will make it dependent.

A complex sentence can have more than one dependent clause—as long as it has one independent clause.

After Jack eats all morning, sleeps all afternoon, and prowls all night, **he is ready to begin all over again,** even when he has the flu.

As discussed in the section on subordination (Chapter 8), complex sentences signal that some ideas merit more emphasis than others.

COMPOUND-COMPLEX SENTENCES

A compound-complex sentence has at least two independent clauses and one dependent clause.

Even though Jack's girlfriend has left town, **he remains optimistic, and he has an active social life.** [*second and third clauses are independent*]

Common Sentence Errors

Any piece of writing is only as good as each of its sentences. Here are common sentence errors, with suggestions for easy repairs.

SENTENCE FRAGMENT

A sentence expresses a logically complete idea. Any complete idea must contain a subject and a verb and must not depend on another complete idea to make sense. Your sentence might contain several complete ideas, but it must have at least one!

> [*incomplete idea*]   [*complete idea*]   [*complete idea*]
> Although Mary was hurt, she grabbed the line, and she saved the boat.

If the idea is not complete—if your reader is left wondering what you mean—you probably have left out some essential element (the subject, the verb, or another complete idea). Such a piece of a sentence is a *fragment*.

> Grabbed the line. [*a fragment because it lacks a subject*]
>
> Although Mary was hurt. [*a fragment because—although it contains a subject and a verb—it needs to be joined with a complete idea to make sense*]

The only exception to the sentence rule applies when we give a command ("Run!") in which the subject (you) is understood. Because "Run!" is a logically complete statement, it is properly called a sentence. So is this one:

> Sam is an electronics technician.

Readers cannot miss your meaning: somewhere is a person; the person's name is Sam; the person is an electronics technician.

Suppose instead we write:

> Sam an electronics technician.

This statement is not logically complete, therefore not a sentence. The reader is left asking, "What **about** Sam the electronics technician?" The verb—the word that makes things happen—is missing. By adding a verb, we can easily change this fragment to a complete sentence.

Simple verb	Sam **is** an electronics technician.
Verb plus adverb	Sam, an electronics technician, **works hard**.
Dependent clause, verb, and subjective complement	**Although he is well paid,** Sam, an electronics technician, **is not happy**.

Do not, however, mistake the following statement—which seems to contain a verb—for a complete sentence:

| Sam being an electronics technician.

Such "-ing" forms do not function as verbs unless accompanied by such other verbs as **is**, **was**, and **will be**. Again, readers are left in a fog unless you complete your idea with an independent clause.

| **Sam,** being an electronics technician, **was responsible for checking the circuitry**.

Likewise, remember that the "to + verb" form (infinitive) does not function as a verb.

| To become an electronics technician.

The meaning is unclear unless you complete the thought.

| To become an electronics technician, **Sam had to complete a two-year apprenticeship**.

Sometimes we inadvertently create fragments by adding certain words (**because**, **since**, **if**, **although**, **while**, **unless**, **until**, **when**, **where**, and others) to an already complete sentence, transforming our independent clause (complete sentence) to a dependent clause.

| **Although** Sam is an electronics technician.

Such words subordinate the words that follow them so that an additional idea is needed to make the first statement complete. That is, they make the statement dependent on an additional idea, which must itself have a subject and a verb and be a complete sentence. (See "Complex Sentences" and "Subordination"—pages 545, 163.) Now we have to round off the statement with a complete idea (an independent clause).

| Although Sam is an electronics technician, **he hopes to become an electrical engineer**.

Note: Be careful not to use a semicolon or a period, instead of a comma, to separate elements in the preceding sentence. Because the incomplete idea (dependent clause) depends on the complete idea (independent clause) for its meaning, you need only a *pause* (symbolized by a comma), not a *break* (symbolized by a semicolon), between these ideas. In fact, many fragments are created when too strong a mark of punctuation (period or semicolon) severs the connection between a dependent and an independent clause. (See the later discussion of punctuation.)

Here are some fragments from students' writing. Each is repaired in several ways. Can you think of other ways of making these statements complete?

Fragment	She spent her first week on the job as a researcher. **Selecting and compiling technical information from digests and journals.**
Revised	She spent her first week on the job as a researcher, selecting and compiling technical information from digests and journals.
	She spent her first week on the job as a researcher. She selected and compiled technical information from digests and journals.
	In her first week on the job as a researcher, she selected and compiled technical information from digests and journals.
Fragment	**Because the operator was careless.** The new computer was damaged.
Revised	Because the operator was careless, the new computer was damaged.
	The operator's carelessness resulted in damage to the new computer.
	The operator was careless; as a result, the new computer was damaged.
Fragment	**When each spool is in place.** Advance your film.
Revised	When each spool is in place, advance your film.
	Be sure that each spool is in place before advancing your film.

ACCEPTABLE FRAGMENTS

For some purposes, a fragmented sentence is acceptable even though it lacks a subject or a verb; in commands or exclamations, the subject ("you") is understood.

Acceptable	Slow down.
	Give me a hand.
	Hurry.
	Look out!

Also, questions and answers sometimes are expressed as incomplete sentences.

Acceptable

How? By investing wisely.

When? At three o'clock.

Who? Bill.

These are the commonest situations that justify fragmented sentences. Some of the sample essays in Section Three show other examples. In general, however, avoid fragments unless you have good reason to use one for special tone or emphasis.

Application A-1

Correct these sentence fragments by rewriting each in two ways.

1. Fred is a terrible math student. But an excellent writer.

2. As they entered the haunted house. The floors began to groan.

3. Hoping for an **A** in biology. Sally studied every night.

4. Although many students flunk out of this college. Its graduates find excellent jobs.

5. Three teenagers out of every ten have some sort of addiction. Whether it is to alcohol or drugs.

COMMA SPLICE

In a comma splice, two complete ideas (independent clauses), which should be *separated* by a period or a semicolon, are incorrectly *joined* by a comma:

Sarah did a great job, she was promoted.

You can choose among several possibilities for correcting this error:

1. Substitute a period followed by a capital letter:

Sarah did a great job. She was promoted.

2. Substitute a semicolon to signal a relationship between the two items:

Sarah did a great job; she was promoted.

3. Use a semicolon with a connecting adverb (a transitional word):

Sarah did a great job; **consequently**, she was promoted.

4. Use a subordinating word to make the less important clause incomplete, thereby dependent on the other:

Because Sarah did a great job, she was promoted.

5. Add a connecting word after the comma:

Sarah did a great job, **and** she was promoted.

Your choice of construction will depend, of course, on the exact meaning or tone you wish to convey. The following comma splices can be repaired in the ways described above.

Comma splice	This is a fairly new product, therefore, some people don't trust it.
Revised	This is a fairly new product. Some people don't trust it.
	This is a fairly new product; therefore, some people don't trust it.
	Because this is a fairly new product, some people don't trust it.
	This is a fairly new product, **and so** some people don't trust it.
Comma splice	Ms. Jones was a strict supervisor, she was well liked by her employees.
Revised	Ms. Jones was a strict supervisor. She was well liked by her employees.
	Ms. Jones was a strict supervisor; **however**, she was well liked by her employees.
	Although Ms. Jones was a strict supervisor, she was well liked by her employees.
	Ms. Jones was a strict supervisor, **but** she was well liked by her employees.
	Ms. Jones was a strict supervisor; she was well liked by her employees.

Application A–2

Correct these comma splices by rewriting each in two ways.

1. Efforts are being made to halt water pollution, however, there is no simple solution to the problem.

2. Bill slept through his final, he had forgotten to set his alarm.

3. Ellen must be a genius, she never studies yet always gets **A**'s.

4. We arrived at the picnic late, there were no hamburgers left.

5. My part-time job is excellent, it pays well, provides good experience, and offers a real challenge.

RUN-ON SENTENCE

The run-on sentence, a cousin to the comma splice, crams too many ideas without needed breaks or pauses.

Run-on   The hourglass is more accurate than the waterclock for the water in a waterclock must always be at the same temperature in order to flow with the same speed since water evaporates it must be replenished at regular intervals thus not being as effective in measuring time as the hourglass.

Like a runaway train, this statement is out of control. Here is a corrected version:

Revised   The hourglass is more accurate than the waterclock because water in a waterclock must always be at the same temperature to flow at the same speed. Also, water evaporates and must be replenished at regular intervals. These temperature and volume problems make the waterclock less effective than the hourglass in measuring time.

Application A–3

Revise these run-on sentences.

1. The gale blew all day by evening the sloop was taking on water.

2. Jennifer felt hopeless about passing English however the writing center helped her complete the course.

3. The professor glared at John he had been dozing in the back row.

4. Our drama club produces three plays a year I love the opening nights.

5. Pets should not be allowed on our campus they are messy and sometimes dangerous.

FAULTY AGREEMENT—SUBJECT AND VERB

The subject should agree in number with the verb. We are not likely to use faulty agreement in short sentences, where subject and verb are not far apart. Thus we are not likely to say "Jack eat too much" instead of "Jack eats too much." But in more complicated sentences—those in which the subject is separated from its verb by other words—we sometimes lose track of the subject-verb relationship.

Faulty   The lion's **share** of diesels **are** sold in Europe.

Although **diesels** is closest to the verb, the subject is **share**, a singular subject that must agree with a singular verb.

Revised   The lion's **share** of diesels **is** sold in Europe.

Agreement errors are easy to correct once subject and verb are identified.

Faulty   There **is** an estimated 29,000 **women** living in our city.

Revised   There **are** an estimated 29,000 **women** living in our city.

Faulty   **A system** of lines **extend** horizontally to form a grid.

Revised   **A system** of lines **extends** horizontally to form a grid.

A second problem with subject-verb agreement occurs when we use indefinite pronouns such as **each**, **everyone**, **anybody**, and **somebody**. They function as subjects and usually take a singular verb.

Faulty   **Each** of the crew members **were** injured during the storm.

Revised   **Each** of the crew members **was** injured during the storm.

Faulty	**Everyone** in the group **have** practiced long hours.
Revised	**Everyone** in the group **has** practiced long hours.

Agreement problems can be caused by collective nouns such as **herd**, **family**, **union**, **group**, **army**, **team**, **committee**, and **board**. A collective noun can call for a singular or plural verb, depending on your intended meaning. When denoting the group as a whole, use a singular verb.

Correct	The **committee meets** weekly to discuss new business.
	The editorial **board** of this magazine **has** high standards.

To denote individual members of the group, however, use a plural verb.

Correct	The **committee disagree** on whether to hire Jim.
	The editorial **board are** all published authors.

Yet another problem occurs when two subjects are joined by **either . . . or** or **neither . . . nor.** Here, the verb is singular if both subjects are singular and plural if both subjects are plural. If one subject is plural and one is singular, the verb agrees with the one that is closer to the verb.

Correct	Neither **John** nor **Bill works** regularly.
	Either **apples** or **oranges are** good vitamin sources.
	Either Felix or his **friends are** crazy.
	Neither the boys nor their **father likes** the home team.

If, on the other hand, two subjects (singular, plural, or mixed) are joined by **both . . . and,** the verb will be plural. Whereas **or** suggests "one or the other," **and** announces a combination of the two subjects, thereby requiring a plural verb.

Correct	**Both** Joe and Bill **are** resigning.
	The **book and** the **briefcase appear** expensive.

A single **and** between subjects makes for a plural subject.

FAULTY AGREEMENT—PRONOUN AND REFERENT

A pronoun can make sense only if it refers to a specific noun (its referent or antecedent), with which it must agree in gender and number. It is easy enough to make most pronouns agree with their respective referents.

Correct	**Jane** lost **her** book.
	The **students** complained that **they** had been treated unfairly.

Some instances, however, are not so obvious. When an indefinite pronoun such as **each**, **everyone**, **anybody**, **someone**, or **none** serves as the pronoun referent, the pronoun itself is singular.

Correct	**Anyone** can get **his** degree from that college.
	Anyone can get **his** or **her** degree from that college.
	Each candidate described **her** plans in detail.

Application A–4

Revise these sentences to make their subjects and verbs agree in number or their pronouns and referents agree in gender and number.

1. Ten years ago the mineral rights to this land was sold to a mining company.

2. Each of the students in our dorm have a serious complaint about living conditions.

3. Neither the students nor the instructor like this classroom.

4. The team meet every Tuesday to discuss new plays.

5. Neither Fred nor Mary expect to pass this course.

6. Anyone wanting to enhance their career should take a computer course.

7. Everyone has their own opinion about nuclear power.

FAULTY PRONOUN CASE

A pronoun's case (nominative, objective, or possessive) is determined by its role in the sentence: as subject, object, or indicator of possession.

If the pronoun serves as the subject of a sentence (**I**, **we**, **you**, **she**, **he**, **it**, **they**, **who**), its case is *nominative*.

> **She** completed her graduate program in record time.
>
> **Who** broke the chair?

When a pronoun follows a version of the verb **to be** (a linking verb), it explains (complements) the subject, and so its case is nominative.

> It was **she**.
>
> The professor who perfected our new distillation process is **he**.

If the pronoun serves as the object of a verb or a preposition (**me**, **us**, **you**, **her**, **him**, **it**, **them**, **whom**), its case is *objective*.

Object of the verb	The employees gave **her** a parting gift.
Object of the preposition	To **whom** do you wish to complain?

If a pronoun indicates possession (**my**, **mine**, **our**, **ours**, **your**, **yours**, **his**, **her**, **hers**, **its**, **their**, **theirs**, **whose**), its case is *possessive*.

> The brown briefcase is **mine**.
>
> **Her** offer was accepted.
>
> **Whose** opinion do you value most?

Here are some frequent errors in pronoun case:

Faulty	**Whom** is responsible to **who**? [*The subject should be nominative and the object should be objective.*]
Revised	**Who** is responsible to **whom**?
Faulty	The debate was between Marsha and **I**. [*As object of the preposition, the pronoun should be objective.*]
Revised	The debate was between Marsha and **me**.
Faulty	**Us** students are accountable for our decisions. [*The pronoun accompanies the subject, "students," and thus should be nominative.*]
Revised	**We** students are accountable for our decisions.

Faulty	A group of **we** students will fly to California. [*The pronoun accompanies the object of the preposition, "students," and thus should be objective.*]
Revised	A group of **us** students will fly to California.

Hint: By deleting the accompanying noun from the two latter examples, we easily can identify the correct pronoun case ("We . . . are accountable . . . "; "A group of us . . . will fly . . . ").

Application A–5

Select the appropriate pronoun case from each of these pairs (in parentheses).

1. Kevin was as fascinated by the Grand Canyon as (me, I).

2. By (who, whom) was the job offer made?

3. The argument was among Bill, Terry, and (I, me).

4. A committee of (we, us) concerned citizens is working to make our neighborhood safer.

5. (Us, we) students are being hurt by federal cuts in loan programs.

6. The liar is (he, him).

SENTENCE SHIFTS

Shifts in point of view damage coherence. If you begin a sentence or paragraph with one subject or person, do not shift to another.

Shift in person	When **you** finish such a great book, **one** will have a sense of achievement.
Revised	When **you** finish such a great book, **you** will have a sense of achievement.
Shift in number	**One** should sift the flour before **they** make the pie.
Revised	**One** should sift the flour before **one** makes the pie. (*Or better: Sift the flour before making the pie.*)

Do not begin a sentence in the active voice and then shift to the passive voice.

Shift in voice	He **delivered** the plans for the apartment complex, and the building site **was also inspected by him.**
Revised	He **delivered** the plans for the apartment complex and also **inspected** the building site.

Do not shift tenses without good reason.

Shift in tense	She **delivered** the blueprints, **inspected** the foundation, **wrote** her report, and **takes** the afternoon off.
Revised	She **delivered** the blueprints, **inspected** the foundation, **wrote** her report, and **took** the afternoon off.

Do not shift from one verb mood to another (as from imperative to indicative mood in a set of instructions).

Shift in mood	**Unscrew** the valve and then steel wool **should be used** to clean the fitting.
Revised	**Unscrew** the valve and then **use** steel wool to clean the fitting.

Do not shift from indirect to direct discourse within a sentence.

Shift in discourse	**Jim** wonders **if he will get the job** and **will he like it?**
Revised	Jim wonders **if he will get the job** and **if he will like it.** [*someone speaking for someone else*]
	Jim wonders, **"Will I get the job, and will I like it?"** [*speaker expressing himself directly*]

Application A–6

Revise these sentences to eliminate shifts in person, mood, voice, tense, number, or discourse.

1. People should keep themselves politically informed; otherwise, you will not be living up to your democratic responsibilities.

2. Barbara made the Dean's List and the Junior Achievement award was also won by her.

3. Professor Jones said that our performance was excellent and that "I am proud to have worked with you all."

4. As soon as he walked into his dorm room, George sees the mess left by his roommate.

5. When one is being stalked by a bear, you should not snack on sardines.

6. First loosen the lug nuts; then you should jack up the car.

7. One should expect that you will face a competitive job market.

Effective Punctuation

Punctuation marks are like road signs and traffic signals. They govern reading speed and provide clues for navigation through a network of ideas; they mark intersections, detours, and road repairs; they draw attention to points of interest along the route; and they mark geographic boundaries. In short, punctuation marks provide us with a practical and simple way of making ourselves understood.

Before we discuss individual punctuation marks in detail, let's review the four used most often (period, semicolon, colon, and comma). These marks can be ranked in order of their relative strengths.

1. *Period.* The strongest mark. A period signals a complete stop at the end of an independent idea (independent clause). The first word in the idea following the period begins with a capital letter.

    Jack is a fat cat. His friends urge him to diet.

2. *Semicolon.* Weaker than a period but stronger than a comma. A semicolon signals a brief stop after an independent idea but does not end the sentence; instead, it announces that the forthcoming independent idea is **closely related** to the preceding idea.

    Jack is a fat cat; he eats too much.

3. *Colon.* Weaker than a period but stronger than a comma. A colon usually follows an independent idea and, like the semicolon, signals a brief stop but does not end the sentence. The colon and semicolon, however, are never interchangeable. A colon provides an important cue: it symbolizes "explanation to follow." Information after the colon (which need not be an independent idea) explains or clarifies the idea expressed before the colon.

> Jack is a fat cat: he weighs forty pounds. [*The information after the colon answers "How fat?"*]

or

> Jack is a fat cat: forty pounds worth! [*The second clause is not independent.*]

Note: As long as any two adjacent ideas are independent, they may correctly be separated by a period. Sometimes a colon or a semicolon may be more appropriate for illustrating the logical relationship between two given ideas. When in doubt, however, use a period.

4. *Comma.* The weakest of these four marks. A comma does not signal a stop at the end of an independent idea, but only a pause within or between ideas in the sentence. A comma often indicates that the word, phrase, or clause set off from the independent idea cannot stand alone but must rely on the independent idea for its meaning.

> Jack, a fat cat, is jolly. [*The phrase within commas depends on the independent idea for its meaning.*]

> **Although he diets often,** Jack is a fat cat. [*Because the first clause depends on the second, any stronger mark would cause the first clause to become a fragment.*]

A comma is used between two independent clauses only if accompanied by a coordinating conjunction (**and, but, or, nor, yet**).

Comma splice   Jack is a playboy, he is loved everywhere.

Correct   Jack is a playboy, **but** he is loved everywhere.

And so we see that punctuation marks, like words, convey specific meanings to the reader. These meanings are further discussed in the sections that follow.

END PUNCTUATION

The three marks of end punctuation—period, question mark, and exclamation point—work like a red traffic light by signaling a complete stop.

Period   A period ends a sentence. Periods end some abbreviations.

Ms.   Assn.   N.Y.

M.D.   Inc.   B.A.

Periods serve as decimal points for figures.

$15.95

21.4%

Question Mark   A question mark follows a direct question.

Where is the balance sheet?

Do not use a question mark to end an indirect question.

Faulty	She asked if all students had failed the test?
Revised	She asked if all students had failed the test. [*someone speaking for someone else*]
	or
	She asked, "Did all students fail the test?" [*speaker expressing herself directly*]

Exclamation Point   Because exclamation points symbolize that you are excited or adamant, don't overuse them. Otherwise you might seem hysterical or insincere.

Use an exclamation point only when expression of strong feeling is appropriate.

Appropriate	Oh, no!
	Pay up!

SEMICOLON

A semicolon usually works like a blinking red traffic light at an intersection by signaling a brief but definite stop.

Semicolons Separating Independent Clauses   Semicolons separate independent clauses (logically complete ideas) whose contents are closely related and are not connected by a coordinating conjunction.

The project was finally completed; we had done a good week's work.

The semicolon can replace the conjunction-comma combination that joins two independent ideas.

> The project was finally completed, and we were elated.
>
> The project was finally completed; we were elated.

The second version emphasizes the sense of elation.

Semicolons Used with Adverbs as Conjunctions and Other Transitional Expressions   Semicolons must accompany conjunctive adverbs and other expressions that connect related independent ideas (**besides, otherwise, still, however, furthermore, moreover, consequently, therefore, on the other hand, in contrast, in fact**, and the like).

> The job is filled; however, we will keep your résumé on file.
>
> Your background is impressive; in fact, it is the best among our applicants.

Semicolons Separating Items in a Series   When items in a series contain internal commas, semicolons provide clear separation between items.

> I am applying for summer jobs in Santa Fe, New Mexico; Albany, New York; Montgomery, Alabama; and Moscow, Idaho.
>
> Members of the survey crew were John Jones, a geologist; Hector
>
> Lightweight, a draftsman; and Mary Shelley, a graduate student.

COLON

Like a flare in the road, a colon signals you to stop and then proceed, paying attention to the situation ahead, the details of which will be revealed as you move along. Usually a colon follows an introductory statement that requires a follow-up explanation.

> We need this equipment immediately: a voltmeter, a portable generator, and three pairs of insulated gloves.
>
> She is an ideal colleague: honest, reliable, and competent.
>
> Two candidates are clearly superior: John and Marsha.

Except for salutations in formal correspondence (e.g. Dear Ms. Jones:, colons follow independent (logically and grammatically complete) statements. Because colons, like end punctuation and semicolons, signal a full stop, they never are used to fragment a complete statement.

| Faulty | My plans include: finishing college, traveling for two years, and settling down in Boston. |

No punctuation should follow "include."
Colons can introduce quotations.

> The supervisor's message was clear enough: "You're fired."

A colon normally replaces a semicolon in separating two related, complete statements when the second statement directly explains or amplifies the first.

> His reason for accepting the lowest-paying job offer was simple: he had always wanted to live in the Northwest.

The statement following the colon explains the "reason" mentioned in the statement preceding the colon.

Application A–7

Insert semicolons or colons as needed in these expressions.

1. June had finally arrived it was time to graduate.

2. I have two friends who are like brothers Sam and Daniel.

3. Joe did not get the job however, he was high on the list of finalists.

4. The wine was superb an 1898 Margaux.

5. Our student senators are Joan Blake, a geology major Helen Simms, a nursing major and Henry Drew, an English major.

COMMA

The comma is the most frequently used—and abused—punctuation mark. Unlike the period, semicolon, and colon, which signal a full stop, the comma signals a *brief pause*. Thus, the comma works like a blinking yellow traffic light, for which you slow down without stopping. Never use a comma to signal a *break* between independent ideas; it is not strong enough.

Comma as a Pause Between Complete Ideas In a compound sentence in which a coordinating conjunction (**and, or, nor, for, but**) connects equal (independent) statements, a comma usually precedes the conjunction.

This is an excellent course, **but** the work is difficult.

This vacant shop is just large enough for our hot-dog stand, **and** the location is excellent for walk-in customer traffic.

Without the conjunction, these previous statements would suffer from a comma splice, unless the comma were replaced by a semicolon or by a period.

Comma as a Pause Between an Incomplete and a Complete Idea   A comma usually is placed between a complete and an incomplete statement in a complex sentence to show that the incomplete statement depends for its meaning on the complete statement. (The incomplete statement cannot stand alone, separated by a break such as a semicolon, colon, or period.)

Because he is a fat cat, Jack diets often.

When he eats too much, Jack gains weight.

Above, the first idea is made incomplete by a subordinating conjunction (**since, when, because, although, where, while, if, until**), which here connects a dependent with an independent statement. The first (incomplete) idea depends on the second (complete) for wholeness. When the order is reversed (complete idea followed by incomplete), the comma usually is omitted.

Jack diets often **because he is a fat cat**.

Jack gains weight **when he eats too much**.

Because commas take the place of speech signals, reading a sentence aloud should tell you whether or not to pause (and use a comma).

Commas Separating Items (Words, Phrases, or Clauses) in a Series   Use a comma to separate items in a series.

Helen, Joe, Marsha, and **John** are joining us on the term project.

The dorm room was **yellow, orange,** and **red**.

He works hard **at home, on the job,** and even **during his vacation**.

The new employee complained **that the hours were long, that the pay was low, that the work was boring, and that the supervisor was paranoid**.

She came, saw, and **conquered**.

Use no commas when **or** or **and** appears between all items in a series.

> She is willing to study in San Francisco or Seattle or even in Anchorage.

Add a comma when **or** or **and** is used only before the final item in the series.

> Our luncheon special for Thursday will be coffee, rolls, steak, beans, and ice cream.

Without the final comma, that sentence might cause the reader to conclude that "beans and ice cream" is an exotic new dessert.

Comma Setting Off Introductory Phrases   Infinitive, prepositional, or verbal phrases introducing a sentence usually are set off by commas.

Infinitive phrase	**To be or not to be,** that is the question.
Prepositional phrase	**In Rome,** do as the Romans do.
Participial phrase	**Being fat**, Jack was a slow runner.
	Moving quickly, the army surrounded the enemy.

When an interjection introduces a sentence, it is set off by a comma.

> **Oh,** is that the final verdict?

When a noun in direct address introduces a sentence, it is set off by a comma.

> **Mary,** you've done a great job.

Commas Setting Off Nonrestrictive Elements   A restrictive phrase or clause modifies or defines the subject in such a way that deleting the modifier would change the meaning of the sentence.

> All students **who have work experience** will receive preference.

The clause **who have work experience** defines **students** and is essential to the meaning of the sentence. Without this clause, the meaning would be entirely different.

> All students will receive preference.

This sentence also contains a restriction.

> All students **with work experience** will receive preference.

The phrase **with work experience** defines **students** and thus specifies the meaning of the sentence. Because this phrase *restricts* the subject by limiting the category **students**, it is essential to the sentence's meaning and so is not separated from the sentence by commas.

A nonrestrictive phrase or clause does not limit or define the subject; a nonrestrictive modifier could be deleted without changing the sentence's basic meaning.

> Our new manager, **who has only six weeks' experience,** is highly competent.
>
> This house, **riddled with carpenter ants,** is falling apart.

In each of those sentences, the modifying phrase or clause does not restrict the subject; each could be deleted.

> Our new manager is highly competent.
>
> This house is falling apart.

Unlike a restrictive modifier, the nonrestrictive modifier does not supply the essential meaning to the sentence; any nonessential clause or phrase is set off from the sentence by commas.

To appreciate how commas can affect meaning, consider this statement:

Restrictive   Office workers **who drink martinis with lunch** have slow afternoons.

Because the restrictive clause limits the subject, **office workers**, we interpret that statement as follows: some office workers drink martinis with lunch, and these have slow afternoons. In contrast, we could write:

Nonrestrictive   Office workers, **who drink martinis with lunch,** have slow afternoons.

Here the subject, **office workers**, is not limited or defined. Thus we interpret that *all* office workers drink martinis with lunch and therefore have slow afternoons.

Commas Setting Off Parenthetical Elements   Items that interrupt the flow of a sentence are called parenthetical and are enclosed by commas.

Expressions such as **of course**, **as a result**, **as I recall**, and **however** are parenthetical and may denote emphasis, afterthought, clarification, or transition.

Emphasis   This deluxe model, **of course,** is more expensive.

Afterthought   Your report format, **by the way,** was impeccable.

Clarification   The loss of my job was, **in a way,** a blessing.

Transition   Our warranty, **however,** does not cover tire damage.

Direct address is parenthetical.

Listen, **my children,** and you shall hear. . . .

A parenthetical expression at the beginning or the end of a sentence is set off by a comma.

Naturally, we will expect a full guarantee.

My friends, I think we have a problem.

You've done a good job, **Jim.**

Yes, you may use my name in your advertisement.

Commas Setting Off Quoted Material   Quoted items included within a sentence often are set off by commas.

The customer said, "I'll take it," as soon as he laid eyes on our new model.

Commas Setting Off Appositives   An appositive, a word or words explaining a noun and placed immediately after it, is set off by commas when the appositive is nonrestrictive. (See page 564.)

Martha Jones, **our new president,** is overhauling all personnel policies.

The new Mercedes, **my dream car,** is priced far beyond my budget.

Alpha waves, **the most prominent of the brain waves,** typically are recorded in a waking subject whose eyes are closed.

Please make all checks payable to Sam Sawbuck, **school treasurer.**

Commas Used in Common Practice   Commas set off the day of the month from the year, in a date.

May 10, 1989

Commas set off numbers in three-digit intervals.

> 11,215
>
> 6,463,657

They also set off street, city, and state in an address.

> Mail the bill to John Smith, 18 Sea Street, Albany, Iowa 01642.

When the address is written vertically, however, the omitted commas are those which would otherwise occur at the end of each address line.

> John Smith
> 18 Sea Street
> Albany, Iowa 01642

If we put "Albany" and "Iowa" on separate lines, we wouldn't have a comma after "Albany," either.
Commas set off an address or date in a sentence.

> Room 3C, Margate Complex, is my summer address.
>
> June 15, 1987, is my graduation date.

They set off degrees and titles from proper nouns.

> Roger P. Cayer, M.D.
>
> Gordon Browne, Jr.
>
> Sandra Mello, Ph.D.

Commas Used Erroneously   Avoid needless or inappropriate commas. In fact, you are probably safer using too few commas than using too many. Reading a sentence aloud is one way to identify inappropriate pause.

Faulty

The instructor told me, that I was late. [*separates the indirect from the direct object*]

The most universal symptom of the suicide impulse, is depression. [*separates the subject from its verb*]

This has been a long, difficult, semester. [*second comma separates the final adjective from its noun*]

John, Bill, and Sally, are joining us on the trip home. [*third comma separates the final subject from its verb*]

An employee, who expects rapid promotion, must quickly prove his or her worth. [*separates a modifier that should be restrictive*]

I spoke by phone with John, and Marsha. [*separates two nouns linked by a coordinating conjunction*]

The room was, 18 feet long. [*separates the linking verb from the subjective complement*]

We painted the room, red. [*separates the object from its complement*]

Application A–8

Insert commas where needed in these sentences.

1. In modern society highways seem as necessary as food water or air.
2. Everyone though frustrated by pollution can play a part in improving the environment.
3. The economic recession is deepening yet real estate continues to be a good investment.
4. Professor Jones who has written three books is considered an authority in her field.
5. Bill my best friend has just left town for the weekend.
6. Amanda Ford of course is the best candidate for governor.
7. When Clem opened the barn door he saw the armadillo scurry behind a hay bale its tail wagging.
8. This car dying of body rot is ready for the junkyard.
9. Terrified by the noise Sally ran never looking back.
10. One book however will not solve all your writing problems.

Application A–9

Eliminate needless or inappropriate commas from these sentences.

1. Students, who smoke marijuana, tend to do poorly in school.
2. As I started the car, I saw him, dash into the woods.

3.   This has been a semester of boring, dreadful, experiences.

4.   Sarah mistakenly made dates on the same evening with Joe, and Bill, even though she had promised herself to be more careful.

5.   In fact, a writer's reaction to criticism, is often defensiveness.

APOSTROPHE

Apostrophes serve three purposes: to indicate the possessive, a contraction, and the plural of numbers, letters, and figures.

Apostrophe Indicating the Possessive   At the end of a singular word, or of a plural word that does not end in **s**, add an apostrophe plus **s** to indicate the possessive. Single-syllable nouns that end in **s** take the apostrophe before an added **s**.

> The people's candidate won.
>
> The chainsaw was Bill's.
>
> The women's locker room burned.
>
> The car's paint job was ruined by the hailstorm.
>
> I borrowed Doris's book.
>
> Have you heard Ray Charles's new song?

Do not add **s** to words that have more than one syllable.

> Aristophanes' death
>
> for conscience' sake

Do not use an apostrophe to indicate the possessive form of either singular or plural pronouns.

> The book was hers.
>
> Ours is the best school in the country.
>
> The fault was theirs.

At the end of a plural word that ends in **s**, add an apostrophe only.

> the cows' water supply
>
> the Jacksons' wine cellar

At the end of a compound noun, add an apostrophe plus **s**.

| my father-in-law's false teeth

At the end of the last word in nouns of joint possession, add an apostrophe plus **s** if both own one item.

| Joe and Sam's lakefront cottage

Add an apostrophe plus **s** to both nouns if each owns specific items.

| Joe's and Sam's passports

Apostrophe Indicating a Contraction   An apostrophe shows that you have omitted one or more letters in a phrase that is usually a combination of a pronoun and a verb.

| I'm   they're
| he's   you'd
| you're   who's

Don't confuse **they're** with **their** or **there**.

| Faulty   there books
| their now leaving
| living their
| Correct   their books
| they're now leaving
| living there

Remember the distinction this way:

| Their friend knows they're there.

Don't confuse **it's** and **its**. **It's** means "it is." **Its** is the possessive.

| It's watching its reflection in the pond.

Don't confuse **who's** and **whose**. **Who's** means "who is," whereas **whose** indicates the possessive.

| Who's interrupting whose work?

Other contractions are formed from the verb and the negative.

isn't	can't
don't	haven't
won't	wasn't

Apostrophe Indicating the Plural of Numbers, Letters, and Figures

The 6's on this new typewriter look like smudged G's, 9's are illegible, and the %'s are unclear.

QUOTATION MARKS

Quotation marks set off the exact words borrowed from another speaker or writer. At the end of a quotation, the period or comma is placed within the quotation marks.

"Hurry up," he whispered.

She told me, "I'm depressed."

The colon or semicolon always is placed outside the quotation marks.

Our student handbook clearly defines "core requirements"; however, it does not list all the courses that fulfill the requirement.

You know what to expect when Honest John offers you a "bargain": a piece of junk.

Sometimes a question mark is used within a quotation that is part of a larger sentence. (Do not follow a question mark with a comma.)

"Can we stop the flooding?" inquired the captain.

When a question mark or exclamation point is part of a quotation, it belongs within the quotation marks, replacing the comma or period.

"Help!" he screamed.

He asked John, "Can't we agree about anything?"

But if the question mark or exclamation point is meant to denote the attitude of the quoter instead of the person being quoted, it is placed outside the quotation mark.

> Why did he wink and tell me, "It's a big secret"?

> He actually accused me of being an "elitist"!

When quoting a passage of 50 words or longer, indent the entire passage ten spaces, and single space between its lines to set it off from the text. Do not enclose the indented passage in quotation marks.

Use quotation marks around titles of articles, paintings, book chapters, and poems.

> The enclosed article, "The Job Market for College Graduates," should provide some helpful insights.

The title of a published work (book, journal, or newspaper) should be underlined or italicized.

Finally, use quotation marks (with restraint) to indicate your ironic use of a word.

> She is some "friend"!

Application A-10

Insert apostrophes and quotation marks as needed in these sentences.

1. Our countrys future, as well as the worlds, depends on everyone working for a cleaner environment.

2. Once you understand the problem, Professor Jones explained, you find its worse than you possibly could have expected.

3. Can we help? asked the captain.

4. Its a shame that my dog had its leg injured in the accident.

5. All the players hats were eaten by the cranky beaver.

ELLIPSES

Use three dots in a row (. . .) to indicate you have omitted some material from a quotation. If the omitted words come at the end of the original sentence, a fourth dot indicates the period. Use several dots centered in a line to indicate that a paragraph or more has been left out. Ellipses help you save time and zero in on the important material within a quotation.

" . . . Three dots . . . indicate you have omitted some material. . . . A fourth dot indicates the period. . . . Several dots centered in a line . . . indicate . . . a paragraph or more. . . . Ellipses help you . . . zero in on the important material. . . ."

ITALICS

In typing or longhand writing, indicate italics by <u>underlining</u>. On a word processor, use italic print for titles of books, periodicals, films, newspapers, and plays; for the names of ships; for foreign words or scientific names; for emphasizing a word (used sparingly); for indicating the special use of a word.

The *Oxford English Dictionary* is a handy reference tool.

The *Lusitania* sank rapidly.

She reads *The Boston Globe* often.

My only advice is *caveat emptor.*

Bacillus anthracis is a highly virulent organism.

Do not inhale these fumes under any circumstances!

Our contract defines a *work-study student* as one who works a minimum of 20 hours weekly.

PARENTHESES

Use commas normally to set off parenthetical elements, dashes to give some emphasis to the material that is set off, and parentheses to enclose material that defines or explains the statement that precedes it.

An anaerobic (airless) environment must be maintained for the cultivation of this organism.

The cost of running our college has increased by 15 percent in one year (see Appendix A for full cost breakdown).

This new calculator (made by Ilco Corporation) is perfect for science students.

Material between parentheses, like all other parenthetical material discussed earlier, can be deleted without harming the logical and grammatical structure of the sentence.

Also, use parentheses to enclose numbers or letters that segment items of information in a series.

This procedure entails three basic steps: (1) . . . , (2) . . . , and (3). . . .

BRACKETS

Use brackets within a quotation to add material that was not in the original quotation but is needed for clarification. Sometimes a bracketed word provides an antecedent (or referent) for a pronoun.

"She [Amy] was the outstanding candidate for the scholarship."

Brackets can enclose information taken from some other location within the context of the quotation.

"It was in early spring [April 2, to be exact] that the tornado hit."

Use brackets to correct a quotation.

"His essay was [full] of mistakes."

Use *sic* ("thus," or "so") when quoting a mistake in spelling, usage, or logic.

The assistant's comment was clear: "He don't [sic] want any."

DASHES

Dashes can be effective—as long as they are not overused. Make dashes on your typewriter by placing two hyphens side by side. Parentheses deemphasize the enclosed material; dashes emphasize it.

Used selectively, dashes can provide dramatic emphasis, but they are no substitute for all other punctuation. When in doubt, do not use a dash!

Dashes can denote an afterthought

Have a good vacation—but don't get sunstroke.

They can enclose an interruption in the middle of a sentence.

The designer of this college building—I think it was Wright—was, above all, an artist.

Our new players—Jones, Smith, and Brown—are already compiling outstanding statistics.

Although they often can be used interchangeably with commas, dashes dramatize a parenthetical statement more than commas do.

> Mary, a true friend, spent hours helping me rehearse.
>
> Mary—a true friend—spent hours helping me rehearse.

Notice the added emphasis in the second version.

Application A–11

Insert parentheses or dashes as appropriate in these sentences.

1. Writing is a deliberate process of deliberate decisions about a writer's purpose, audience, and message.

2. Have fun but be careful.

3. She worked hard summers at three jobs actually to earn money for agricultural school.

4. To achieve peace and contentment that is the meaning of success.

5. Fido a loyal pet saved my life during the fire.

Effective Mechanics

Correctness in abbreviation, hyphenation, capitalization, use of numbers, and spelling is an important sign of your attention to detail.

ABBREVIATIONS

Whenever you abbreviate, consider your audience; never use an abbreviation that might confuse your reader. Often, abbreviations are not appropriate in formal writing. When in doubt, write the word out.

Abbreviate some words and titles when they precede or immediately follow a proper name.

Correct

Mr. Jones	Raymond Dumont, Jr.
Dr. Jekyll	Wendy White, Ph.D.
St. Simeon	

Do not, however, write abbreviations such as these:

Faulty

Mary is a Dr.

Pray, and you might become a St.

In general, do not abbreviate military, religious, and political titles.

Correct   Reverend Ormsby

                   Captain Hook

                   President Clinton

Abbreviate time designations only when they are used with actual times.

Correct   400 B.C.

                   5:15 A.M.

Do not abbreviate these designations when they are used alone.

Faulty   Plato lived sometime in the B.C. period.

                   She arrived in the A.M.

In formal writing, do not abbreviate days of the week, individual months, words such as **street** and **road**, or names of disciplines such as **English**. Avoid abbreviating states, such as **Me.** for **Maine**; countries, such as **U.S.** for **United States**; and book parts, such as **Chap.** for **Chapter**, **p.** for **page**, and **fig.** for **figure**.

Use **no.** for **number** only when the actual number is given.

Correct   Check switch No. 3.

For abbreviations of other words, consult your dictionary. Most dictionaries have a list of abbreviations at the front or rear or alphabetically with the word entry.

For correct abbreviations in documentation of research sources, see pages 455–464.

HYPHEN

Use a hyphen to divide a word at the right-hand margin. Consult your dictionary for the correct syllable breakdown:

com-puter

comput-er

Actually, it is best to avoid altogether this practice of dividing words at the ends of lines in a typewritten text.

Use a hyphen to join compound modifiers (two or more words preceding the noun as a single adjective),

> the rough-hewn wood
>
> the well-written novel
>
> the all-too-human error

Do not hyphenate these same words if they *follow* the noun.

> The wood was rough hewn.
>
> The novel is well written.
>
> The error was all too human.

Hyphenate an adverb-participle compound preceding a noun.

> the high-flying glider

Do not hyphenate compound modifiers if the adverb ends in **-ly**.

> The finely tuned engine.

Hyphenate most words that begin with the prefix **self-**. (Check your dictionary.)

> self-reliance
>
> self-discipline
>
> self-actualizing

Hyphenate to avoid ambiguity.

> re-creation [*a new creation*]
>
> recreation [*leisure activity*]

Hyphenate words that begin with **ex** only if **ex** means "past."

> ex-faculty member
>
> excommunicate

Hyphenate all fractions, along with ratios that are used as adjectives and that precede the noun.

a **two-thirds** majority

In a **four-to-one** vote, the student senate defeated the proposal.

Do not hyphenate ratios if they do not immediately precede the noun.

The proposal was voted down **four to one**.

Hyphenate compound numbers from twenty-one through ninety-nine.

Thirty-eight windows were broken.

Hyphenate a series of compound adjectives preceding a noun.

The subjects for the motivation experiment were **fourteen-, fifteen-,** and **sixteen-year-old** students.

CAPITALIZATION

Capitalize these proper nouns: titles of people, books, and chapters; languages; days of the week; the months; holidays; names of organizations or groups; races and nationalities; historical events; important documents; and names of structures or vehicles. In titles of books, films, and the like, capitalize the first word and all those following except articles or prepositions.

Joe Schmoe	Russian
A Tale of Two Cities	Labor Day
Protestant	Dupont Chemical Company
Wednesday	Senator Barbara Boxer
the *Queen Mary*	France
the Statue of Liberty	The War of 1812

Do not capitalize the seasons (**spring, winter**) or general groups (**the younger generation, the leisure class**).

Capitalize adjectives that are derived from proper nouns.

Chaucerian English

Capitalize titles preceding a proper noun but not those following.

State Senator Marsha Smith

Marsha Smith, state senator

Capitalize words such as **street**; **road**, **corporation**, and **college** only when they accompany a proper noun.

> Bob Jones University
>
> High Street
>
> The Rand Corporation

Capitalize **north**, **south**, **east**, and **west** when they denote specific locations, not when they are simply directions.

> the South
>
> the Northwest
>
> Turn east at the next set of lights.

Begin all sentences with capitals.

USE OF NUMBERS

If numbers can be expressed in one or two words, you can write them out or you can use the numerals.
For larger numbers, use numerals.

> 4,364   2,800,357
>
> 543

Use numerals to express decimals, fractions, precise technical figures, or any other exact measurements. Numerals are more easily read and better remembered than numbers that are spelled out.

> $3^1/_4$ 15 pounds of pressure
>
> 50 kilowatts   4000 rpm

Express these in numerals: dates, census figures, addresses, page numbers, exact units of measurement, percentages, ages, times with A.M. or P.M. designations, and monetary and mileage figures.

> page 14   1:15 P.M.
>
> 18.4 pounds   9 feet
>
> 115 miles   12 gallons
>
> the 9-year-old motorcycle $15

Do not begin a sentence with a numeral.

> Six hundred students applied for the 102 available jobs.

If your figure consumes more than two words, revise your word order.

> The 102 available jobs brought 780 applicants.

Do not use numerals to express approximate figures, time not designated as A.M. or P.M., or streets named by numbers less than 100.

> about seven hundred fifty
>
> four fifteen
>
> 108 East Forty-second Street

If one number immediately precedes another, spell out the first, and use a numeral for the second:

> Please deliver twelve 16-inch anchovy pizzas.

In contracts and other documents in which precision is vital, a number can be stated both in numerals and in words:

> The tenant agrees to pay a rental fee of three hundred seventy-five dollars ($375.00) monthly.

SPELLING

If you are bothered by spelling weaknesses, take the time to use your dictionary for all writing assignments. And when you read, notice the spelling of words that have given you trouble. Compile a list of troublesome words. Your college may have a learning laboratory where you can get assistance. Or your instructor may suggest books for spelling improvement.

Application A–12

In these sentences, make any needed mechanical corrections in abbreviations, hyphens, numbers, or capitalization.

1. Dr. Jones, our english prof., drives a Volkswagen Jetta.

2. Eighty five students in the survey rated self-discipline as essential for success in college.

3. Since nineteen seventy seven, my goal has been to live in the northwest.

4. Senator Tarbell has collected forty five hand made rugs from the middle east.

5. During my third year at Margate university, I wrote twenty three page papers on the Russian revolution.

Appendix B: Guidelines for Collaborative Writing, Reviewing, and Editing*

Writing Collaboratively
- **Reviewing and Editing the Work of Peers**
  - **Works Cited for Appendix B**

Countless documents in the workplace are produced collaboratively: by people working in teams or groups, sharing information, ideas, and responsibilities. Effective collaboration enables a group to synthesize the *best* from each member. With today's electronic communications, collaboration occurs more and more routinely.

Your instructor might ask you to work on some assignments collaboratively, as a way of experiencing the benefits—and the pitfalls—of group efforts. Here are some major benefits of collaboration:

---

*Adapted from Alred, Oliu, and Brusaw, page 37; Bogert and Butt, page 51; Bruffee, page 652; Burnett, pages 533–34; Debs, pages 38, 41; Hill-Duin, pages 45–46; Morgan, pages 540–41; Nelson and Smith, page 61. Full citations appear in Works Cited, page 588.

- We test and sharpen our ideas.

- We get a chance to examine more objectively our biases and assumptions.

- We receive feedback from group members.

- Instead of the stress of working alone, we enjoy group support.

- We share in new perspectives.

- Writing for a peer audience can seem less intimidating than writing for the English teacher.

- We have the chance to discuss our writing.

Despite benefits of collaboration, certain pressures and conflicts present rhetorical challenges for all group members:

- Some people might not get along because of differences in personality, working style, commitment, standards, or ability to take criticism.

- Some people might disagree about exactly what or how much the group should accomplish or who should do what or who should make the final decisions.

- Some people might feel intimidated or hesitant to speak out.

Group members have to find ways of expressing their views persuasively, of accepting constructive criticism, of getting along and reaching agreement with others who hold different views. These all are essential rhetorical skills for overcoming personal differences so we can work together toward common goals.

Writing Collaboratively

A collaborative writing project includes any or all of these activities: generating ideas (through brainstorming and so on), researching information; planning the essay or report; producing, reviewing, and editing drafts, and revising.

Whether your project is an essay, a research report, or some other writing, most of the following guidelines apply.

1. *Appoint a group manager.* Your instructor might serve as manager, or the group might select a person to assign tasks, enforce deadlines, conduct meetings, consult with the instructor, and generally "run the show."

2. *Identify a clear purpose.* Compose a purpose statement (pages 31, 32) that spells out the project's goal and the group's plan for achieving the goal.

3. *Decide how the group will be organized.* Some possibilities:

   a. The group researches and plans together, but each person writes a different part of the document.

   b. Some members plan and research; one person writes a complete draft; others review, edit, revise, and produce the final version.

   c. Some other arangement.

   Keep in mind that the final revision should display one consistent style throughout—as if written by one person only.

4. *Divide the task.* Who will be responsible for which parts of the essay or report or which phases of the project? Should only one person be responsible for the final revision? Which jobs are hardest? Who is best at doing what (writing, editing, using a word processor)?

5. *Establish a timetable.* Specific completion dates for each phase will keep everyone focused on what is due and when.

6. *Decide on a meeting schedule and format.* How often will the group meet, and for how long? In or out of class? Who will take notes, or will people take turns? Will the instructor attend, or participate?

7. *Establish a procedure for responding to the work of other members.* Will reviewing and editing (pages 78–85) be done in writing, face-to-face, as a group, one-on-one, or even via computer? Will this process be supervised by the project manager or the instructor?

8. *Establish procedures for dealing with group problems.* How will gripes and disagreements be aired (to the manager, the whole group, the "offending" individual)? How will disputes be resolved (by vote, the manager, the instructor)? How will irrelevant discussion be avoided or curtailed? Expect some conflict, but try to use it positively.

9. *Decide how to evaluate fairly each member's contribution.* Will the manager assess each member's performance and, in turn, be evaluated by each member? Will members evaluate each other? What are the criteria for evaluation? Figure B.1 depicts one possible form for a manager's evaluation of members. Equivalent

---

Performance Appraisal

Performance Appraisal for_____

(After each item, place an X in the column that applies.)

	Superior	Acceptable	Unacceptable
Dependability			
Cooperation			
Effort			
Quality of work			
Ability to meet deadlines			

_____
Project Manager's signature

Figure B.1 A Possible Form for Evaluating Team Members

criteria for evaluating the manager could include "ability to organize the team," "fairness in assigning tasks," "ability to resolve conflicts," "ability to motivate," or other essential traits.

10. *Prepare a project management plan.* Figure B.2 depicts a sample plan sheet. Distribute copies of the plan to members and the instructor.

Beyond these guidelines, showing respect for other people's views and being willing to listen are essential ingredients for successful collaboration.

Reviewing and Editing the Work of Peers

All writing can benefit from feedback. In the workplace, for example, writers routinely depend on peers to review and edit their various drafts.

Reviewing means evaluating how well a written piece achieves its purpose in terms of its intended audience. Is the content worthwhile? Is the piece well organized? Is the style readable? In a peer review, you are explaining to the writer how you respond as a reader. This feedback helps writers envision ways of revising (Chapter 4). Criteria for reviewing an essay are spelled out on page 79; for an argument, on pages 394–395; and for a Research Report, on pages 464–465.

Editing means actually "fixing" the piece: rephrasing or reorganizing sentences, choosing a better word, correcting spelling or usage or

Management Plan Sheet

Title of paper: _____

Audience: _____

Project manager: _____

Team members: _____

_____

Purpose statement _____

_____

Specific Assignments   ## Due Dates

Research: Research due:

Planning: Plan and outline due:

Drafting: First draft due:

Revising: Reviews due:

Preparing final draft: Revision due:

                                 Final draft due:

Work Schedule

Group meetings: date   place   time   note-taker

#1

#2

#3

etc.

Meetings with instructor

#1

#2

etc.

Miscellaneous

How will disputes be settled?_____

_____

How will performance be evaluated?_____

_____

Other Issues? _____

_____

_____

_____

Figure B.2 Sample Plan Sheet for Managing a Collaborative Project punctuation, clarifying a topic sentence , and so on. Criteria for editing are listed in Table A.1, page 540.

Your writing course may include workshops, during which the class discusses writing done by students. Workshops usually include peer reviewing and editing. The following guidelines should help the process run smoothly.

1. *Read the entire piece at least twice before you comment.* Get a clear sense of the assignment's purpose and its intended audience. View the whole before evaluating its parts.

2. *Remember that mere correctness offers no guarantee of effectiveness.* Poor grammar, usage, punctuation, or mechanics do distract readers and harm the writer's credibility. However, a "correct" piece of writing still could contain inappropriate rhetorical elements (content, organization, or style).

3. *Understand the acceptable limits of editing.* Student editors usually are not expected to be co-authors. In the workplace, "editing" can range from fine-tuning to an in-depth rewrite (in which case editors are cited prominently as consulting editors or co-authors). In school, however, rewriting a piece to the extent that it becomes no longer the writer's own may constitute plagiarism.

4. *Be honest but diplomatic.* All of us (including this writer) benefit from honest feedback, but we still are sensitive to criticism—even the most constructive! Begin with something positive before moving to material needing improvement. Try to be supportive instead of judgmental.

5. *Always explain "why" something doesn't work.* Instead of "this paragraph is confusing," say "because this paragraph lacks a clear topic sentence, I had trouble discovering the main idea." Use the criteria for reviewing and editing (pages 79, 394, 465).

6. *Make specific recommendations for improvements.* Reviewing and editing is a process of "diagnosing" a problem and "prescribing" a cure. Write out your evaluation and suggestions in enough detail to give the writer a clear sense of how to proceed.

7. *Be aware that not all feedback has equal value.* Even professional reviewers and editors sometimes disagree on matters of content, organization, or style. When your own writing is being reviewed or edited, you may receive conflicting opinions from different readers. In such cases, seek the advice of your instructor.

In the broadest sense, skills in collaboration enable us to contribute to the kinds of conversations in which all participants benefit.

Works Cited for Appendix B

Alred, Gerald J., Walter E. Oliu, and Charles T. Brusaw. *The Professional Writer: A Guide for Advanced Technical Writing.* New York: St. Martin's, 1992.

Bogert, Judith, and David Butt. "Opportunities Lost, Challenges Met: Understanding and Applying Group Dynamics in Writing Projects." *Bulletin of the Association for Business Communication* 53.2 (1990): 51–53.

Bruffee, Kenneth A. "Collaborative Learning and the 'Conversation of Mankind'." *College English* 46.7 (1984): 635–52.

Burnett, Rebecca E. "Substantive Conflict in a Cooperative Context: A Way to Improve the Collaborative Planning of Workplace Documents." *Technical Communication* 38.4 (1991): 532–39.

Debs, Mary Beth. "Collaborative Writing in Industry." *Technical Writing: Theory and Practice.* Ed. Bertie E. Fearing and W. Keats Sparrow. New York: Modern Language Assn., 1989, 33–42.

Hill-Duin, Ann. "Terms and Tools: A Theory and Research-Based Approach to Collaborative Writing." *Bulletin of the Association for Business Communication* 53.2 (1990): 45–50.

Morgan, Meg. "Patterns of Composing: Connections between Classroom and Workplace Collaborations." *Technical Communication* 38.4 (1991): 540–42.

Nelson, Sandra J., and Douglas C. Smith. "Maximizing Cohesion and Minimizing Conflict in Collaborative Writing Groups." *Bulletin of the Association for Business Communication* 53.2 (1990): 540–42.

Appendix C: Guidelines for Writing with a Computer

Computers continue to revolutionize the way we write and communicate. This appendix focuses on the major benefits and limitations of writing with a computer.

The Computer as Multipurpose Tool

As a multipurpose tool, the computer can enhance our writing by streamlining our research, planning, drafting, and revising.

RESEARCH AND REFERENCE

Instead of thumbing through newspapers, journals, reference books, or printed card catalogs, you can do much of your research at the computer terminal. See Chapter 20 for detailed descriptions of computerized research and reference tools (card catalogs, on-line databases, electronic encyclopedias, and so on).

WORD PROCESSING

Essentially a typewriter with a memory, a word processor reduces the drudgery of writing and revising. Working directly on the computer screen, you can brainstorm, develop different outlines, and design countless versions of a document without retyping the entire piece. The latest word-processing packages allow you to insert, delete, or move blocks of text; change formats; search the document to change a word or phrase; or have your document examined automatically for correct spelling, accurate word choice, and readable style. By eliminating so many mechanical tasks, word processors leave you more time to think, to experiment, and to refine both the content and and the "look" of your writing. You then can file your finished document electronically, for easy retrieval.

COLLABORATIVE WRITING

Computers facilitate collaborative writing. For instance, group members might review, edit, or proofread your writing directly from a disk you have provided. The latest software even enables readers to comment on your writing without altering the text itself. Using "groupware" (a group authoring system), writers in different locations can edit, proofread, compare drafts, and comment on each other's work (Brittan 44; Easton et al. 35–36). Using an *electronic mail* network, you can transmit copies of your writing to any computer screen on that network. Alerted by an on-screen signal, your recipient "opens" her or his mailbox, reads the message on the computer screen, and then responds, files the message, or erases it. In the workplace collaborative groups often communicate via electronic mail as they plan, draft, and revise a document.

Computer Guidelines for Writers

In order to use electronic writing tools to full advantage, we need to recognize their limitations:

- Whether a message finally appears on a computer screen or on a printed page, it still needs to be *written*. A computer can transmit data, but it cannot give *meaning* to the information—only the writer and reader can do so. The task of sorting, organizing, and interpreting information still belongs to the writer.

- A computer makes writing easier, but not necessarily better. No computerized device can convert bad writing to good. Moreover, the ease of "fixing" our writing on a computer might encourage minimal revision. (Sometimes the very act of rewriting an entire page in longhand or type causes us to rethink that whole page or discover something new.)

- A computer is not a substitute brain. When you struggle through that first draft, it makes no difference whether you use quill and ink or the most sophisticated word processor; if the thinking is shabby, the writing will be useless.

The following guidelines will help insure that you capitalize on all the benefits a computer can offer.

1. *Explore your school's computer facilities.* Sign up for training sessions on your school's word processors. Visit the computer clusters and learn about the available hardware (Macintosh, IBM compatible, or mainframe) and software. Ask which software packages are supported by your school's computing services (MS Word, MS Word/Windows, Excel, Pagemaker, and so on). Learn about your school's computer network. If possible, attend a workshop on *Internet,* a worldwide information network. If you own a computer, ask about a modem connection to your school's mainframe computer.

2. *Decide whether to draft by hand or on the computer.* Some writers prefer to produce a draft by hand before working on the computer. Others like to compose directly on the computer. Experiment with each approach before deciding which works best for you.

3. *Beware of computer junk.* The ease of cranking out words on a computer sometimes can produce long, windy pieces that say nothing. Edit your final drafts to eliminate anything that fails to advance your meaning. (See pages 170–177 for ways to achieve conciseness.)

4. *Never confuse style with substance.* With laser printers and choices of typefaces, type sizes, and other highlighting options, documents can be made highly attractive. But not even the most attractive formatting can redeem a document whose content is worthless, organization chaotic, or style unreadable. The value of any writing ultimately depends on elements that are more than skin deep.

5. *Save and print your work often.* One way to court disaster is to write without saving or printing often enough. One wrong keystroke might cause pages of writing to disappear forever—unless you have saved them beforehand. Save each paragraph as you write it and print out each page as you complete it.

6. *Make a backup disk.* A single electrical surge or other malfunction can destroy the contents of an entire file, or even an
entire floppy disk or hard disk! Whether you save your files on a
hard or floppy disk, always make a backup disk.

7. *Always revise from hard copy.* Nothing beats scribbling and
scratching on the printed page with pen or pencil. The hard copy
provides the whole text, right in front of you.

8. *Never depend only on automated "checkers."* Page 209
summarizes the limitations of many computerized aids. A
synonym offered up in an electronic thesaurus may not accurately
convey your intended meaning. The spell checker cannot
differentiate among correct or incorrect usage of correctly spelled
words such as "their," "they're" or "there" or "it's" versus "its,"
and so on. And even though spell and grammar checkers can
enhance a document's *correctness,* they are incapable of evaluating style *appropriateness,* (the subtle choices of phrasing that
determine tone and emphasis). Even the most sophisticated
writing aids are no substitute for careful proofreading.

9. *Print your final copy on good paper.* Inexpensive computer paper
crinkles, smudges, and is hard to write on.

10. *Always print two final copies.* With all the paperwork that writing
instructors shuffle, papers sometimes get misplaced. Or sometimes a late paper is stuffed in the wrong mailbox or shoved under
the wrong office door. Submit one copy and keep one for
yourself—just in case!

11. *Never assume that your electronic mail is private.* A message that
you address to a particular recipient might very well end up on the
computer screen of unintended readers as well. If privacy is
essential, use some other medium for transmitting your message.

Works Cited for Appendix C

Brittan, David. "Being There: The Promise of Multimedia
Communications." *Technology Review* May/June 1992: 43–50.

Easton, Annette, "Supporting Group Writing with Compter Software." *Bulletin of the Association for Business Communication*
39.2 (1992): 264–66.

Appendix D: Format Guidelines for Submitting Your Manuscript

Format is the look of a page, the visual arrangement of words and spacing. A well-formatted manuscript invites readers in, guides them through the material, and helps them understand it.

One's first impression of a manuscript tends to be purely visual. Readers expect writing that looks neat, carefully typed or printed, and arranged for easy access. They are annoyed by writing that looks carelessly produced and hard to follow.

Whether you write with a typewriter, a computer, or by hand, the following guidelines will enable your formats to satisfy reader's expectations.

1. *Use the right paper and ink.* Type or print in black ink, on $8^1/_2 \times 11$ inch, low-gloss, white paper. Use rag-bond paper (2 pounds or heavier) with a high fiber content (25 percent minimum). Shiny paper produces glare and tires the eyes. Do not use onion skin or erasable paper because these smudge easily and are difficult for instructors to write on.

    If your instructor allows handwritten papers, use looseleaf paper—not pages torn out of a spiral bound notebook. Write legibly in blue or black ink—not in pencil.

2. *Use high-quality type or print.* On typewritten or handwritten copy, keep erasures to a minimum, and redo all smudged pages. Typewriter erasures with opaquing fluid or opaquing film

(correction tape) are neatest. Use a fresh ribbon and keep typewriter keys clean. On a computer, print your hard copy on a letter-quality printer, a laser printer, or a dot-matrix printer (with a fresh ribbon) in the letter-quality mode. Many older dot-matrix printers produce copy that is hard to read.

3. *Use standard type sizes and typefaces.* Word-processing programs offer a variety of typesizes. Standard type sizes for manuscripts run from 10 to 12 points—depending on the particular typeface. (Certain typefaces, such as "pica," usually call for a 10-point typesize whereas others, such as "elite," call for a 12-point typesize.) Use larger or smaller sizes only for headings, titles, or special emphasis.

   Typeface is the style of individual letters and characters. Word-processing programs offer a variety of typefaces (or fonts). Except for special emphasis, use conservative typefaces; the more ornate ones are harder to read and are generally inappropriate for a manuscript.

4. *Number pages consistently.* Number your first and subsequent pages with arabic numerals (1, 2, 3). Place all page numbers one-half inch from page top and aligned with the right margin or centered in the top or bottom margin. (Some word processors may limit page-number placement; check the manual.) For numbering pages in a research report or other long documents, see pages 474–501.

5. *Provide ample margins.* Small margins make a page look crowded and difficult, and allow no room for peer or instructor comments. Provide margins of at least $1^1/_2$ inches top and bottom, and $1^1/_4$ inches right and left. If the manuscript is to be bound in some kind of cover, widen your left margin to 2 inches.

   For a handwritten paper, provide $1^1/_2$-inch margins, both right and left, to allow room for comments.

   Word processing programs usually offer a choice between *unjustified* text (uneven right margins—as in a typewritten manuscript) and justified text (a straight, vertical, right margin—as in most of this book). Justified text is preferred in printed books, but in a manuscript, unjustified text is considered easier to read.

6. *Keep line spacing and indentation consistent.* Double space within and between paragraphs. Indent the first line of each paragraph five spaces from the left margin. (Indent five spaces on a computer by striking the Tab key.) Set off quotations of four lines or longer by indenting the entire passage ten spaces and omitting the quotation marks.

7. *Design the first and subsequent pages.* If your instructor requires a title page, see pages 474. For the first pages of a manuscript without a separate title page, follow the format your instructor recommends, or this one:

```
                                                                    1


Your name
Instructor's name
Course and section number
Day/month/year

                          Title (centered)

     Your text begins two spaces below the title, with the first line

of each paragraph indented five spaces and all lines double spaced.
```

Label each subsequent page with a running head (your last name and page number, one-half inch below page top and aligned with the right margin.

```
                                              Name   2

Your text continues two spaces below the running head, with all

lines double spaced.
```

For designing "Works Cited" pages in a research report, see pages 500–505.

8. *Cite and document each of your sources.* All sources must be properly and clearly credited. Consult pages 455–456 for parenthetical-reference formats, and pages 456–463 for Works-Cited formats.

9. *Proofread your final manuscript.* Even for professional writers, a final proofreading usually uncovers an occasional typographical

error. On a computer, spell checkers and grammar checkers can reveal certain errors, but are no substitute for your own careful evaluation.

If you need to make a few handwritten corrections on your final copy, use a caret (^) to denote the insertion:

make
If you need to ^ a few handwritten. . . .

Any page requiring more than three or four such corrections should be retyped or reprinted.

10. *Bind your manuscript for readers' convenience.* Do not use a cover unless your instructor so requests. Do not staple your pages or fold the top corner. Bind your pages with a large paper clip in the upper-left corner.

11. *Make a backup copy.* Print out or photocopy a backup paper, which you keep—just in case the original you submit gets lost or misplaced.

Format Checklist

Before submitting any manuscript, evaluate its format by using the following checklist.

☐   Do paper and ink meet quality standards?

☐   Is the type or print neat, crisp, and easy to read?

☐   Are type sizes and typefaces appropriate and easy to read?

☐   Are pages numbered consistently?

☐   Are all margins adequate?

☐   Are line spacing and indentation consistent?

☐   Are the first and subsequent pages appropriately designed?

☐   Is each source correctly cited and documented?

☐   Has the manuscript been proofread carefully?

☐   Is the manuscript bound for readers' convenience?

☐   Has a backup copy been made?

Acknowledgments

Jay Allison. "About Men: Back at the Ranch" by Jay Allison from *The New York Times Magazine*, May 27, 1990, page 14. Copyright © 1990 by The New York Times Company. Reprinted by permission.

Roger Angell. Excerpt from *Five Seasons* by Roger Angell. Copyright © 1972, 1973, 1974, 1975, 1976, 1977 by Roger Angell. Reprinted by permission of Simon & Schuster, Inc.

Isaac Asimov. Excerpt adapted from "The Case Against Man" in *Science Past-Science Future*. Copyright © 1970 by Field Enterprises, Inc. Reprinted by permission of Doubleday & Company, Inc.

Russell Baker. "Meaningful Relationships" by Russell Baker from *The New York Times Magazine*, March 19, 1978. Copyright © 1978 by The New York Times Company. Reprinted by permission.

David Blum. "The Evils of Gentrification" by David Blum from *Newsweek*, January 3, 1983. Copyright © 1983 by David Blum. Reprinted by permission of the author.

Roberta F. Borkat. "A Liberating Curriculum" by Roberta F. Borkat originally appeared in *Newsweek*, April 12, 1993. Reprinted by permission of the author.

John Brooks. Excerpt from *Telephone: The First Hundred Years* by John Brooks. Copyright © 1975, 1976 by John Brooks. Reprinted by permission of Harper & Row, Publishers, Inc.

Rachel Carson. Excerpt from *The Edge of the Sea* by Rachel Carson. Copyright © 1955 by Rachel L. Carson. Copyright renewed © 1983 by Roger Christie. Reprinted by permission of Houghton Mifflin Company.

Rachel Carson. Excerpt from *The Silent Spring* by Rachel Carson. Copyright © 1962 by Rachel L. Carson. Reprinted by permission of Houghton Mifflin Company.

Norman Cousins. Excerpt from "How to Make People Smaller Than They Are," *Saturday Review*, December 1978. Reprinted by permission of the author.

Joan Didion. Excerpt from "Los Angeles Notebook" from *Slouching Towards Bethlehem* by Joan Didion. Copyright © 1967, 1968 by Joan Didion. Reprinted by permission of Farrar, Straus and Giroux, Inc.

Annie Dillard. "Seeing" and "Cruelty at Tinker Creek" from *Pilgrim at Tinker Creek* by Annie Dillard. Copyright © 1974 by Annie Dillard. Reprinted by permission of Harper & Row.

Lars Eighner. Copyright © 1993 by Lars Eighner. From *Travels with Lizbeth* and reprinted with permission from St. Martin's Press, Inc. This essay first appeared in *The Threepenny Review*, in Fall 1991.

Lloyd Garver. "No, You Can't Have Nintendo" by Lloyd Garver from *Newsweek*, June 11, 1990, "My Turn Column," page 8.

Daniel Goleman. Excerpt from "Why the Brain Blocks Daytime Dreams." Reprinted by permission from *Psychology Today* Magazine, March 1976, copyright © 1976.

Ellen Goodman. "The Belated Father" from *Close to Home* by Ellen Goodman. Copyright © 1979 by The Washington Post Company. Reprinted by permission of Simon & Schuster, Inc.

Rose Dell Castillo Guilbault. "Americanization is Tough on 'Macho'" by Rose Dell Castillo Guilbault from *This World*. Reprinted by the author.

Ernest Hemingway. Excerpt from "Bull Fighting: A Tragedy" from *By-Line: Ernest Hemingway*, edited by William White (New York: Charles Scribner's Sons, 1967). Reprinted by permission.

Hendrick Hertzberg and David C. K. McClelland. Excerpt from "Paranoia." Copyright © 1974 by *Harper's Magazine*. All rights reserved. Reprinted from the June 1974 issue by special permission.

Thomas H. Holmes and R. H. Rahe. Table reprinted with permission from *Journal of Psychonomic Research*, Vol. 11, "The Social Readjustment Rating Scale." Copyright © 1967, Pergamon Press Inc.

Aldous Huxley. Excerpt from "Brave New World Revisited: Proleptic Meditations on Mother's Day, Euphoria and Pavlov's Pooch" as it appeared in *Esquire* Magazine. Copyright © 1956 by Esquire, Inc. Reprinted by permission of Laura Huxley.

Lewis P. Johnson. "For My Indian Daughter" by Lewis P. Johnson. From *Newsweek*, September 5, 1983.

James R. Kelly. Excerpt from "The Limits of Reason," *Commonweal*. September 12, 1975. Reprinted by permission.

Harry Kemelman. Excerpt from *Common Sense in Education* by Harry Kemelman. Copyright © 1970 by Harry Kemelman. Reprinted by permission of Crown Publishers, Inc.

Virak Khiev. "Breaking the Bonds of Hate" by Virak Khiev from *Newsweek*, April 27, 1992. Reprinted by permission of the author.

Martin Luther King, Jr. Excerpt from "Letter from Birmingham Jail, April 16, 1963" in *Why We Can't Wait* by Martin Luther King, Jr. Copyright © 1963 by Martin Luther King, Jr. Reprinted by permission of Harper & Row Publishers, Inc.

Robert Jay Lifton and Eric Olson. Excerpts from *Living and Dying*. Copyright © 1974 by Robert Jay Lifton and Eric Olson. Reprinted by permission of Holt, Rinehart and Winston, Inc.

Anne Morrow Lindbergh. From *Gift from the Sea* by Anne Morrow Lindbergh. Copyright © 1955 by Anne Morrow Lindbergh. Reprinted by permission of Pantheon Books, a division of Random House, Inc.

Norman Mailer. Excerpt from *The Presidential Papers*. Copyright © 1960, 1961, 1962, 1963 by Norman Mailer. Reprinted by permission of the author and the author's agents, Scott Meredith Literary Agency, 845 Third Avenue, New York, New York 10022.

Marya Mannes. Excerpt from "Television: The Splitting Image," *Saturday Review*, November 14, 1970. Reprinted by permission of Harold Ober Associates, Inc. Copyright © 1970 by Marya Mannes.

Peter Marin. Excerpt from "The New Narcissism," *Harper's Magazine*, October 1975. Reprinted by permission of International Creative Management, Inc.

Karl Menninger. Excerpt from *The Crime of Punishment* by Karl Menninger, M.D.

Atlantic-Little Brown. Copyright © 1959 James Thurber. Copyright © 1987 Rosemary A. Thurber. Reprinted by permission.

Carll Tucker. "Fear of Dearth," *Saturday Review*, October 27, 1979. Copyright © 1979 by *Saturday Review*. All rights reserved. Reprinted by permission.

Thomas Tutko and William Bruns. Excerpt from *Winning Is Everything and Other American Myths*, published by Macmillan Publishing Company. Copyright © 1976 by Thomas Tutko and William Bruns. Reprinted by permission of the authors.

John Updike. "Beer Can." Copyright © 1964 by John Updike. Reprinted from *Assorted Prose.* by John Updike, by permission of Alfred A. Knopf, Inc. Originally appeared in *The New Yorker.*

Judith Viorst. "Friends, Good Friends–and Such Good Friends" by Judith Viorst from *Redbook Magazine*, October 1977. Copyright © 1977 by Judith Viorst. Originally appeared in *Redbook.*

Glen Waggoner. "How to Press Flesh." Reprinted with permission from *Esquire* (July 1986). Copyright © 1986 by Esquire Associates.

Alan Watts. From *In My Own Way* by Alan Watts. Copyright © 1972 by Alan Watts. Reprinted by permission of Pantheon Books, a division of Random House, Inc.

E. B. White. Excerpt from "Here Is New York" in *Essays of E. B. White.* Copyright © 1949 by E. B. White. Reprinted by permission of Harper & Row Publishers, Inc.

Frank Lloyd Wright. Excerpt adapted from Frank Lloyd Wright, "Away with the Realtor," *Esquire* (October 1958). Copyright © 1958 by Esquire Publishing Inc. Used by permission of *Esquire.*

Index